CW01220585

BBC CHILDREN'S BOOKS
Published by the Penguin Group
Penguin Books Ltd, 80 Strand, London, WC2R 0RL, England
Penguin Group (USA), Inc., 375 Hudson Street, New York, New York 10014, USA
Penguin Books (Australia) Ltd, 250 Camberwell Road, Camberwell, Victoria 3124, Australia.
(A division of Pearson Australia Group Pty Ltd)
Canada, India, New Zealand, South Africa.
Individual files first published as part of the Doctor Who Files, published by BBC Children's Books, 2006.
Published by BBC Children's Books, 2009
Text and design © Children's Character Books, 2009
Images © BBC 2004
The Doctor, Rose, The Slitheen and The Sycorax written by Jacqueline Rayner.
Mickey, Martha and The Ood written by Moray Laing
K-9, The Daleks, The Cybermen, Captain Jack and The Sontarans written by Justin Richards
Cult of Skaro and The Master written by Matt Kemp
Donna and additional material by Annabel Gibson
10 9 8 7 6 5 4 3 2 1
Doctor Who logo © BBC 2004. TARDIS image © BBC 1963. Dalek image © BBC/Terry Nation 1963.
BBC logo TM & © BBC 1996. Licensed by BBC Worldwide Limited.
DOCTOR WHO, TARDIS and DALEK and the DOCTOR WHO, TARDIS and DALEK logos
are trade marks of the British Broadcasting Corporation and are used under licence.
Printed in China.
ISBN-13: 978-1-40590605-0

DOCTOR·WHO

THE DOCTOR WHO FILES
COLLECTOR'S EDITION

CONTENTS

The Doctor	7
Rose	37
The Slitheen	67
The Sycorax	97
Mickey	127
K-9	157
The Daleks	187
The Cybermen	217
Martha	247
Captain Jack	277
The Cult of Skaro	307
The TARDIS	337
The Sontarans	367
The Ood	397
The Master	427
Donna	457
Travelling On...	487

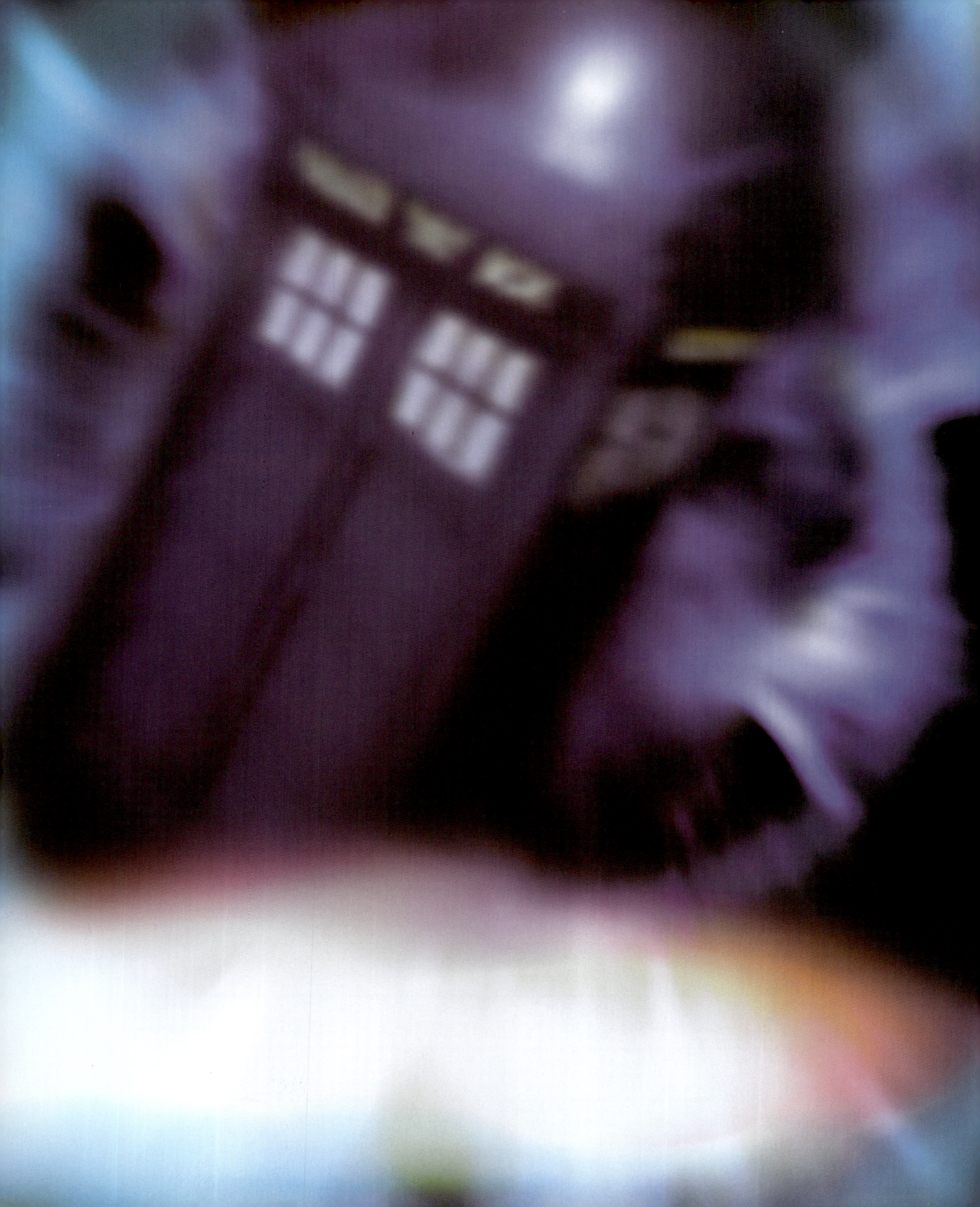

DOCTOR·WHO

THE DOCTOR

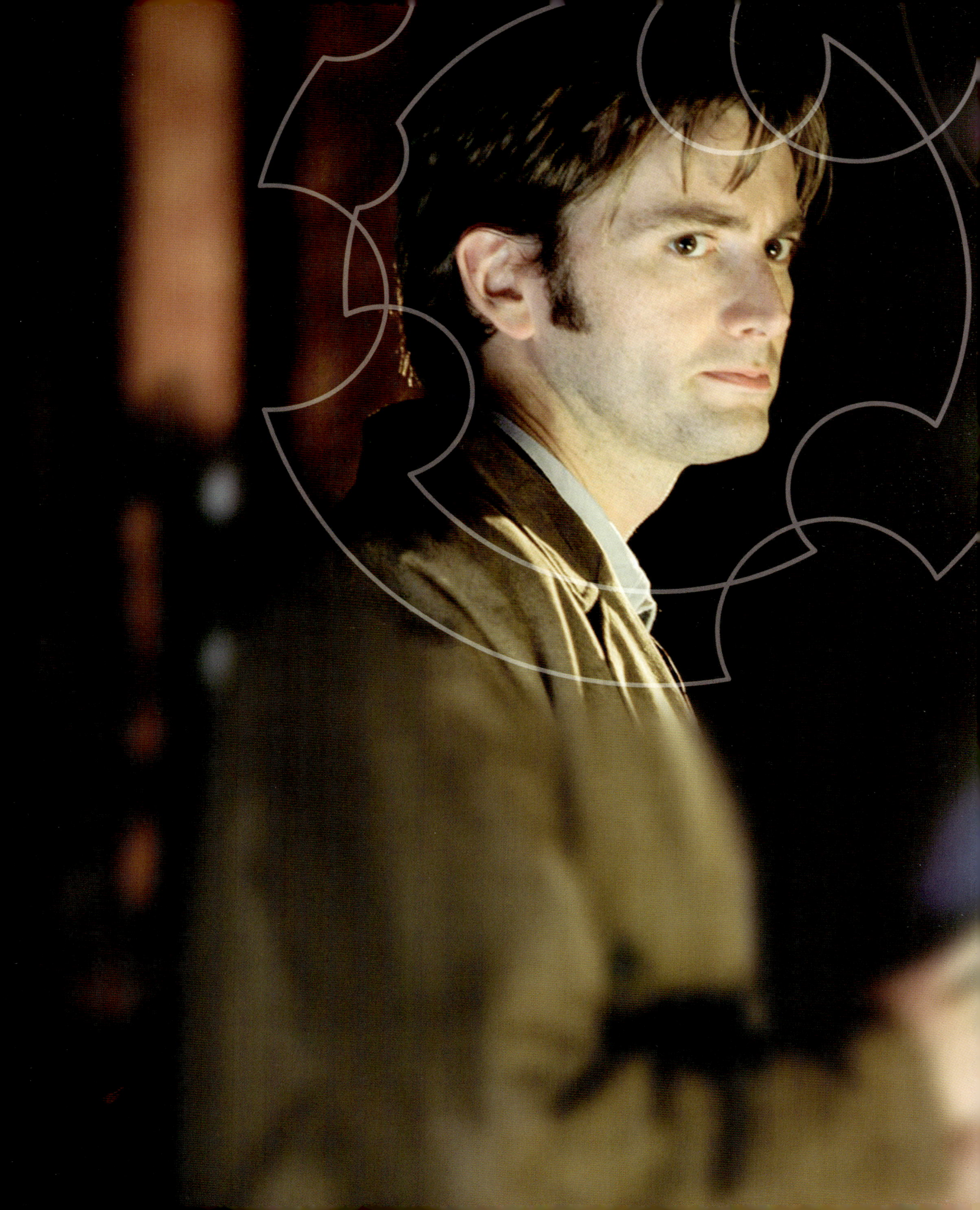

CONTENTS

Meet the Doctor
Introduction 10
Doctor Data 12
Doctor Anatomy 14
◆ Test your Knowledge

Companions
Rose 16
Sarah Jane 17
K-9, Mickey 18
Adam, Captain Jack 19
◆ Test your Knowledge

Enemies
The Daleks 20
The Cybermen 21
Repair Droids 22
The Sycorax 23
◆ Test your Knowledge

Time Lords
The Time War 24
Regeneration 26
Tea 27
◆ Test your Knowledge

Technology and Transport
The TARDIS 28
Numbers 29
Sonic Screwdriver 30
Psychic Paper 31
◆ Test your Knowledge

Tenth Doctor Travels 32
◆ Test your Knowledge

Test your Knowledge Answers 36

MEET THE DOCTOR

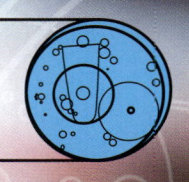

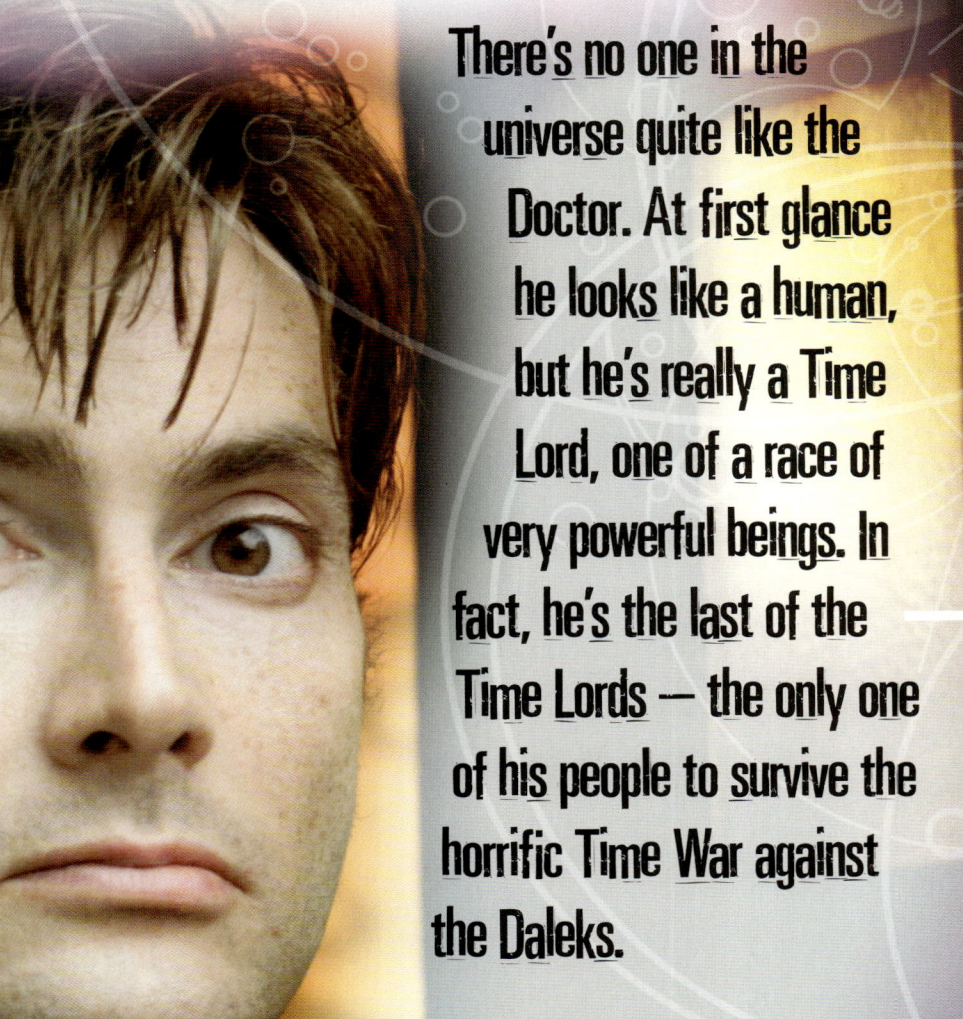

There's no one in the universe quite like the Doctor. At first glance he looks like a human, but he's really a Time Lord, one of a race of very powerful beings. In fact, he's the last of the Time Lords — the only one of his people to survive the horrific Time War against the Daleks.

But even before the destruction of his people, the Doctor was unique. Instead of staying at home, he chose to 'borrow' a time machine and explore the universe. Instead of just observing other planets, he chose to get involved in their affairs. And instead of following the easy path, he chose to stand up for what is right. Whatever the cost.

11

Luckily for us, Earth is the Doctor's favourite planet. He sometimes despairs of the human race, but he will always be there to defend them from harm. The Doctor may have had ten bodies and travelled with dozens of different companions, but one thing doesn't change, he'll always be a hero.

DOCTOR DATA

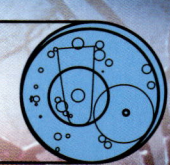

Name: No one knows! He's always called just 'the Doctor'
Age: approx. 900 years old
Height: 1.85m (6'1")
Hair: Brown
Eyes: Brown
Home planet: Gallifrey, now destroyed
Current home: The TARDIS
Species: Time Lord
Profession: Adventurer

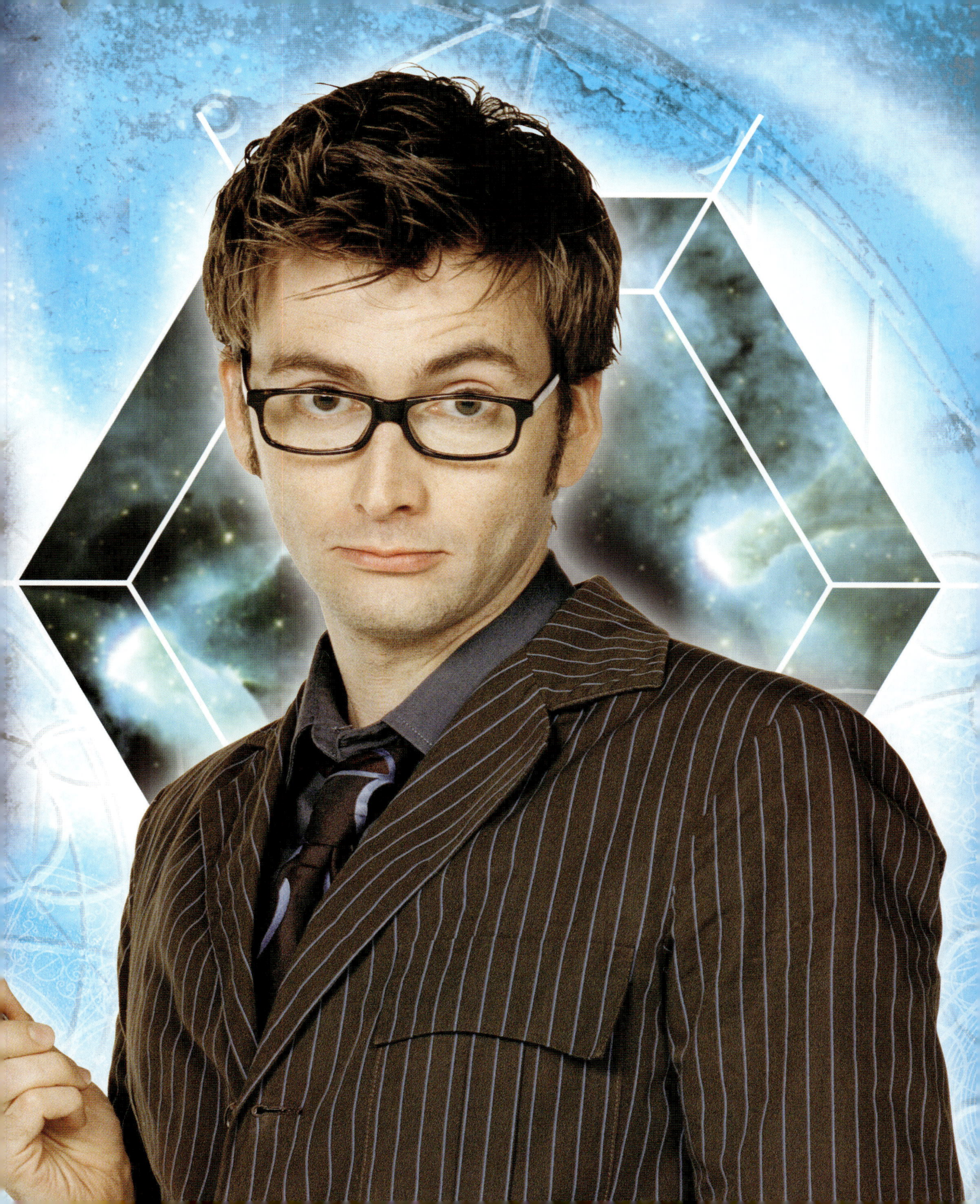

14 DOCTOR ANATOMY

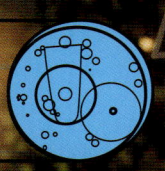

Trendy sideburns

Glasses for examining things closely

New 'fighting' hand, grown to replace the one cut off by the Sycorax Leader

Suit lets him blend in on present-day Earth

1.85m tall (6'1")

Mole between his shoulder blades

Ever-useful sonic screwdriver

Respiratory bypass system allows the Doctor to go without oxygen for a short time

Comfy plimsolls

TEST YOUR KNOWLEDGE

1. **WHAT PART OF THE DOCTOR'S BODY DID THE SYCORAX LEADER CUT OFF?**
   A. Ear
   B. Hand
   C. Foot

2. **WHAT PLANET DOES THE DOCTOR COME FROM?**
   A. Gallifrey
   B. Earth
   C. Griffoth

3. **HOW MANY HEARTS DOES THE DOCTOR HAVE?**
   A. Two
   B. Three
   C. One

4. **WHAT IS THE NAME OF THE DOCTOR'S SHIP?**
   A. The TOASTER
   B. The TURTLE
   C. The TARDIS

5. **WHO WERE THE DOCTOR'S PEOPLE?**
   A. The Space Sentinels
   B. The Time Lords
   C. The Vortex Guardians

COMPANIONS

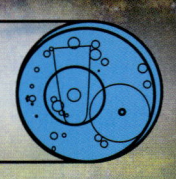

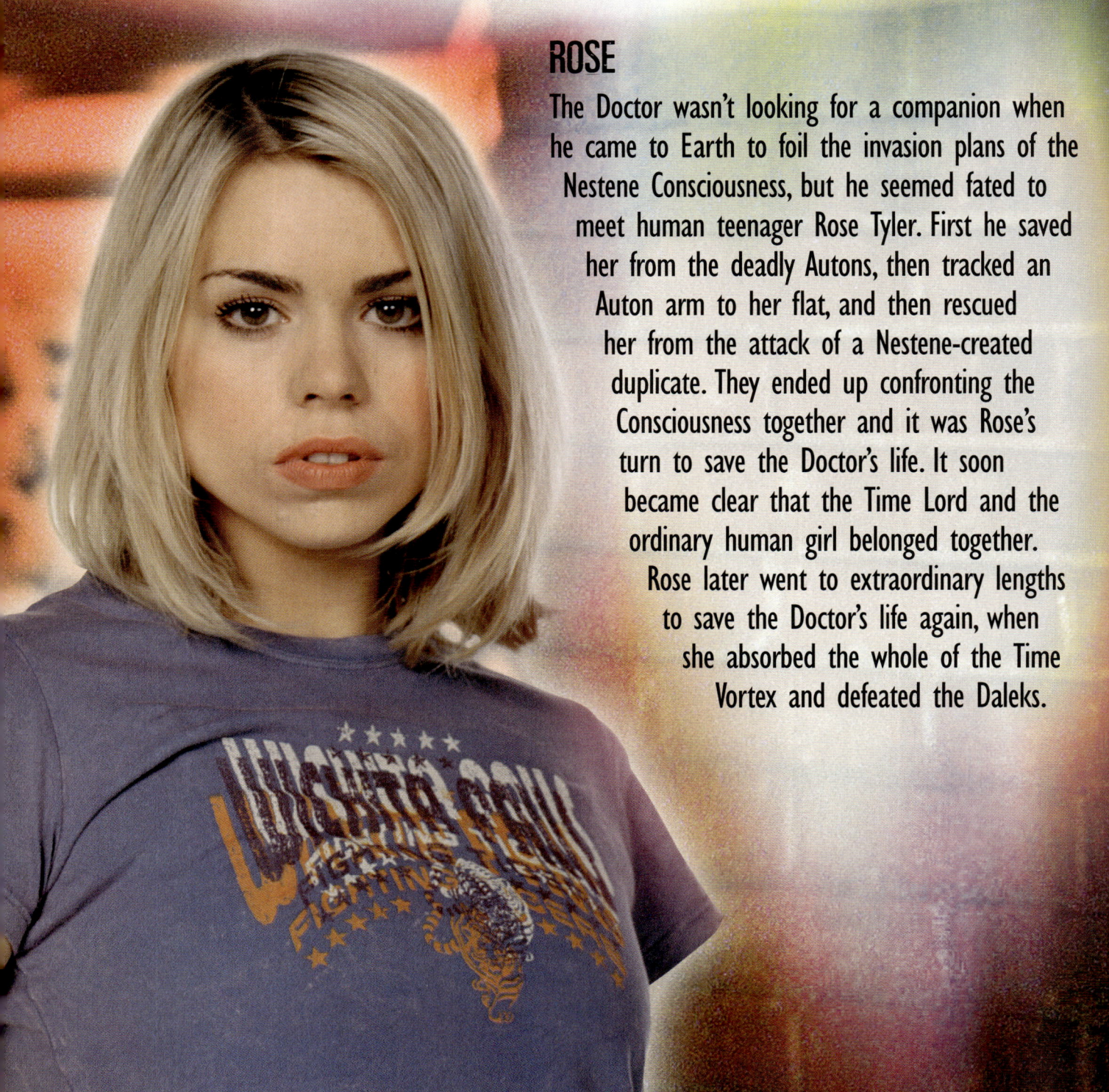

ROSE

The Doctor wasn't looking for a companion when he came to Earth to foil the invasion plans of the Nestene Consciousness, but he seemed fated to meet human teenager Rose Tyler. First he saved her from the deadly Autons, then tracked an Auton arm to her flat, and then rescued her from the attack of a Nestene-created duplicate. They ended up confronting the Consciousness together and it was Rose's turn to save the Doctor's life. It soon became clear that the Time Lord and the ordinary human girl belonged together. Rose later went to extraordinary lengths to save the Doctor's life again, when she absorbed the whole of the Time Vortex and defeated the Daleks.

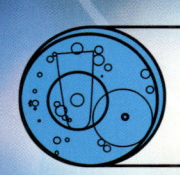

SARAH JANE

Journalist Sarah Jane Smith first met the third Doctor when she was working undercover to get a story. To start with, she thought the Doctor was a baddie! But they soon became firm friends and Sarah and the Doctor had many exciting adventures together. Until the Doctor left Sarah on Earth when he was summoned to his home planet, and never came back for her. Sarah was stunned to meet the tenth Doctor many years later, when she was once more investigating a story, and was soon caught up in the fight against the Krillitanes. Although the Doctor invited Sarah to travel with him again, she decided that her place was on Earth, but no matter what, Sarah will always occupy a very special place in the Doctor's hearts.

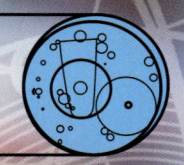

K-9

K-9 — the Doctor's 'second best friend' — is a mobile computer in the shape of a dog. He originally came from the year 5000, having been built by a scientist called Professor Marius who was missing his pet. The Doctor travelled with two different K-9s before building a third to send to his friend, Sarah Jane Smith, on Earth. K-9 is as loyal as a real dog, and will defend his master, the Doctor, and his mistress, Sarah Jane, to the end. But he has several things that a real dog doesn't have, like a blaster in his nose, a tail antenna and extensive databanks. K-9 sacrificed himself to defeat the Krillitanes, but the Doctor once again replaced him with a new and improved model.

MICKEY

The Doctor offered Mickey the chance to travel in the TARDIS soon after they met, but scared Mickey turned it down. However Mickey gradually realised what a great opportunity he was missing and asked to join the TARDIS crew, travelling with the Doctor until he decided to stay to defeat the Cybermen on a parallel Earth.

ADAM

The Doctor met Adam Mitchell on Earth in 2012, and Rose persuaded him to let Adam come with them in the TARDIS. However it soon became clear that Adam wasn't cut out for the time travelling life, and was unceremoniously dumped back home.

CAPTAIN JACK

Con man Captain Jack Harkness travelled with the Doctor until he was killed by the Daleks on the Game Station. Rose brought Jack back to life, but the TARDIS flew off without him. The Doctor decided not to go back for Jack, thinking he would be busy rebuilding the Earth.

TEST YOUR KNOWLEDGE

1. WHAT DOES K-9 CALL THE DOCTOR?
A. Mr Who
B. Master
C. Boss man

2. WHO DID THE DOCTOR DECIDE WASN'T CUT OUT TO BE HIS COMPANION?
A. Rose
B. K-9
C. Adam

3. WHAT IS SARAH JANE'S JOB?
A. Dinner lady
B. Journalist
C. Dog trainer

4. WHO SAVED THE DOCTOR FROM THE NESTENE CONSCIOUSNESS?
A. K-9
B. A Dalek
C. Rose

5. WHICH OF THE DOCTOR'S COMPANIONS WAS KILLED BY THE DALEKS?
A. Captain Jack
B. Adam
C. Sarah Jane

20 ENEMIES

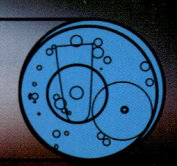

THE DALEKS

In the ancient legends of the Dalek Homeworld the Doctor is known as the Oncoming Storm — the only person in the universe that the Daleks fear. The Doctor was there for the birth of the Daleks on the planet Skaro and he thought he was there for their destruction at the end of the Time War, but he was wrong. He was distressed when he found a single surviving Dalek in 21st century Utah, believing that his sacrifices in the war had all been in vain. But this was nothing compared to the revelation that a Dalek ship had fallen through time and the fearsome Emperor Dalek had created a new army out of dead humans.

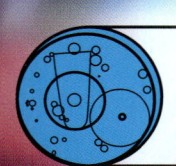

THE CYBERMEN

The people of Earth's twin planet, Mondas, grew weak, so Mondasian scientists began replacing feeble human parts with strong metal ones. Over time, the only piece that was left of each Mondasian was the brain, with all emotions removed. Every other part was cybernetic. These flesh and metal creatures became known as Cybermen and they embarked on universal conquest. It was up to the Doctor to defeat their many plans. The Doctor fought the Cybermen again and again in this universe, but he was shocked to land on a parallel Earth, and find that the monsters were being created there, too. Dying genius John Lumic had found a way to preserve his life and create an army. He told the Doctor that the Cybermen would bring peace but the Doctor knows from experience that they only cause pain and fear.

REPAIR DROIDS

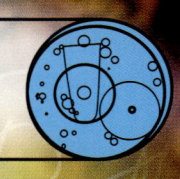

These terrifying clockwork robots have just one purpose — to repair their damaged spaceship. They are programmed to use whatever they can find to make repairs, and to them a human being is just a walking set of spare parts. First the human is knocked out using the hypodermic needle that springs from the droid's hand, then its wrist-blade can be used to dismember the body.

The robots disguised themselves with wigs and masks to infiltrate 18th-century France to find the last part they needed: Madame de Pompadour's brain. But underneath the masks, they have no faces. All that can be seen is the clockwork mechanism that drives them. As long as they are wound up, the droids can go on for ever. Well, unless the Doctor's on the case.

THE SYCORAX

The cruel Sycorax travel through space targeting the planets of weaker species. They employ techniques such as blood control to gain power, but if that fails, they have the full might of the Sycorax Armada behind them. When the Sycorax turned their attention to Earth, thinking it was weak and undefended, it seemed as though they would succeed in their plan to plunder its minerals and take its people into slavery. But they'd reckoned without the Doctor. Even the Sycorax's deadly flesh-searing whips held no fear for the newly regenerated Time Lord, who sent the message to aliens everywhere. The Earth is defended.

TEST YOUR KNOWLEDGE

1. HOW IS THE DOCTOR KNOWN IN DALEK LEGEND?
   A. The Hideous Hurricane
   B. The Oncoming Storm
   C. The Windy Man

2. IN OUR UNIVERSE, WHERE DID THE CYBERMEN COME FROM?
   A. Mondas
   B. Earth
   C. New Earth

3. WHO CREATED THE PARALLEL EARTH CYBERMEN?
   A. Mickey Smith
   B. John Lumic
   C. Cyril Cybus

4. WHAT WAS THE FINAL PART NEEDED BY THE REPAIR DROIDS?
   A. The Doctor's right heart
   B. Rose's nose
   C. Madame de Pompadour's brain

5. WHO PLANNED TO ENSLAVE EARTH'S PEOPLE?
   A. Repair Droids
   B. The Sycorax
   C. The Cybermen

24 TIME LORDS

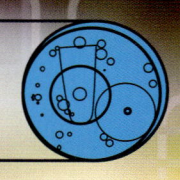

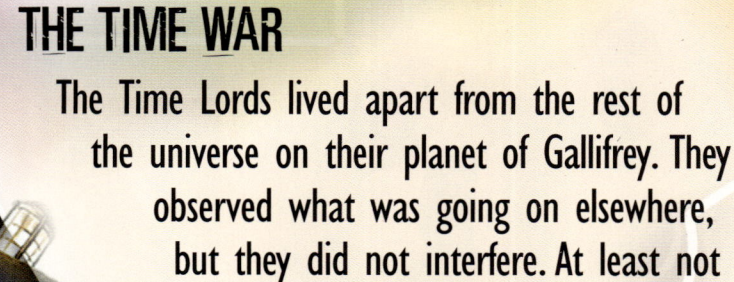

THE TIME WAR

The Time Lords lived apart from the rest of the universe on their planet of Gallifrey. They observed what was going on elsewhere, but they did not interfere. At least not officially. If there was something that needed to be done, they called on the Doctor to do their dirty work.

But then the threat to the Time Vortex became so great that the Time Lords had to act themselves to save it. The Time War, the most terrible of all Time Wars, was fought between the Time Lords and the evil Daleks. It led to tragedy for both races and for many more caught up in the war.

The Doctor fought alongside his people in the war, and desperately tried to save the many planets that were caught up in the conflict, such as the homeworld of the Nestene Consciousness. He finally ended the war, destroying the Daleks in an inferno. But the Time Lords and their planet burnt at the same time. The Doctor hadn't planned to survive, but he did, the last of his race.

The war took a terrible toll on the Doctor. Having lost his home planet and all his people, he was haunted by the terrible memories of what happened, and his inability to stop it. For the first time in his many lives, he was unsure of himself. But salvation came in the form of Rose Tyler. She helped the Doctor embrace life again, and be happy...

26

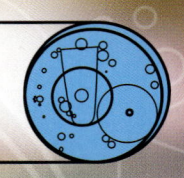

REGENERATION

A Time Lord can live for hundreds of years, but over that length of time his body may wear out and if so, he can decide to change it for another one. This is called regeneration.

It's not always a matter of choice, though. If a Time Lord has a fatal accident the same process allows him to cheat death. Every cell in his body is renewed, and the Time Lord becomes a completely new person. In emergencies like this, the Time Lord has no choice over what new body he gets, and the forced regeneration may go wrong, causing the Doctor to become ill. The Doctor has regenerated nine times, for many different reasons:

1. Body wearing out.

2. Appearance changed by the Time Lords.

3. Poisoned by radiation.

4. Falling off a radio telescope.

5. Infected with Spectrox Toxaemia.

6. Hitting his head on the TARDIS console.

7. Shot by a street gang.

8. We don't know. Was the Doctor hurt defeating the Daleks in the Time War?

9. Absorbing the energy of the Time Vortex to save Rose.

TEA

When the Doctor absorbed the Time Vortex, he cheated death by regenerating. But what helped him recover from the regeneration itself? The answer is simple — tea!

The drink tea is made from the leaves and berries of the tea plant, which are dried and then brewed with boiling water. Many people then add milk, lemon or sugar to make the tea taste nicer.

Tea fights free radicals, which are dangerous molecules. They occur naturally in the body, but are also produced by pollution. Substances called antioxidants help stop free radicals doing too much damage. Tannin is an antioxidant. It also helps fight bacteria and viruses. Tannin tastes very bitter, and funnily enough a lot of plants contain it to stop animals eating them, but it doesn't stop people drinking tea!

It's not just the Doctor who needs tea to wake him up, lots of humans like to have a cup of tea first thing in the morning as well!

TEST YOUR KNOWLEDGE

1. WHO WAS THE TIME WAR BETWEEN?
A. Time Lords and Daleks
B. Cybermen and Slitheen
C. Time Lords and Krillitanes

2. HOW MANY TIMES HAS THE DOCTOR REGENERATED?
A. 1
B. 13
C. 9

3. WHAT HELPED THE DOCTOR RECOVER FROM HIS NINTH REGENERATION?
A. Lemonade
B. Cake
C. Tea

4. WHICH OF THESE DID NOT CAUSE THE DOCTOR TO REGENERATE?
A. Shot by a street gang
B. Stung by a bee
C. Poisoned by radiation

5. WHO DID THE DOCTOR SAVE BY ABSORBING THE ENERGY FROM THE TIME VORTEX?
A. Rose
B. Sarah Jane
C. The Time Lords

28 | TECHNOLOGY AND TRANSPORT

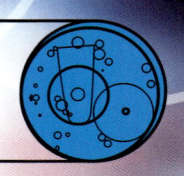

THE TARDIS

The TARDIS is not just a spaceship, it's the Doctor's home. The initials TARDIS stand for 'Time and Relative Dimension in Space' and the ship is dimensionally transcendental, which means it's bigger on the inside than the outside. The TARDIS has a chameleon circuit which is supposed to disguise the ship so it fits in with its surroundings, but the circuit got stuck during a visit to the 1960s, and now the TARDIS always looks like a police box. It doesn't fly like a normal spaceship, but dematerialises in one place and appears somewhere else.

By the way, did we mention? It also travels in time.

29

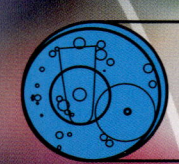

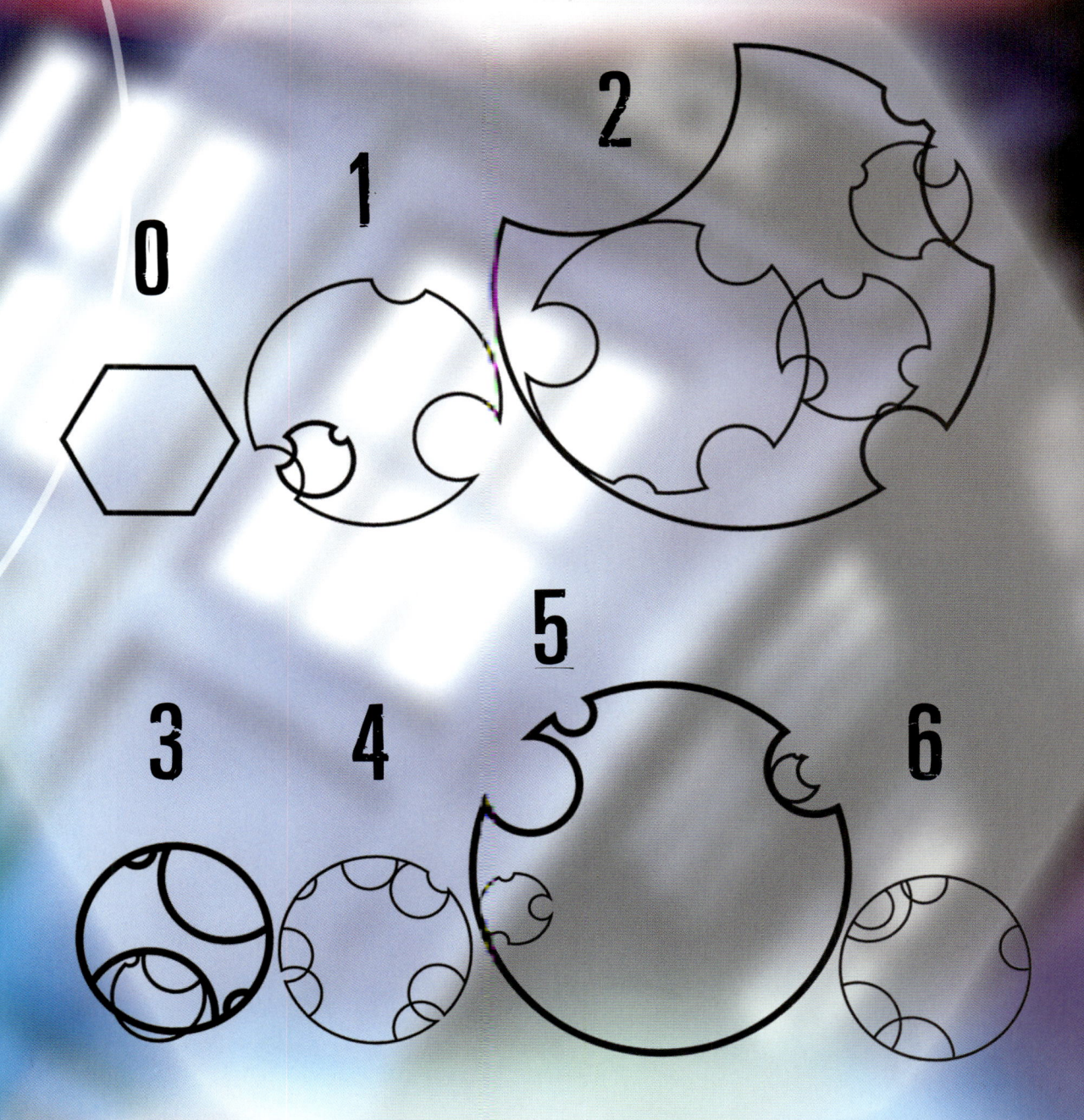

NUMBERS

The Doctor is an expert in maths and science, which allows him to understand advanced technology like the TARDIS. But the TARDIS isn't programmed using Earth numbers — the Doctor uses a Gallifreyan method of counting.

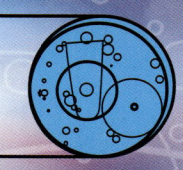

THE SONIC SCREWDRIVER

The Doctor would be in a hole without his sonic screwdriver. This marvellous device can do almost anything, apart from triplicate the flammability of alcohol! It can:

- Reattach barbed wire
- Cut off remote signals
- Reverse teleportation
- Resonate concrete
- Open any lock — except a deadlock seal
- Burn through rope
- Disable security cameras
- Operate the TARDIS by remote control
- And of course, put up cabinets!

PSYCHIC PAPER

If the Doctor needs to get into a restricted area, assume a fake identity or just crash a party, his psychic paper is invaluable. When someone looks at it, they see whatever the Doctor wants them to see. It's come to his rescue on many occasions: from gaining access to the Earthdeath ceremony on Platform One, to persuading people he's working for the management of Satellite Five or has been appointed as protector to Queen Victoria. It even carries messages, such as when the Face of Boe summoned him to New Earth. With psychic paper in his wallet and a sonic screwdriver in his pocket, the Doctor can't be stopped!

TEST YOUR KNOWLEDGE

1. WHAT IS SUPPOSED TO DISGUISE THE TARDIS?
   A. Chameleon circuit
   B. Psychic paint
   C. Sonic circuit

2. WHICH OF THESE THINGS CAN THE SONIC SCREWDRIVER DO?
   A. Resonate concrete
   B. Open a deadlock seal
   C. Triplicate the flammability of alcohol

3. WHO SENT THE DOCTOR A MESSAGE VIA HIS PSYCHIC PAPER?
   A. Sarah Jane
   B. Cassandra
   C. The Face of Boe

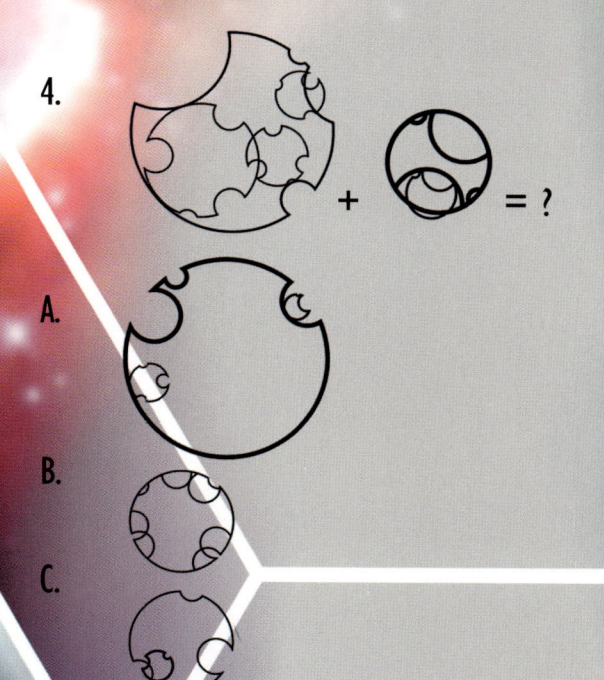

4.
   A.
   B.
   C.

32 | TENTH DOCTOR TRAVELS

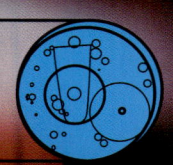

THE CHRISTMAS INVASION
The TARDIS first brought the new Doctor to Earth, on Christmas Eve, just as the evil Sycorax launched an attack on the planet. But the Doctor, recovering from his recent regeneration, had to wake up before he could try to defeat the aliens!

ATTACK OF THE GRASKE
The alien Graske take over a planet by replacing its population with duplicates. The Doctor discovered a Graske had infiltrated a family Christmas on present-day Earth, and then followed it back to London in 1883. The Graske escaped to its home planet, Griffoth, and the Doctor followed to rescue the humans who'd been replaced.

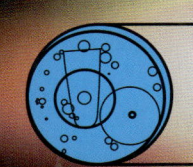

NEW EARTH

When the Doctor and Rose visited the planet of New Earth, they found their old enemy Cassandra lurking in a hospital basement. But she wasn't responsible for the deadly secret that the cat-like nurses were hiding in the intensive care ward...

TOOTH AND CLAW

In 1879, Her Majesty Queen Victoria, together with the Doctor and Rose, sought shelter in a Scottish manor house. Little realising that they'd been deliberately lured there by werewolves who wanted a lycanthrope on the throne. For their help, the Doctor and Rose were dubbed Sir Doctor of TARDIS and Dame Rose of the Powell Estate.

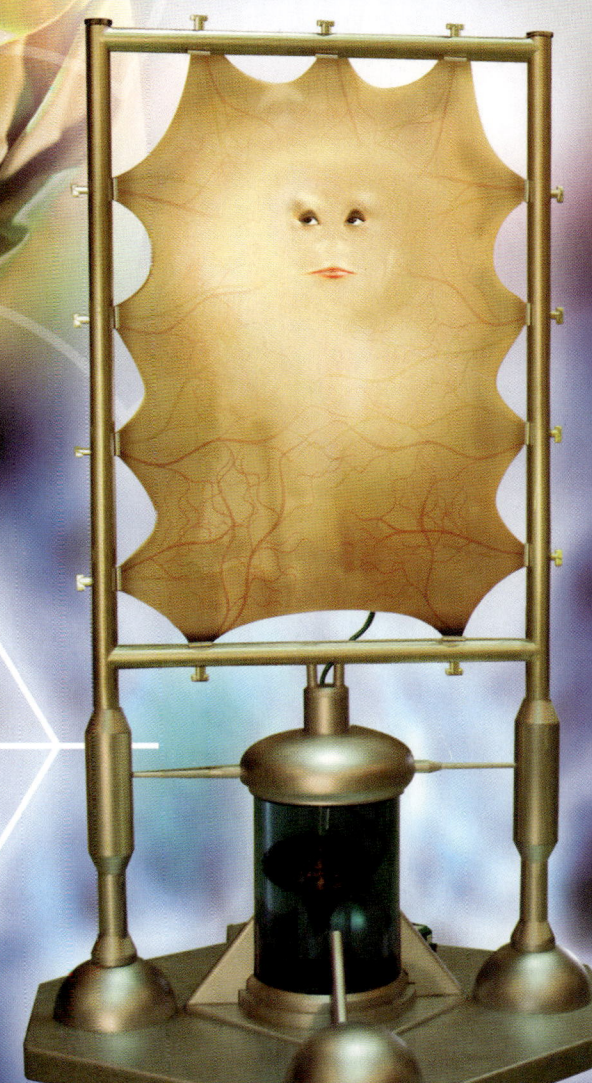

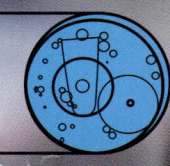

SCHOOL REUNION

Reports of UFOs from Mickey and a school that got record results brought the Doctor and Rose to present-day Earth, where they had to defeat the evil Krillitanes. But the Doctor's old friend Sarah Jane was also investigating the strange goings-on, and the Doctor discovered what effect he has on the people he leaves behind.

THE GIRL IN THE FIREPLACE

A strange conduit between a spaceship and 18th-century France led to the Doctor's life becoming entwined with that of the beautiful Madame de Pompadour, whom he had to save from terrifying clockwork robots of the future which had been tracking her since childhood.

RISE OF THE CYBERMEN/ THE AGE OF STEEL

The TARDIS fell through the Vortex and landed on a parallel Earth, in time for the Doctor to witness the birth of one of his deadliest enemies. In this universe, John Lumic's Cybus Industries was poised to take over the world — by 'upgrading' every human into an emotionless metal Cyberman.

OTHER ADVENTURES

The Doctor has had many other adventures, such as investigating the disappearance of faces in 1950s England and helping the alien Isolus during the 2012 Olympics. And you can guarantee there are plenty more to come. Wherever there's danger and excitement, you're sure to find the Doctor!

TEST YOUR KNOWLEDGE

1. WHAT ENEMIES DID THE DOCTOR FACE AT CHRISTMAS?
   A. Cybermen and Daleks
   B. Sycorax and Graske
   C. Krillitanes and Werewolves

2. WHICH OLD ENEMY DID THE DOCTOR FIND ON NEW EARTH?
   A. Cassandra
   B. Sarah Jane
   C. Cybermen

3. WHO DID THE DOCTOR MEET IN 18TH-CENTURY FRANCE?
   A. Queen Victoria
   B. Madame de Pompadour
   C. Cassandra

4. WHAT TITLE DID QUEEN VICTORIA GIVE TO THE DOCTOR?
   A. Lord Doctor of Time
   B. Baron Doctor of Space
   C. Sir Doctor of TARDIS

5. WHICH OLD FRIEND DID THE DOCTOR MEET WHILE INVESTIGATING THE KRILLITANES?
   A. Sarah Jane
   B. John Lumic
   C. Jackie Tyler

TEST YOUR KNOWLEDGE

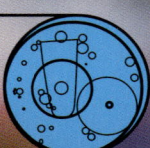

ANSWERS

Meet the Doctor
1(b) 2(a) 3(a) 4(c) 5(b)

Companions
1(b) 2(c) 3(b) 4(c) 5(a)

Enemies
1(b) 2(a) 3(b) 4(c) 5(b)

Time Lords
1(a) 2(c) 3(c) 4(b) 5(a)

Technology and Transport
1(a) 2(a) 3(c) 4(a)

Tenth Doctor Travels
1(b) 2(a) 3(b) 4(c) 5(a)

DOCTOR·WHO

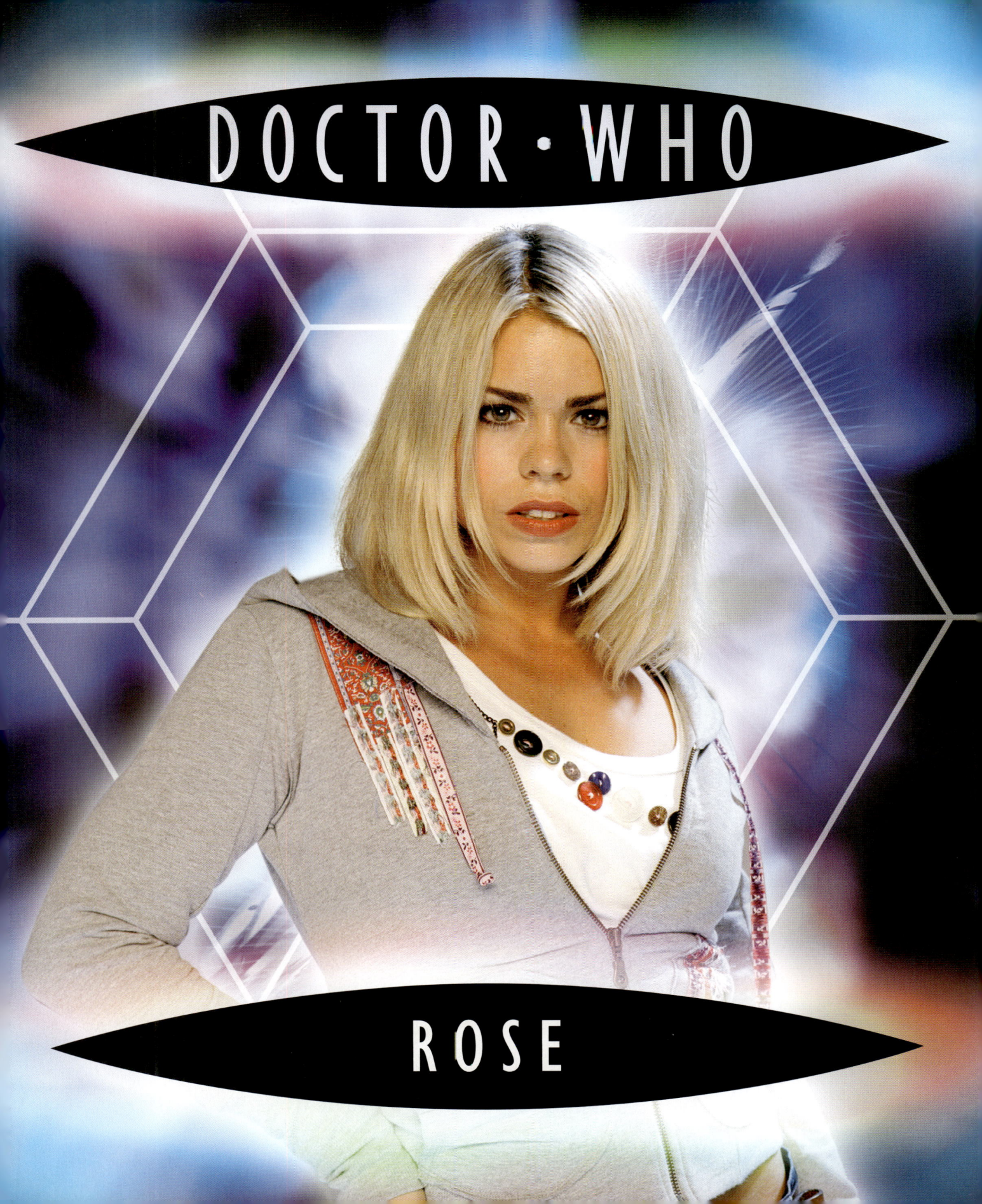

ROSE

BIOHAZARD
MUST BE WORN IN THIS AREA
PERSONNEL ONLY

CONTENTS

Meet Rose

Introduction..................................40
Rose Data....................................42
Rose Anatomy...............................44
◆ Test your Knowledge

Friends and Family

The Doctor...................................46
Mickey..47
Jackie and Pete.............................48
Captain Jack.................................48
◆ Test your Knowledge

Enemies and Rivals

The Daleks...................................50
The Cybermen...............................51
The Slitheen.................................52
Cassandra....................................52
◆ Test your Knowledge

No Place Like Home

Earth..54
Travels Through Time.....................56
◆ Test your Knowledge

Transport and Technology

The TARDIS..................................58
Bad Wolf.....................................59
Jack's Gadgets..............................60
Mobile Phone................................60
◆ Test your Knowledge

Adventures at Home 62
◆ Test your Knowledge

Test your Knowledge Answers 66

40 MEET ROSE

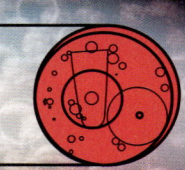

If you passed Rose Tyler in the street, you'd think she was an ordinary teenager. And in many ways you'd be right. Rose went to school like everyone else. She left school after her GCSEs and eventually got a job in a department store called Henrik's. The rest of the time she liked going clubbing with her friends and seeing her boyfriend, Mickey Smith. She lived in a flat with her mum, Jackie, but her dad, Pete, died when she was small.

But one day, something incredible happened. A mysterious stranger rescued Rose from a horde of killer shop dummies, and the ordinary 19 year old girl from Earth found herself caught up in an alien invasion! After Rose helped the Doctor to foil the aliens' plans, he invited her to join him on his travels through time and space.

41

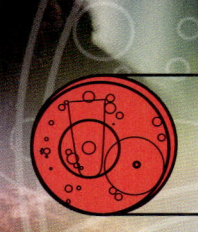

So, Rose joined the Doctor in his incredible spaceship, the TARDIS, and they flew off to have exciting adventures together. She's met all sorts of people, and fought all sorts of monsters. She's been to the past and the future. She's proved herself to be brave, resourceful, caring and loyal, in fact, she's even saved the world. Rose might be an ordinary teenager, but she's definitely an extraordinary person!

42 ROSE DATA

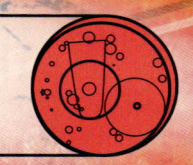

Name: Rose Marion Tyler
Date of birth: 27 April 1987
Parents: Jackie and Pete Tyler
Height: 1.63m (5'4")
Hair: Blonde
Eyes: Brown
Home planet: Earth
Home address: 48 Bucknall House, Powell Estate, London SE15 7GO
Species: Human
Profession: Adventurer

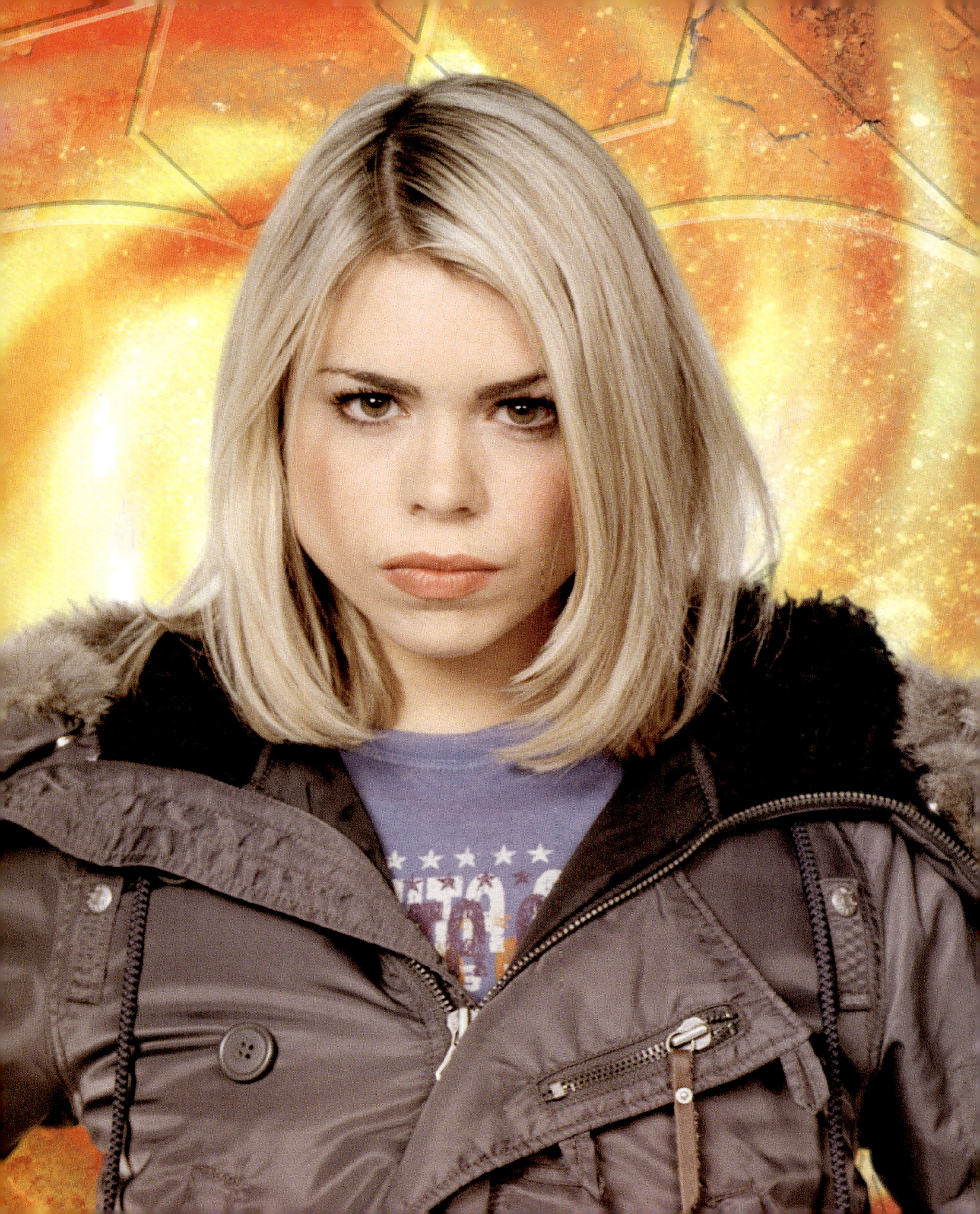

44 ROSE ANATOMY

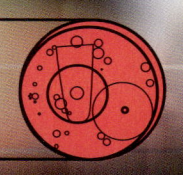

1.63m tall

Eyes inherited from dad Pete

The TARDIS puts a telepathic field inside her brain so she can understand different languages

Chin that pokes out, according to Cassandra

Handy pocket for carrying mobile phone and TARDIS key

Trainers for running fast

TEST YOUR KNOWLEDGE

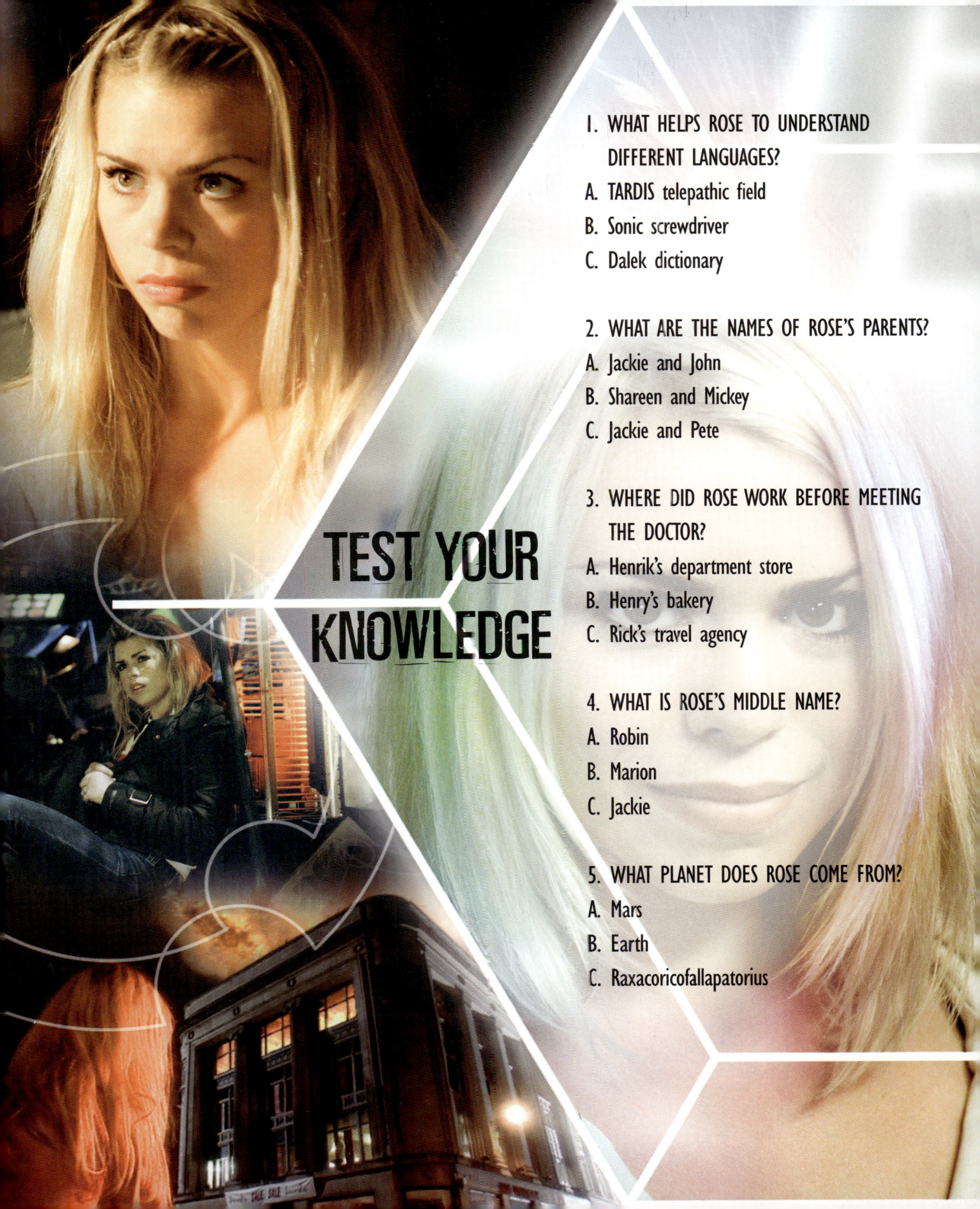

1. **WHAT HELPS ROSE TO UNDERSTAND DIFFERENT LANGUAGES?**
   A. TARDIS telepathic field
   B. Sonic screwdriver
   C. Dalek dictionary

2. **WHAT ARE THE NAMES OF ROSE'S PARENTS?**
   A. Jackie and John
   B. Shareen and Mickey
   C. Jackie and Pete

3. **WHERE DID ROSE WORK BEFORE MEETING THE DOCTOR?**
   A. Henrik's department store
   B. Henry's bakery
   C. Rick's travel agency

4. **WHAT IS ROSE'S MIDDLE NAME?**
   A. Robin
   B. Marion
   C. Jackie

5. **WHAT PLANET DOES ROSE COME FROM?**
   A. Mars
   B. Earth
   C. Raxacoricofallapatorius

46 FRIENDS AND FAMILY

THE DOCTOR

Rose's best friend is the Doctor. He's the last of the Time Lords, a powerful race who were destroyed in the Time War against the Daleks. A Time Lord has the amazing ability to save himself from death by changing every cell in his body — this is called regeneration. Since Rose met the Doctor, he has been forced to regenerate and Rose has had to get used to a completely new Doctor. Luckily, she likes him just as much as the old one!

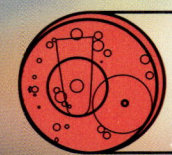

MICKEY

Mickey Smith has been Rose's on-off boyfriend for years, they first started going out when Rose was 14. Mickey's computer skills have proved invaluable to the Doctor, and he's helped to save Earth from the Slitheen and the Krillitane among others. After Mickey helped to defeat John Lumic and Cybus Industries on a parallel Earth, he decided to stay behind to help fight the Cybermen and look after his other-universe grandmother, Rita-Anne. Rose was sad to say goodbye, but proud of Mickey and his choice.

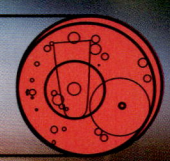

JACKIE AND PETE

Jacqueline Andrea Suzette Prentice and Peter Alan Tyler got married in 1982, and five years later had a daughter, Rose. Pete was a wheeler-dealer, and Jackie was often frustrated by his money-making schemes, but they loved each other and Jackie was devastated when Pete was killed in an accident in November 1987. Rose put everyone in danger when she travelled back to the past to try to save his life, and released the Reapers by opening up a rift in time. But Pete proved himself a hero when he sacrificed himself to save the world. Jackie can be bossy and irritating, as the Doctor discovered very early on, but she loves Rose very much and would do anything for her.

CAPTAIN JACK

Rose met con man of the future Jack Harkness in 1941, when he was pretending to be a Royal Air Force captain during the Second World War. Rose and Jack became good friends (and they fancied each other too!) but Jack was killed by the Daleks while trying to save the Earth. Rose used her Bad Wolf powers to bring him back to life, but Jack was left behind on the Game Station when the Doctor and Rose departed in the TARDIS.

TEST YOUR KNOWLEDGE

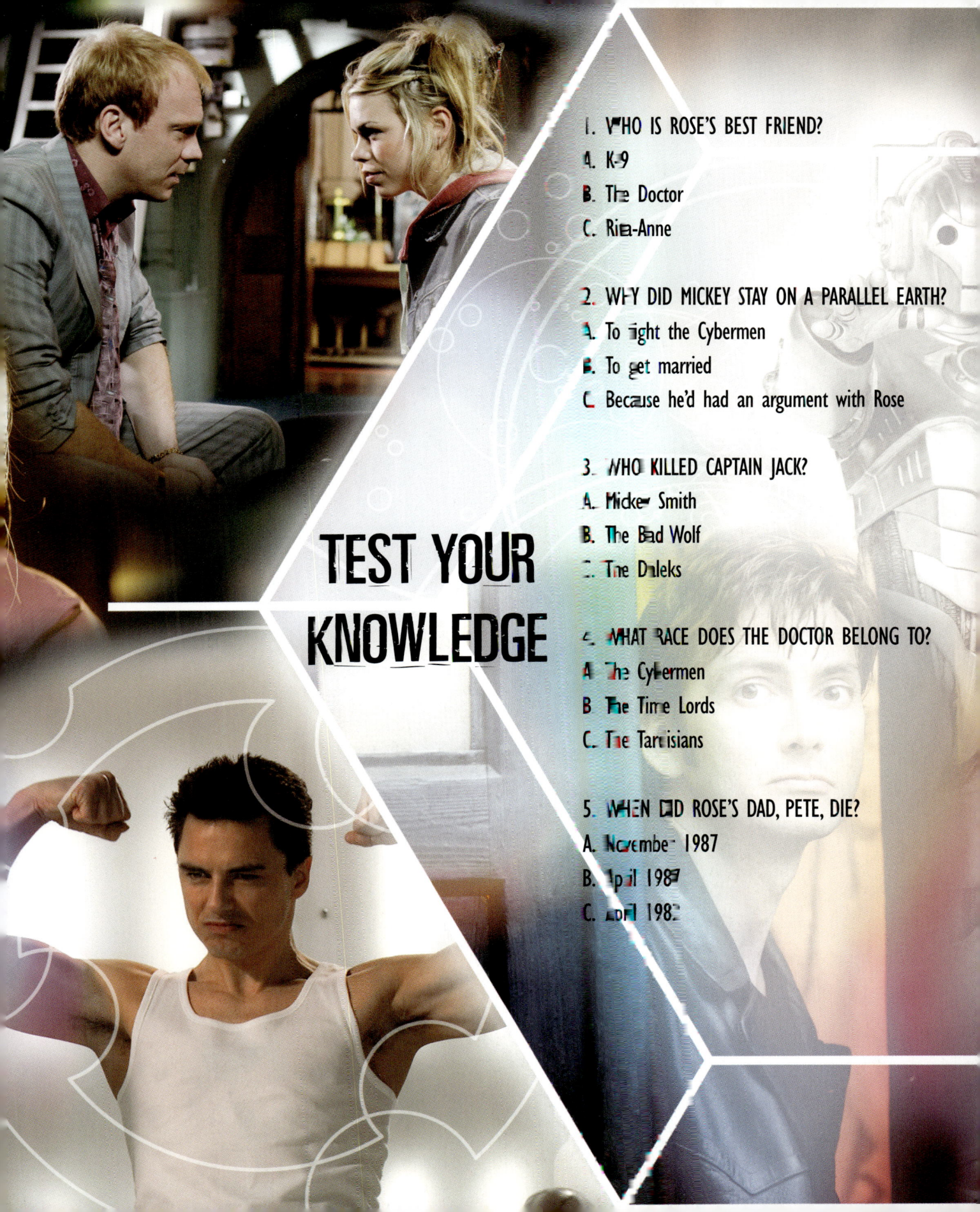

1. WHO IS ROSE'S BEST FRIEND?
A. K-9
B. The Doctor
C. Rita-Anne

2. WHY DID MICKEY STAY ON A PARALLEL EARTH?
A. To fight the Cybermen
B. To get married
C. Because he'd had an argument with Rose

3. WHO KILLED CAPTAIN JACK?
A. Mickey Smith
B. The Bad Wolf
C. The Daleks

4. WHAT RACE DOES THE DOCTOR BELONG TO?
A. The Cybermen
B. The Time Lords
C. The Tardisians

5. WHEN DID ROSE'S DAD, PETE, DIE?
A. November 1987
B. April 1987
C. April 1982

50 ENEMIES AND RIVALS

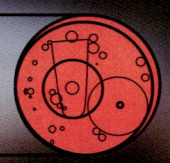

THE DALEKS

The Daleks are evil mutant creatures living inside deadly metal machines. Everyone dreads hearing their terrible battle cry 'Exterminate!' Rose first met a Dalek in Utah, 2012, when the injured creature used her DNA to heal itself. She felt sorry for this Dalek — but she certainly didn't feel sorry for the Dalek army she encountered in 200,100, when billions of Daleks, under the control of their mad Emperor, tried to destroy Earth and turn all humans into Daleks. Rose unleashed the power of the Time Vortex from the TARDIS and used it to annihilate the Daleks. Is she now their greatest enemy?

THE CYBERMEN

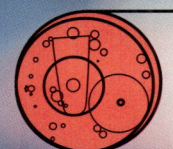

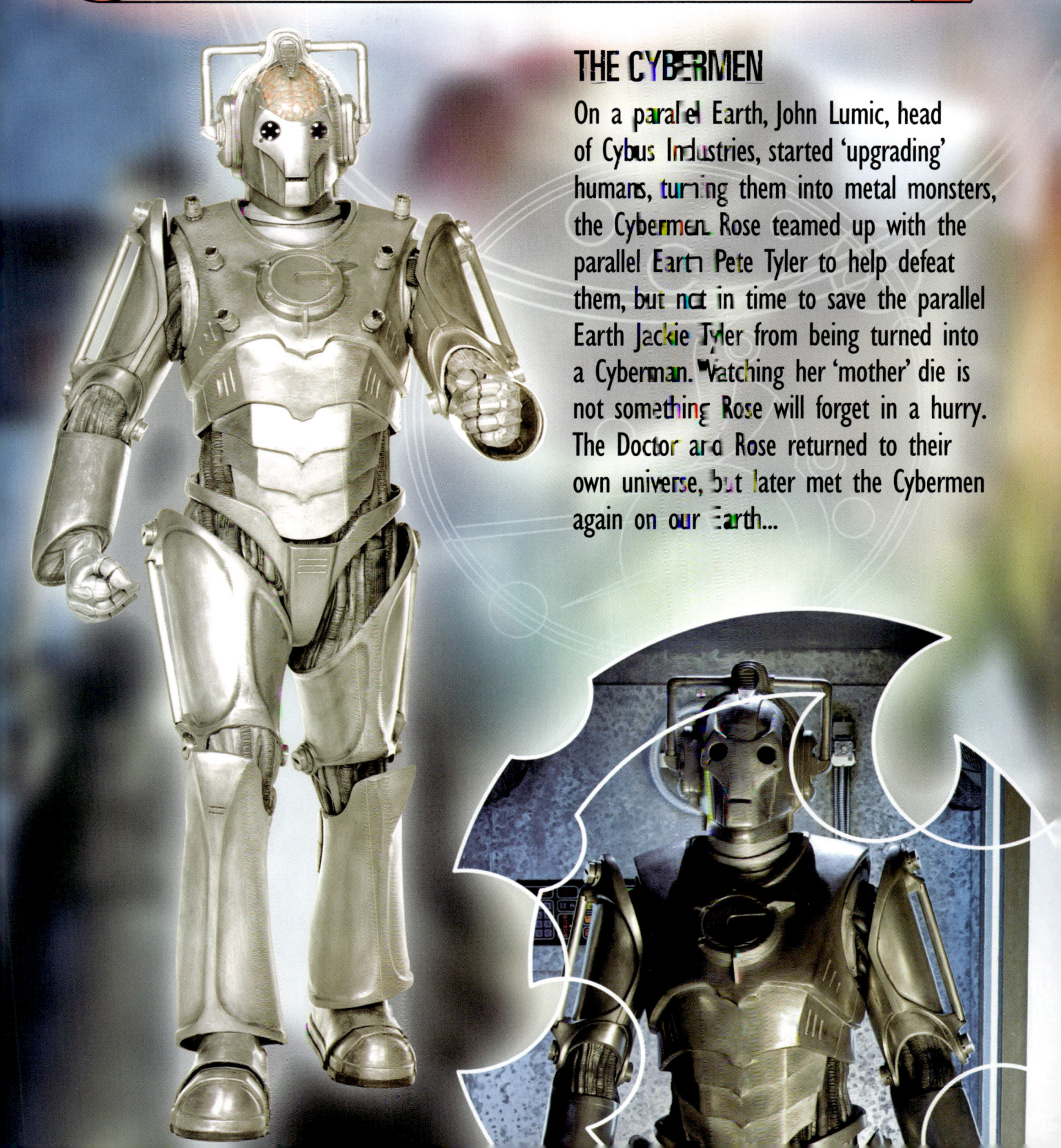

On a parallel Earth, John Lumic, head of Cybus Industries, started 'upgrading' humans, turning them into metal monsters, the Cybermen. Rose teamed up with the parallel Earth Pete Tyler to help defeat them, but not in time to save the parallel Earth Jackie Tyler from being turned into a Cyberman. Watching her 'mother' die is not something Rose will forget in a hurry. The Doctor and Rose returned to their own universe, but later met the Cybermen again on our Earth...

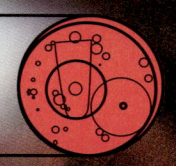

SLITHEEN

The Slitheen are a family of criminals from the planet Raxacoricofallapatorius. Rose became very unpopular with them when she helped the Doctor to foil their plan to destroy the Earth and then sell the remaining radioactive chunks as starship fuel. She later helped to defeat the one remaining monster, Blon Fel Fotch Pasameer-Day Slitheen, whose attempts to leave the planet threatened to blow up Earth — again!

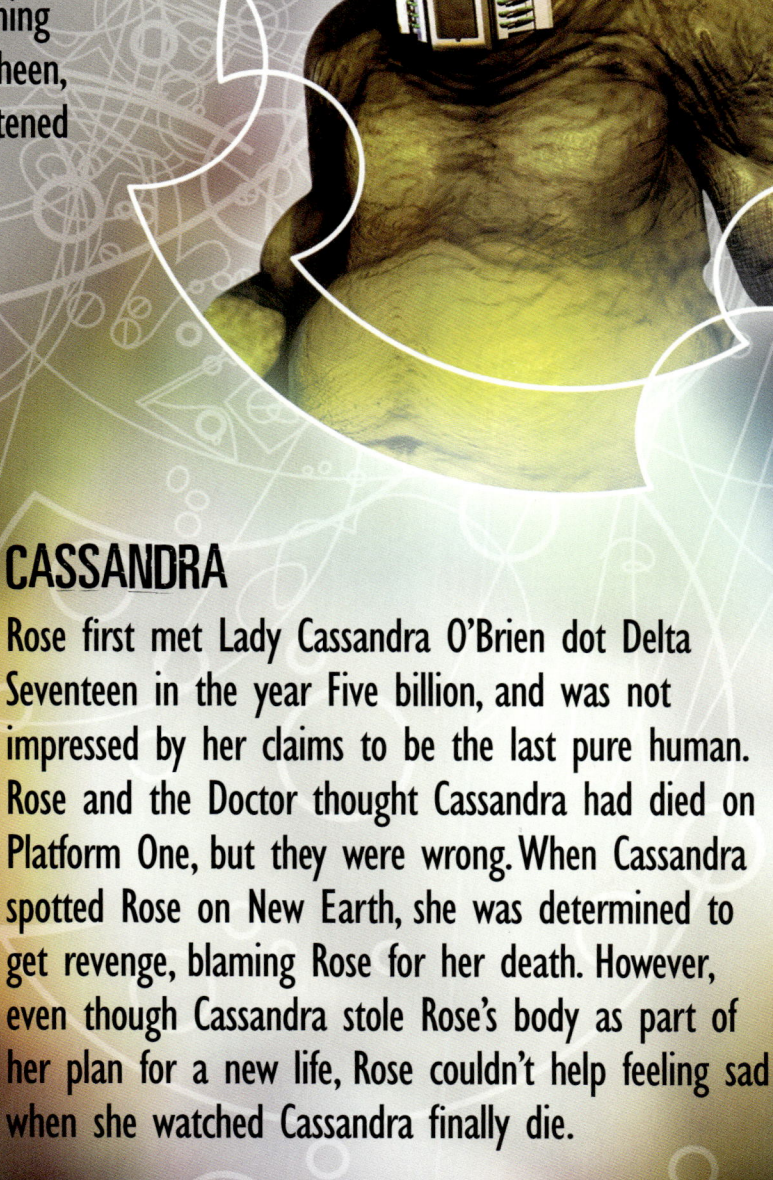

CASSANDRA

Rose first met Lady Cassandra O'Brien dot Delta Seventeen in the year Five billion, and was not impressed by her claims to be the last pure human. Rose and the Doctor thought Cassandra had died on Platform One, but they were wrong. When Cassandra spotted Rose on New Earth, she was determined to get revenge, blaming Rose for her death. However, even though Cassandra stole Rose's body as part of her plan for a new life, Rose couldn't help feeling sad when she watched Cassandra finally die.

TEST YOUR KNOWLEDGE

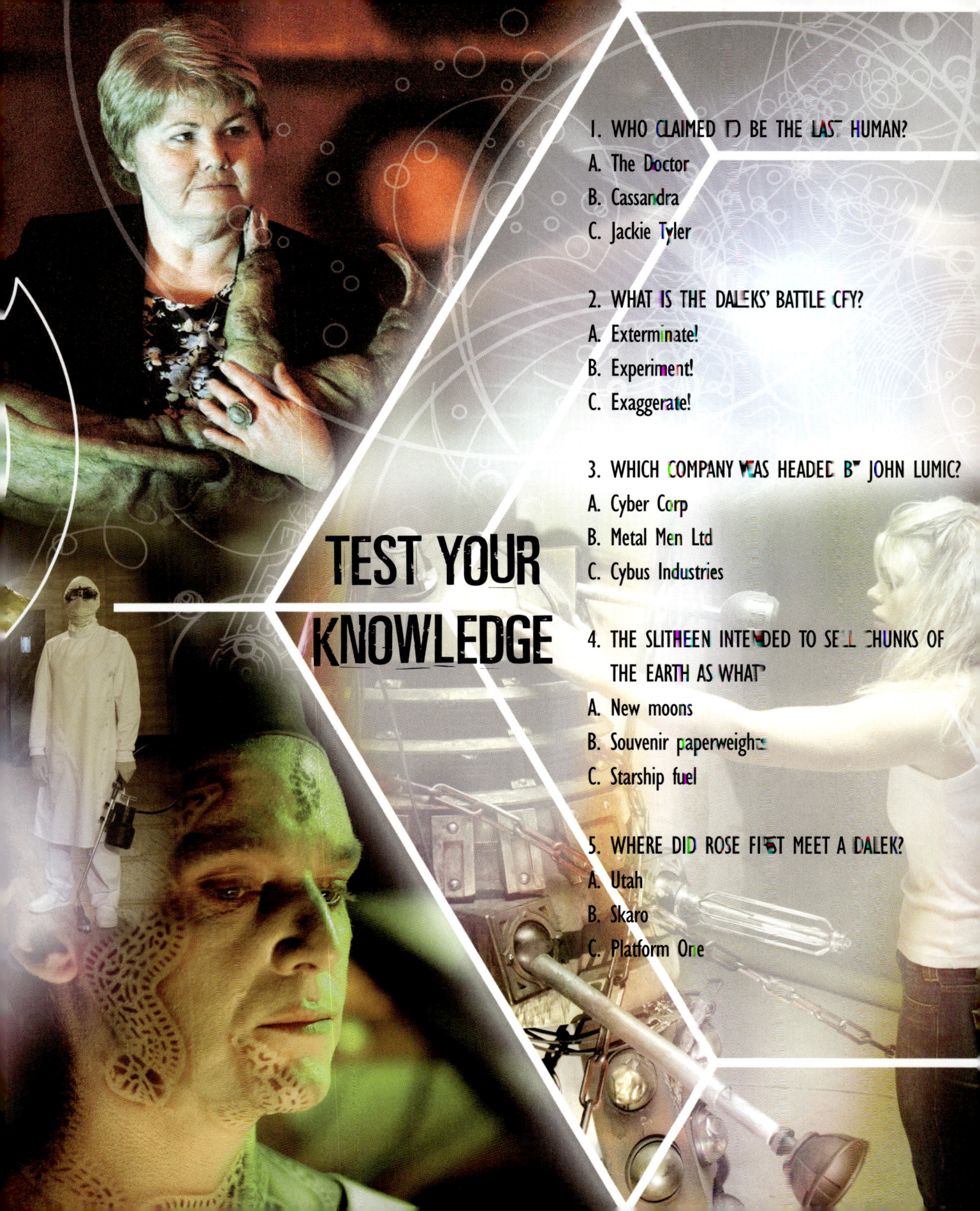

1. WHO CLAIMED TO BE THE LAST HUMAN?
A. The Doctor
B. Cassandra
C. Jackie Tyler

2. WHAT IS THE DALEKS' BATTLE CRY?
A. Exterminate!
B. Experiment!
C. Exaggerate!

3. WHICH COMPANY WAS HEADED BY JOHN LUMIC?
A. Cyber Corp
B. Metal Men Ltd
C. Cybus Industries

4. THE SLITHEEN INTENDED TO SELL CHUNKS OF THE EARTH AS WHAT?
A. New moons
B. Souvenir paperweights
C. Starship fuel

5. WHERE DID ROSE FIRST MEET A DALEK?
A. Utah
B. Skaro
C. Platform One

54 NO PLACE LIKE HOME

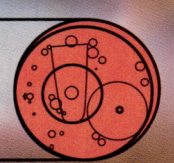

EARTH

Rose comes from the planet Earth — you might have heard of it!

Earth is part of our solar system, which is in the outer reaches of the Milky Way galaxy. It is the third planet out from the sun, and the fifth largest in the solar system. Most humans believe Earth is the only planet in the solar system capable of supporting life, but the Doctor might not agree with them!

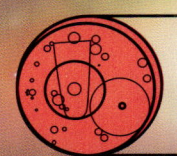

Earth has one satellite, the moon. The moon doesn't have an atmosphere, so a human being needs to wear a spacesuit there in order to survive. The first man to step on to its surface was Captain Neil Armstrong, in July 1969.

Approximately 70 per cent of Earth is covered in water. Around 6 billion people live on the land that makes up the other 30 per cent of Earth's surface. The land is divided into seven continents: North America, South America, Europe, Asia, Africa, Australia and Antarctica.

Rose comes from London, in the United Kingdom, which is part of the continent of Europe.

TRAVELS THROUGH TIME

The TARDIS is a time machine, and the Doctor loves the planet Earth, so he's taken Rose to see her planet's past, and its future. Rose has visited prehistoric times, Ancient Rome and London in the 1930s, and seen Earth from space in the year 200,000. And that's not all...

Rose made friends with novelist Charles Dickens when the Doctor took her to Victorian Cardiff in 1869. The famous writer even helped the Doctor and Rose to defeat the terrifying Gelth. But Dickens is not the only well-known Victorian Rose has encountered. Queen Victoria, the most famous Victorian of them all, was not amused to find there were werewolves in Scotland, 1855, but Rose was very impressed to meet the monarch who reigned from 1837 to 1901.

Rose had learnt about the Second World War in History lessons, but that didn't prepare her for landing in the middle of it. In September 1939, Britain and France declared war after Germany invaded Poland. The war lasted until 1945, and millions of people were killed, but the Doctor and Rose managed to save a few lives when they arrived in war-torn England in 1941.

By 200,000, Earth has five moons and a population of 96 billion. A hundred years later, the Daleks destroy the continents of Europa, Pacifica, the New American Alliance and Australasia, but by the time Rose arrives on Platform One in the year Five billion, the National Trust has restored Earth to its 'classic' state, and the continents have returned to their twenty-first-century positions. The sun finally expands and Earth explodes. Rose's planet is no more.

TEST YOUR KNOWLEDGE

Earth may have gone, but that's not the end. Nostalgic humans find a planet the same size as Earth, with the same atmosphere and the same orbit, and they create New Earth — Earth Two. When the TARDIS lands near the city of New New York in the year five billion and twenty-three, it's clear to Rose that although her planet has been destroyed, Earth, and humanity, will go on.

1. HOW MANY MOONS DOES EARTH HAVE BY THE YEAR 200,000?
   A. Eight
   B. Five
   C. One

2. WHICH FAMOUS NOVELIST DID ROSE MEET IN VICTORIAN CARDIFF?
   A. Charles Dickens
   B. Charles Gelth
   C. Queen Victoria

3. HOW MUCH OF EARTH'S SURFACE IS COVERED BY WATER?
   A. 70 per cent
   B. 30 per cent
   C. 50 per cent

4. WHAT GALAXY IS EARTH IN?
   A. Mars
   B. Milky Bottle
   C. Milky Way

5. IN HOW MANY YEARS IN THE FUTURE DOES EARTH EXPLODE?
   A. 5 million
   B. 50 million
   C. 5 billion

58 TRANSPORT AND TECHNOLOGY

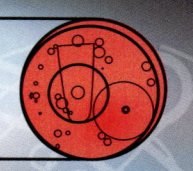

THE TARDIS

When she started travelling with the Doctor, Rose swapped cars and buses for a spaceship! The TARDIS may be disguised as an old Earth police box, but it can travel anywhere in time and space. Though it doesn't always arrive exactly where the Doctor planned, such as the time it brought Rose back home a year after she'd left, instead of the next day! The Doctor suspected that Rose only started travelling with him because he told her the TARDIS travelled in time, which meant she could go back to the past to see her dad. Even if that was the truth, Rose proved herself to be the perfect TARDIS passenger time and time again.

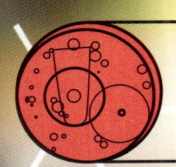

BAD WOLF

Rose has been closer to the TARDIS than any other companion of the Doctor. Desperate to rescue the Doctor from the Daleks, she enlisted Mickey and Jackie's help to access the heart of the TARDIS. She looked into the Time Vortex and absorbed it, gaining power over life and death. Rose became the Bad Wolf, spreading a message to herself across all of time and space, leading her to a certain moment in time. She destroyed the Daleks and saved the Doctor, but the vortex was killing her. The Doctor gave up his own life to save Rose, draining the power from his best friend through a kiss.

JACK'S GADGETS

Despite being surrounded by alien technology, Rose wished the Doctor could be a bit more 'sci-fi' occasionally. So she was pretty impressed when she met Captain Jack with his invisible spaceship, tractor beams and scans for alien tech — not to mention his all-in-one sonic blaster, sonic cannon and triple-enfolded sonic disruptor!

MOBILE PHONE

The Doctor modified Rose's ordinary phone so it worked anywhere in time and space and across any distance. It not only allowed Rose to keep in touch with her home, but it played a vital role in many of her adventures, from enabling the Doctor to communicate with Mickey in order to defeat the Slitheen, to providing the codes that would destroy the Cybermen. Mickey kept the phone when he stayed behind on the parallel Earth to help in his continuing fight against the metal monsters.

TEST YOUR KNOWLEDGE

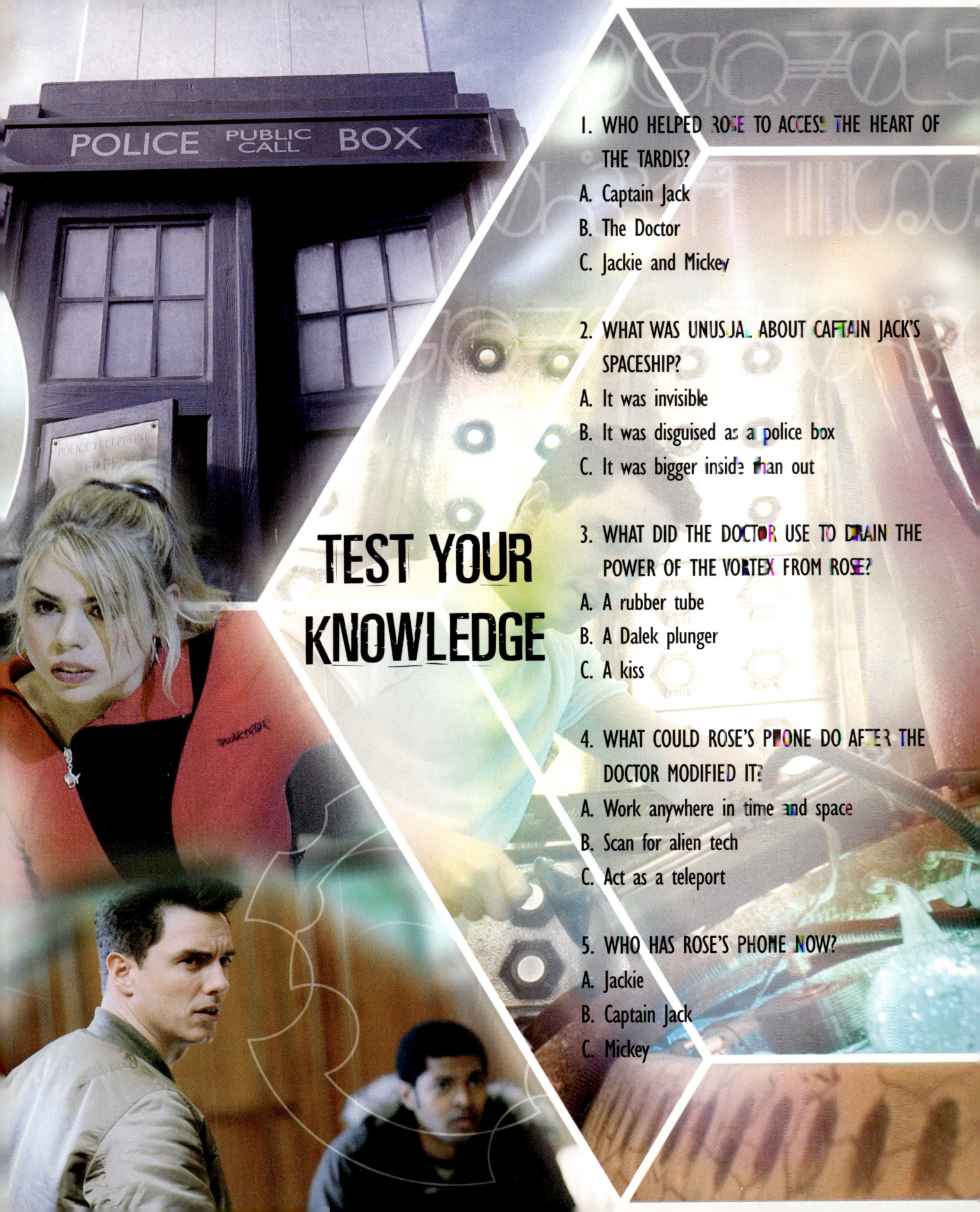

1. WHO HELPED ROSE TO ACCESS THE HEART OF THE TARDIS?
   A. Captain Jack
   B. The Doctor
   C. Jackie and Mickey

2. WHAT WAS UNUSUAL ABOUT CAPTAIN JACK'S SPACESHIP?
   A. It was invisible
   B. It was disguised as a police box
   C. It was bigger inside than out

3. WHAT DID THE DOCTOR USE TO DRAIN THE POWER OF THE VORTEX FROM ROSE?
   A. A rubber tube
   B. A Dalek plunger
   C. A kiss

4. WHAT COULD ROSE'S PHONE DO AFTER THE DOCTOR MODIFIED IT?
   A. Work anywhere in time and space
   B. Scan for alien tech
   C. Act as a teleport

5. WHO HAS ROSE'S PHONE NOW?
   A. Jackie
   B. Captain Jack
   C. Mickey

62 ADVENTURES AT HOME

When the Doctor tracked the Nestene Consciousness to twenty-first-century Earth, he had no idea he was about to meet a girl who was to become one of the most important people in his many lives. Rose Tyler, along with mum Jackie and boyfriend Mickey, soon found herself caught up in an incredible adventure. First she was attacked by shop dummies, then the store she worked in was blown up, and then her boyfriend was kidnapped and duplicated by aliens! But throughout it all, the Doctor was on hand. First he rescued Rose and then, in the end, she rescued him. The Doctor asked Rose to travel with him in the TARDIS and she said no. But luckily, she very soon changed her mind...

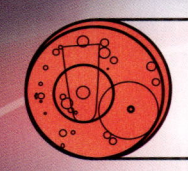

The Doctor took Rose home for a visit, but a miscalculation meant she'd been gone a year. She'd been reported missing, and Mickey had even been questioned about murdering her. Luckily everyone was distracted when a spaceship plummeted into the Thames. Soon Rose, Mickey and Jackie were caught up in the Slitheen's plot to destroy Earth, which was foiled when Mickey sent a missile to blow up 10 Downing Street. Rose decided to keep travelling with the Doctor, but she met up with Mickey again on her next visit home and once again the Slitheen were involved. The escaped Blon Fel Fotch had disguised herself as Lord Mayor of Cardiff, but they managed to capture her before she did any damage.

Jackie and Mickey tried to comfort Rose when the Doctor sent her home from the Game Station without him. But Rose was determined to go to his rescue and both Jackie and Mickey displayed great selflessness by helping her operate the TARDIS, even though they wanted her to stay on Earth in safety. They were overjoyed when the TARDIS arrived back on Christmas Eve, with Rose safe and sound, although with a new Doctor! Jackie helped look after the newly regenerated Doctor, while Mickey got caught up in the fight against the evil Sycorax. But with the menace defeated, the Doctor, Rose, Mickey and Jackie were able to celebrate Christmas together.

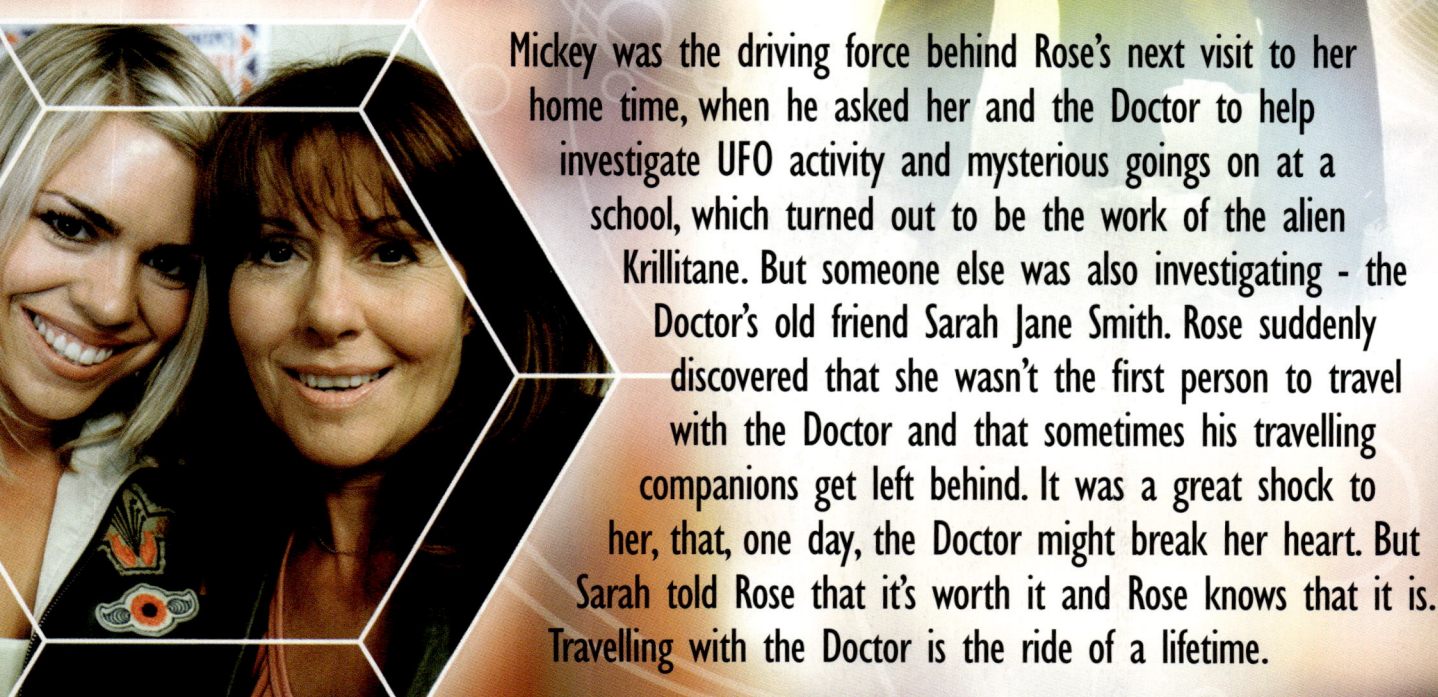

Mickey was the driving force behind Rose's next visit to her home time, when he asked her and the Doctor to help investigate UFO activity and mysterious goings on at a school, which turned out to be the work of the alien Krillitane. But someone else was also investigating - the Doctor's old friend Sarah Jane Smith. Rose suddenly discovered that she wasn't the first person to travel with the Doctor and that sometimes his travelling companions get left behind. It was a great shock to her, that, one day, the Doctor might break her heart. But Sarah told Rose that it's worth it and Rose knows that it is. Travelling with the Doctor is the ride of a lifetime.

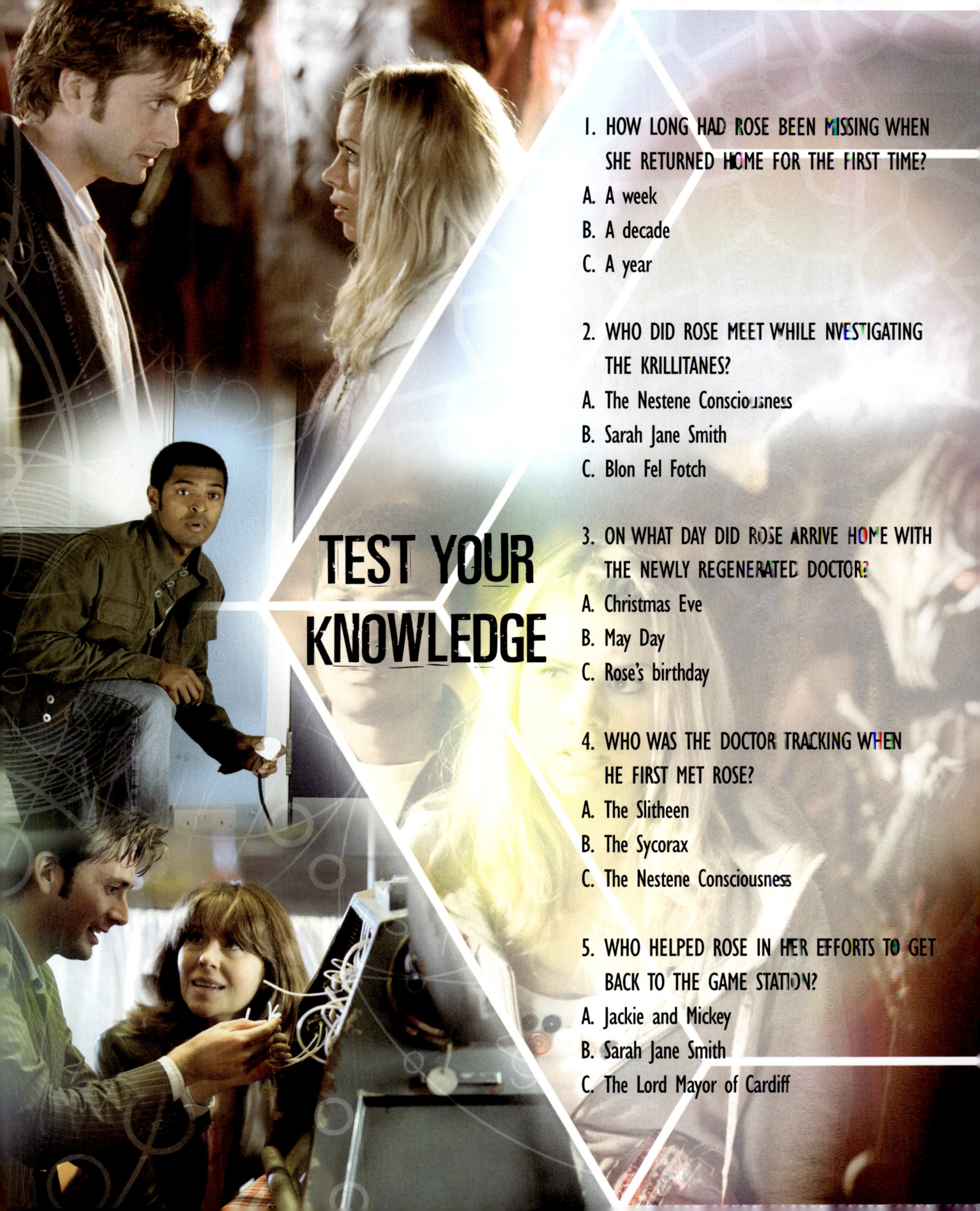

TEST YOUR KNOWLEDGE

1. HOW LONG HAD ROSE BEEN MISSING WHEN SHE RETURNED HOME FOR THE FIRST TIME?
   A. A week
   B. A decade
   C. A year

2. WHO DID ROSE MEET WHILE INVESTIGATING THE KRILLITANES?
   A. The Nestene Consciousness
   B. Sarah Jane Smith
   C. Blon Fel Fotch

3. ON WHAT DAY DID ROSE ARRIVE HOME WITH THE NEWLY REGENERATED DOCTOR?
   A. Christmas Eve
   B. May Day
   C. Rose's birthday

4. WHO WAS THE DOCTOR TRACKING WHEN HE FIRST MET ROSE?
   A. The Slitheen
   B. The Sycorax
   C. The Nestene Consciousness

5. WHO HELPED ROSE IN HER EFFORTS TO GET BACK TO THE GAME STATION?
   A. Jackie and Mickey
   B. Sarah Jane Smith
   C. The Lord Mayor of Cardiff

TEST YOUR KNOWLEDGE

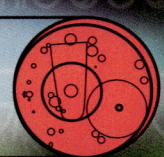

ANSWERS

Meet Rose
1 (a) 2 (c) 3 (a) 4 (b) 5 (b)

Friends and Family
1 (b) 2 (a) 3 (c) 4 (b) 5 (a)

Enemies and Rivals
1 (b) 2 (a) 3 (c) 4 (c) 5 (a)

No Place Like Home
1 (b) 2 (a) 3 (a) 4 (c) 5 (c)

Transport and Technology
1 (c) 2 (a) 3 (c) 4 (a) 5 (c)

Adventures at Home
1 (c) 2 (b) 3 (a) 4 (c) 5 (a)

DOCTOR·WHO

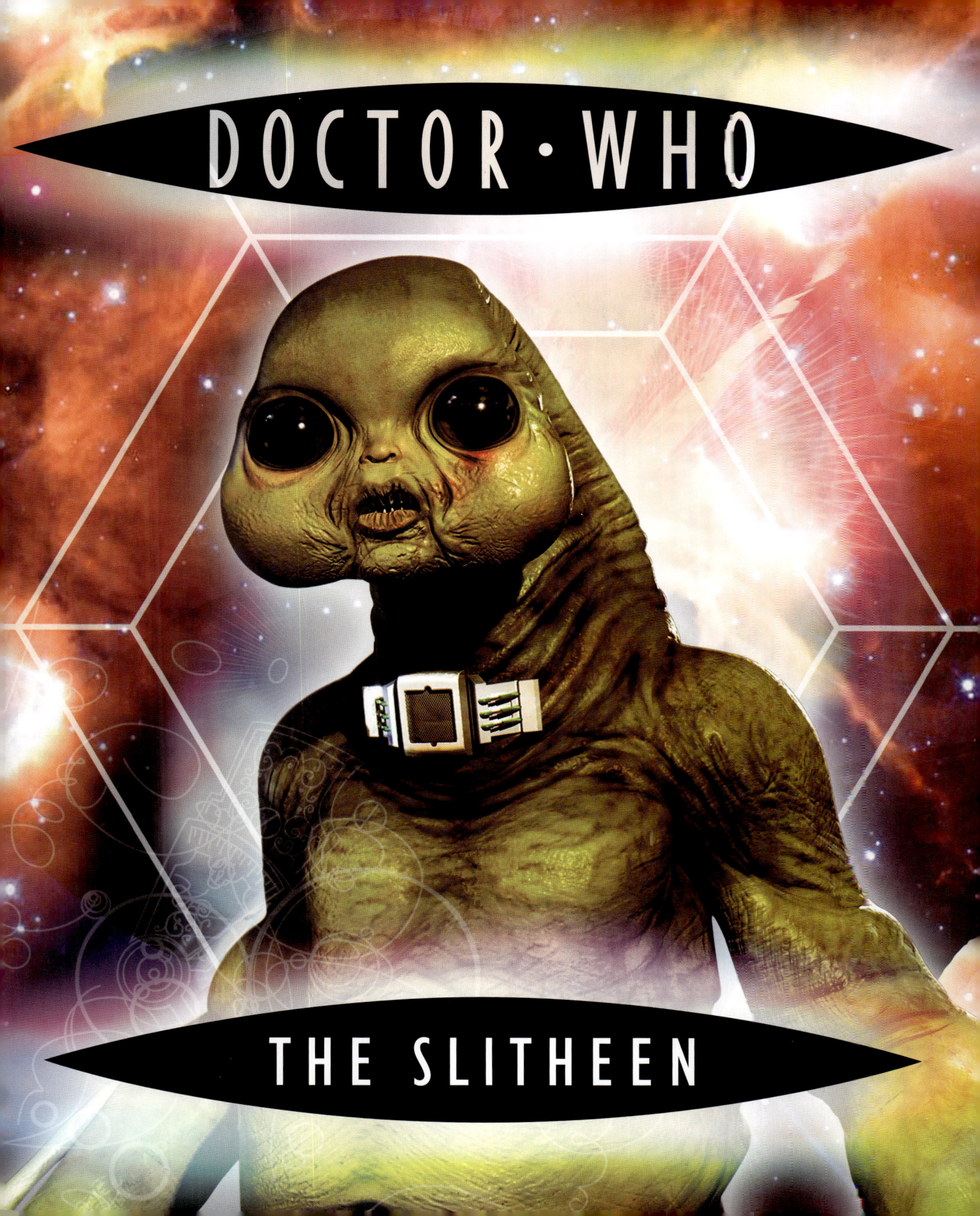

THE SLITHEEN

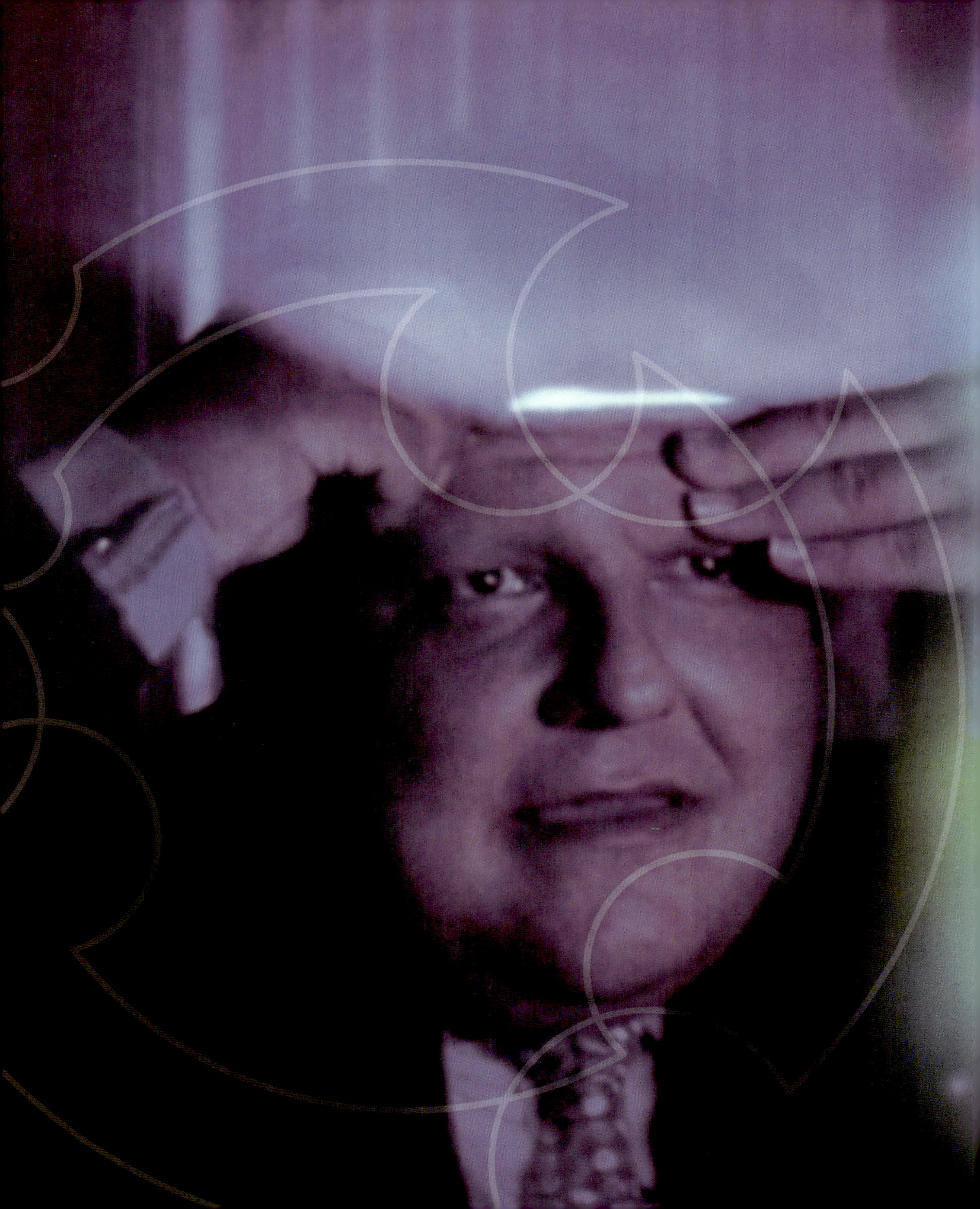

CONTENTS

Meet the Slitheen
Introduction..................................70
Slitheen Data...............................72
Slitheen Anatomy........................74
◆ Test your Knowledge

We Are Family
The Family Slitheen.....................76
Blon Fel Fotch.............................78
The Blathereen............................79
◆ Test your Knowledge

Human Enemies
The Doctor and Rose..................80
Jackie Tyler................................81
Mickey Smith..............................82
Harriet Jones..............................82
◆ Test your Knowledge

Background
Raxacoricofallapatorius...............84
Execution....................................85
The Slitheen's Weakness............86
◆ Test your Knowledge

Transport and Technology
Compression Field......................88
Teleportation...............................89
Spaceships and Space Pigs.......90
The Extrapolator.........................90
◆ Test your Knowledge

Adventures with the Slitheen
The Slitheen's Plan....................92
Blon's Second Chance..............94
Slitheen of the Future................95
◆ Test your Knowledge

Test your Knowledge Answers.......96

70 | MEET THE SLITHEEN

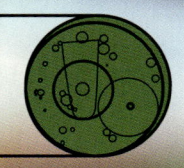

The Slitheen may have baby-like faces, but they're certainly not cute! Slitheens love the thrill of the chase and will happily hunt down humans and with their enormous claws and pointed teeth, humans don't stand much of a chance against them.

'Slitheen' isn't the name of an alien race, it's the surname of a family of alien criminals who come from the planet Raxacoricofallapatorius. The Slitheen are on the run from their home planet, where they have been sentenced to death for their criminal activities. Now they roam through space, looking for ways to make a profit and they don't care who they hurt along the way.

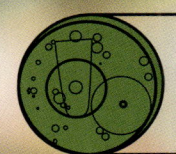

To remain undetected, a Slitheen disguises itself by using a compression field to squash down its giant form until it's small enough to fit inside a bodysuit made from the skin of a murdered human. Unfortunately a lot of the mass is converted into gas, which then escapes with an unpleasant noise and a nasty smell of decaying carbon. That's one way to detect a disguised Slitheen! Another is to look for the telltale zip across its forehead.

SLITHEEN DATA

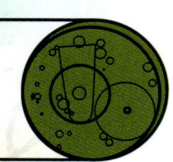

Name: The Slitheen family
Close relations: The Blathereen family, the Rackateen family
Height: approx. 2.44m (8')
Skin: Green
Eyes: Black
Weakness: Acetic acid (vinegar)
Home planet: Raxacoricofallapatorius
Species: Raxacoricofallapatorian
Profession: Criminals

73

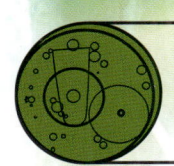

74 SLITHEEN ANATOMY

- Nearly two and a half metres tall
- Scarily sharp teeth
- Compression field controller
- Fearsome claws
- Body made of living calcium
- Excellent sense of smell helps to track prey
- Threatened female can exhale poison through her mouth, from her lungs
- Threatened female can manufacture and shoot a poison dart from within her finger

TEST YOUR KNOWLEDGE

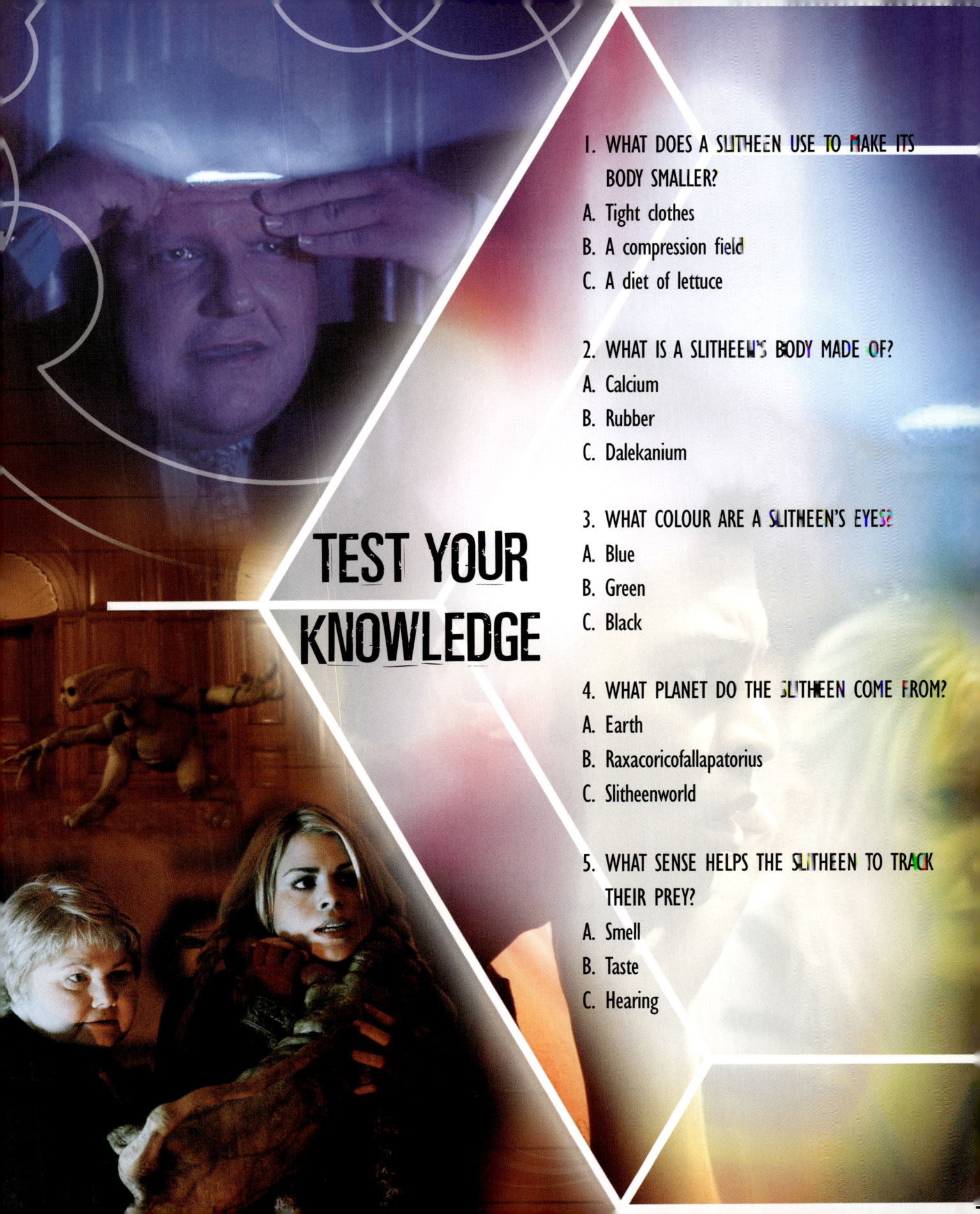

1. WHAT DOES A SLITHEEN USE TO MAKE ITS BODY SMALLER?
   A. Tight clothes
   B. A compression field
   C. A diet of lettuce

2. WHAT IS A SLITHEEN'S BODY MADE OF?
   A. Calcium
   B. Rubber
   C. Dalekanium

3. WHAT COLOUR ARE A SLITHEEN'S EYES?
   A. Blue
   B. Green
   C. Black

4. WHAT PLANET DO THE SLITHEEN COME FROM?
   A. Earth
   B. Raxacoricofallapatorius
   C. Slitheenworld

5. WHAT SENSE HELPS THE SLITHEEN TO TRACK THEIR PREY?
   A. Smell
   B. Taste
   C. Hearing

76 | WE ARE FAMILY

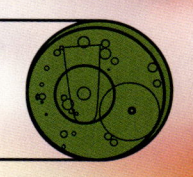

Members of the Slitheen family are scattered across the galaxy, all looking for ways to make money and survive while on the run from the other Raxacoricofallapatorians and the fearsome Wrarth Warriors, the police of their star system. One branch of the family, led by Jocrassa Fel Fotch Pasameer-Day Slitheen, moved into the fuel-supply business, and came to Earth...

Jocrassa Fel Fotch Pasameer-Day Slitheen disguised himself as Joseph Green, MP for Hartley Dale (who became Acting Prime Minister). He tried to persuade the United Nations to give him the nuclear access codes.

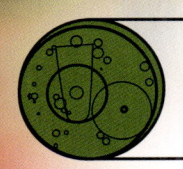

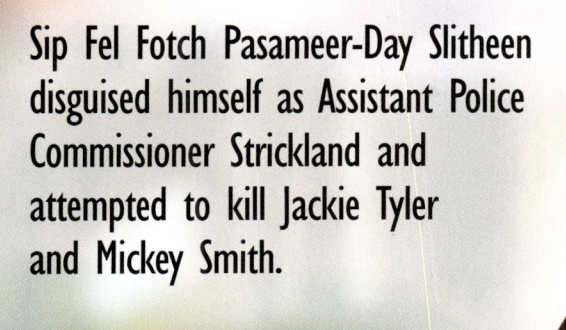

Sip Fel Fotch Pasameer-Day Slitheen disguised himself as Assistant Police Commissioner Strickland and attempted to kill Jackie Tyler and Mickey Smith.

Another Slitheen disguised himself first as Oliver Charles, Transport Liaison, then as General Asquith.

Other Slitheen disguised themselves as Group Captain Tennant James of the Royal Air Force, Ewan McAllister, Deputy Secretary for the Scottish Assembly and Sylvia Dillane, Director of the North Sea Boating Club.

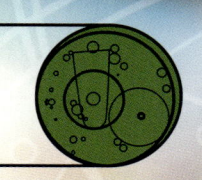

BLON FEL FOTCH PASAMEER-DAY SLITHEEN

Blon Fel Fotch disguised herself as Margaret Blaine of MI5, and was the only Slitheen to escape from 10 Downing Street. Still disguised, she became Lord Mayor of Cardiff, and set up the Blaidd Drwg (Welsh for 'Bad Wolf') Project in an attempt to get a nuclear power station built in the city.

Nearly everyone who stood in her way died mysteriously and painfully, but she showed a rare compassionate side to her nature when she let a pregnant journalist go free.

THE BLATHEREEN

The Slitheen's greatest rivals are their cousins, the Blathereen. Each side is forever trying to get the better of the other with their dodgy business deals. It was the Blathereen who forced the Slitheen out of their fuel business by undercutting prices.

Blathereen disguises in the year 2501 are more impressive than those their cousins used 500 years earlier. They can fit into the skins of humans of any size, and have small vertical zips on the top of their heads, which are easy to hide. The Doctor and Rose encountered a number of Blathereen on the penal colony Justicia, under the control of the Blathereen Patriarch, Don Arco.

TEST YOUR KNOWLEDGE

1. WHO ARE THE SLITHEEN'S GREATEST BUSINESS RIVALS?
   A. The Blathereen
   B. The Halloween
   C. The Aberdeen

2. WHO WAS THE ONLY SLITHEEN TO ESCAPE FROM 10 DOWNING STREET?
   A. Jocrassa Fel Fotch
   B. Don Arco
   C. Blon Fel Fotch

3. WHO TRIED TO KILL JACKIE AND MICKEY?
   A. Sip Fel Fotch
   B. Blon Fel Fotch
   C. Rose

4. WHAT IS THE TRANSLATION OF 'BLAIDD DRWG'?
   A. Bad Doctor
   B. Naughty Dog
   C. Bad Wolf

5. WHO DID JOCRASSA FEL FOTCH DISGUISE HIMSELF AS?
   A. Joseph Green
   B. Sylvia Dillane
   C. General Asquith

80 HUMAN ENEMIES

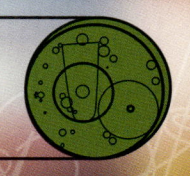

THE DOCTOR AND ROSE

The Doctor and Rose managed to thwart both the Slitheen's plan to turn Earth into starship fuel, and Blon Fel Fotch's plan to escape the planet by causing a nuclear explosion in Cardiff's time/space rift.

Although the Doctor later became friendly with two Slitheen who were fellow prisoners on Justicia, it's fair to say that the Doctor and Rose will never be favourites of the Slitheen family.

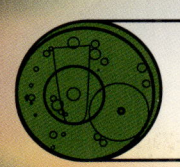

JACKIE TYLER

Rose's mum, Jackie, was terrified when she discovered that the policeman who was interviewing her was really an alien. But when the Doctor told her how to defeat the monster, Jackie put aside her fear to create one big vinegary mixture containing gherkins, pickled onions and pickled eggs. resulting in Sip Fel Fotch exploding messily, and Jackie becoming the first human to kill a Slitheen.

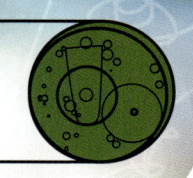

MICKEY SMITH

Rose's boyfriend Mickey played a big part in defeating the Slitheen invasion of Downing Street. With the Doctor's help, Mickey hacked into the Royal Navy's computer systems, and launched a missile from submarine *HMS Taurean* which he guided towards 10 Downing Street. The Slitheen were destroyed along with the building, thanks to Mickey.

The Doctor, Rose and Harriet Jones survived, safe inside the steel walls of the Cabinet Room.

HARRIET JONES

Harriet Jones, MP for Flydale North, was the first person to discover that the Slitheen had infiltrated Downing Street. She helped the Doctor and Rose to fight the monsters, and convinced the Doctor that he had to carry out his plan to blow up the building and wipe out the Slitheen — whatever the cost.

Her part in the Slitheen defeat helped Harriet become Prime Minister of Great Britain and while she's running the country, it would be a brave Slitheen who dared to set foot there again.

TEST YOUR KNOWLEDGE

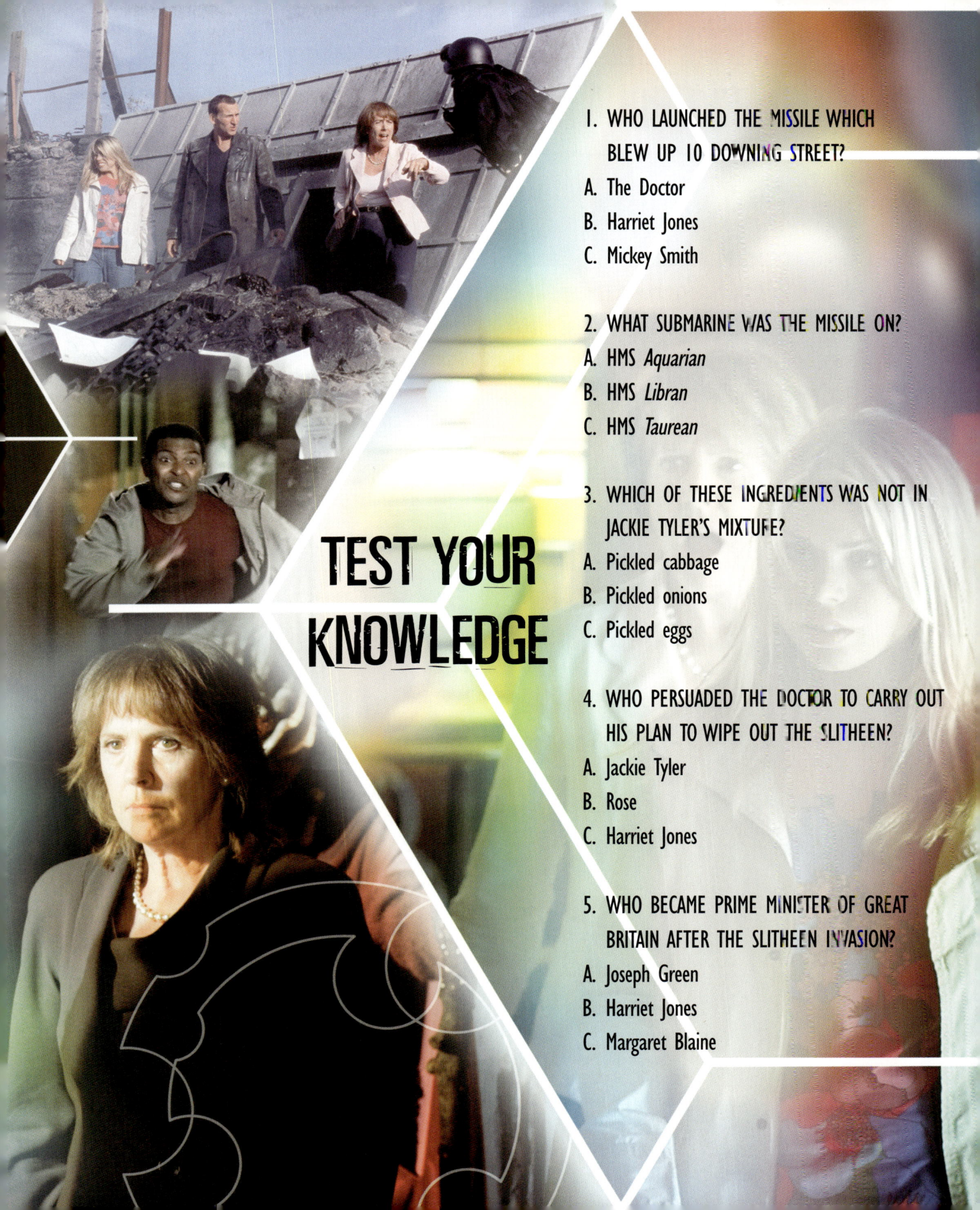

1. WHO LAUNCHED THE MISSILE WHICH BLEW UP 10 DOWNING STREET?
   A. The Doctor
   B. Harriet Jones
   C. Mickey Smith

2. WHAT SUBMARINE WAS THE MISSILE ON?
   A. HMS *Aquarian*
   B. HMS *Libran*
   C. HMS *Taurean*

3. WHICH OF THESE INGREDIENTS WAS NOT IN JACKIE TYLER'S MIXTURE?
   A. Pickled cabbage
   B. Pickled onions
   C. Pickled eggs

4. WHO PERSUADED THE DOCTOR TO CARRY OUT HIS PLAN TO WIPE OUT THE SLITHEEN?
   A. Jackie Tyler
   B. Rose
   C. Harriet Jones

5. WHO BECAME PRIME MINISTER OF GREAT BRITAIN AFTER THE SLITHEEN INVASION?
   A. Joseph Green
   B. Harriet Jones
   C. Margaret Blaine

BACKGROUND

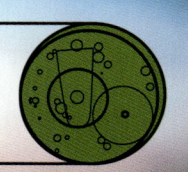

RAXACORICOFALLAPATORIUS

The planet Raxacoricofallapatorius is a beautiful place — not the sort of world you'd associate with criminals like the Slitheen. In fact most Raxacoricofallapatorians are peaceful and law-abiding. Raxacoricofallapatorians hatch from eggs, which are kept in hatcheries. Adult Raxacoricofallapatorians sleep in nests.

Most children are taught mathematics and poetry, except the Slitheen children, who are taught to hunt and kill. The Slitheen have declared that one day they will return home and claim this paradise for themselves!

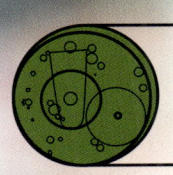

EXECUTION

The Slitheen have been sentenced to death, which means that any member of the family who returns to Raxacoricofallapatorius faces a painful public execution. First a thin acetic acid is prepared. Then the criminal is lowered into the Cauldron of Atonement and boiled. The acetic acid eats away at the skin until it is all gone, after which the internal organs fall into the solution. Gradually the Slitheen is turned into soup while he's still alive. Finally the soup is drunk by Raxacoricofallapatorian officials.

Needless to say, the Slitheen will do anything possible to prevent being sent back to their home planet. For now.

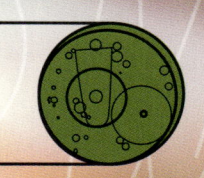

THE SLITHEEN'S WEAKNESS

When Jackie and Mickey were attacked by a Slitheen, the Doctor had to think fast to save them. He needed to know the Slitheen's weakness and he found it. As the Slitheen are made out of living calcium, which would be weakened by their compression field, they could be destroyed by a mild solution of acetic acid, such as vinegar.

Harriet Jones likened the Doctor's plan to that of Hannibal. Hannibal was a Carthaginian general who crossed the Alps with a large army (and 40 elephants!) in 218BC. A historian called Livy tells how Hannibal cleared a path through the mountains by heating the rocks that were in his way with fire, and then pouring vinegar over them so they dissolved.

Even the ordinary sort of vinegar that gets put on chips contains some acetic acid. Vinegar is made by fermenting an alcoholic liquid like wine or beer with a certain sort of bacteria. The alcohol turns into acetic acid, and the wine or beer becomes vinegar. Pure acetic acid can be distilled from vinegar, but it's very strong and would cause nasty burns to humans as well as hurting Slitheen!

TEST YOUR KNOWLEDGE

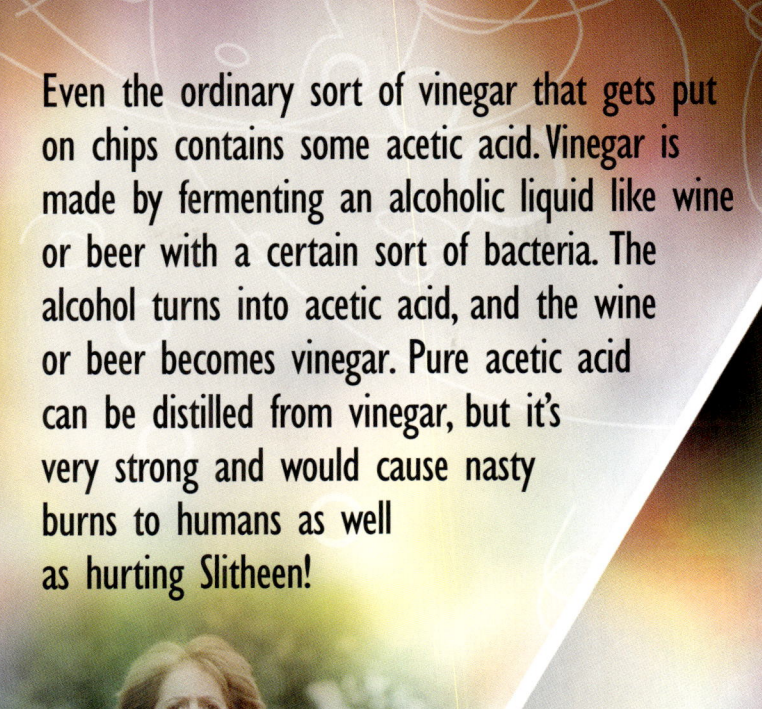

1. HOW ARE CRIMINALS EXECUTED ON RAXACORICOFALLAPATORIUS?
A. Eaten by crocodiles
B. Turned into stone
C. Boiled alive

2. WHICH OF THESE LIQUIDS CONTAINS ACETIC ACID?
A. Water
B. Vinegar
C. Milk

3. WHERE DO ADULT RAXACORICOFALLAPATORIANS SLEEP?
A. In bunk beds
B. In nests
C. In burrows

4. WHAT SUBJECTS ARE MOST RAXACORICOFALLAPATORIAN CHILDREN TAUGHT?
A. Poetry and Mathematics
B. French and Ballet
C. Needlework and Geography

5. WHAT IS A HATCHERY?
A. A place where Raxacoricofallapatorian eggs are kept
B. A Slitheen hat shop
C. A place of execution

TRANSPORT AND TECHNOLOGY

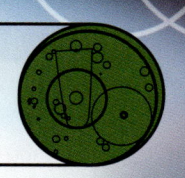

COMPRESSION FIELD

The Slitheen wear devices around their necks which enable them to control a compression field. The compression field allows them to shrink their bodies enough to fit inside a human skin. When a Slitheen is released from the compression field, a bright blue light surrounds it.

The neck device also establishes a connection between Slitheen. When the Slitheen used electrified identity cards to kill a roomful of alien experts, the Doctor turned the tables by inserting a card into Jocrassa Fel Fotch's neck device, and all the Slitheen were electrocuted.

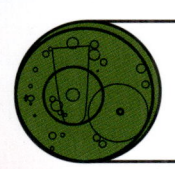

TELEPORTATION

Blon Fel Fotch used an emergency one-person teleport to escape from the exploding 10 Downing Street, but unfortunately for her, without coordinates, she ended up in a skip on the Isle of Dogs.

She was better organised when the Doctor came looking for her in Cardiff, using the teleport device (its components disguised as a brooch and a pair of earrings) to get away — but each time she tried it, the Doctor used his sonic screwdriver to reverse the teleport and bring her back, so eventually she gave up.

SPACESHIPS AND SPACE PIGS

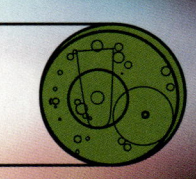

Humans were astonished when a spaceship careered through the London sky and crashed into the Thames, especially when it destroyed Big Ben along the way! But the Doctor realised the ship was a decoy. It had been launched from Earth, done a slingshot manoeuvre around the planet and come back down to Earth again.

Inside this ship was an Earth pig that the Slitheen had adapted to make it appear alien. Its brain was wired up and it was made to walk upright and wear a spacesuit. The pig was taken to Albion Hospital to be examined, but the scared creature was shot by a soldier when it tried to run away. The Slitheen also had their own spaceship, complete with slipstream engine, parked in the Thames.

THE EXTRAPOLATOR

Blon Fel Fotch built a nuclear power station on top of the space-time rift in Cardiff. The planet would explode, but she had a stolen alien device, a tribophysical waveform macro-kinetic extrapolator, to keep her safe. Not only would it protect her with a force field, it would enable her to ride the power waves to take her off the planet and out of the solar system, just like a pan-dimensional surfboard.

The Doctor foiled that plan, but didn't realise what would happen next. The extrapolator locked on to the TARDIS and began to open the rift using the ship's power supply. However Blon hadn't reckoned with what would happen when she started to pull the TARDIS apart...

TEST YOUR KNOWLEDGE

1. **BLON'S EXTRAPOLATOR RESEMBLED WHAT SPORTING EQUIPMENT?**
   A. A tennis racquet
   B. A surfboard
   C. A cricket ball

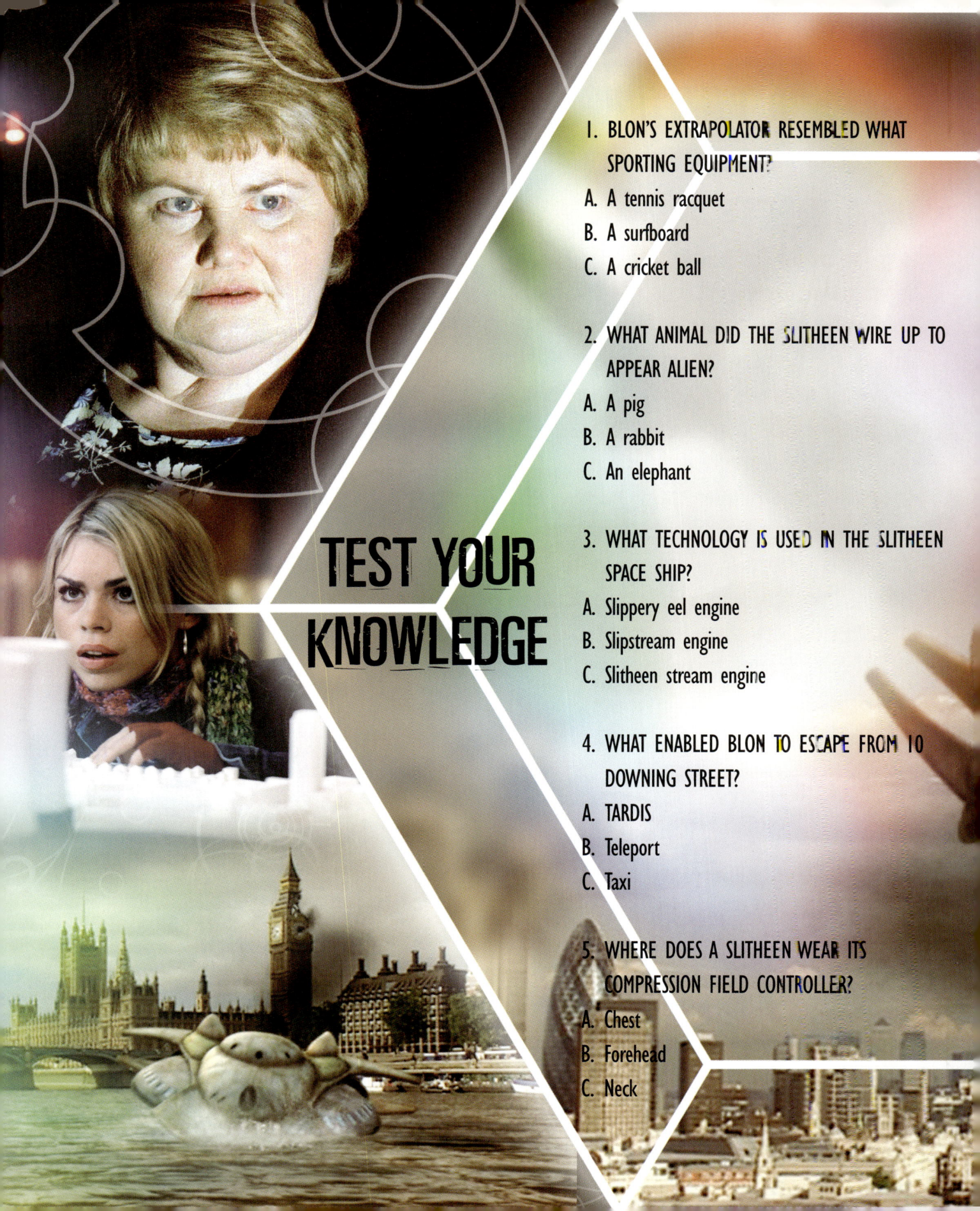

2. **WHAT ANIMAL DID THE SLITHEEN WIRE UP TO APPEAR ALIEN?**
   A. A pig
   B. A rabbit
   C. An elephant

3. **WHAT TECHNOLOGY IS USED IN THE SLITHEEN SPACE SHIP?**
   A. Slippery eel engine
   B. Slipstream engine
   C. Slitheen stream engine

4. **WHAT ENABLED BLON TO ESCAPE FROM 10 DOWNING STREET?**
   A. TARDIS
   B. Teleport
   C. Taxi

5. **WHERE DOES A SLITHEEN WEAR ITS COMPRESSION FIELD CONTROLLER?**
   A. Chest
   B. Forehead
   C. Neck

ADVENTURES WITH THE SLITHEEN

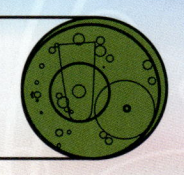

THE SLITHEEN'S PLAN

After landing on Earth, the Slitheen began attempting to infiltrate the British Government. When a satellite detected a Slitheen signal under the North Sea, a decoy ship and alien pilot was sent up to act as a diversion from the real Slitheen ship. But that wasn't all it did. Having killed the Prime Minister, the Slitheen were now able to assemble all Earth's top alien experts together in one place. They thought they had come to Downing Street to discuss the new alien threat, but every expert except the Doctor was killed by the Slitheen.

93

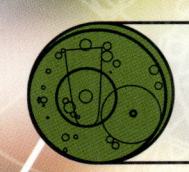

The evidence of the ship and the death of the alien experts could then be used to persuade the United Nations to release the nuclear codes to the disguised Slitheen, who would use them to start World War Three and destroy the planet. Then they planned to sit back and wait for customers to turn up to buy their advertised starship fuel, made from the molten, radioactive chunks of Earth. If only the Doctor hadn't turned up just in time to foil their plans!

BLON'S SECOND CHANCE

Arriving in Cardiff, the Doctor, Rose, Mickey and Captain Jack were surprised to see a photo of the new Lord Mayor — Margaret Blaine, aka Blon Fel Fotch Pasameer-Day Slitheen. The Doctor decided to take Blon back to Raxacoricofallapatorius, where she would be executed.

Blon tried to persuade him that she regretted her past and had changed, but this didn't seem likely when she revealed her intention of using the power of the TARDIS to destroy Earth so she could escape from the planet.

However when she looked into the heart of the TARDIS, she was transformed into an egg. Perhaps the TARDIS realised she really did want to change, and was giving her the chance to start again.

SLITHEEN OF THE FUTURE

According to Dram and Ecktosca Fel Fotch, who the Doctor met in the year 2501, the Slitheen gave up selling radioactive chunks of exploded planets soon after the Doctor foiled their plans on Earth. They turned to chizzle-waxing for a while, but gave it up as it was too messy. Don't be fooled, though, the Slitheen haven't turned their back on a life of crime. They have plenty more money-making schemes up their (borrowed) sleeves and they won't let anyone stand between them and a quick profit...

TEST YOUR KNOWLEDGE

1. WHERE WAS THE SLITHEEN SIGNAL BEING TRANSMITTED FROM?
   A. 10 Downing Street
   B. The North Sea
   C. Raxacoricofallapatorius

2. WHAT FATE AWAITED BLON ON RAXACORICOFALLAPATORIUS?
   A. Marriage
   B. Imprisonment
   C. Execution

3. WHAT DID THE SLITHEEN WANT FROM THE UNITED NATIONS?
   A. An ice cream
   B. The nuclear codes
   C. A free pardon

4. WHAT MESSY CRIMINAL ACTIVITY DID THE SLITHEEN BRIEFLY TURN TO?
   A. Pig-polishing
   B. Chizzle-waxing
   C. Dazzle-dusting

5. WHAT HAPPENED WHEN BLON LOOKED INTO THE HEART OF THE TARDIS?
   A. She became an egg
   B. The TARDIS exploded
   C. She was teleported home

TEST YOUR KNOWLEDGE

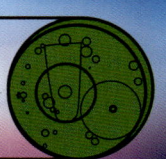

ANSWERS

Meet the Slitheen
1(b) 2(a) 3(c) 4(b) 5(a)

We Are Family
1(a) 2(c) 3(a) 4(c) 5(a)

Human Enemies
1(c) 2(c) 3(a) 4(c) 5(b)

Background
1(c) 2(b) 3(b) 4(a) 5(a)

Transport and Technology
1(b) 2(a) 3(b) 4(b) 5(c)

Adventures with the Slitheen
1(b) 2(c) 3(b) 4(b) 5(a)

DOCTOR·WHO

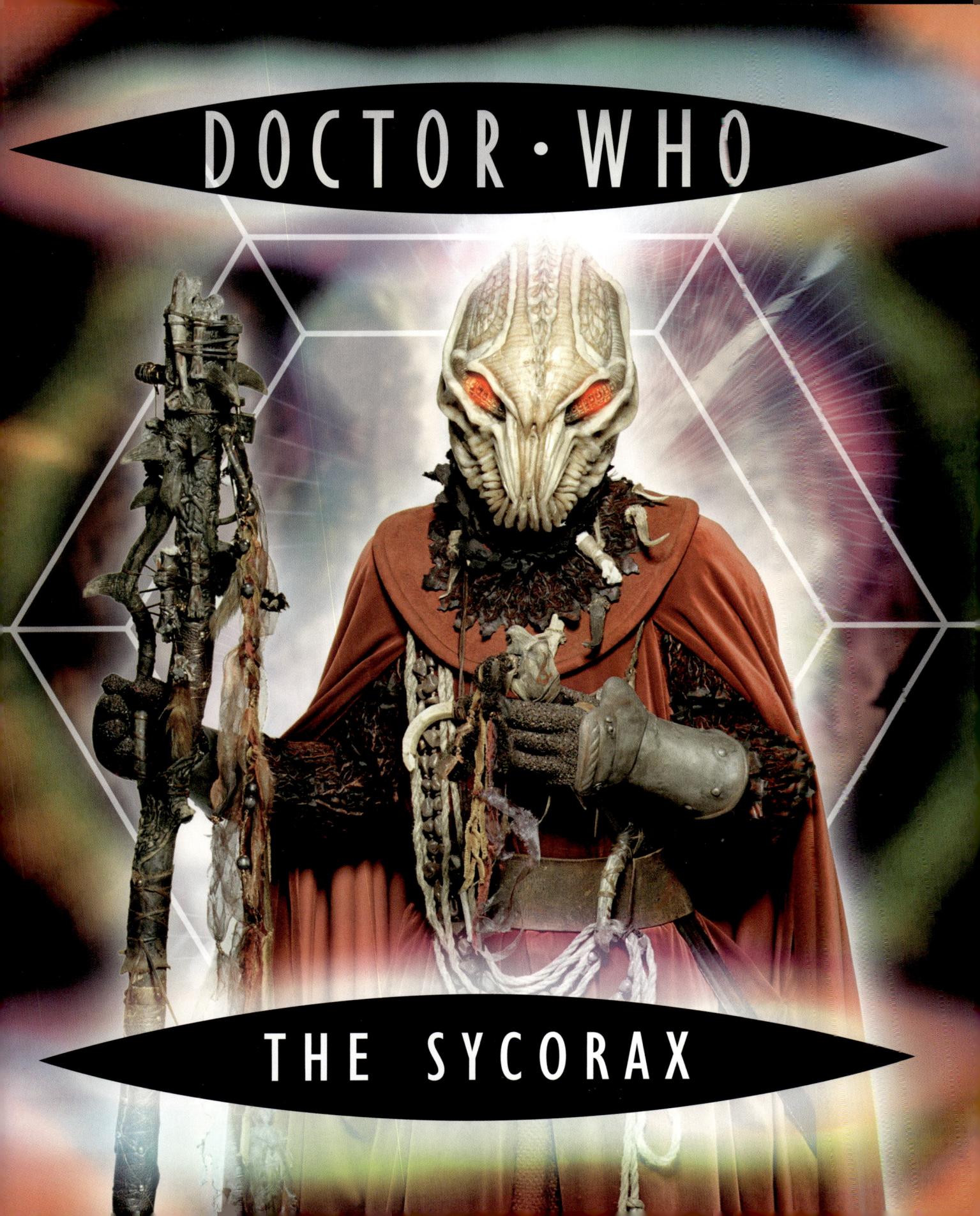

THE SYCORAX

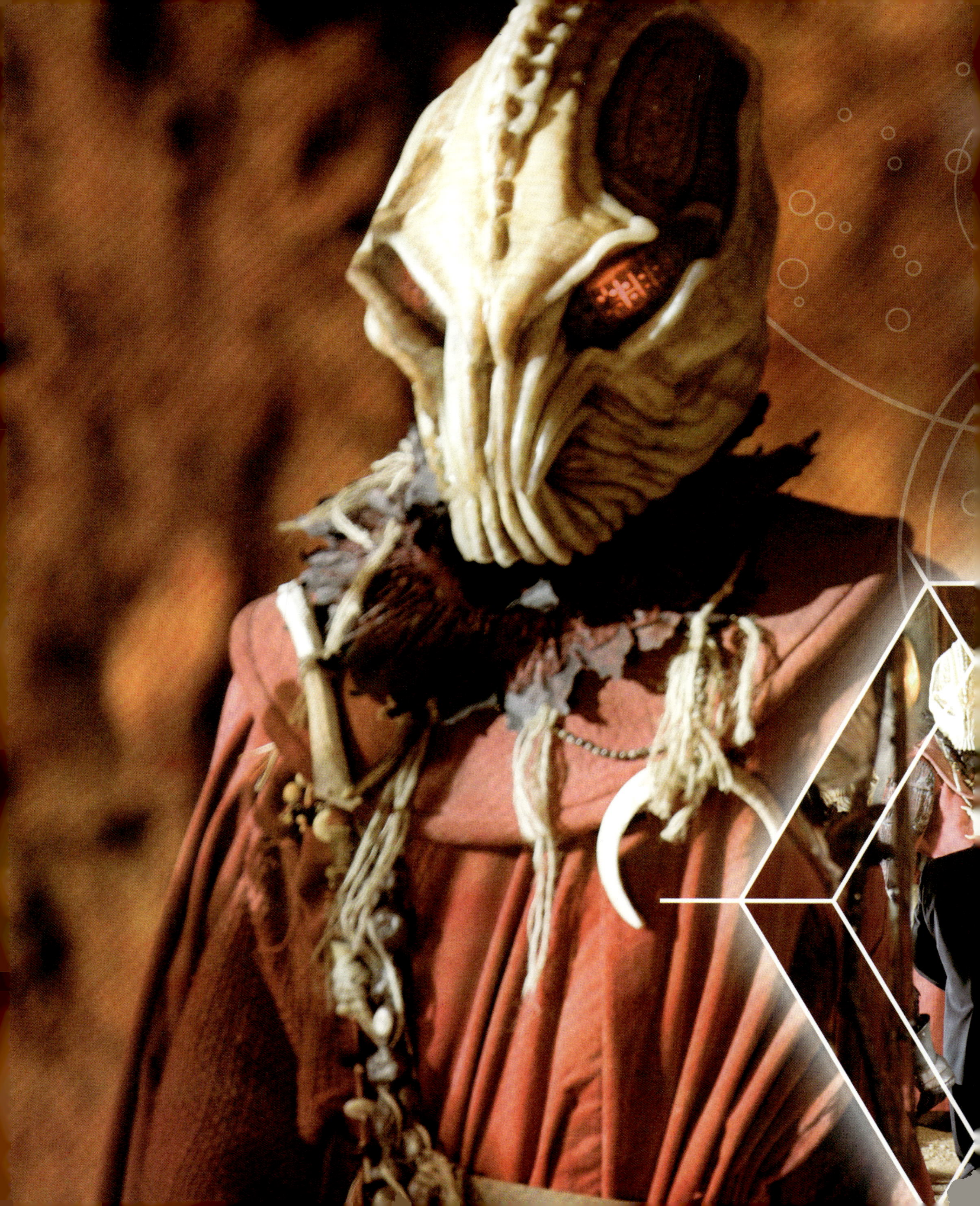

CONTENTS

Meet the Sycorax
Introduction..................................100
Sycorax Data.................................102
Sycorax Anatomy...........................104
◆ Test your Knowledge

History of the Sycorax
History of the Sycorax....................106
◆ Test your Knowledge

Enemies and Rivals
Rose..110
The Doctor...................................111
Harriet Jones................................112
Torchwood....................................113
◆ Test your Knowledge

No Place Like Home
'Pilot Fish' Aliens..........................114
Sycoraxic....................................116
◆ Test your Knowledge

Weapons and Technology
Weaponry....................................118
Blood Control..............................120
Messages to Aliens.......................121
◆ Test your Knowledge

The Christmas Invasion..............122
◆ Test your Knowledge

Test your Knowledge Answers........126

100 MEET THE SYCORAX

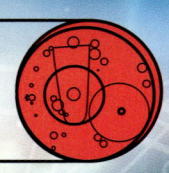

The scavenging Sycorax travel through space searching for worlds to ransack. Planets which are taking their first steps into space are ideal targets for the Sycorax, as they usually have a suitably advanced level of technology to make attacking them worthwhile, but not so high as to make them able to withstand an invasion.

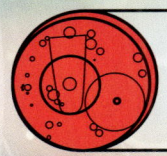

Ritual and superstition play a large part in the Sycorax way of life and since they have embraced technology they can guarantee that their spells and curses really work. Blood and bones play a large part in Sycorax ceremonies. The rite of blood control is a particular favourite, guaranteed to spread fear and panic in the Sycorax's victims.

The Sycorax are a warlike people, although they prefer to subjugate a planet with no resistance, their love of fighting means they will not turn away from combat. Single combat, with its rules and rituals, appeals to their warrior spirit, but their desire for victory at any price often wins out over honour.

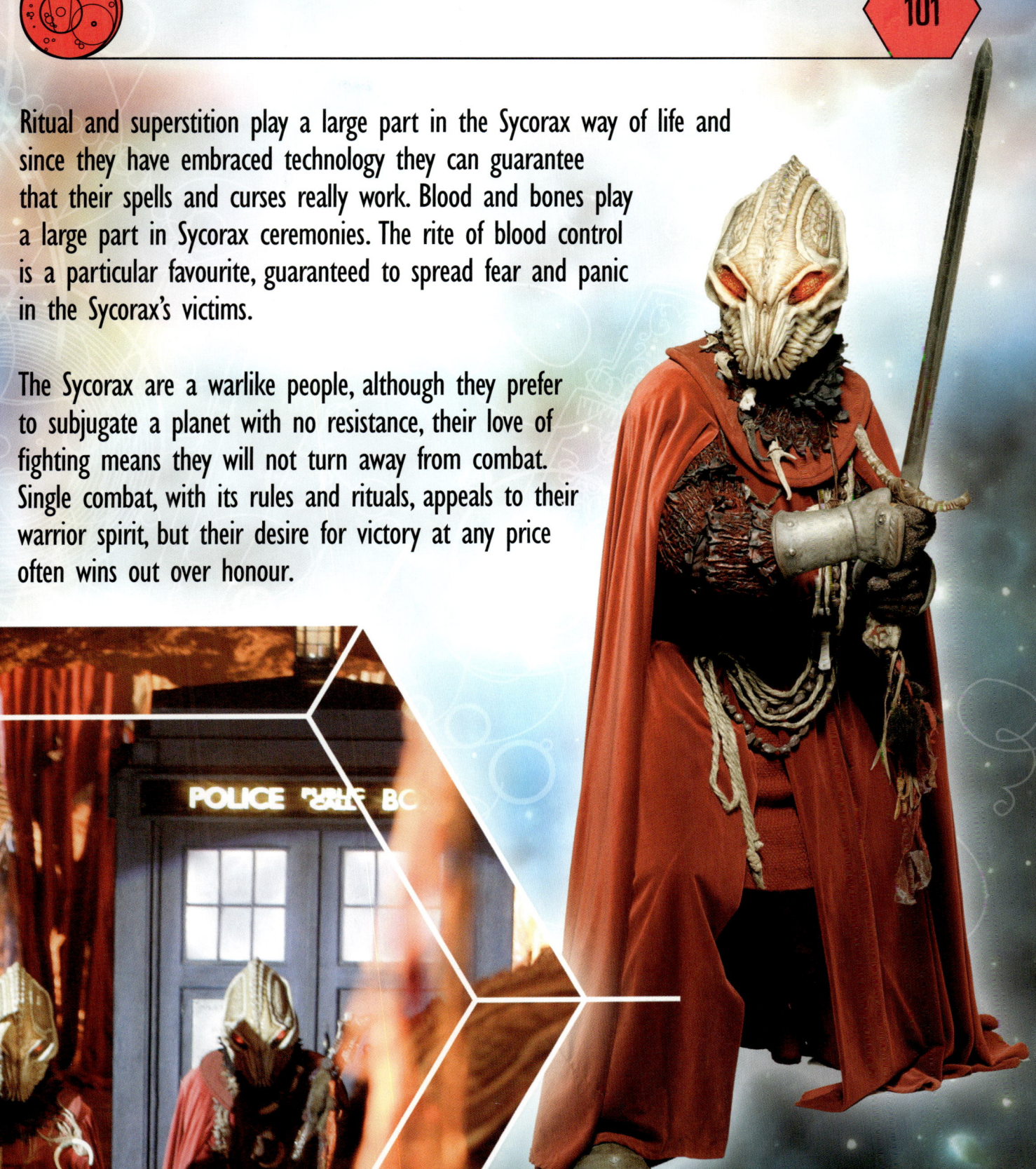

102 SYCORAX DATA

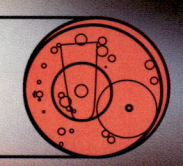

Name: The Sycorax

Height: approx. 1.90m (6'2")

Skin: Muscle and bone

Eyes: Red

Home planet: Sycorax

Language: Sycoraxic

Profession: Scavengers

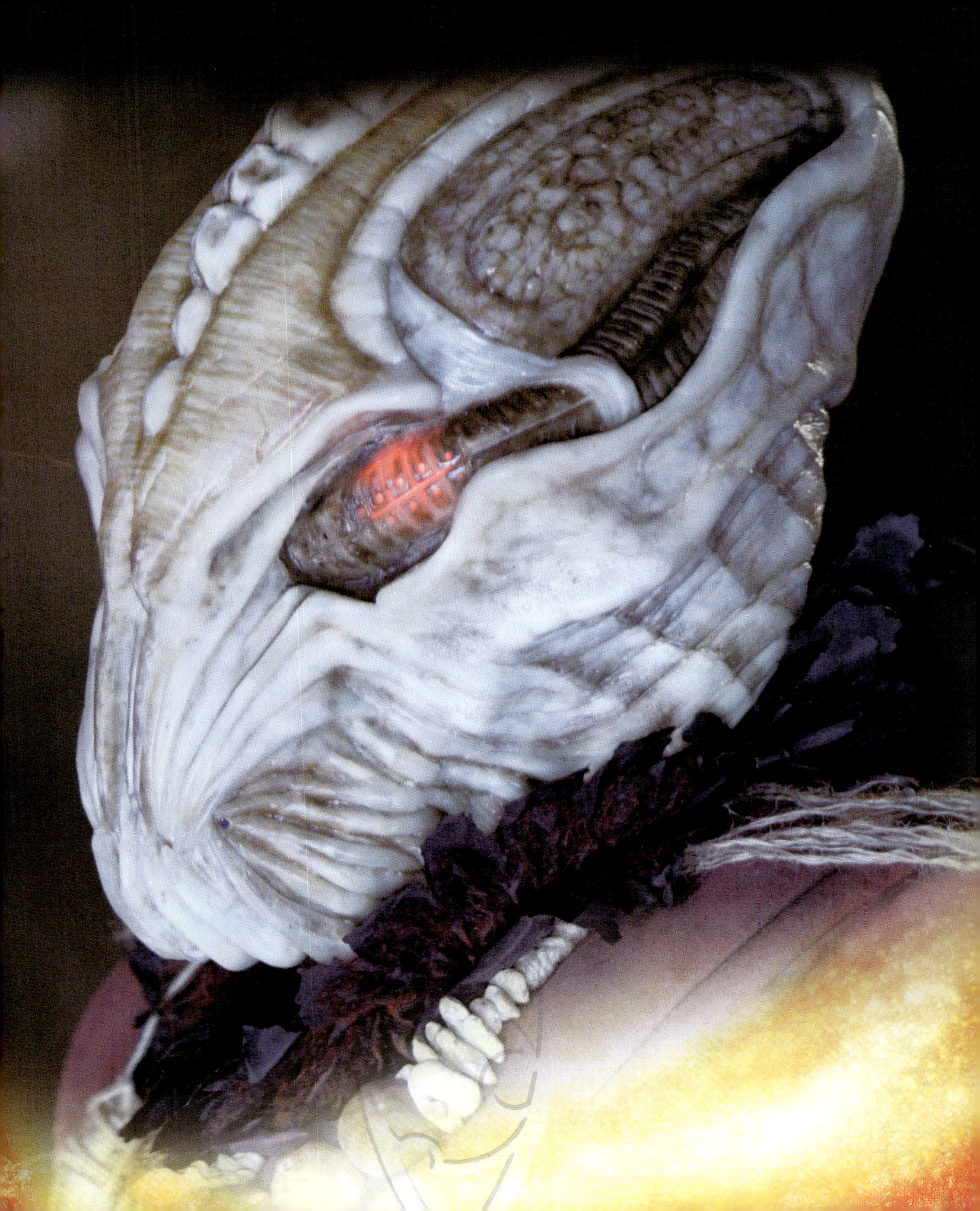

104 SYCORAX ANATOMY

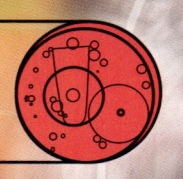

Skull helmet to inspire fear.

Trophies from conquests

Red eyes that glow

Totems and decorations on staff show tribe and tribal status

Blood-red velvet robe indicates wealth

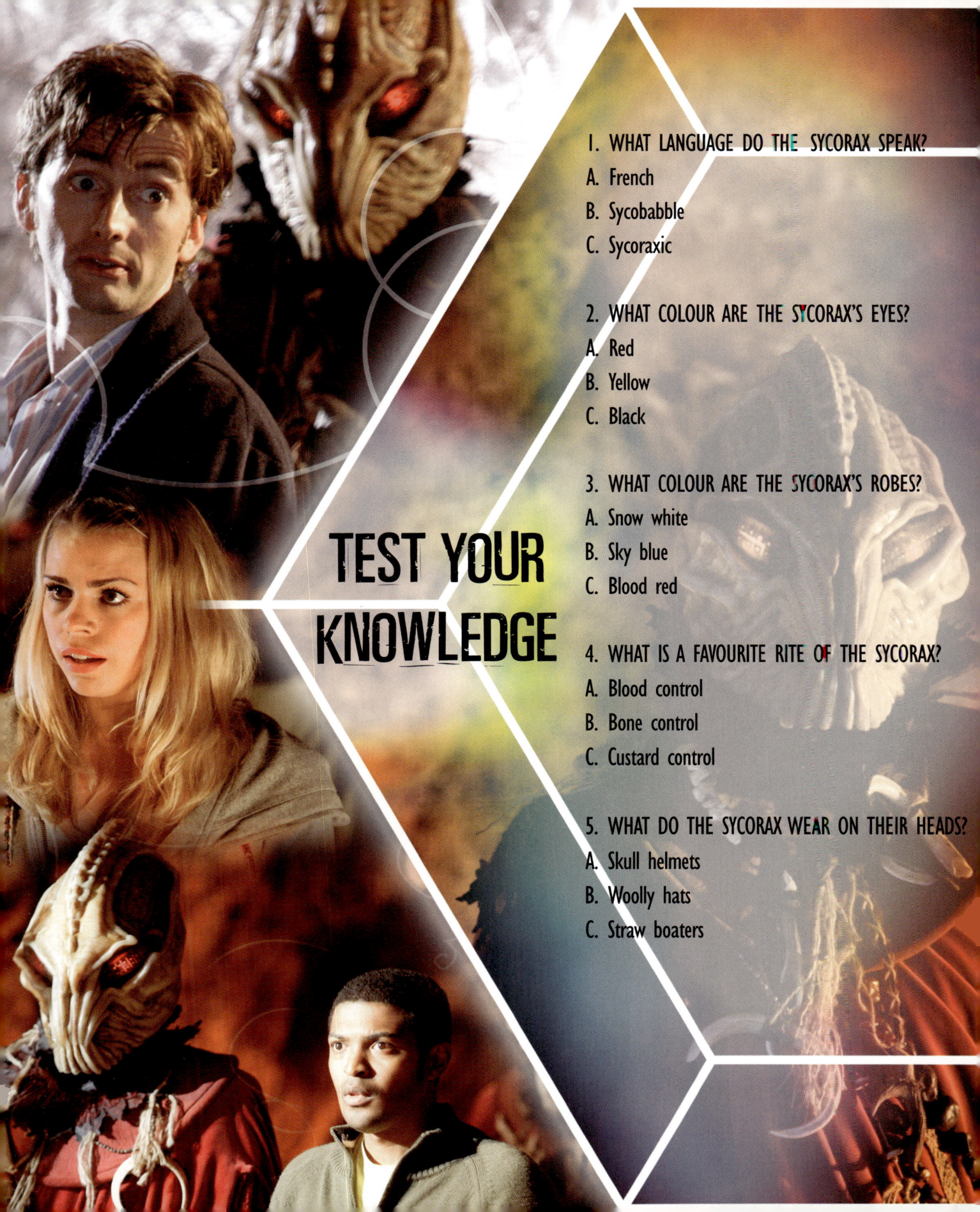

TEST YOUR KNOWLEDGE

1. WHAT LANGUAGE DO THE SYCORAX SPEAK?
   A. French
   B. Sycobabble
   C. Sycoraxic

2. WHAT COLOUR ARE THE SYCORAX'S EYES?
   A. Red
   B. Yellow
   C. Black

3. WHAT COLOUR ARE THE SYCORAX'S ROBES?
   A. Snow white
   B. Sky blue
   C. Blood red

4. WHAT IS A FAVOURITE RITE OF THE SYCORAX?
   A. Blood control
   B. Bone control
   C. Custard control

5. WHAT DO THE SYCORAX WEAR ON THEIR HEADS?
   A. Skull helmets
   B. Woolly hats
   C. Straw boaters

106 | HISTORY OF THE SYCORAX

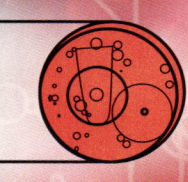

The Sycorax come from a distant planet, far out in the wastelands of the galaxy. Nobody on Earth was aware of its existence, until one fateful Christmas day...

The many tribes of the Sycorax lived just beneath the surface of a small asteroid that was composed mainly of rock and ice. This inhospitable world had few natural resources, but the warlike Sycorax forged an existence there, tribe fighting tribe for scraps of food and metal. These primitive Sycorax worshipped Astrophia, goddess of darkness and death, each tribe trying to outdo the others in reverence and offerings. Sycorax shamen, the tribal wise men, carried out rites of blood and sacrifice to implore Astrophia to bring favour to their tribes and misfortune to others in battle.

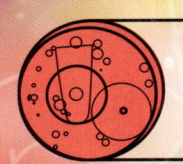

After many centuries of tribal conflict, the Sycorax became aware of the existence of other beings in the universe. A spaceship crash-landed on the surface of their world, bringing them into contact with another species for the first time. The Halvinor Tribe enslaved the survivors, and forced them to teach the Sycorax of their technology. This threatened to bring terrible war to the Sycorax, as the other tribes both resented and feared the Halvinor's discovery. But the shaman of the Halvinor persuaded them that instead of fighting among themselves, the Sycorax should unite in order to exploit the newly discovered universe, so full of riches.

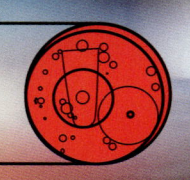

Working together, the Sycorax developed their new-found technology. With little metal on their planet, they hit on an ambitious plan — to pilot the tiny asteroid from world to world, plundering their wealth and enslaving their people. This they did for many generations, growing richer and richer, until finally the mechanism controlling the travel systems failed and the asteroid became trapped in the orbit of a planet at the far outer reaches of our solar system. But the Sycorax refused to give up their space-scavenging ways and return to a life of hardship.

Each tribe broke off a piece of the asteroid and fitted it with the necessary systems until the Sycorax had created an armada of vast, rocky ships. The tribal shamen resurrected the lost rites of Astrophia, now supplemented with their technological discoveries, and used them to control the races whose planets they wanted to ransack and if that failed, the rest of the fleet could be summoned to take the planet by force. The Sycorax Armada swept through the galaxy, leaving devastated worlds in its wake. None stood against it. Until, of course, a tribe made the mistake of targeting a planet defended by the Doctor...

TEST YOUR KNOWLEDGE

1. WHERE DO THE SYCORAX COME FROM?
A. Leeds
B. A distant planet
C. The moon

2. WHO WAS WORSHIPPED BY THE SYCORAX?
A. Astrophia
B. Zeus
C. The Doctor

3. WHAT IS THE SYCORAX ASTEROID MADE OF?
A. Snow and sand
B. Rock and ice
C. Molten lava

4. WHAT ARE THE SYCORAX SHIPS MADE FROM?
A. Iron
B. Diamond
C. Pieces of asteroid

5. WHAT ARE SYCORAX WISE MEN CALLED?
A. Shampoos
B. Shamen
C. Shark

ENEMIES AND RIVALS

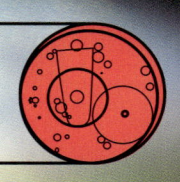

ROSE

With the Doctor out of action, Rose bravely stepped into the breach and tried to convince the Sycorax to leave Earth in peace. Calling on the authority of monsters she has met, she challenged them in the name of the Slitheen Parliament of Raxacoricofallapatorius and the Gelth Confederacy, as sanctioned by the Mighty Jagrafess and the Daleks. The Sycorax laughed — but perhaps they would have taken her more seriously had they known the fate of these aliens, all defeated at the hands of Rose and the Doctor.

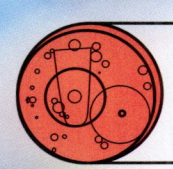

THE DOCTOR

It was straight back to work for the Doctor, who woke up from his regenerative coma to find himself in the middle of an invasion. But if the Sycorax thought they'd get an easy ride from the recovering Time Lord, they were mistaken. After removing the threat of the Sycorax's blood control, the Doctor stood as champion of Earth and challenged the leader of the Sycorax to single combat — with the planet as the prize. The Doctor won, but the Sycorax Leader proved he was not to be trusted when he attempted to kill the Doctor after the combat had ended.

HARRIET JONES

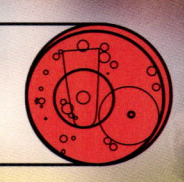

Since Harriet Jones met the Slitheen during their invasion of 10 Downing Street, she's known that Earth faces a serious threat from extraterrestrials — and she knows that the Doctor won't always be on hand to save the day. As Prime Minister she attempted to negotiate with the Sycorax following their threats and refused to surrender the planet to them. When there was no sign of the Doctor she called on Torchwood, hoping they would be able to destroy the aliens.

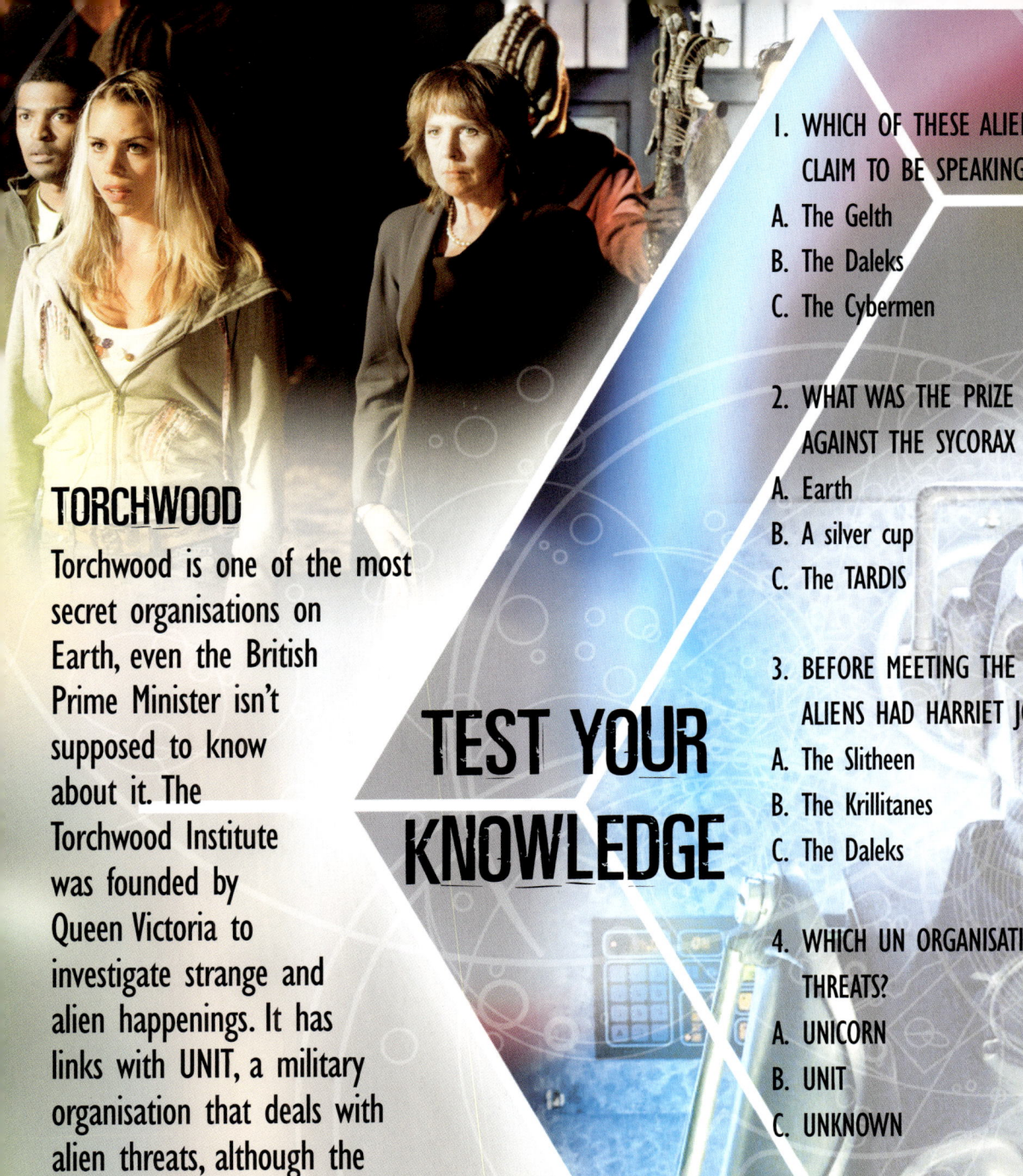

TORCHWOOD

Torchwood is one of the most secret organisations on Earth, even the British Prime Minister isn't supposed to know about it. The Torchwood Institute was founded by Queen Victoria to investigate strange and alien happenings. It has links with UNIT, a military organisation that deals with alien threats, although the existence of Torchwood has been kept from the UN itself. Torchwood collects alien technology that comes to Earth and adapts it for their own use, such as defending the planet. The weapon that destroyed the Sycorax ship had been adapted from alien technology, from a ship that had fallen to Earth ten years before.

TEST YOUR KNOWLEDGE

1. WHICH OF THESE ALIENS DID ROSE NOT CLAIM TO BE SPEAKING FOR?
A. The Gelth
B. The Daleks
C. The Cybermen

2. WHAT WAS THE PRIZE IN THE DOCTOR'S FIGHT AGAINST THE SYCORAX LEADER?
A. Earth
B. A silver cup
C. The TARDIS

3. BEFORE MEETING THE SYCORAX, WHICH OTHER ALIENS HAD HARRIET JONES ENCOUNTERED?
A. The Slitheen
B. The Krillitanes
C. The Daleks

4. WHICH UN ORGANISATION DEALS WITH ALIEN THREATS?
A. UNICORN
B. UNIT
C. UNKNOWN

5. WHO FOUNDED THE TORCHWOOD INSTITUTE?
A. Queen Victoria
B. Harriet Jones
C. The Doctor

NO PLACE LIKE HOME

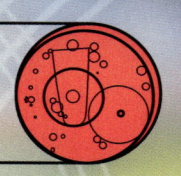

'PILOT FISH' ALIENS

In nature, 'pilot fish' swim with much more powerful sharks, knowing they'll be led to food. The robotic space 'pilot fish' aliens keep close to fearsome space travellers such as the Sycorax, who will lead them to energy-rich planets. As the Sycorax focused on Earth, the 'pilot fish' aliens that travelled alongside them detected the Doctor's regenerative energy and hijacked the Sycorax's teleportation technology to track him down. The 'pilot fish' aliens tried to take out the Doctor's defences, first by disguising themselves as Santa Clauses and attacking Rose and Mickey, then by sending a remote-controlled homicidal Christmas tree to Jackie's flat. With his defenders out of the way, it would have been easier to steal the Doctor's energy — a power source large enough to feed the pilot fish for several years.

115

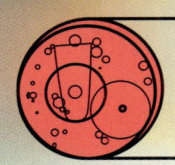

WEAPONS

Disguised as a carol-playing brass trio, the robots caused mayhem with their deadly instruments, making sure it wasn't a *Silent Night* for Rose and Mickey.

Trombone of Terror
really a flame thrower!

Tricky Trumpet
a machine gun in disguise!

Terrible Tuba acts as a missile launcher!

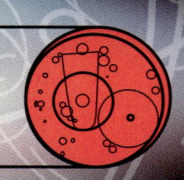

SYCORAXIC

Harriet Jones and her team needed a computer to translate the Sycorax's language into English, but this handy guide to Sycoraxic words and phrases should make things easier next time the Sycorax try to invade the Earth!

Sycoraxic	English	Sycoraxic	English
Astrofaaa	Astrophia	jalvaaan	surrender
codrafee	we are	ka	now
codsyla	choice	padskaa	welcome
col	or	potrosca	third
con	of	practeel	funny
fadros-pallujikaa	tribal leader	stapeen	stolen
foraxi	aboard	Sycorafan Staa	Sycorax Armada
gan	very	tass	yes
gatrosca	half	vol	words
gilfane	clever		

Tass, conafee tedro soo — Yes, we know who you are.

Sycora jak! Sycora telpo! Sycora faa! — Sycorax strong! Sycorax mighty! Sycorax rock!

Jalvaaan, col chack chiff — Surrender, or they will die.

Crel stat foraxi — Bring it on board.

Codrafee Sycora. Codrafee gassac tel dashfellik — We are the Sycorax. We stride the darkness.

TEST YOUR KNOWLEDGE

1. WHICH OF THESE INSTRUMENTS WAS NOT USED BY THE 'PILOT FISH' ALIENS?
   A. Trumpet
   B. Trombone
   C. Triangle

2. WHAT DEADLY FESTIVE OBJECT DID THE 'PILOT FISH' ALIENS SEND TO JACKIE'S FLAT?
   A. Plum pudding
   B. Christmas tree
   C. Holly wreath

3. WHAT DID THE 'PILOT FISH' ALIENS SENSE THAT BROUGHT THEM TO EARTH?
   A. Jackie's cooking
   B. Mickey's aftershave
   C. The Doctor's energy

4. WHAT DOES THE SYCORAXIC PHRASE 'SYCORA JAK!' MEAN IN ENGLISH?
   A. Sycorax strong!
   B. Sycorax rock!
   C. Sycorax sorry!

5. WHAT DOES THE SYCORAXIC PHRASE 'CODRAFEE GASSAC TEL DASHFELLIK' MEAN IN ENGLISH?
   A. Coffee and a doughnut, please
   B. We stride the darkness
   C. Give us your precious stones

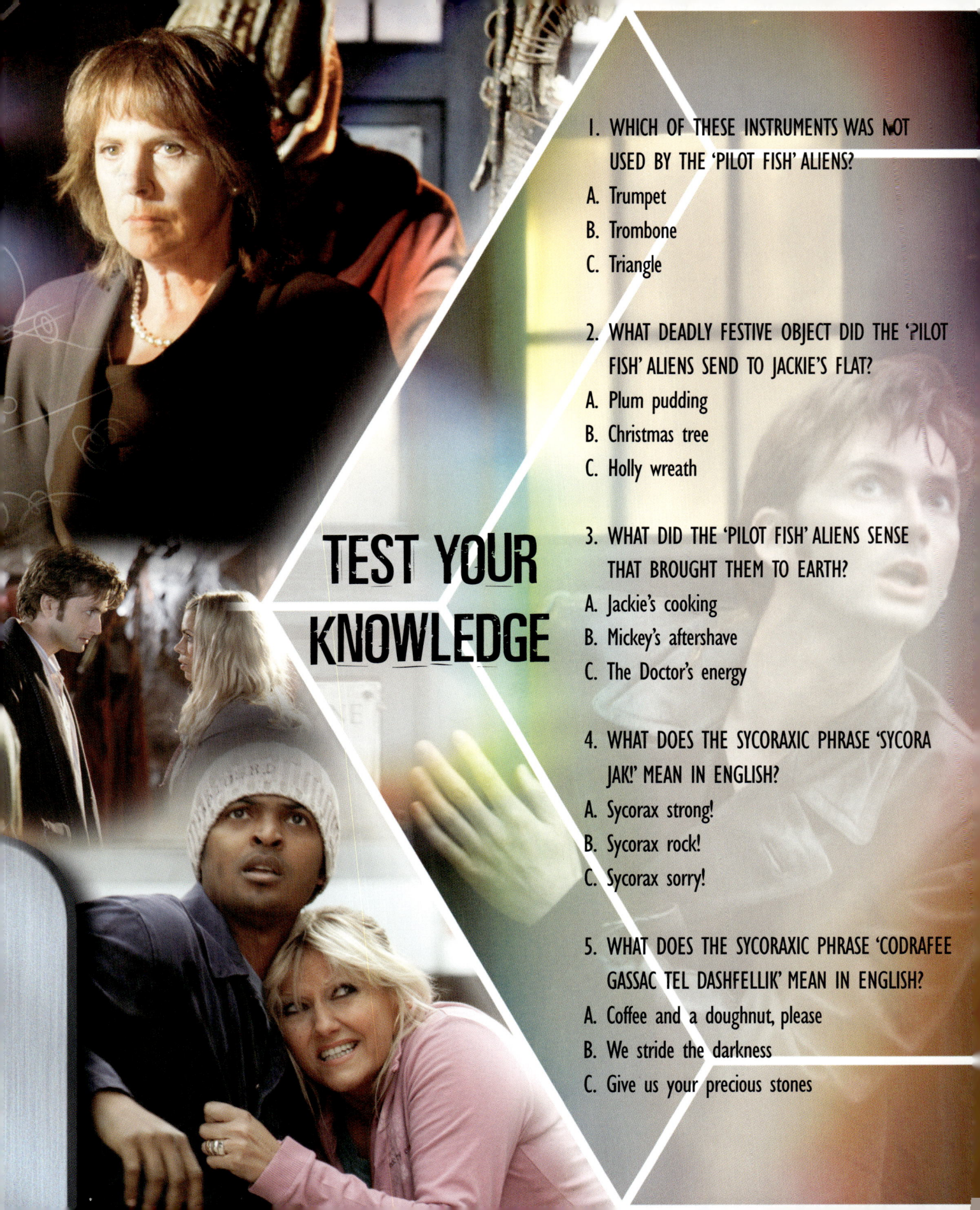

118 WEAPONS AND TECHNOLOGY

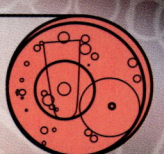

SWORD

The Sycorax's favoured weapon is the broadsword, especially for hand-to-hand combat. The Sycorax claim to abide by the sanctified rules of combat. An elected champion of one side may issue a challenge to an agreed representative of the other side (in the case of the Sycorax, usually the tribal leader). If accepted, the champions will face each other in single combat, with the winner's side being declared the victors of the conflict. However, if the rules of combat are violated in any way, such as if one combatant receives assistance from his side, the challenge is invalidated and his opponent automatically wins. Challengers should beware that the Sycorax view mercy as weakness, and may choose to ignore the sanctified rules and refuse to accept defeat.

WHIP

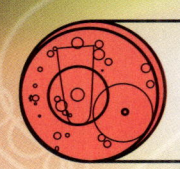

The Sycorax whip is one of the most fearsome weapons in existence, causing immediate death. A single touch of the whiplash instantaneously disintegrates every atom of human flesh, leaving only a burnt skeleton. The Sycorax use this to punish prisoners or inspire fear rather than in a combat situation.

STAFF

The Sycorax's staff may be used as a weapon, but it has another important function. The totems which adorn the staff indicate tribal allegiance, while the trophies and decorations show the status within the tribe of the Sycorax who wields it. Destroying the staff of a Sycorax is a terrible insult, implying that they are not worthy of the position they claim.

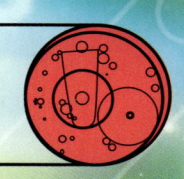

BLOOD CONTROL

When the Sycorax took the Guinevere One probe on to their ship, they discovered a plaque which was intended to identify the human race to any aliens who might encounter it. The probe contained maps, music, wheat seeds, water, and A+ human blood. The Sycorax used the blood to feed a control matrix, which gave them power over everyone on Earth who had that blood type.

Types of blood are usually sorted into groups according to the ABO system and the Rhesus (Rh) system, depending on what antigens they contain.

In the ABO system, blood can be either A, B, AB or O. A blood contains A antigens, B blood contains B antigens, AB blood contains both and O blood contains neither. In the Rh system, blood can be either positive or negative. Positive blood contains Rh antigens, negative blood does not. So blood can be A+, A-, B+, B-, AB+, AB-, O+ or O-.

About one third of the people on Earth have A+ blood. Do you know what type you have? Would the Sycorax have been able to control you?

MESSAGES TO ALIENS

In the 1970s, two spacecraft, Pioneer 10 and Pioneer 11, both carried metal plaques that would tell any aliens who found them where the craft came from.

A few years later, Voyager 1 and Voyager 2 were sent into space. They each contained a 'golden record' containing lots of information about the Earth, in both images and sounds. If an alien managed to play the record, it would hear thunder, bird song, greetings in 55 different languages and much more.
It even contained music by composers such as Bach and Beethoven, and rock star Chuck Berry!

Voyagers 1 and 2 should reach other star systems where there might be life in about 40,000 years — that is, unless aliens like the Sycorax find them first!

TEST YOUR KNOWLEDGE

1. WHAT IS THE SYCORAX'S FAVOURED WEAPON IN HAND-TO-HAND COMBAT?
A. Whip
B. Broadsword
C. Staff

2. WHICH OF THE SYCORAX'S WEAPONS CAN DISINTEGRATE HUMAN FLESH?
A. Whip
B. Broadsword
C. Staff

3. WHICH OF THE SYCORAX'S WEAPONS IS ALSO A STATUS SYMBOL?
A. Whip
B. Broadsword
C. Staff

4. OVER WHICH TYPE OF BLOOD DID THE SYCORAX GAIN CONTROL?
A. A+
B. O+
C. A-

5. WHICH OF THESE WAS NOT ON THE GUINEVERE ONE IDENTITY PLAQUE?
A. Wheat seeds
B. Water
C. Chocolate

122 THE CHRISTMAS INVASION

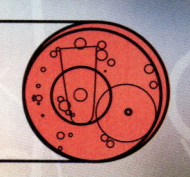

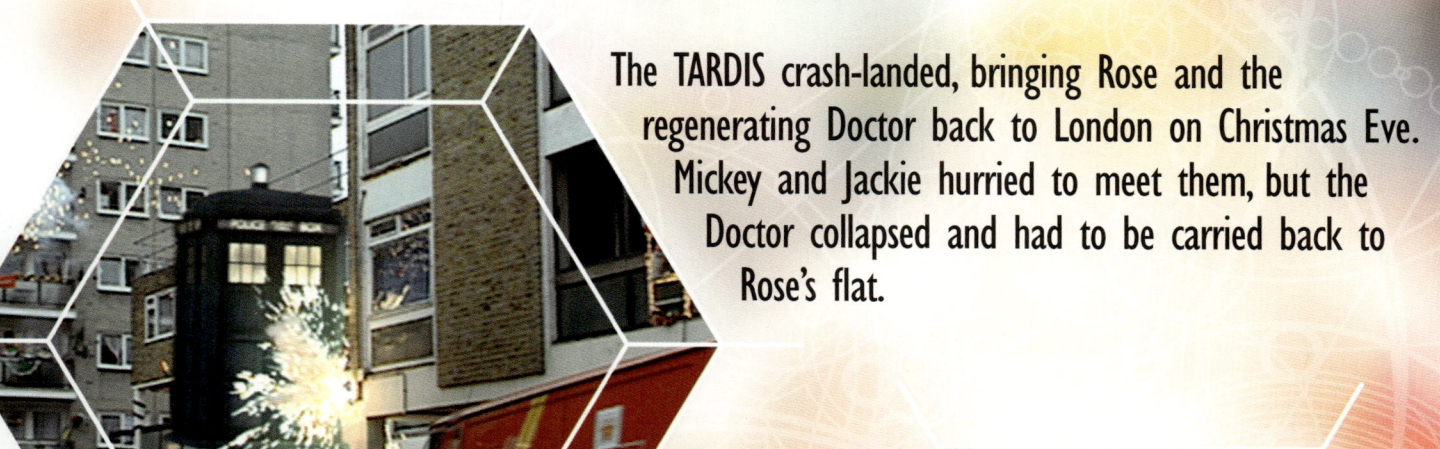

The TARDIS crash-landed, bringing Rose and the regenerating Doctor back to London on Christmas Eve. Mickey and Jackie hurried to meet them, but the Doctor collapsed and had to be carried back to Rose's flat.

While the unconscious Doctor laid in bed exhaling regenerative energy, the British Rocket Group waited for news of unmanned space probe Guinevere One, which was due to land on Mars. But the probe had been waylaid — hijacked by a mysterious spaceship.

Rose and Mickey were Christmas shopping in town when they were attacked by a group of homicidal robot Santa Clauses. They escaped and returned home, where a killer Christmas tree was lying in wait for them.

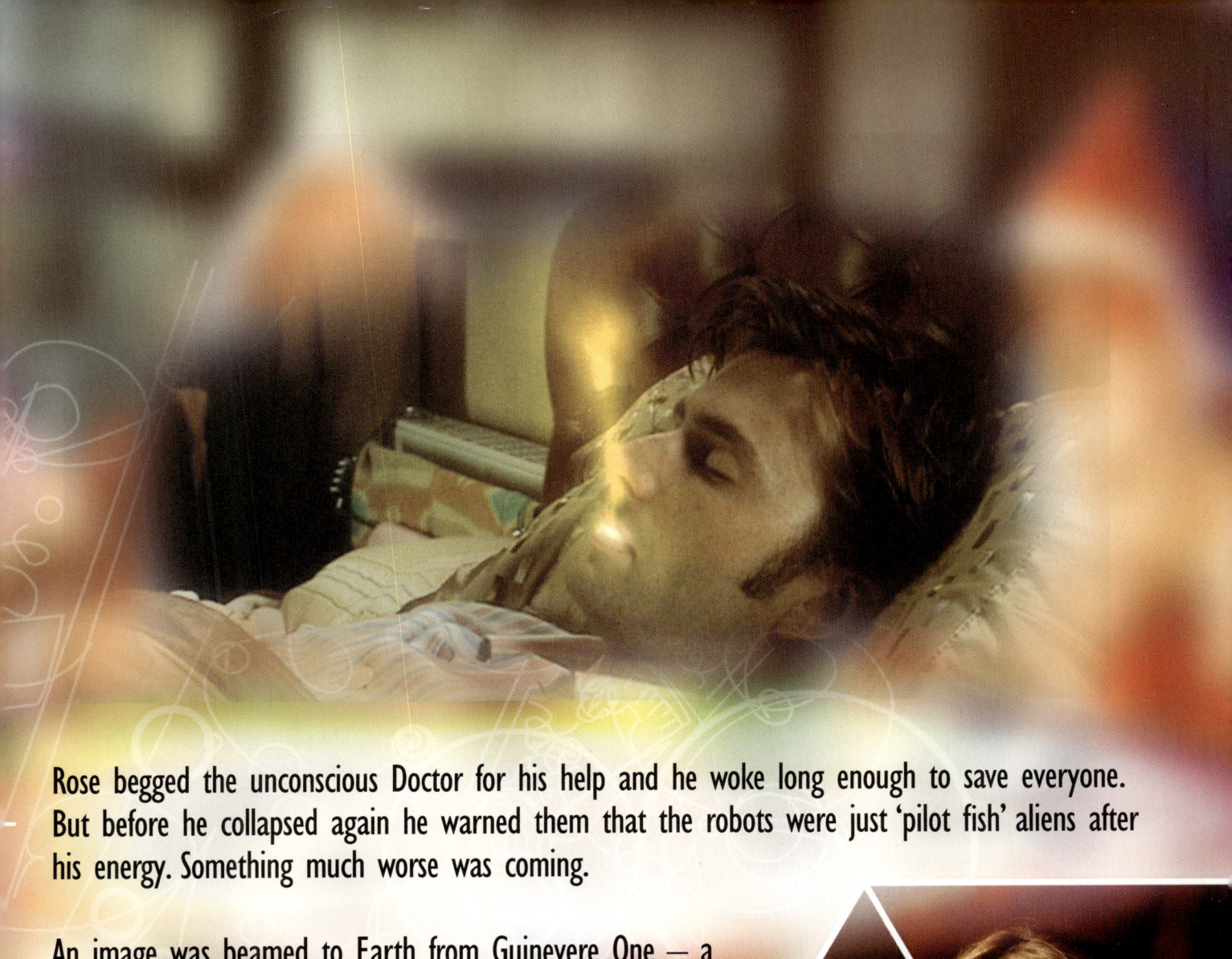

Rose begged the unconscious Doctor for his help and he woke long enough to save everyone. But before he collapsed again he warned them that the robots were just 'pilot fish' aliens after his energy. Something much worse was coming.

An image was beamed to Earth from Guinevere One — a terrifying alien face. UNIT detected a ship heading towards the Earth, and the alien Sycorax demanded the surrender of Earth's people. Prime Minister Harriet Jones refused.

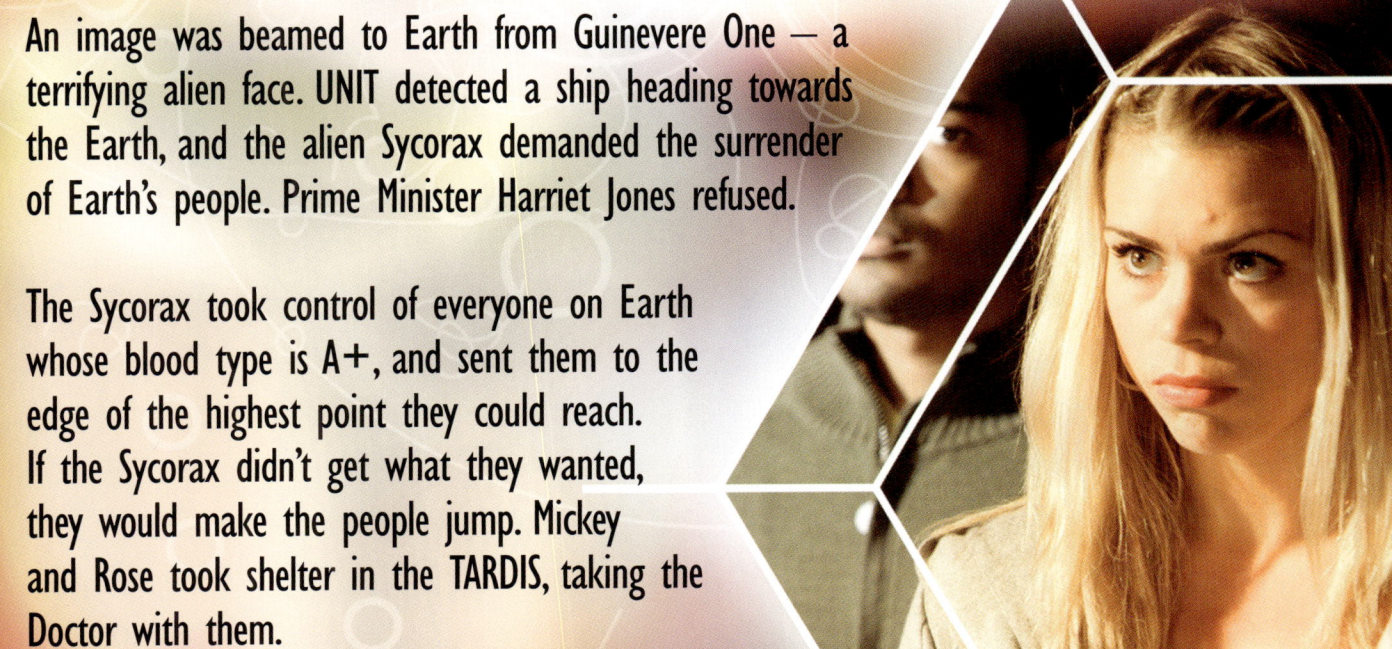

The Sycorax took control of everyone on Earth whose blood type is A+, and sent them to the edge of the highest point they could reach. If the Sycorax didn't get what they wanted, they would make the people jump. Mickey and Rose took shelter in the TARDIS, taking the Doctor with them.

124

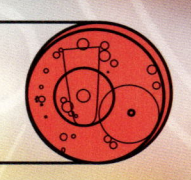

Prime Minister Harriet Jones and her colleagues were teleported aboard the Sycorax ship and so was the TARDIS. Rose tried to face up to the Sycorax, but just as all hope seemed to be lost, the TARDIS door opened. The Doctor was back, reinvigorated by tea!

The Doctor activated the Sycorax's blood control matrix, but no one jumped. The human instinct for survival is too strong. With the threat removed, the Doctor challenged the Sycorax leader to single combat, to decide ownership of the planet.

The fight was fierce. The Doctor was knocked over and the Sycorax leader cut off his hand! But the Doctor had enough residual cellular energy from his regeneration to grow a new one. He continued the fight and the Sycorax leader was defeated.

The Doctor offered to spare the leader's life if he left Earth, never to return. The Sycorax leader agreed, but betrayed the Doctor by attempting to kill him again. The Doctor merely tossed a satsuma and the leader fell to his death.

The Sycorax retreated, taking the Doctor's warning with them - Earth is defended. But Harriet Jones, worried that the Doctor won't always be around to protect the planet, ordered Torchwood to destroy the Sycorax ship as it left. The furious Doctor called her a murderer...

The Doctor and Rose celebrated Christmas with Jackie and Mickey. Ash from the Sycorax ship fell from the sky, bringing a white Christmas to London. But soon it was time for the time travellers to leave again, on their way to new adventures.

TEST YOUR KNOWLEDGE

1. ON WHAT PLANET IS GUINEVERE ONE SUPPOSED TO LAND?
   A. Mars
   B. Pluto
   C. Venus

2. HOW DOES HARRIET JONES TRAVEL TO THE SYCORAX SHIP?
   A. Teleport
   B. TARDIS
   C. Rocket

3. WHAT FRUIT BRINGS ABOUT THE DEATH OF THE SYCORAX LEADER?
   A. Apple
   B. Satsuma
   C. Banana

4. WHAT IMAGE DOES GUINEVERE ONE SEND TO EARTH?
   A. An alien face
   B. A comet
   C. A black hole

5. WHAT BRINGS A WHITE CHRISTMAS TO LONDON?
   A. Snow
   B. White paint
   C. Ash

TEST YOUR KNOWLEDGE

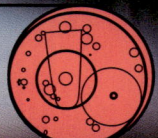

ANSWERS

Meet the Sycorax
1(c) 2(a) 3(c) 4(a) 5(a)

History of the Sycorax
1(b) 2(a) 3(b) 4(c) 5(b)

Enemies
1(c) 2(a) 3(a) 4(b) 5(a)

No Place Like Home
1(c) 2(b) 3(c) 4(a) 5(b)

Weapons and Technology
1(b) 2(a) 3(c) 4(a) 5(c)

The Christmas Invasion
1(a) 2(a) 3(b) 4(a) 5(c)

DOCTOR·WHO

MICKEY

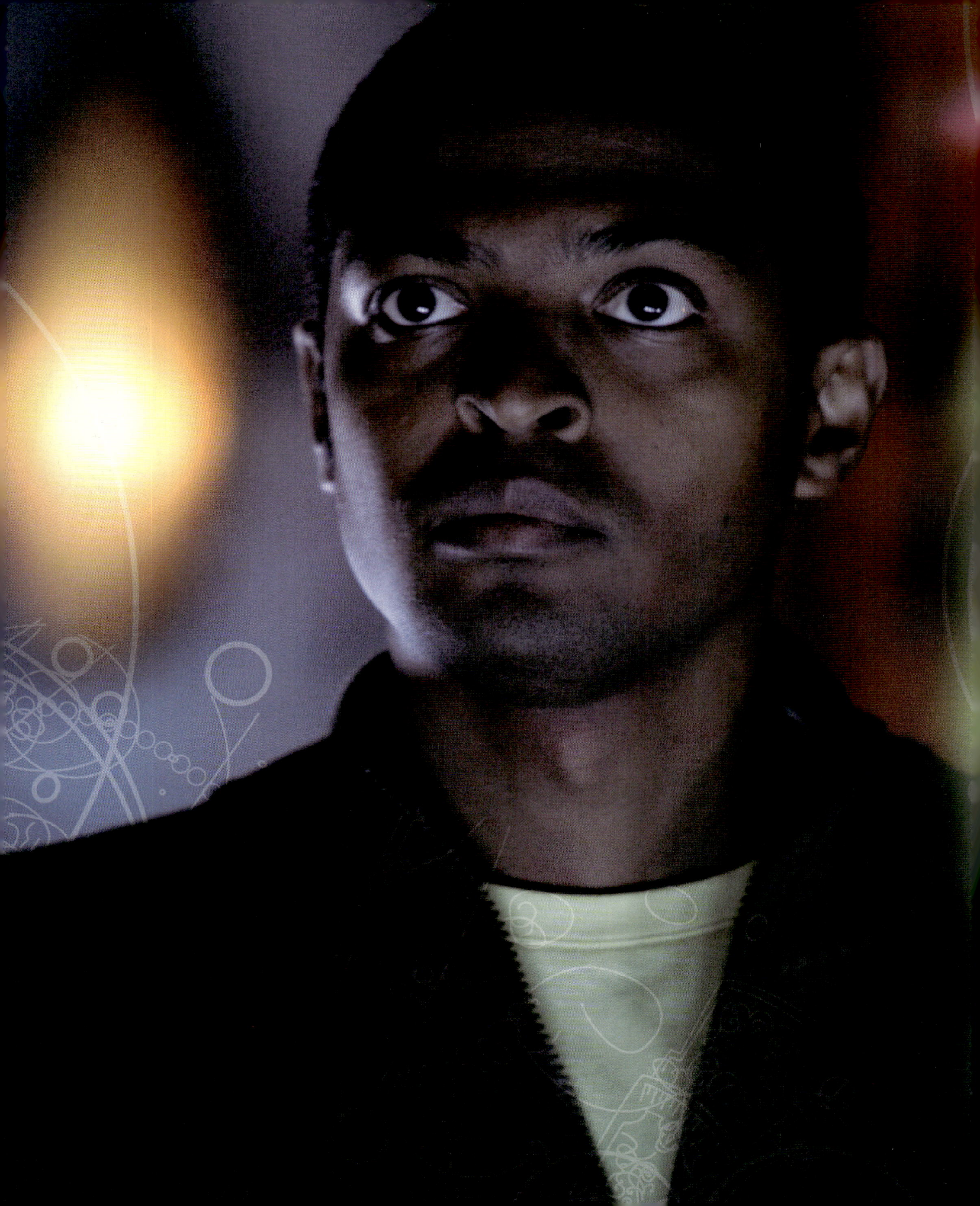

CONTENTS

Meet Mickey
Introduction...130
Mickey Data..132
Mickey Anatomy.....................................134
◆ Test your Knowledge

Friends and Family
Rose..136
The Doctor..136
Jackie Tyler...137
Parents...138
Rita-Anna..138
Ricky...139
◆ Test your Knowledge

Enemies and Rivals
Living Plastic..140
The Slitheen...140
The Krillitanes..141
The Cybermen..142
The Daleks..143
◆ Test your Knowledge

No Place Like Home
Earth...144
Earth and Parallel Earth.......................146
◆ Test your Knowledge

Transport and Technology
Cars, Trucks and Zeppelins................148
The TARDIS..150
The Internet...150
Mobile Phone..151
◆ Test your Knowledge

Adventures at Home
Rose..152
Aliens of London/World War Three..........152
Boom Town..153
Parting of the Ways..............................153
The Christmas Invasion......................154
School Reunion......................................154
The Age of Steel/Rise of the Cybermen....154
Army of Ghosts/Doomsday..............155
◆ Test your Knowledge

Test your Knowledge Answers...................156

MEET MICKEY

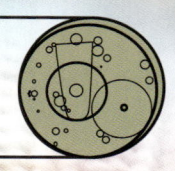

When Mickey Smith was a young boy, he discovered that things didn't always turn out how he'd like them to. His mum died when he was six, and his father went to Spain and never came back. Years later his adventurous girlfriend went off into time and space and left him behind too. So, luckily, Mickey learned how to adapt at an early age.

Mickey was brought up by his gran, a lovely woman called Rita-Anne, who he was extremely close to. He was devastated when she died after she had an accident at home.

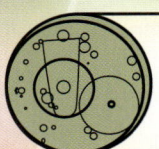

On leaving school, Mickey became a car mechanic, at a garage not far from his flat. He started going out with a girl called Rose Tyler and the pair had an on-off relationship for five years. He always thought they were good together and had something special. All that changed, though, when Rose met a time traveller known as the Doctor. An upset Mickey watched as his girlfriend chose to go travelling with a complete stranger in a time machine disguised as a Police Box.

Over a year later, Mickey got the chance to travel with Rose and the Doctor in the TARDIS, and it was during his travels that he ended up in a parallel universe where his gran was still alive. Fed up of always being second best to the Doctor in Rose's affections, he decided to stay there. Somewhere where he could make a difference.

132 | MICKEY DATA

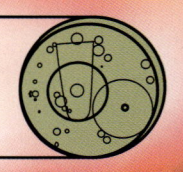

Name: Mickey Smith
Date of birth: 22nd May 1984
Parents: Pauline and Jackson Smith
Height: 1.65 (5'5")
Hair: Black
Eyes: Brown
Home planet: Earth
Home address: 10 Bucknall House, Powell Estate, London SE15
Species: Human
Profession: Car mechanic turned adventurer

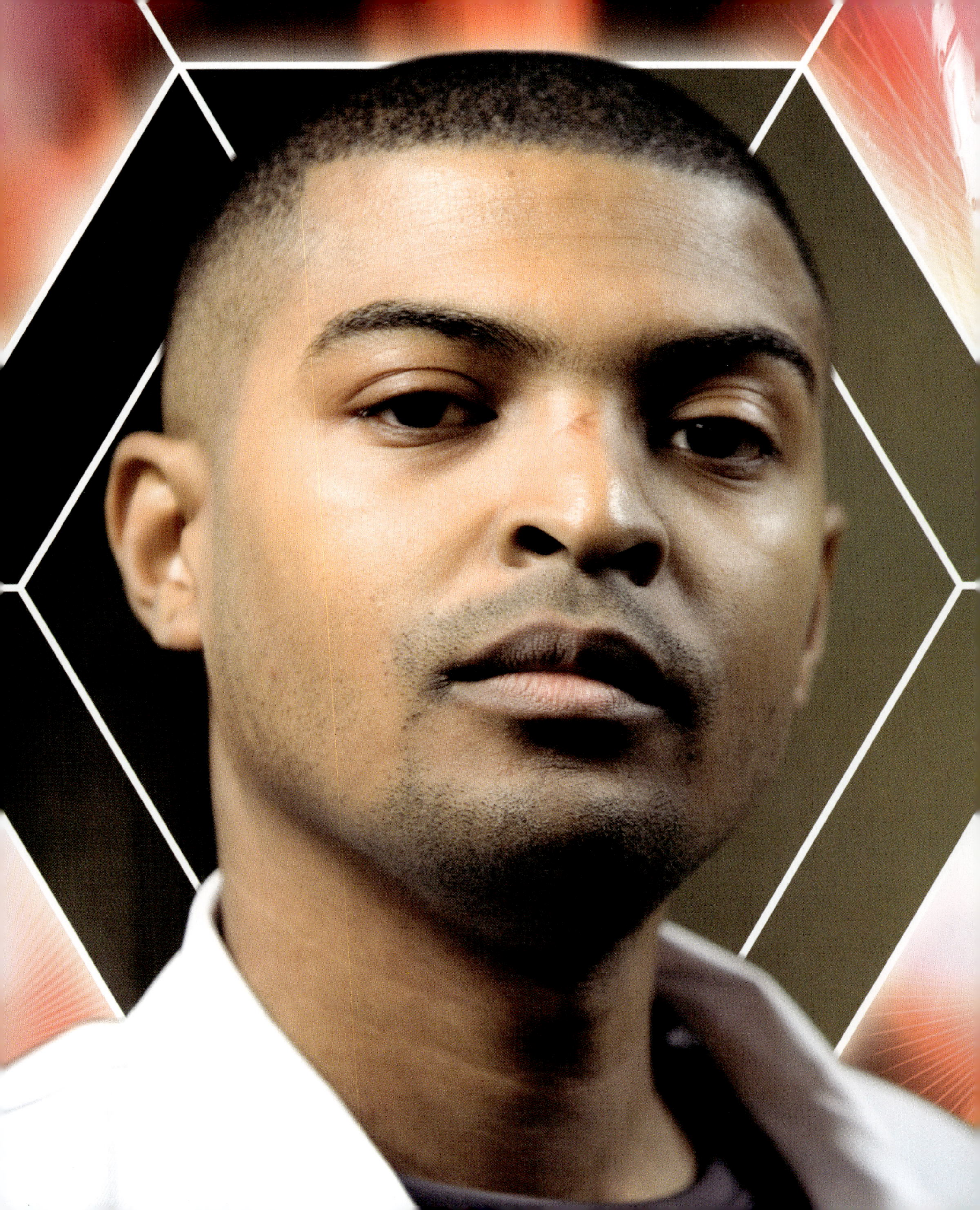

134 MICKEY ANATOMY

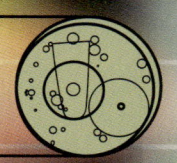

1.65m tall

Heart — broken several times by Rose…

Fit body — from working out and working hard as a mechanic

The TARDIS puts a telepathic field inside his brain so he can understand different languages

Contains his mobile phone, which he is always checking to see if Rose has called…

TEST YOUR KNOWLEDGE

1. **WHAT IS MICKEY'S LAST NAME?**
   A. Smith
   B. Smart
   C. Tyler

2. **WHAT IS THE NAME OF MICKEY'S FATHER?**
   A. Jimmy
   B. Jackson
   C. James

3. **WHAT JOB DID MICKEY DO WHEN HE LEFT SCHOOL?**
   A. A hairdresser
   B. A car mechanic
   C. An actor

4. **WHAT WAS MICKEY'S GRAN CALLED?**
   A. Rita-Anne
   B. Rita-Sue
   C. Rita-Jane

5. **WHAT IS THE NAME OF THE ESTATE MICKEY COMES FROM?**
   A. Paddington
   B. Powell
   C. Padbury

FRIENDS AND FAMILY

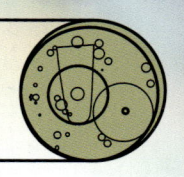

ROSE

One of the best things to happen to Mickey was meeting Rose Tyler. She lived in the same block of flats as him on the Powell Estate and he really fancied her. He was heartbroken when she chose to go off into time and space with the Doctor. But Mickey knew that Rose had to do what was best for her... and, unfortunately for Mickey that meant travelling with the Doctor.

THE DOCTOR

The last of the Time Lords, a powerful race who were destroyed in the Time War against the Daleks. The Doctor didn't take to Mickey at first. He thought he was a coward, which, to be fair, he was! But Mickey didn't exactly like him either. After all, the Doctor stole his girlfriend. Before the Doctor regenerated, the Doctor liked to call Mickey 'Ricky' to wind him up!

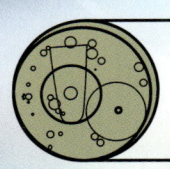

JACKIE TYLER

Rose's mum, Jackie, always got on well with Mickey. Until the Doctor took Rose away, that is. When Rose went missing for a year, Jackie blamed Mickey for her disappearance. She started up a hate campaign around the estate, which led to a miserable life for the innocent Mickey. When Jackie discovered the truth, that her daughter had become a time and space adventurer, Mickey and she became friends again. She would cook for him most Sundays and both of them would sit there wondering what Rose and the Doctor were up to, and if they'd ever come home...

PARENTS

Mickey's mum died when he was very young. His dad, Jackson Smith, worked in the key cutters in Clifton Parade, but Mickey was never very close to him. He never got the chance, as his dad disappeared off to Spain and never returned.

RITA-ANNE

With no parents around, Mickey's gran, Rita-Anne, became a big part of his life. He lived with her and loved her very much. Mickey was devastated when his gran, who was blind, tripped over at home and died as a result. When the TARDIS arrived in a parallel Earth, Mickey discovered that in this other world Rita-Anne was still alive. Upset but happy, he chose to stay there. A world where he could fit in and not feel alone.

TEST YOUR KNOWLEDGE

1. WHAT WAS ONE OF THE BEST THINGS TO HAPPEN TO MICKEY?
   A. Winning the lottery
   B. Meeting Rose Tyler
   C. Becoming a mechanic

2. WHAT DID THE DOCTOR CALL MICKEY TO ANNOY HIM?
   A. Dicky
   B. Ricky
   C. Vicky

3. WHAT DID MICKEY'S DAD DO FOR A LIVING?
   A. A time traveller
   B. A fitness instructor
   C. A key cutter

4. WHAT KILLED RICKY?
   A. A zeppelin
   B. Rose
   C. A cyberman

5. WHERE DID MICKEY'S DAD GO?
   A. Wales
   B. Spain
   C. Australia

RICKY

Ricky, although physically identical to him, was completely different to Mickey. They met on the parallel Earth. He was brave and courageous, but was killed by a Cyberman. His death shook Mickey — and changed his life. From that day on his days of being the coward and being left behind were certainly over. A new, stronger and braver Mickey emerged, leading to his decision to stay behind and start a new life without Rose and fight the Cybermen.

ENEMIES AND RIVALS

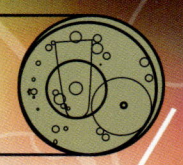

LIVING PLASTIC

The Nestene Consciousness is able to bring anything made of plastic to life, as Mickey discovered when he opened a wheelie bin! The bin swallowed Mickey, kept him trapped underground, and made a plastic replica of him to trick Rose into telling them where the Doctor was. Later, a terrified Mickey was rescued by the Doctor and Rose in the TARDIS.

THE SLITHEEN

The Slitheen are a family of criminals from Raxacoricofallapatorious. Mickey first met one when it turned up in Jackie Tyler's flat and tried to kill her. They destroyed the alien by throwing vinegar over it and got covered in Slitheen slime as a result! Later that year he met one of the escaped Slitheen in Cardiff, but was more concerned about losing Rose than helping return Blon Fel Fotch Pasameer-Day Slitheen to her home planet...

THE KRILLITANES

Mickey brought the Doctor and Rose back to Earth when there were reports of UFO activity and strange happenings at a school. There they discovered the Krillitanes, gargoyle-like aliens made up from all the races they'd ever conquered. They could morph into human form and were posing as school teachers. Their leader, Mr Finch, enlisted the help of school children, against their will, to crack the Skasas Paradigm in order to gain control over time, space and matter! The Krillitanes put special oil in school lunches to accelerate the children's learning power. They were destroyed when the oil, which was toxic to them, covered them and the school was blown up.

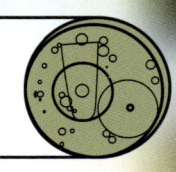

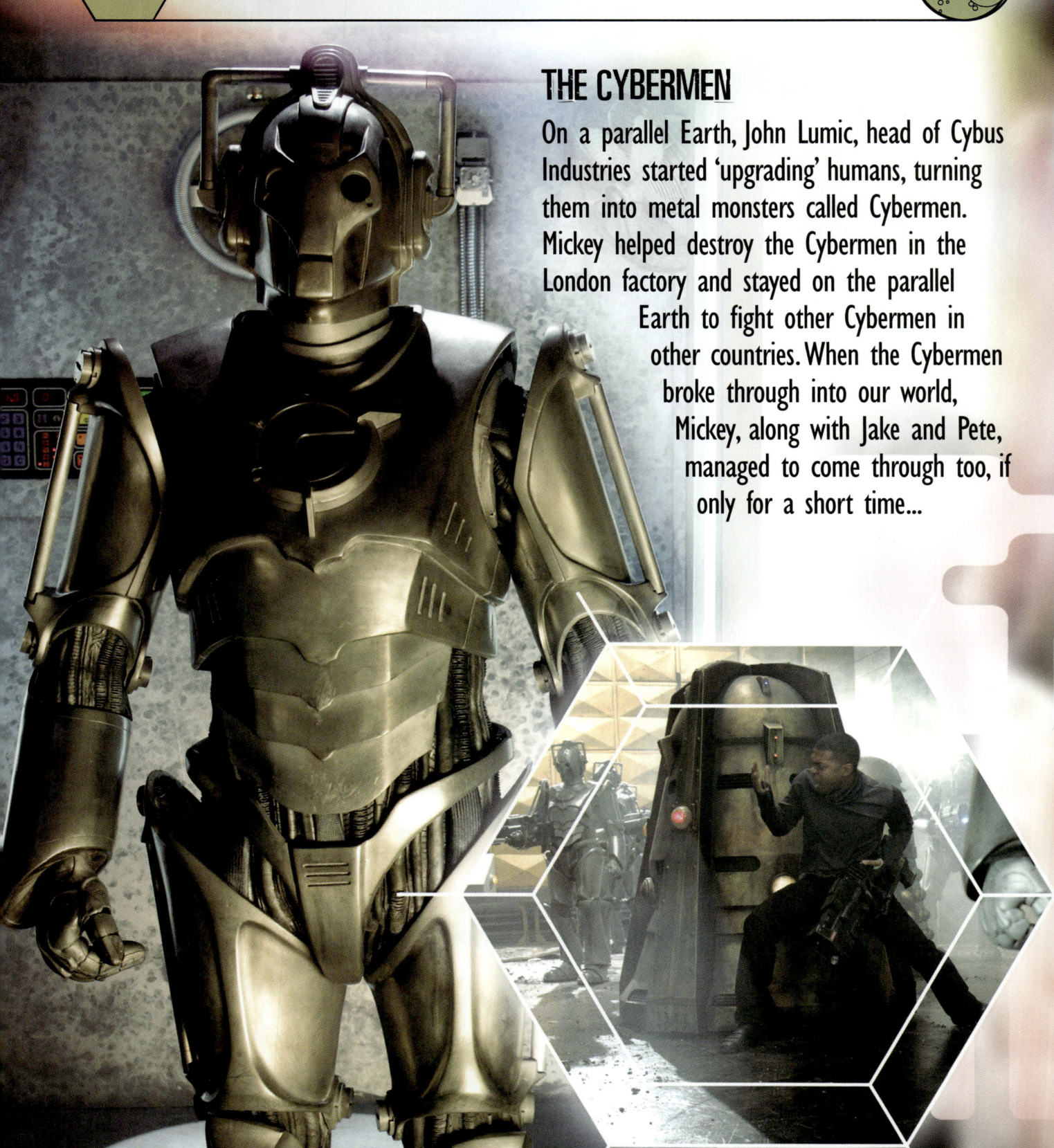

THE CYBERMEN

On a parallel Earth, John Lumic, head of Cybus Industries started 'upgrading' humans, turning them into metal monsters called Cybermen. Mickey helped destroy the Cybermen in the London factory and stayed on the parallel Earth to fight other Cybermen in other countries. When the Cybermen broke through into our world, Mickey, along with Jake and Pete, managed to come through too, if only for a short time...

THE DALEKS

The Daleks are mutant creatures and one of the most evil races in the entire universe. While the Dalek army in 200,100 was trying to destroy Earth and turn all humans into Daleks, Mickey was comforting his girlfriend Rose, who the Doctor had sent back to the past to the safety of life at home. If it hadn't been for his efforts in returning Rose to the future to help the Doctor, the Daleks would have succeeded, so Mickey can be proud that he played a big part in saving Earth! Later, he met the Daleks properly when the Cybermen broke through into our world. Mickey accidentally unleashed the Daleks when he fell against the Genesis Ark (their prison capsule), unlocking it and releasing the Daleks.

TEST YOUR KNOWLEDGE

1. THE SLITHEEN ARE A FAMILY OF WHAT?
A. Doctors
B. Accountants
C. Criminals

2. WHO DID THE NESTENE CONSCIOUSNESS MAKE A REPLICA OF?
A. Rose
B. The Doctor
C. Mickey

3. WHAT WERE THE KRILLITANES TRYING TO SOLVE?
A. The Skasas Paradigm
B. Pythagoras' Theorem
C. The Meaning of Life

4. WHAT DID MICKEY OPEN TO RELEASE THE DALEKS?
A. A door inside the TARDIS
B. The Genesis Ark
C. Aladdin's lamp

5. WHAT ALLOWED MICKEY TO COME BACK TO OUR WORLD?
A. The TARDIS
B. The Cybermen breaking through into our world
C. A Slitheen teleporter

144 NO PLACE LIKE HOME

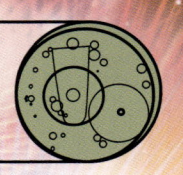

EARTH

Mickey's home planet is Earth. A generally friendly planet, Earth is the third planet from the Sun in our solar system, positioned between Venus and Mars. It has one satellite — the Moon. It's not a young planet, it's over 4.5 billion years old!

Earth travels around the sun at a speed of 108,000km per hour. As it orbits the Sun, Earth rotates. This takes 24 hours (giving us day and night, day as it's facing the Sun and night when it's not). Earth's journey around the sun takes a total of 364 days.

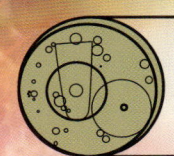

Many different kinds of creatures live here and over 6 billion humans call Earth their home. Non-human travellers haven't been included in this figure, but the planet does tend to attract the odd visitor or two! Many aliens have tried to invade the planet over the last few billion years…

Earth is the only planet in the solar system where water exists on the surface. It's a good planet to live on as a result and many aliens like the Daleks, Sycorax and Slitheen try to invade, destroy or control it in some way. Thankfully, the planet has had the help of the Doctor on more than one occasion.

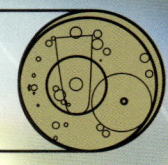

EARTH AND PARALLEL EARTH

Since Mickey met the Doctor, Earth has been invaded by several aliens. Alongside Rose, he has played a big part in helping defeat them. He saved Earth from the Slitheen using the computer in his bedroom; he helped Rose and the newly regenerated Doctor attack the mysterious 'pilot fish' who appeared ahead of the Sycorax; and finally, he played a huge part in ridding the world of the Cybermen and Daleks. Which was only fair, as he was accidentally responsible for bringing the Daleks back in the first place!

On the parallel Earth in the early 21st century things are slightly different to our world. There are zeppelins in the sky. Technology is more advanced. Advertisement posters can move and everyone wears Ear Pods through which they can receive news, information, and later, sinister instructions.

More shocking is that Rose's dad and Mickey's gran are still alive, and Rose doesn't exist, although Jackie and Pete Tyler have a dog with her name!

TEST YOUR KNOWLEDGE

1. WHAT PLANET DOES MICKEY COME FROM?
A. Earth
B. Venus
C. Mars

2. APPROXIMATELY HOW MANY PEOPLE LIVE ON EARTH?
A. Seventeen Billion
B. Six Billion
C. One Billion

3. IN THE PARALLEL EARTH, WHAT IS THE NAME OF JACKIE AND PETE'S DOG?
A. Mickey
B. Rose
C. Trisha

4. HOW OLD IS EARTH?
A. 2000 years old
B. 10,000 millions years old
C. 4.5 billion years old

5. WHAT ARE YOU LIKELY TO FIND IN THE SKY IN THE PARALLEL EARTH?
A. Helicopters
B. Zeppelins
C. Spaceships

148 | TRANSPORT AND TECHNOLOGY

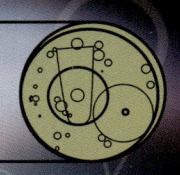

BEETLE

Being a mechanic, Mickey is good with vehicles. He knows them inside out. His previous car was a yellow Volkswagen Beetle. He used it to take Rose to visit a man called Clive, who supposedly knew all about the Doctor. Mickey waited patiently in his car while Rose talked to Clive, but was lured out of it by a wheelie bin that swallowed him and then made a replica of him. When Rose returned to the car a 'plastic' Mickey drove off with her…!

MINI

Mickey used a Mini to try to open up the heart of the TARDIS. Mickey and Rose tied a chain to the TARDIS controls and tried to break it open with sheer force. The little car wasn't powerful enough though.

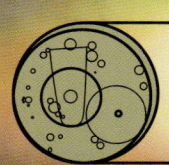

TRUCK

Mickey proudly claimed he once saved the world in a big yellow pick-up truck. When the Mini wasn't strong enough, Jackie found a truck and Mickey managed, eventually, to open up the heart of the TARDIS, which allowed Rose to get back to the Doctor.

ZEPPELIN

Mickey bravely took the controls of a zeppelin while helping battle against the Cybermen. He was able to rescue the Doctor, Rose and Pete with it and enjoyed flying it. When asked where he had learned to fly such a craft, he said it was all down to playing PlayStation games!

THE TARDIS

The TARDIS may be disguised as an old Earth police box, but it can travel anywhere in time and space, although it doesn't always arrive exactly where the Doctor planned. It took a while for Mickey to get used to the idea. His first trip in it was after being rescued by the Doctor and Rose, but he was too scared to appreciate the experience…

THE INTERNET

Mickey is a big fan of the Internet and has used it several times to help the Doctor and Rose. Initially, when Rose first left, he used it to try and find out about the Doctor. Later, he broke into a government database and helped to destroy the Slitheen; learnt about 'pilot fish' to prepare for the Sycorax attack; and wiped all traces of the Doctor from the Internet.

TEST YOUR KNOWLEDGE

MOBILE PHONE

Mickey, like most people, depends on his mobile. When Mickey and Jackie were attacked by a Slitheen, he took a picture of the creature and sent it to Rose. The Doctor adapted Rose's ordinary phone so it worked anywhere in time and space, and across any distance. Mickey kept the phone when he stayed behind on the parallel Earth to help in his continuing fight against the Cybermen, as the phone contained codes that could destroy them.

1. WHAT VEHICLE WAS USED TO OPEN THE HEART OF THE TARDIS?
   A. A London bus
   B. A Beetle
   C. A pick-up truck

2. WHERE DID MICKEY SAY HE'D LEARNED TO FLY A ZEPPELIN?
   A. Playing PlayStation games
   B. He did a course
   C. Jake taught him

3. WHAT COLOUR WAS MICKEY'S BEETLE?
   A. Red
   B. Black
   C. Yellow

4. WHAT DID MICKEY TAKE A PICTURE OF WITH HIS PHONE?
   A. A Dalek
   B. A Cyberman
   C. A Slitheen

5. WHAT IS THE TARDIS DISGUISED AS?
   A. A Police Box
   B. A pick-up truck
   C. A sofa

152 ADVENTURES AT HOME

ROSE

After being eaten by a wheelie bin, Mickey was dumped in the underground lair of the Nestene Consciousness. He watched, helpless, scared and not believing what he saw, as Rose saved the Doctor and the Nestene was destroyed. It was all too much for him. While he was desperate to get away from the Doctor and get home to safety, Rose had other ideas. Mickey got a quick kiss, and Rose ran into the TARDIS and disappeared…

ALIENS OF LONDON/WORLD WAR THREE

Rose had been missing a year. During that time Mickey had been arrested and accused of her disappearance — even though he was completely innocent. He didn't tell anybody about the Doctor. Who would believe him? When Rose and the Doctor returned, Mickey helped them by launching a missile via his computer and destroying the Slitheen, but then they left him behind. The Doctor did ask him if he wanted to go with them but he thought that their dangerous life was too much for him. The Doctor gave Mickey a disc containing a virus that, when put online, would delete any mention of him from the Internet.

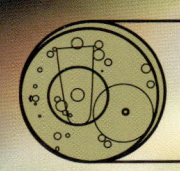

BOOM TOWN

Rose said she needed her passport, but it was really just an excuse to see Mickey again. He spent a day with the Doctor, Rose and Captain Jack, and they captured one of the Slitheen who'd escaped and was posing as the Mayor of Cardiff. Mickey was quite willing to trek all the way across to Wales to see Rose, but found himself bored of her constant talking about her travels. So he told her about Trisha, a girl he'd started seeing… and disappeared home to London, upset, without saying goodbye to the time travellers.

PARTING OF THE WAYS

Hearing the TARDIS land, Mickey couldn't help running towards the sound. He found a tearful Rose by the Police Box. The Doctor, to protect her, had sent her back through time, where he wanted her to stay safe and out of danger. When Rose thoughtlessly told Mickey that there was nothing left for her on Earth, however much he loved her, he knew he had to help her get back. So they eventually opened the heart of the TARDIS and off she went. Leaving Mickey behind for a fourth time.

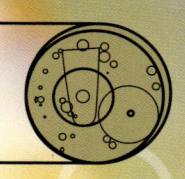

THE CHRISTMAS INVASION

That Christmas Eve, while he was still at work, Mickey heard the sound of the TARDIS and once again rushed to see Rose. He and Jackie were almost squashed by the Police box, which contained a shaken Rose and a new Doctor. After fighting the Sycorax, the Doctor, Rose, Mickey and Jackie celebrated Christmas together. Mickey, along with Jackie, finally saw what Rose got from travelling with the Doctor.

SCHOOL REUNION

Mickey called Rose and the Doctor home to help investigate UFO activity and mysterious goings on at a school, which turned out to be the work of the Krillitanes. But someone else was also investigating, the Doctor's old friend Sarah Jane Smith and K-9, the robot dog that the Doctor had given her. Seeing Rose again and meeting Sarah Jane convinced Mickey that this time he wasn't going to be left behind. He asked if he could travel in the TARDIS and suddenly Mickey Smith was travelling in time and space!

THE AGE OF STEEL/THE RISE OF THE CYBERMEN

Mickey was quick to realise the TARDIS had brought the Doctor, Rose and him to a parallel time and place. He'd seen it in films, where everything looks the same but is really a little bit different. In this alternative world, he found one of the biggest differences was that his gran was still alive and that he had an alternative self called Ricky! Being braver and stronger than ever before, Mickey helped bring down the Cybermen and chose to stay in this world to destroy other Cyberfactories. Keeping Rose's phone, containing codes to stop the Cybermen, he said goodbye to his girlfriend and the Doctor, thinking he'd never see them again...

ARMY OF GHOSTS/DOOMSDAY

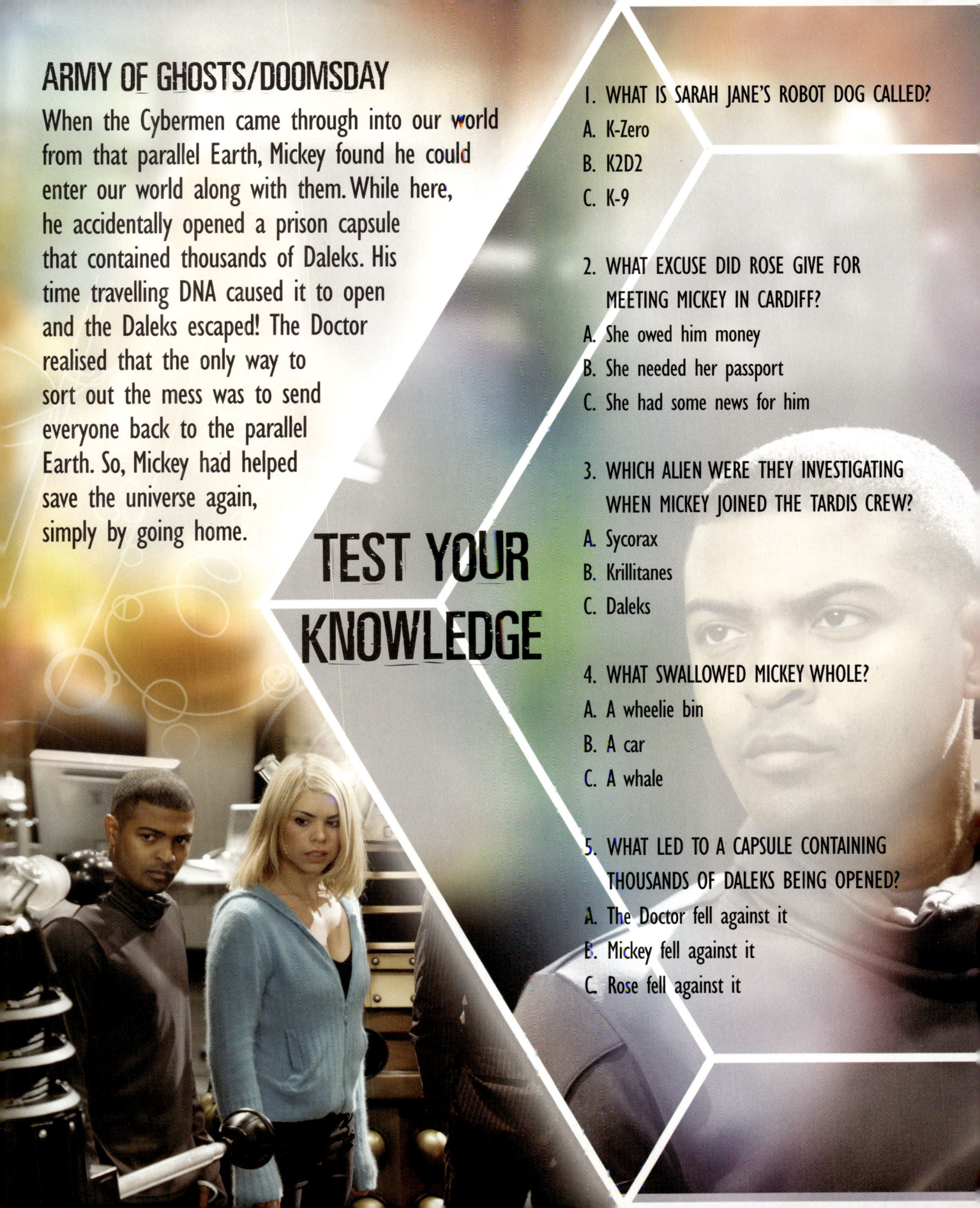

When the Cybermen came through into our world from that parallel Earth, Mickey found he could enter our world along with them. While here, he accidentally opened a prison capsule that contained thousands of Daleks. His time travelling DNA caused it to open and the Daleks escaped! The Doctor realised that the only way to sort out the mess was to send everyone back to the parallel Earth. So, Mickey had helped save the universe again, simply by going home.

TEST YOUR KNOWLEDGE

1. WHAT IS SARAH JANE'S ROBOT DOG CALLED?
A. K-Zero
B. K2D2
C. K-9

2. WHAT EXCUSE DID ROSE GIVE FOR MEETING MICKEY IN CARDIFF?
A. She owed him money
B. She needed her passport
C. She had some news for him

3. WHICH ALIEN WERE THEY INVESTIGATING WHEN MICKEY JOINED THE TARDIS CREW?
A. Sycorax
B. Krillitanes
C. Daleks

4. WHAT SWALLOWED MICKEY WHOLE?
A. A wheelie bin
B. A car
C. A whale

5. WHAT LED TO A CAPSULE CONTAINING THOUSANDS OF DALEKS BEING OPENED?
A. The Doctor fell against it
B. Mickey fell against it
C. Rose fell against it

TEST YOUR KNOWLEDGE

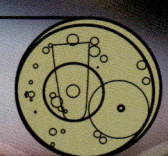

ANSWERS

Meet Mickey
1 (a) 2 (b) 3 (b) 4 (a) 5 (b)

Friends and Family
1 (b) 2 (b) 3 (c) 4 (c) 5 (b)

Enemies and Rivals
1 (c) 2 (c) 3 (a) 4 (b) 5 (b)

No Place Like Home
1 (a) 2 (b) 3 (b) 4 (c) 5 (b)

Transport and Technology
1 (c) 2 (a) 3 (c) 4 (c) 5 (a)

Adventures at Home
1 (c) 2 (b) 3 (b) 4 (a) 5 (b)

DOCTOR · WHO

K-9

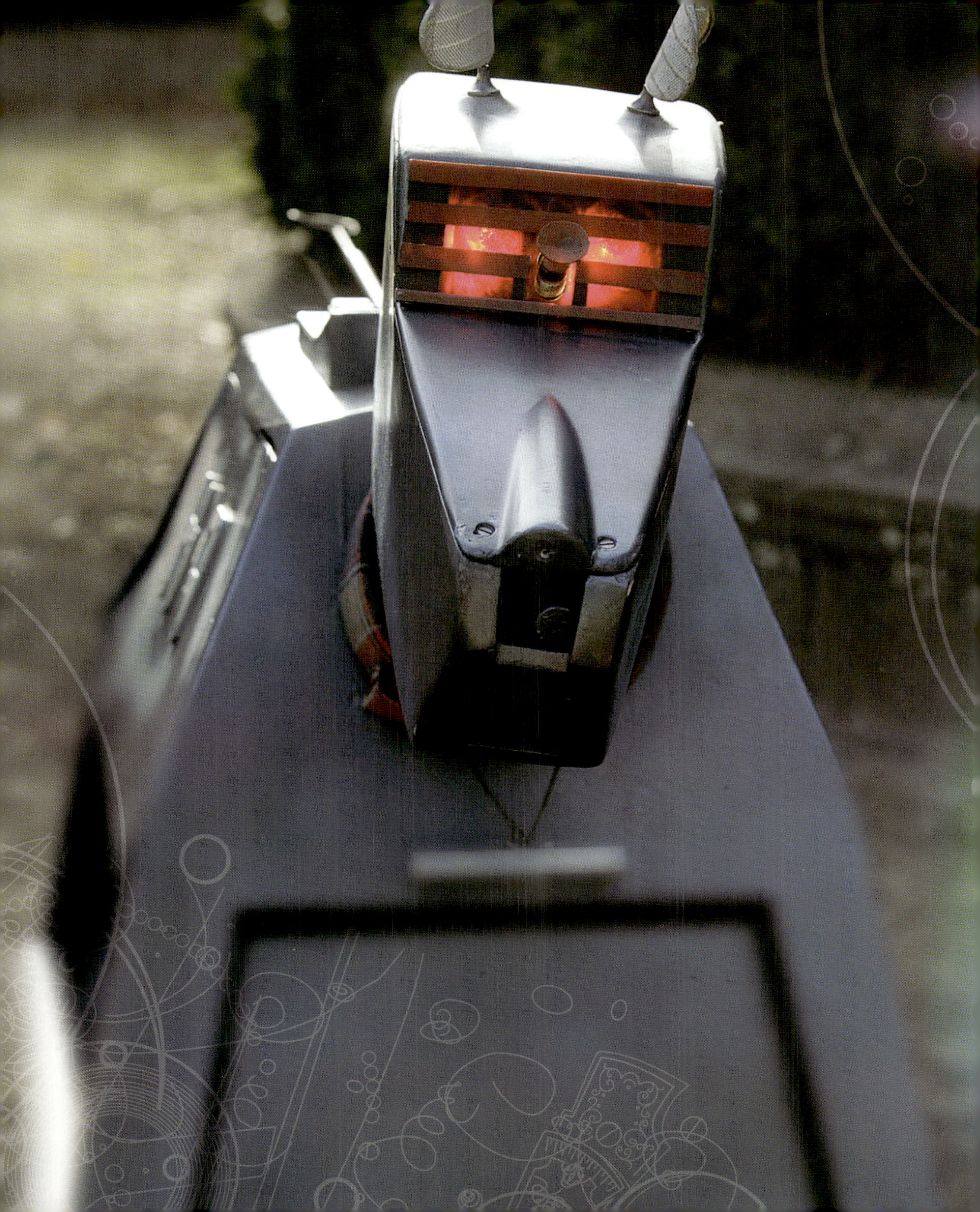

CONTENTS

K-9
Meet K-9 160
K-9 Data 162
K-9 Anatomy 164
◆ Test your Knowledge

K-9's Friends
The Doctor 166
Sarah Jane Smith 167
Rose Tyler 168
Mickey Smith 169
◆ Test your Knowledge

K-9's Enemies
The Krillitanes 170
Mr Finch 172
◆ Test your Knowledge

Biography of K-9
Earlier K-9s 174
Repairing K-9 176
◆ Test your Knowledge

K-9's Technology
Capabilities 178
Computer brain 180
Weaponry 181
◆ Test your Knowledge

The Adventures of K-9 182
◆ Test your Knowledge

Test your Knowledge Answers 186

MEET K-9

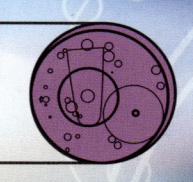

K-9 is a robot dog, originally designed in the year 5,000. He has an incredibly powerful computer for his brain, and talks in a high-pitched voice. K-9 is armed with a laser gun that is hidden in his nose, and can use his probes and sensors to detect all sorts of transmission and sounds. He originally belonged to the Doctor, who gave him to his friend Sarah Jane Smith to look after.

Sarah Jane lives in Croydon on present day Earth. She was surprised and excited when she found the Doctor had left K-9 for her as a present — it meant he had not forgotten all the adventures they had together in time and space. Sarah Jane and K-9 travelled with the Doctor at different times, so they had never met before. But they had lots of adventures together, including having to defeat a group of people involved in black magic in Gloucestershire.

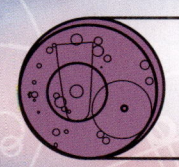

But as time went on, K-9 began to wear out. Since he was a robot from the future, Sarah Jane couldn't just go and buy spare parts for him, or take him to be repaired. So gradually, K-9 stopped working. Then one day, when Sarah Jane was investigating a strange school with creepy teachers who turned out to be aliens, she met the Doctor again. He had changed his appearance, but it was still the same Doctor. So he repaired K-9 and he was even better than ever.

162 K-9 DATA

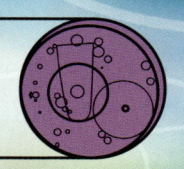

Name: K-9

Species: Computerised robot dog

Created by: Professer Marius

Other owners: The Doctor and Sarah Jane Smith

Weaponry: Nose blaster emits a photon beam

Protection: Armoured casing

Sensors: Articulated sensors ('ears') for hearing, visual circuits ('eyes') and probe

Power source: Electricity — can recharge from any available power source

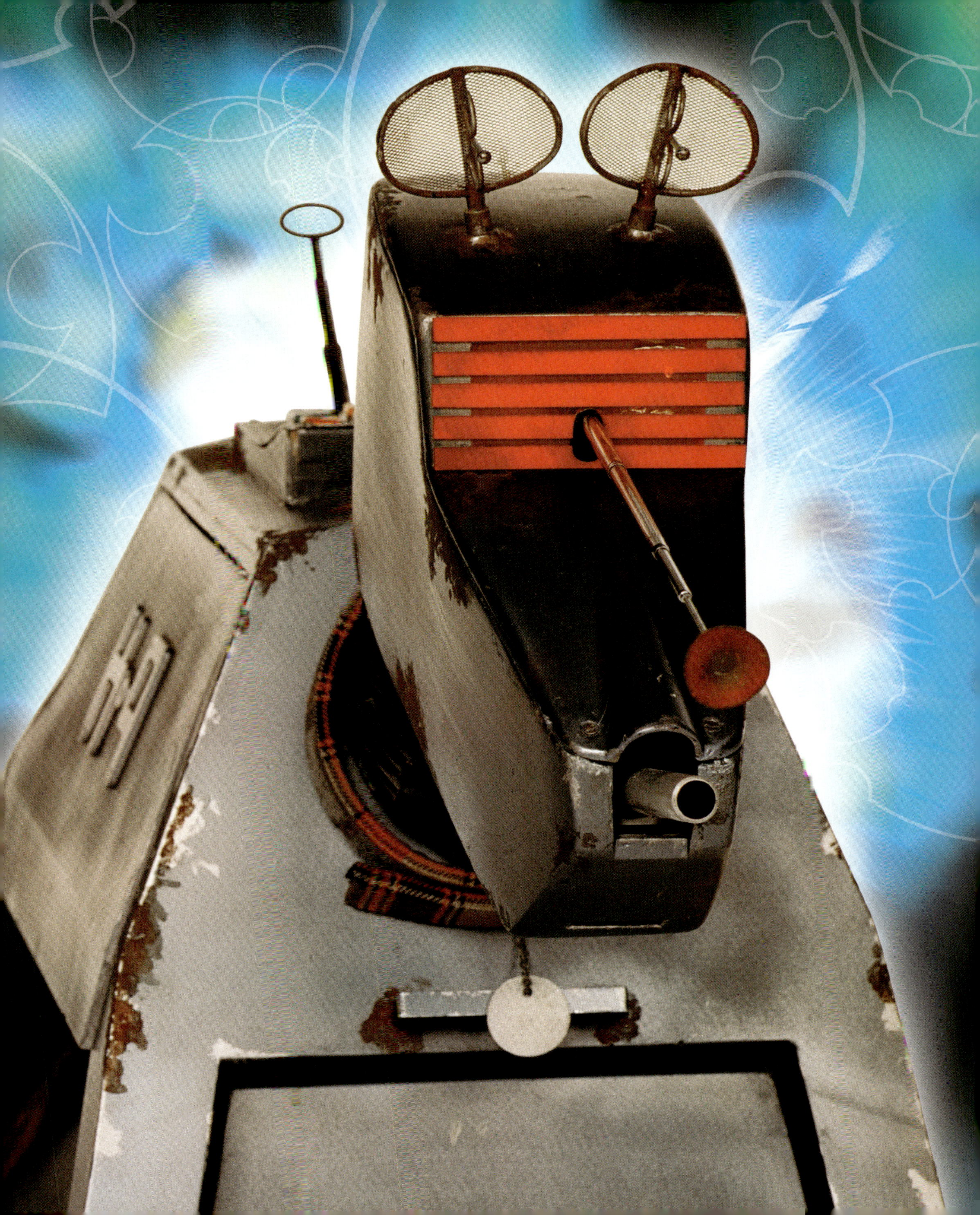

164 K-9 ANATOMY

Operator console for manual programming

Articulated sensors

Communications antenna

Visual orientation circuits (eyes)

Photon blaster

Sensor probe, can link to other online systems

Ticker tape read-out

TEST YOUR KNOWLEDGE

1. WHAT YEAR WAS K-9 ORIGINALLY BUILT?
A. 1066
B. 55BC
C. 5,000

2. WHERE IS K-9'S BLASTER WEAPON HIDDEN?
A. Under his collar
B. In a special holster
C. Up his nose

3. HOW DOES K-9 COMMUNICATE WITH SARAH JANE AND THE DOCTOR?
A. Written memos
B. In a high-pitched voice
C. Email

4. WHO GAVE K-9 TO SARAH JANE SMITH?
A. The Doctor
B. Sarah Jane's Aunt Lavinia
C. A boy called Brendan

5. HOW DOES K-9 RECHARGE?
A. He plugs into a special socket in the TARDIS
B. He can link to any available power source
C. He gets top-up cards from the local newsagent

166 K-9'S FRIENDS

THE DOCTOR

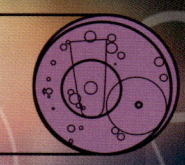

A long time ago, K-9 used to travel through time and space with the Doctor in his TARDIS and they had many adventures together. The Doctor is the last of the Time Lords, a powerful race who were destroyed in the Time War. A Time Lord can save himself from death by changing every cell in his body — this is called regeneration. Since K-9 travelled with the Doctor, he has been forced to regenerate several times so he now looks quite different. But K-9 knew at once who he was when they met again and the Doctor repaired him.

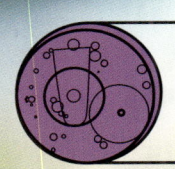

SARAH JANE SMITH

Sarah Jane used to travel with the Doctor too, but that was before the Doctor met K-9. By then, Sarah Jane had already gone home and was carrying on with her job as a journalist. But one day she found the Doctor had left her a present in a crate in the attic. When she opened the crate, she found K-9 inside, and knew at once that he was from the Doctor. Sarah Jane was rather surprised to be given a robot dog from the future, but she and K-9 became great friends and had many adventures of their own.

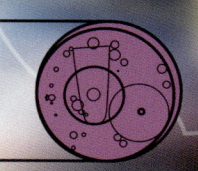

ROSE TYLER

Rose travels with the Doctor now, just like Sarah Jane and K-9 used to long ago. She met Sarah Jane and K-9 when they all investigated the same strange school where odd things were happening. Rose's friend Mickey discovered there were lots of UFOs seen in the area and it turned out some of the teachers had been replaced by aliens! At first, Sarah Jane and Rose did not get along too well, as they were each jealous of the other's friendship with the Doctor. But they are now the best of friends and Rose is very fond of K-9 too.

MICKEY SMITH

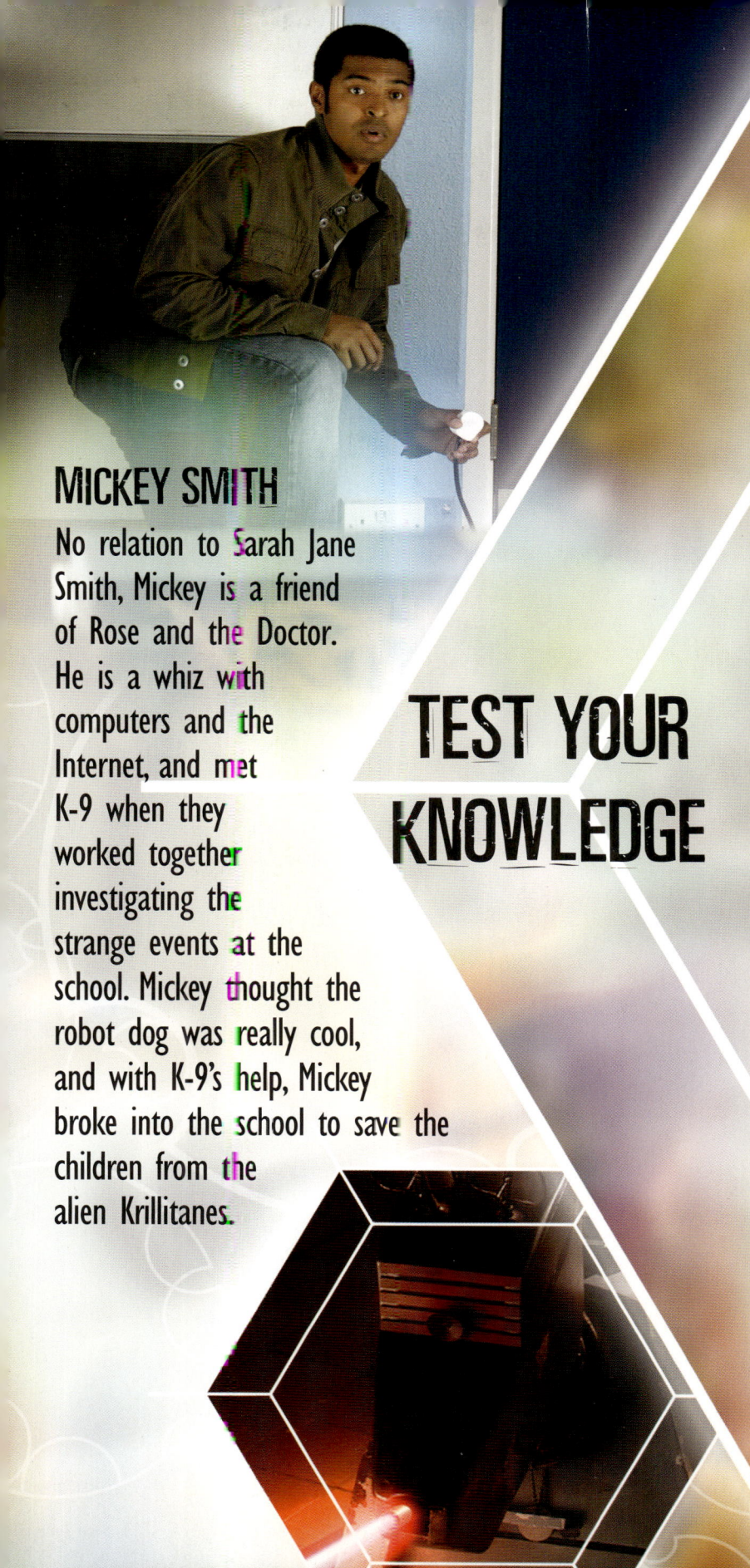

No relation to Sarah Jane Smith, Mickey is a friend of Rose and the Doctor. He is a whiz with computers and the Internet, and met K-9 when they worked together investigating the strange events at the school. Mickey thought the robot dog was really cool, and with K-9's help, Mickey broke into the school to save the children from the alien Krillitanes.

TEST YOUR KNOWLEDGE

1. WHEN DID K-9 AND SARAH JANE MEET THE DOCTOR, ROSE AND MICKEY?
A. When they investigated a mystery at a school
B. When the TARDIS landed in Croydon
C. When they were at the local shops buying milk

2. WHERE DID SARAH JANE FIND K-9?
A. In the TARDIS
B. In a crate in the attic
C. At the supermarket

3. WHO IS MICKEY SMITH?
A. The school caretaker
B. A friend of the Doctor and Rose
C. Sarah Jane Smith's brother

4. WHAT IS SARAH JANE'S JOB?
A. Teacher
B. Police officer
C. Journalist

5. WHO BROKE INTO THE SCHOOL WITH K-9 TO SAVE THE CHILDREN?
A. Mickey
B. The Doctor
C. The army

170 K-9'S ENEMIES

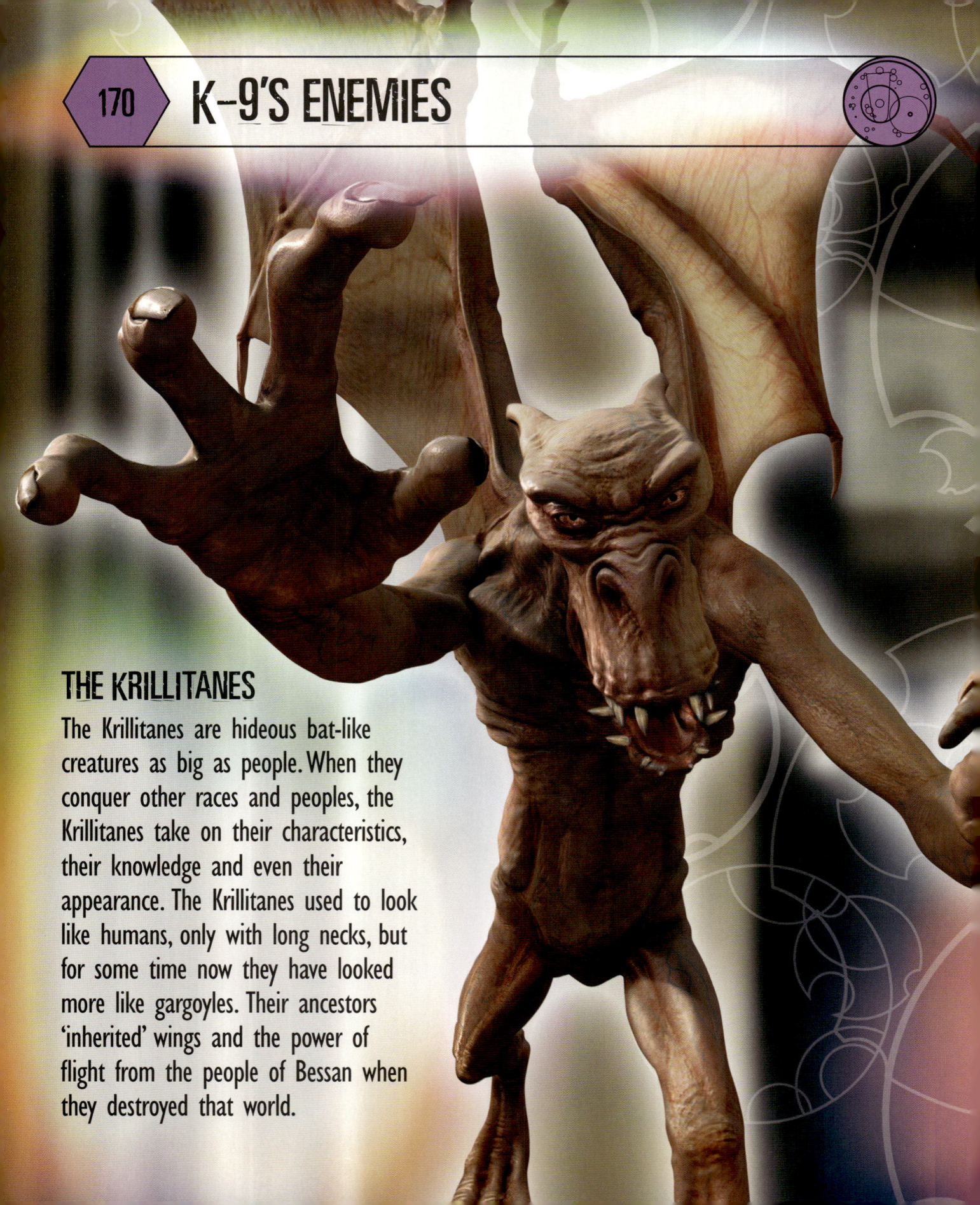

THE KRILLITANES

The Krillitanes are hideous bat-like creatures as big as people. When they conquer other races and peoples, the Krillitanes take on their characteristics, their knowledge and even their appearance. The Krillitanes used to look like humans, only with long necks, but for some time now they have looked more like gargoyles. Their ancestors 'inherited' wings and the power of flight from the people of Bessan when they destroyed that world.

The Krillitanes are able to disguise themselves so they look like ordinary people. But it is just an illusion, a trick. Really the Krillitanes are carnivores that will eat anything from a dead rat to a human child!

The Krillitanes that K-9 and his friends fought against had taken over a school by disguising themselves as teachers and dinner ladies. The headmaster was really the Krillitanes leader. They were making the children really clever by cooking the chips for school dinners in special oil, which made people brainier. They wanted the children to work out a formula to solve the Skasas Paradigm, which would give the Krillitanes power over the whole universe. But K-9's friend the Doctor found out what was happening and they stopped the Krillitanes.

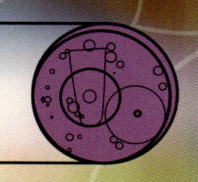

MR FINCH

When the head teacher of the school had to leave suddenly, a new head teacher arrived. He was called Mr Finch. But he was actually the leader of the Krillitanes and his real name was Brother Lassar.

The day after Mr Finch's arrival, half the other teachers mysteriously fell ill with very bad flu. They had to be replaced with new teachers, who were all secretly Krillitanes working for Mr Finch.

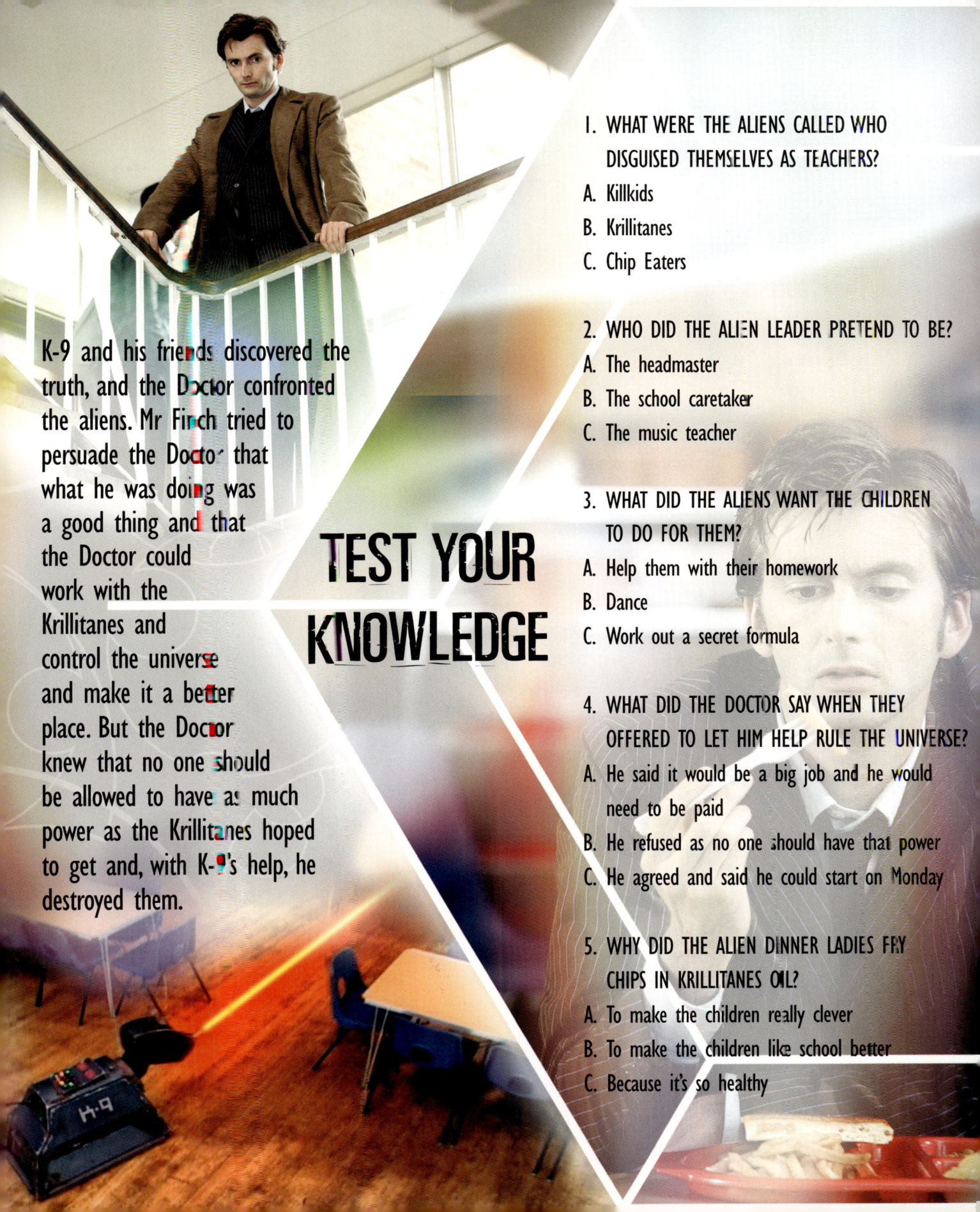

K-9 and his friends discovered the truth, and the Doctor confronted the aliens. Mr Finch tried to persuade the Doctor that what he was doing was a good thing and that the Doctor could work with the Krillitanes and control the universe and make it a better place. But the Doctor knew that no one should be allowed to have as much power as the Krillitanes hoped to get and, with K-9's help, he destroyed them.

TEST YOUR KNOWLEDGE

1. WHAT WERE THE ALIENS CALLED WHO DISGUISED THEMSELVES AS TEACHERS?
   A. Killkids
   B. Krillitanes
   C. Chip Eaters

2. WHO DID THE ALIEN LEADER PRETEND TO BE?
   A. The headmaster
   B. The school caretaker
   C. The music teacher

3. WHAT DID THE ALIENS WANT THE CHILDREN TO DO FOR THEM?
   A. Help them with their homework
   B. Dance
   C. Work out a secret formula

4. WHAT DID THE DOCTOR SAY WHEN THEY OFFERED TO LET HIM HELP RULE THE UNIVERSE?
   A. He said it would be a big job and he would need to be paid
   B. He refused as no one should have that power
   C. He agreed and said he could start on Monday

5. WHY DID THE ALIEN DINNER LADIES FRY CHIPS IN KRILLITANES OIL?
   A. To make the children really clever
   B. To make the children like school better
   C. Because it's so healthy

174 BIOGRAPHY OF K-9

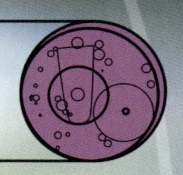

EARLIER K-9S

Actually, K-9 is really K-9 Mark III because there were two other K-9's before him. K-9 Mark I was built by Professor Marius who worked at the Bi-Al Foundation — a huge hospital built into an asteroid in space. When he lived on Earth, Professor Marius used to have a dog, but he was not allowed to take it with him into space. So he built K-9 to be his friend, as well as his computer.

After the Doctor helped Professor Marius defeat a deadly alien virus swarm that wanted to take people over, the Professor gave K-9 to the Doctor, as he was due to go home to Earth soon.

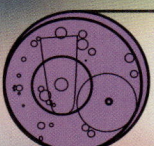

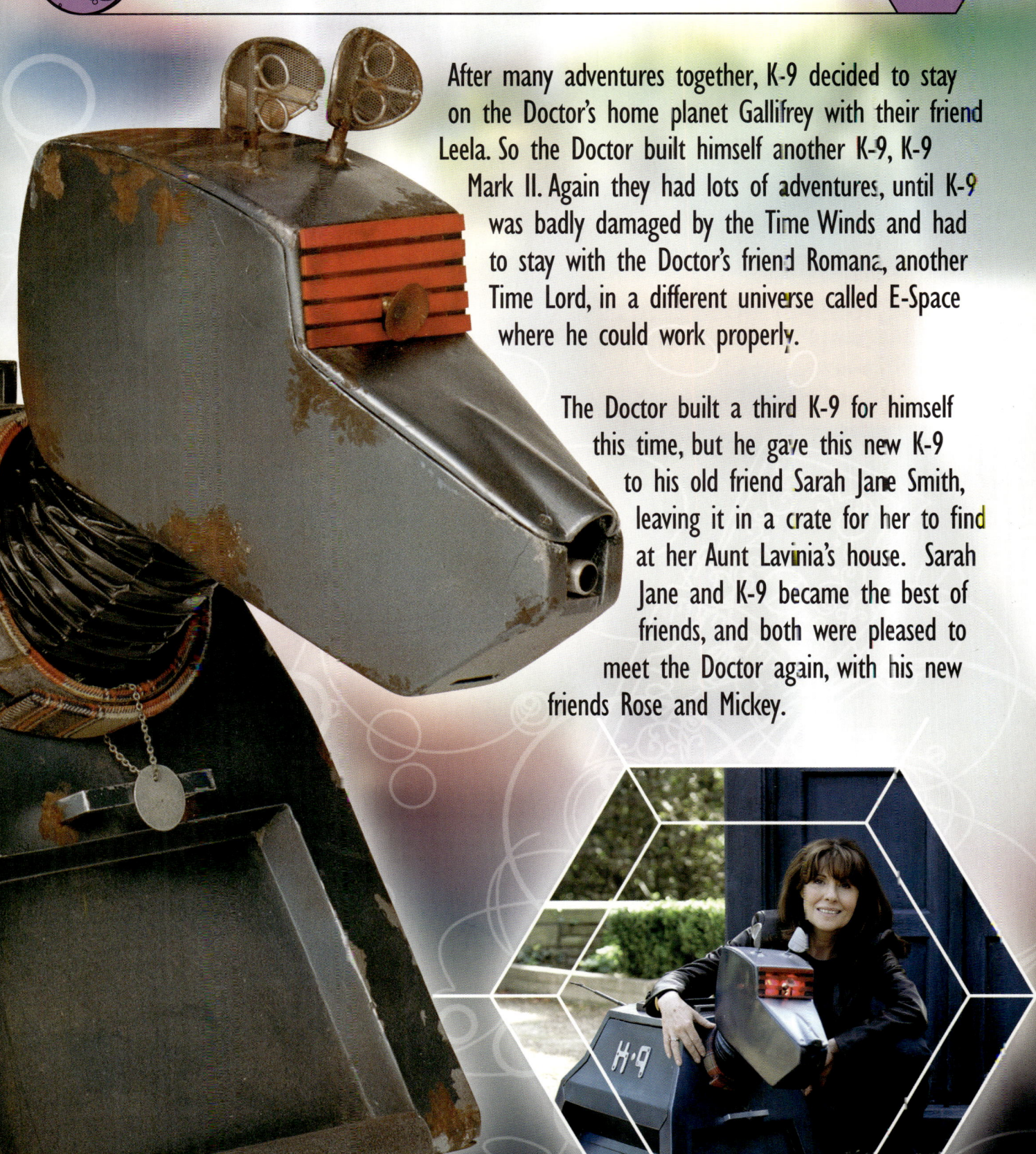

After many adventures together, K-9 decided to stay on the Doctor's home planet Gallifrey with their friend Leela. So the Doctor built himself another K-9, K-9 Mark II. Again they had lots of adventures, until K-9 was badly damaged by the Time Winds and had to stay with the Doctor's friend Romana, another Time Lord, in a different universe called E-Space where he could work properly.

The Doctor built a third K-9 for himself this time, but he gave this new K-9 to his old friend Sarah Jane Smith, leaving it in a crate for her to find at her Aunt Lavinia's house. Sarah Jane and K-9 became the best of friends, and both were pleased to meet the Doctor again, with his new friends Rose and Mickey.

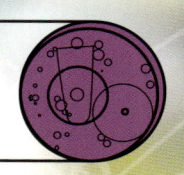

REPAIRING K-9

There have been lots of times when K-9 has broken down and the Doctor has had to repair him. Once he went into the sea and the water upset his electrical circuits and he blew up! Another time he got a robot version of laryngitis and couldn't speak. He's even been crushed by the alien Ogri, a creature made of stone. On many occasions he has run out of power and had to recharge.

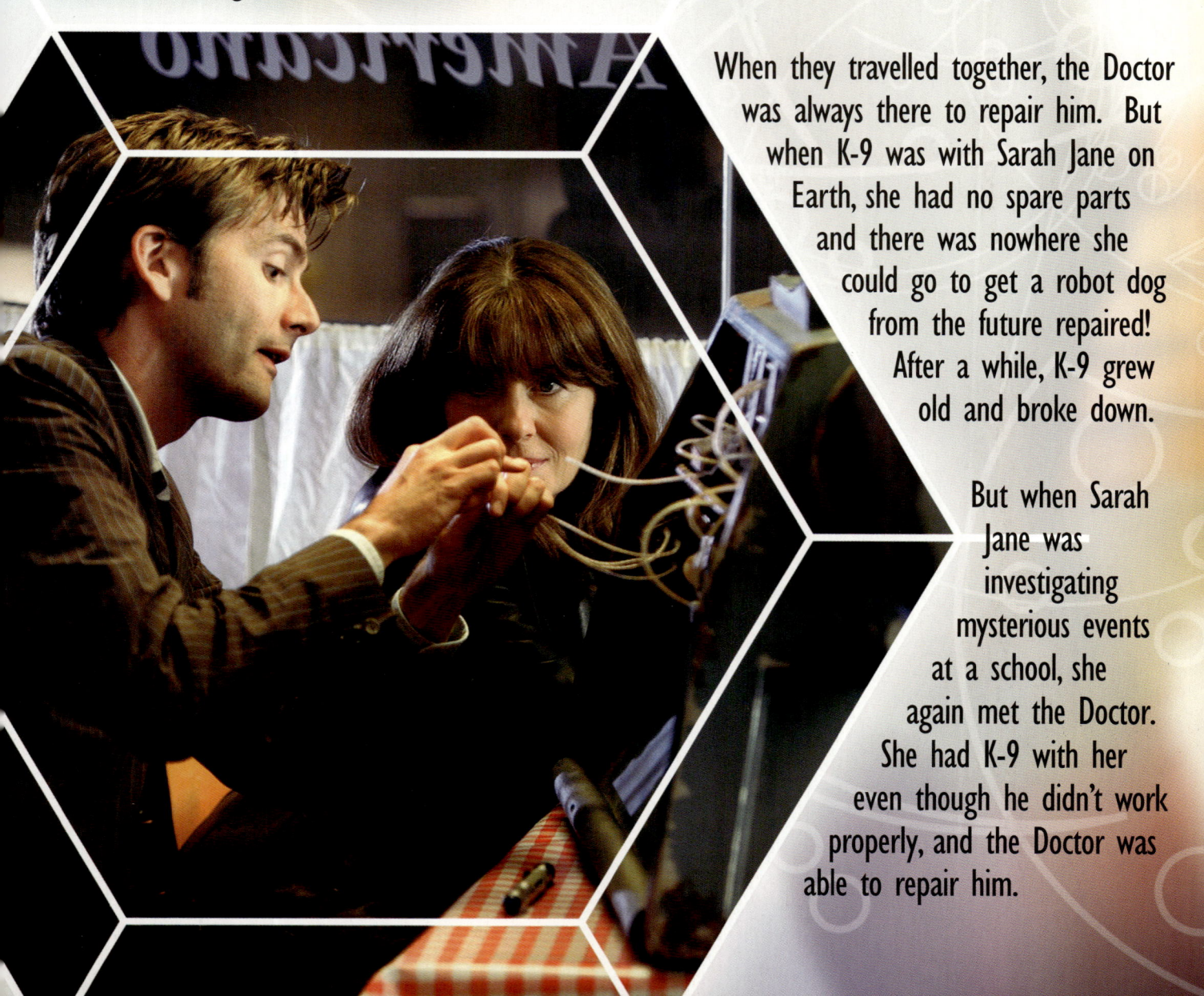

When they travelled together, the Doctor was always there to repair him. But when K-9 was with Sarah Jane on Earth, she had no spare parts and there was nowhere she could go to get a robot dog from the future repaired! After a while, K-9 grew old and broke down.

But when Sarah Jane was investigating mysterious events at a school, she again met the Doctor. She had K-9 with her even though he didn't work properly, and the Doctor was able to repair him.

But to defeat the evil Krillitanes, K-9 had to fire his blaster at explosive Krillitanes oil from close range, and he was caught in the explosion. Sarah Jane was very sad to think K-9 was gone. She was happy and surprised when the Doctor left in the TARDIS and there was K-9 — as good as new. The Doctor had repaired him again and made him even better. K-9 now has omni flexible hyperlink facilities, though Sarah Jane doesn't really know what that means! But she does know that she will have many more adventures with K-9 in the future.

TEST YOUR KNOWLEDGE

1. WHO ORIGINALLY BUILT K-9?
A. The Doctor
B. The Cybermen
C. Professor Marius

2. WHY DID HE BUILD K-9?
A. He used to have a dog but had to leave it on Earth
B. He wanted a present to give the Doctor
C. A deadly alien virus swarm made him do it

3. WHAT HAPPENED TO K-9 MARK I?
A. He blew up on Jupiter
B. He stayed on the Doctor's planet, Gallifrey
C. He retired to an old dogs' home

4. WHAT IS THE NAME OF SARAH JANE'S AUNT?
A. Dodie Smith
B. Lavinia Smith
C. Harriet Jones

5. WHO REPAIRED K-9 FOR SARAH JANE?
A. Mickey
B. Professor Marius
C. The Doctor

178 K-9'S TECHNOLOGY

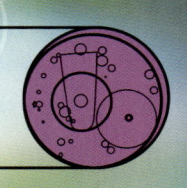

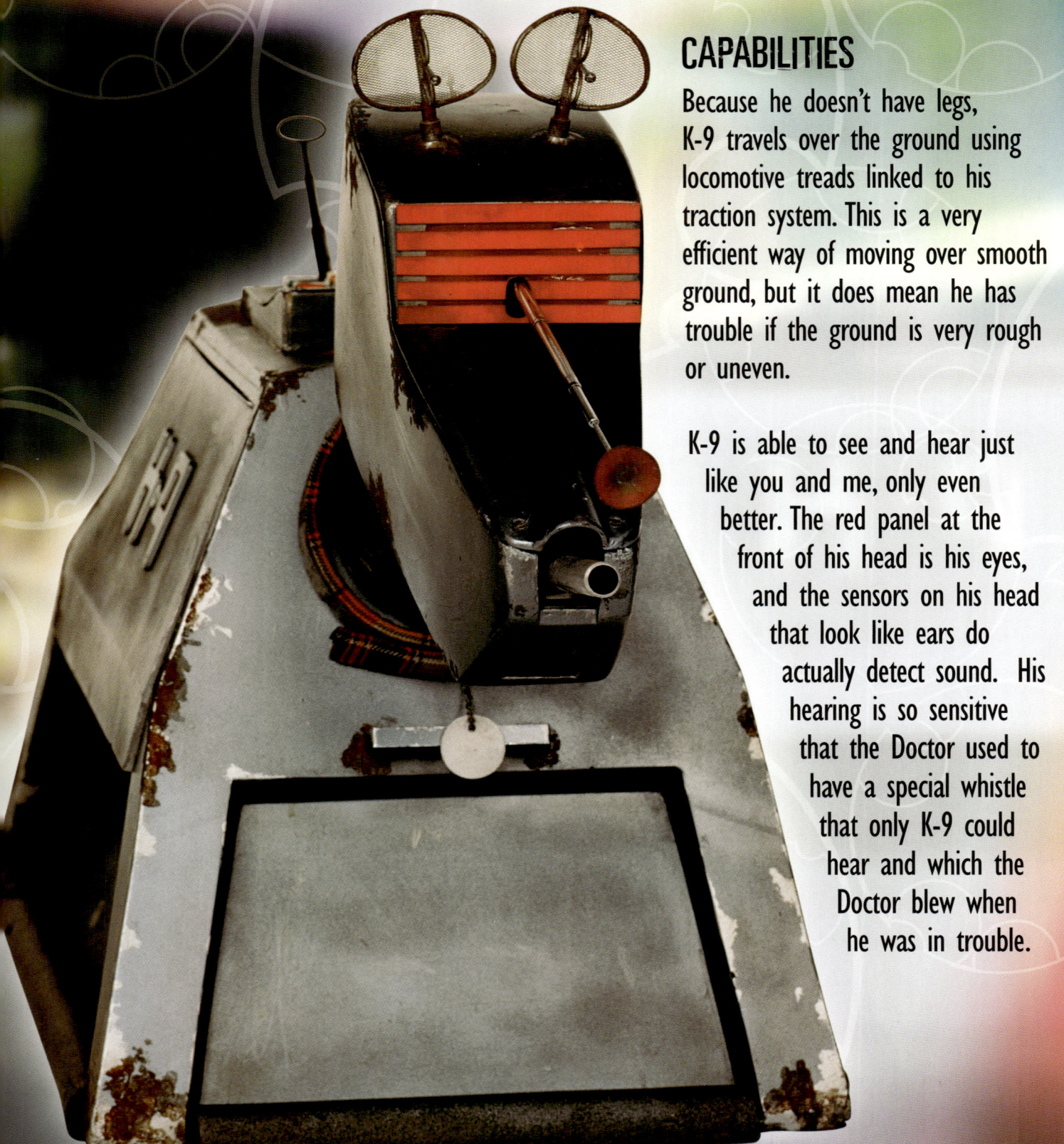

CAPABILITIES

Because he doesn't have legs, K-9 travels over the ground using locomotive treads linked to his traction system. This is a very efficient way of moving over smooth ground, but it does mean he has trouble if the ground is very rough or uneven.

K-9 is able to see and hear just like you and me, only even better. The red panel at the front of his head is his eyes, and the sensors on his head that look like ears do actually detect sound. His hearing is so sensitive that the Doctor used to have a special whistle that only K-9 could hear and which the Doctor blew when he was in trouble.

He can also smell, in a way, as he can detect particles in the air and identify people by their blood, scent, tissue and the alpha-wave patterns of their brains. He can find the Doctor by listening for the distinctive sound of his two hearts beating!

The probe on his head can extend to examine things, or to connect to other computers. Sometimes the circuit controlling this jams, and to reset it someone has to waggle K-9's tail, which is actually a communications aerial.

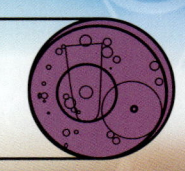

COMPUTER BRAIN

K-9's brain is an incredibly powerful computer that can analyse data and make decisions very fast. He can interface between other computers and robots and talk to them directly in their own machine language, and he can get information from any computer storage. K-9 is so clever he can even beat the Doctor at chess, and his memory wafers hold details of all chess championship tournaments since 1866. K-9's memory is huge — he remembers everything that happens as well as all the historical and scientific data he has been programmed with. Although, because of a misunderstanding with the Doctor's friend Romana, K-9 has no knowledge at all about tennis!

WEAPONRY

K-9 is equipped with a powerful photon beam blaster that is tucked away inside his nose. It extends when he needs to use it either for defence or attack. The blaster has four different intensity levels. K-9 can use it to cut through solid material like doors or walls, or to stun or even kill people. At its highest setting it can melt rock, but using the blaster quickly drains K-9's power.

As well as his blaster, K-9 is protected by a very strong outer casing. People have used hammers and chisels to try to open him up before now, but without success.

TEST YOUR KNOWLEDGE

1. WHAT DOES K-9 USE TO TRAVEL OVER THE GROUND?
   A. Legs
   B. Locomotive treads
   C. Techno-sledge

2. WHAT HAS BEEN ACCIDENTALLY REMOVED FROM K-9'S MEMORY?
   A. All knowledge about tennis
   B. The storage wafer at the back on the left
   C. An articulated sensor

3. HOW CAN THE DOCTOR SIGNAL THAT HE NEEDS K-9?
   A. He shouts: "K-9, I need you!" very loudly
   B. He blows a special whistle
   C. He jumps up and down and waves a mauve flag

4. HOW MANY LEVELS OF INTENSITY DOES K-9'S BLASTER HAVE?
   A. 4
   B. 6
   C. 117

5. WHAT DO YOU NEED TO DO IF K-9'S PROBE CIRCUIT JAMS?
   A. Get him mended by a qualified robotics dealer
   B. Reprogram his data input keypad
   C. Waggle his tail

182 — THE ADVENTURES OF K-9

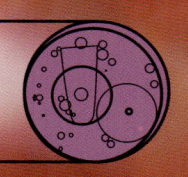

Long before he became Sarah Jane's friend and companion, K-9 travelled with the Doctor in the TARDIS. They had many adventures together, on Earth and on alien planets and even in another universe. The Doctor and K-9 first met when the Doctor was infected by an alien virus, which K-9 and the Doctor's friend Leela helped to defeat. K-9 also helped the Doctor fight tyranny on Pluto in the far future and battle against an evil computer called the Oracle at the very edge of the galaxy. After defeating an invasion of the Doctor's home planet Gallifrey by the warlike Sontarans, K-9 stayed there with Leela.

The Doctor built a new version of K-9 — K-9 Mark II. Together with Time Lady Romana, they found the hidden pieces of the legendary Key to Time. Romana and K-9 shared many more adventures with the Doctor, both in our own universe and an other universe called E-Space. When K-9 was damaged, he had to stay in E-Space with Romana. That was when the Doctor decided to leave a new K-9 Mark III with his friend Sarah Jane Smith on Earth. Sarah and K-9 were at once great friends and they also had many adventures together, although K-9 was getting old and needed repairing.

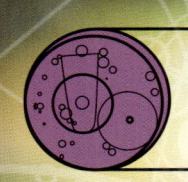

184

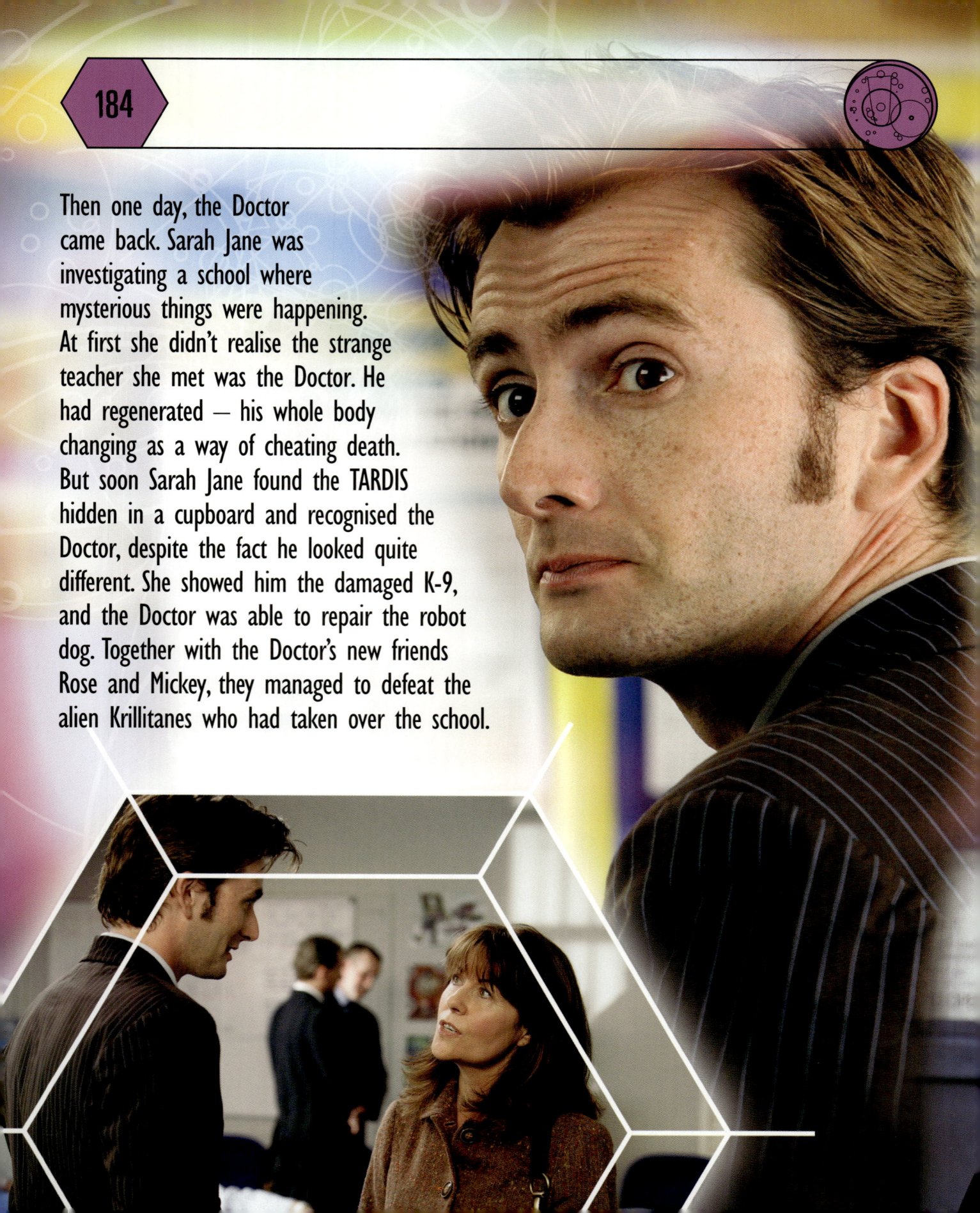

Then one day, the Doctor came back. Sarah Jane was investigating a school where mysterious things were happening. At first she didn't realise the strange teacher she met was the Doctor. He had regenerated — his whole body changing as a way of cheating death. But soon Sarah Jane found the TARDIS hidden in a cupboard and recognised the Doctor, despite the fact he looked quite different. She showed him the damaged K-9, and the Doctor was able to repair the robot dog. Together with the Doctor's new friends Rose and Mickey, they managed to defeat the alien Krillitanes who had taken over the school.

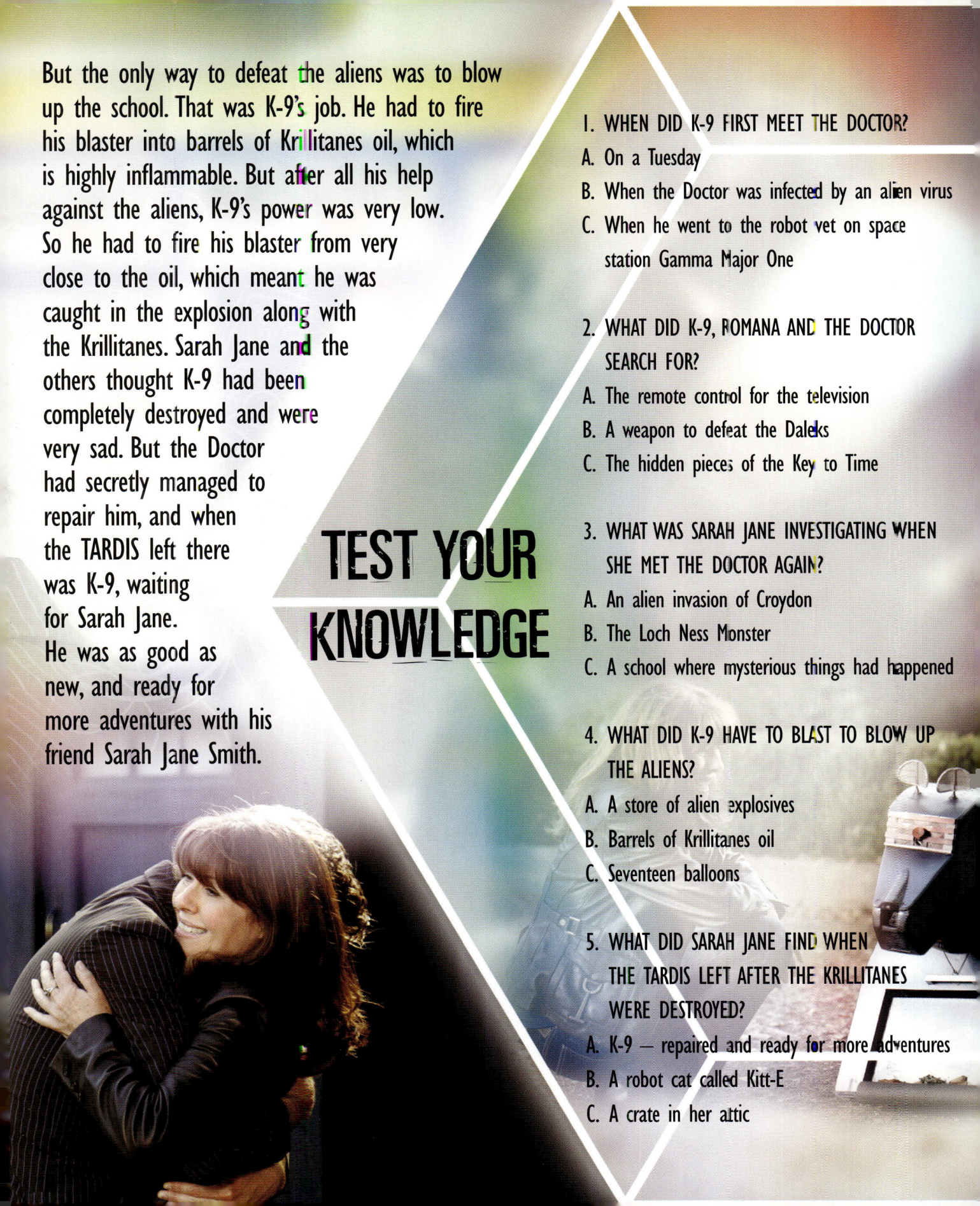

But the only way to defeat the aliens was to blow up the school. That was K-9's job. He had to fire his blaster into barrels of Krillitanes oil, which is highly inflammable. But after all his help against the aliens, K-9's power was very low. So he had to fire his blaster from very close to the oil, which meant he was caught in the explosion along with the Krillitanes. Sarah Jane and the others thought K-9 had been completely destroyed and were very sad. But the Doctor had secretly managed to repair him, and when the TARDIS left there was K-9, waiting for Sarah Jane. He was as good as new, and ready for more adventures with his friend Sarah Jane Smith.

TEST YOUR KNOWLEDGE

1. **WHEN DID K-9 FIRST MEET THE DOCTOR?**
A. On a Tuesday
B. When the Doctor was infected by an alien virus
C. When he went to the robot vet on space station Gamma Major One

2. **WHAT DID K-9, ROMANA AND THE DOCTOR SEARCH FOR?**
A. The remote control for the television
B. A weapon to defeat the Daleks
C. The hidden pieces of the Key to Time

3. **WHAT WAS SARAH JANE INVESTIGATING WHEN SHE MET THE DOCTOR AGAIN?**
A. An alien invasion of Croydon
B. The Loch Ness Monster
C. A school where mysterious things had happened

4. **WHAT DID K-9 HAVE TO BLAST TO BLOW UP THE ALIENS?**
A. A store of alien explosives
B. Barrels of Krillitanes oil
C. Seventeen balloons

5. **WHAT DID SARAH JANE FIND WHEN THE TARDIS LEFT AFTER THE KRILLITANES WERE DESTROYED?**
A. K-9 — repaired and ready for more adventures
B. A robot cat called Kitt-E
C. A crate in her attic

TEST YOUR KNOWLEDGE

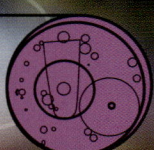

ANSWERS

Meet K-9
1 (c) 2 (c) 3 (b) 4 (a) 5 (b)

K-9's Friends
1 (a) 2 (b) 3 (b) 4 (c) 5 (a)

K-9's Enemies
1 (b) 2 (a) 3 (c) 4 (b) 5 (a)

Biography of K-9
1 (c) 2 (a) 3 (b) 4 (b) 5 (c)

K-9's Technology
1 (b) 2 (a) 3 (b) 4 (a) 5 (c)

The Adventures of K-9
1 (b) 2 (c) 3 (c) 4 (b) 5 (a)

DOCTOR·WHO

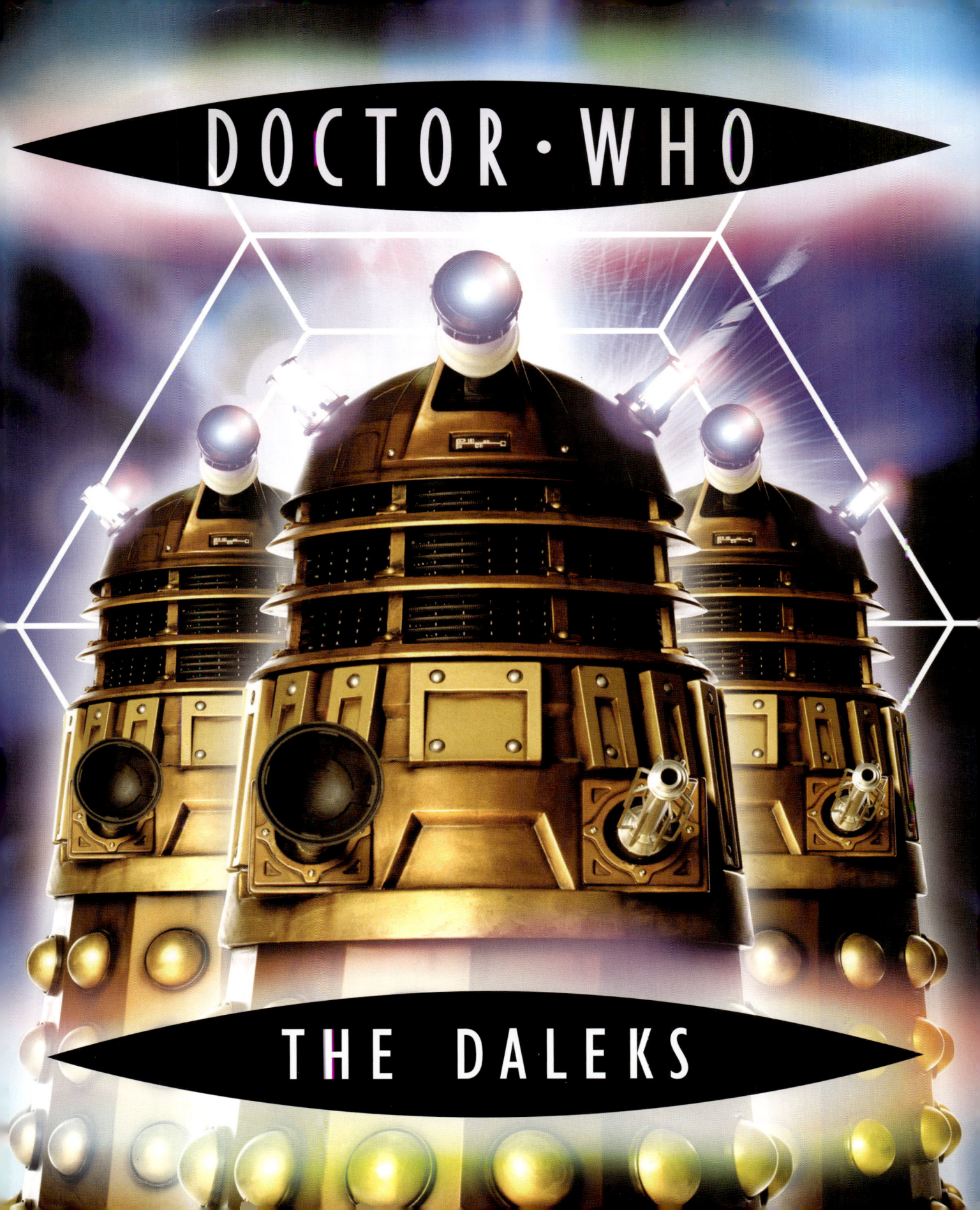

THE DALEKS

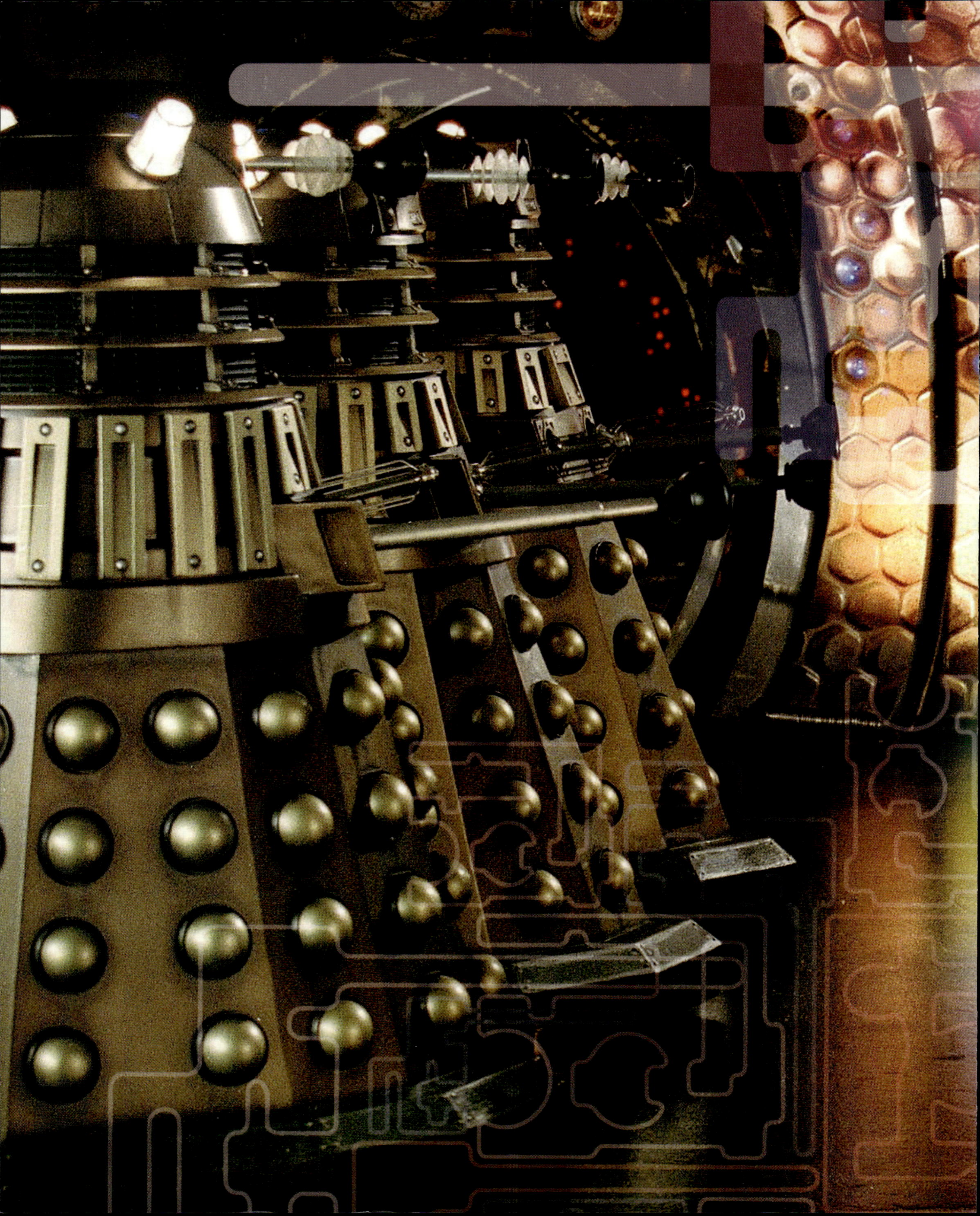

CONTENTS

The Daleks
Meet the Daleks 190
Dalek Data 192
Dalek Anatomy 194
◆ Test your Knowledge

Dalek Allies
The Emperor Dalek 196
The Game Station 197
Torchwood 198
The Cult of Skaro 199
◆ Test your Knowledge

Dalek Enemies
The Doctor 200
Rose Tyler and Captain Jack 201
Henry Van Statten 202
The Cybermen 203
◆ Test your Knowledge

History of the Daleks
The Great Time War 204
Dalek Survival 206
◆ Test your Knowledge

Weapons and Technology
Dalek Space Saucers 208
Tool Attachments 210
The Genesis Ark 211
◆ Test your Knowledge

Dalek Encounters 212
◆ Test your Knowledge

Test your Knowledge Answers 216

190 MEET THE DALEKS

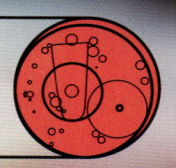

Hated and feared throughout the whole universe, the Daleks are the most ruthless and evil creatures in all creation. They might look like robots, but inside that protective, armoured shell is a living creature.

The Daleks were once like us, but after a thousand year war with their enemies the Thals on their home planet Skaro, they mutated and changed into grotesque, ugly beings that are totally dependent on their machines to stay alive and move. Now they want to exterminate or conquer every other life form. They want their empire to include every planet and every time.

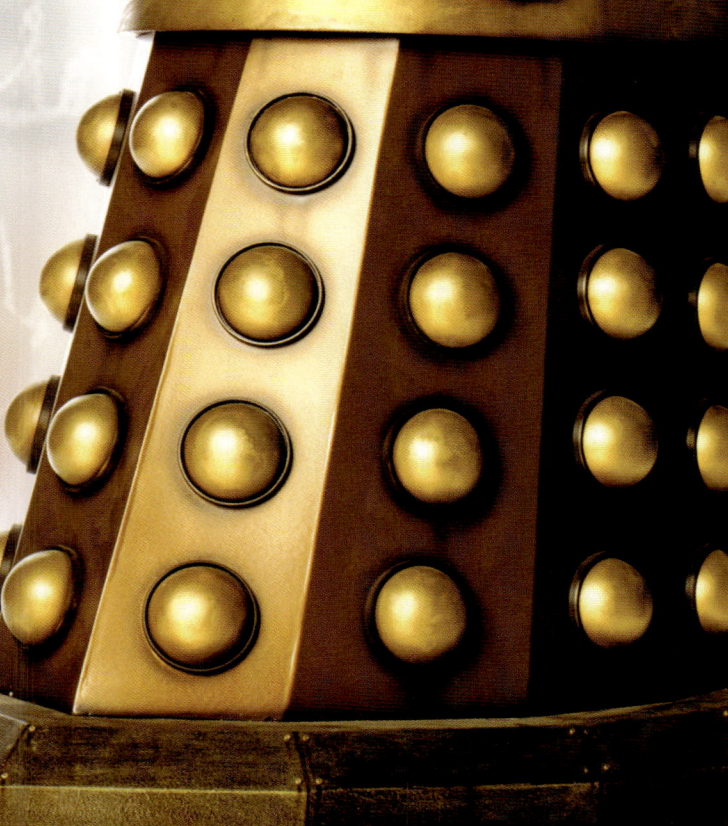

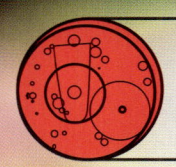

The Dalek casing is an awesome war machine as well as a life-support system. It provides the Dalek creature inside with armoured protection, sensory information like sight and hearing, powerful weaponry, and even the ability to levitate and fly. The Dalek's force field can stop bullets and energy blasts.

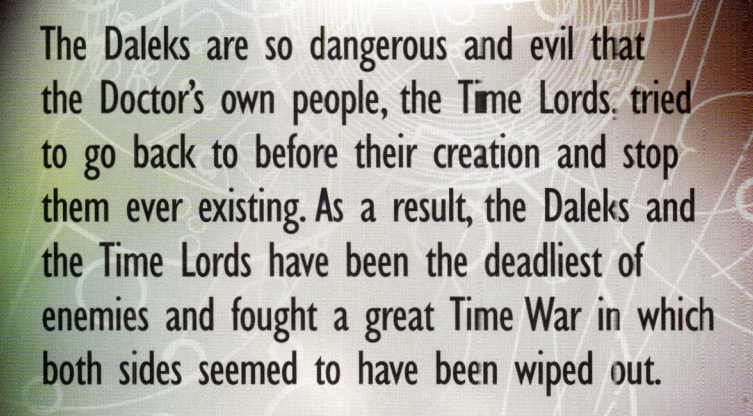

The Daleks are so dangerous and evil that the Doctor's own people, the Time Lords, tried to go back to before their creation and stop them ever existing. As a result, the Daleks and the Time Lords have been the deadliest of enemies and fought a great Time War in which both sides seemed to have been wiped out.

But the Daleks survived, and they are out to exterminate everyone and everything. Especially their greatest enemy, the last of the Time Lords: the Doctor.

192 DALEK DATA

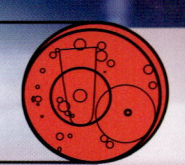

Name: Daleks

Species: Mutated humanoid inside battle casing

Height: 1.68m (5'6")

Home planet: Skaro

Weaponry: Ruby-ray blaster

Protection: Armoured casing and force field

Construction: Dalekanium casing

Power source: Static electricity

Leader: The Emperor Dalek

Battle cry: 'Exterminate!'

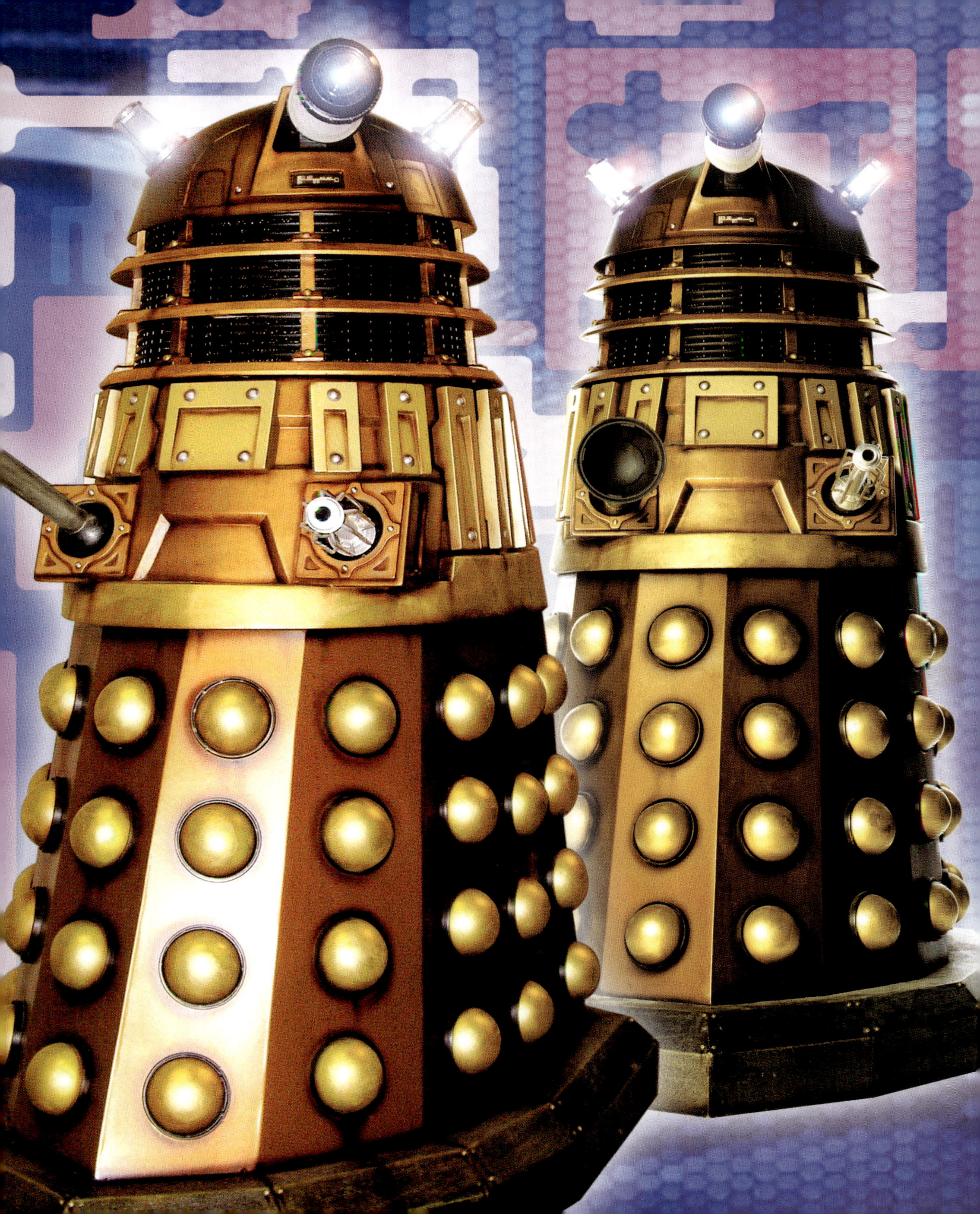

194 DALEK ANATOMY

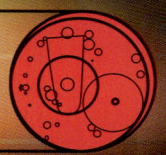

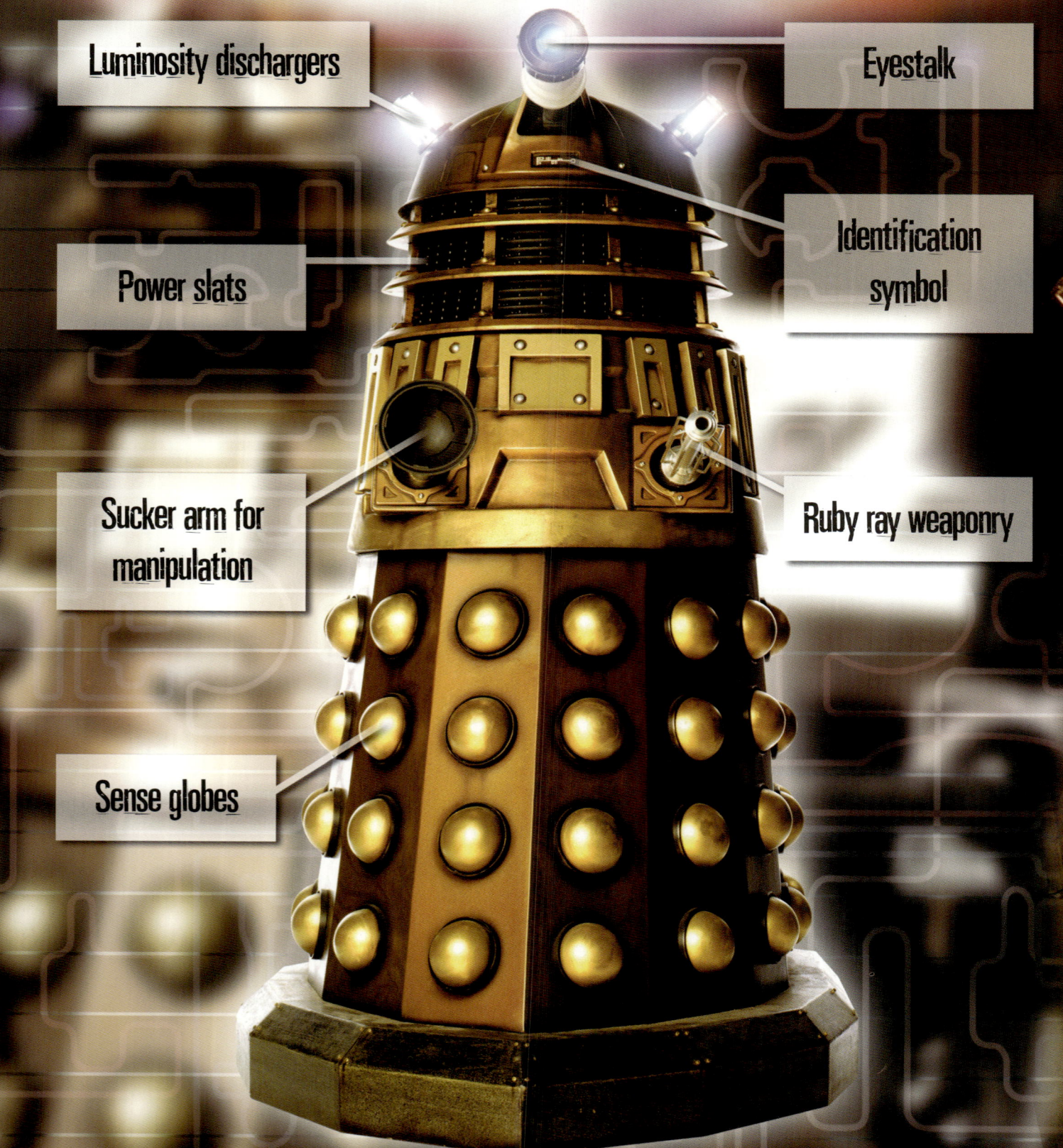

- Luminosity dischargers
- Eyestalk
- Power slats
- Identification symbol
- Sucker arm for manipulation
- Ruby ray weaponry
- Sense globes

TEST YOUR KNOWLEDGE

1. WHAT PLANET ARE THE DALEKS ORIGINALLY FROM?
   A. Raxacoricofallapatorius
   B. Skaro
   C. New Earth

2. WHAT IS THE DALEK BATTLE CRY?
   A. Annihilate!
   B. Conquer!
   C. Exterminate!

3. WHAT IS THE DALEK CASING MADE FROM?
   A. Plastic
   B. Dalekanium
   C. Wood

4. WHAT DO THE DALEKS WANT TO DO?
   A. Conquer all other life forms and rule the universe
   B. Organise cake sales and be nice to everyone
   C. Go into the music industry

5. WHAT DID THE TIME LORDS TRY TO DO?
   A. Make peace with the Daleks
   B. Hide
   C. Stop the Daleks ever being created

196 DALEK ALLIES

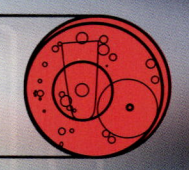

THE EMPEROR DALEK

The Doctor believed that all the Daleks had been destroyed in the Great Time War, and that he was the only survivor. But then he discovered a single Dalek held captive on Earth. Even this did not prepare him for the terrible truth. In the year 200,100 he discovered a whole fleet of Dalek spaceships. Half a million new Daleks were preparing to invade Earth, and they were led by another survivor of the Time War — the Dalek Emperor.

The Emperor had survived, and slowly built up a new army of Daleks by converting humans kidnapped from a space station — the Game Station.

But the Emperor and his army were not the only Dalek survivors...

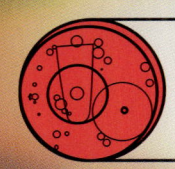

THE GAME STATION

Satellite Five was the main news station for Earth, broadcasting 600 channels of constant news reports. The Daleks worked secretly with the Mighty Jagrafess to manipulate the media so that the satellite broadcasted what they wanted.

A hundred years after the Doctor destroyed the Jagrafess, Satellite Five became the Game Station, and the Daleks were still secretly in control. They used the unpleasant game shows to teleport humans to the Dalek fleet, to be converted into Daleks.

The games were run by the Controller. She has been linked into the computer system since she was a little girl, and every broadcast was channelled through her brain. But she knew the Daleks were evil, and betrayed them. She managed to bring the Doctor to the Game Station, knowing that he would fight and defeat the Daleks.

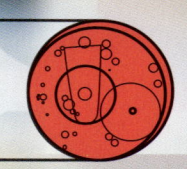

TORCHWOOD

Queen Victoria set up the Torchwood Institute in 1879. She wanted an organisation that would combat alien invaders and use captured alien technology to keep the British Empire in power. Today, Torchwood still exists — its headquarters are in Canary Wharf, in London.

Of course, Torchwood would never knowingly help the Daleks. But with their motto 'If it's alien it's ours' they collect all sorts of alien devices and ships. One thing they collected was a huge sphere, and they tried to discover its secrets. But the sphere was a Dalek Void Ship — a spaceship designed to travel through the empty space between parallel worlds and universes. Without knowing it, Torchwood provided the ship with the power it needed…

THE CULT OF SKARO

Before the Great Time War, the Daleks set up a secret order whose job was to think the unthinkable — to dare to *imagine*. More important even than the Dalek Emperor, the Cult of Skaro was made up of four Daleks who tried to think like the enemy, to get inside enemy minds and predict their strategies, so as to give the Daleks an advantage in their wars. These Daleks even had names. They were called Thay, Sec, Jast and Caan. It was all part of becoming enough like the enemy to predict and counter their actions.

When the Daleks realised that they could not defeat the Time Lords without being totally destroyed themselves, it was the Cult of Skaro that devised a plan for survival. The four Daleks hid in the space between universes in a special Void Ship, waiting for the war to end. They took with them a terrible secret — something they had stolen from the Time Lords themselves, something that would guarantee the survival of the Dalek race: the Genesis Ark.

TEST YOUR KNOWLEDGE

1. WHAT IS THE NAME OF THE LEADER OF THE DALEKS?
   A. The Emperor Dalek
   B. The Mighty Jagrafess
   C. Gerald

2. WHAT DID THE DALEKS CONVERT INTO NEW DALEKS?
   A. Antimatter
   B. The Mighty Jagrafess
   C. Kidnapped human beings

3. WHAT WAS THE NAME OF THE WAR IN WHICH THE DALEKS WERE ALMOST WIPED OUT?
   A. Space War One
   B. The Great Time War
   C. The War of the Daleks

4. WHO SET UP THE TORCHWOOD INSTITUTE?
   A. The Daleks
   B. Queen Victoria
   C. Abraham Lincoln

5. WHAT MADE THE DALEKS OF THE CULT OF SKARO DIFFERENT?
   A. They had names
   B. They were all pink in colour
   C. They liked to play trains

200 DALEK ENEMIES

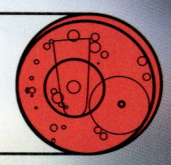

THE DOCTOR

The Doctor is the last of the Time Lords — the race that the Daleks fought in the Great Time War. He is their greatest enemy and has defeated them in many times and places.

The Doctor can change his appearance. When his body is worn out or damaged he can change into a new one. Travelling through space and time in his TARDIS and with the help of various companions, the Doctor fights against evil and injustice. That makes the Daleks his number one enemy. When he was forced to change after defeating the Daleks on the Game Station, he must have known it would not be long before he had to fight them again…

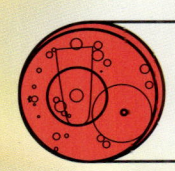

ROSE TYLER AND CAPTAIN JACK

Rose is the Doctor's best friend. She is a 19 year old girl that the Doctor met on Earth in our time when she was working in a shop. Then she went travelling with the Doctor in the TARDIS through time and space. When the Daleks attacked the Game Station and Earth in 200,100 it was Rose who defeated them. She looked into the heart of the TARDIS and used the power that was inside to wipe out the Dalek fleet.

Rose's friend, Captain Jack, a former time agent from the future, also helped defeat the Daleks. With the power from the TARDIS, Rose was able to bring him back to life after the Daleks exterminated him!

HENRY VAN STATTEN

A ruthless multi-millionaire, Henry Van Statten collected anything alien he could find. And his most treasured item was an alien he called a 'Metaltron', which was discovered in a crater in the USA after it fell to Earth.

He didn't know that his 'Metaltron' was really a Dalek and had been torturing it to try to make it talk. Van Statten kept the Dalek chained up in a cell deep underground. But the Dalek was just waiting for a chance to escape and exterminate everyone. It got that chance after the Doctor and Rose arrived…

THE CYBERMEN

The Daleks have known of the Cybermen for many years. But it was only on present day Earth, when the cult of Skaro emerged from their Void Ship that the two races met for the first time.

These Cybermen were from a parallel Earth – human beings like us but whose bodies had been replaced with metal and plastic. Their brains had been changed to remove all emotions and feelings. So they have no love or hate or fear… They followed the Dalek Void Ship through to our Earth, and invaded.

But the Daleks were not impressed. They knew that even one Dalek could wipe out the armies of Cybermen on Earth.

TEST YOUR KNOWLEDGE

1. WHAT CAN THE DOCTOR DO WHEN HIS BODY WEARS OUT OR IS DAMAGED?
A. He can go to Time Lord hospital
B. He can change his body into a new one
C. He can pass on his knowledge to a friend or relative

2. HOW DID ROSE TYLER DEFEAT THE DALEKS IN 200,100?
A. She used the power at the heart of the Doctor's TARDIS
B. She told them to go away
C. She invented an anti-Dalek neutraliser ray

3. WHAT DID HENRY VAN STATTEN COLLECT?
A. Stamps
B. Alien artefacts
C. Coins from the Roman Empire

4. WHAT DID HENRY VAN STATTEN CALL HIS CAPTIVE DALEK?
A. Galactus
B. Malcolm
C. Metaltron

5. HOW MANY DALEKS ARE NEEDED TO ATTACK AN ARMY OF CYBERMEN?
A. Only a dozen
B. A mere hundred
C. Just one

204 HISTORY OF THE DALEKS

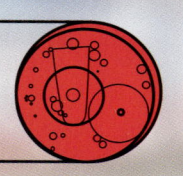

THE GREAT TIME WAR

Long ago, the Time Lords of the planet Gallifrey tried to prevent the Daleks from ever existing by sending the Doctor back in time to stop them being created. Although the Doctor failed, he knew that many future races would become allies, not enemies, because of their shared fear of their common enemy; the Daleks.

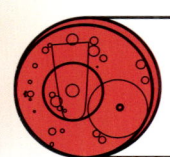

But as their empire and their strength grew, and the Daleks realised what the Time Lords had tried to do, they began to retaliate. Negotiations broke down, and a full-scale war erupted within the Time Vortex and beyond that in the Ultimate Void. The Time Lords reached back into history for ever more terrible weapons, while the Daleks unleashed the Deathsmiths of Goth.

For centuries the war raged, unseen by most of the Universe. But the Higher Species, it is said, watched and wept.

When the war was over, a single survivor walked alone through the carnage of Gallifrey and Skaro — the Time Lord who had brought the War to its terrible end: The Doctor. Although he did not know it at the time, the Daleks had also survived…

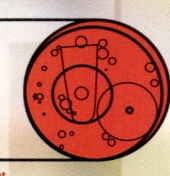

DALEK SURVIVAL

After the Tenth Dalek Occupation, the Daleks disappeared. They were fighting the Time Lords in the Great Time War. The Time Lords were destroyed, but they took the Daleks with them — or so they thought.

In fact, the Dalek Emperor survived. Using kidnapped humans to create new Dalek creatures, he slowly built up an enormous Dalek army. All the time, the Daleks were hiding in our solar system, and manipulating events through their agents on Satellite Five and later the Game Station.

After Rose Tyler destroyed the Dalek Emperor and his fleet, it seemed that once again the Daleks were gone. But other Daleks had survived. The so-called Cult of Skaro, a group of four very special Daleks, had hidden away in the void between universes. When they were ready, their Void Ship appeared on Earth in the 21st century and the Daleks emerged.

They brought with them the Genesis Ark — a large casket that contained the future of the Dalek race and the means of its survival. Battling against the Doctor and his friends and millions of Cybermen, the Daleks were still able to open the Genesis Ark.

The Doctor and Rose were eventually able to defeat the Daleks. But they knew that if just one Dalek survived, then the universe would never be safe from their evil...

TEST YOUR KNOWLEDGE

1. WHAT DID THE TIME LORDS TRY TO DO TO THE DALEKS?
A. Destroy their Emperor
B. Prevent them from ever existing
C. Lock them up on a prison space station

2. WHO WAS THE AGENT THE TIME LORDS SENT TO CHANGE HISTORY?
A. The Doctor
B. Rose Tyler
C. Captain Jack

3. WHAT DID THE DALEKS DO ONCE THEY WERE POWERFUL ENOUGH?
A. They negotiated for peace
B. They retaliated
C. They forgot all about it

4. WHEN DID THE DALEKS DISAPPEAR FROM THE UNIVERSE?
A. At 7 o'clock on a Saturday evening
B. When the Time Lords landed on Skaro
C. After the Tenth Dalek Occupation

5. WHERE DID THE CULT OF SKARO HIDE TO ESCAPE BEING DESTROYED IN THE TIME WAR?
A. In the dark space at the edge of our solar system
B. In the void between universes
C. Behind the sofa

208 WEAPONS AND TECHNOLOGY

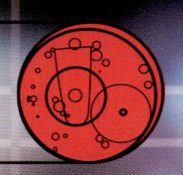

DALEK SPACE SAUCERS

The Dalek fleet that attacked the Game Station was made up of 200 ships. Shaped like upturned saucers, each ship can carry an army of 2,000 Daleks ready to disembark and form an attack force at any time. The Dalek saucers are powered by vast, incredibly powerful anti-gravity engines that spin them through space at great speed, and they can hide from detection using a transmitted signal that masks their presence.

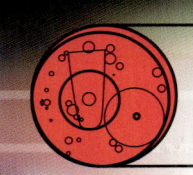

The interior of the Dalek saucers is divided into many separate floors, with a central shaft running down the middle. Daleks use their levitation abilities to move between floors. The vast and impressive Dalek Emperor is housed in the central area of their flagship. It also has compartments where kidnapped humans can be kept until they are needed.

Like Daleks, the ships are protected by force fields, and are armed with impressive weaponry, including target-seeking missiles, which home in on their prey using a thronic aura beam, and explode with more power than an erupting volcano.

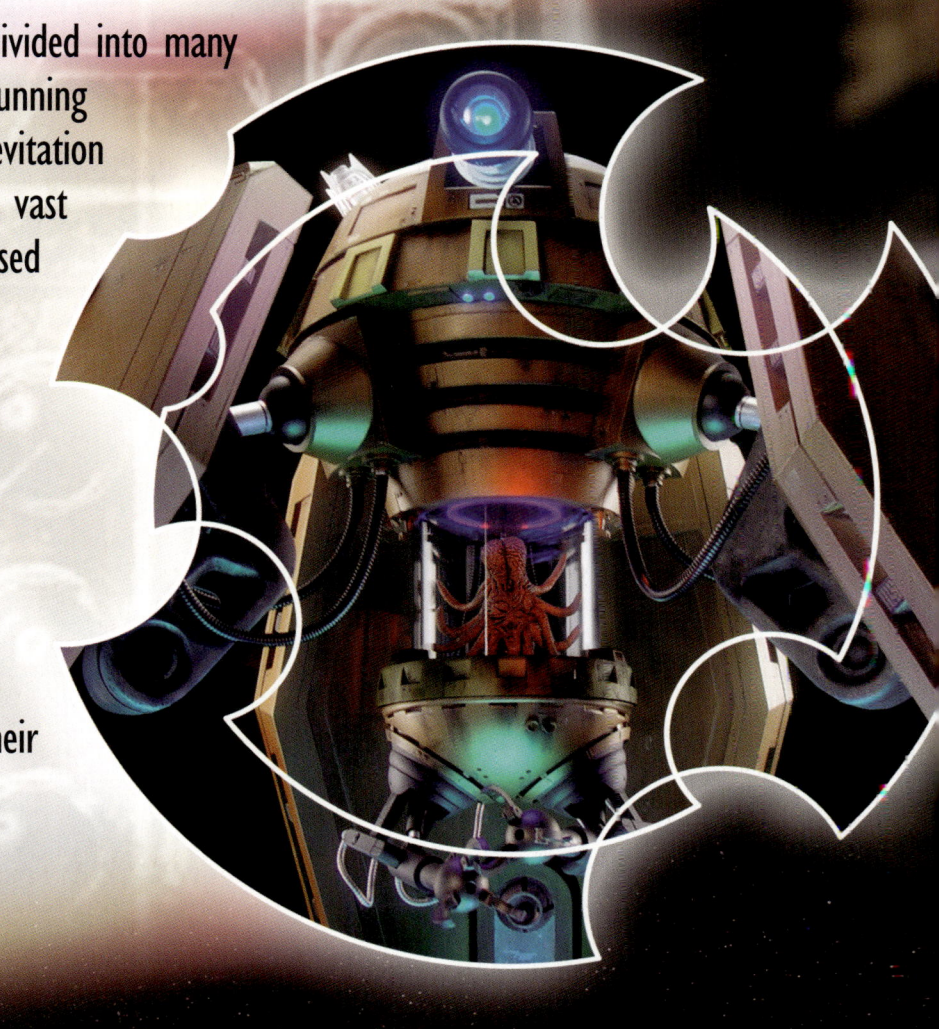

210

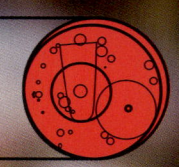

TOOL ATTACHMENTS

As well as a standard ruby ray blaster gun, most Daleks have a sucker arm, which they use in the same way as we use our hands. The sucker is flexible enough to pick up even small, delicate objects. There is a direct link from the sucker to the Dalek control systems, so it can use this attachment to decode a numeric keypad and open a locked door, or to absorb information from people's brains.

These suckers can also be replaced with other attachments, such as special cutting tools to slice through metal doors. The Emperor's personal guard Daleks have a second, even more powerful blaster gun. These Daleks are also distinguished from other Daleks by their black domes.

THE GENESIS ARK

Daleks take no prisoners unless they need them as slaves or for experimentation or interrogation. But during the Great Time War the Time Lords took many Daleks prisoner. Faced with the problem of what to do with these prisoners of war, the Time Lords locked them all in a huge prison, the Genesis Ark. The Time Lords know how to fit enormous spaces into tiny containers, just like the Doctor's TARDIS, which is so much bigger inside than on the outside. In the same way, the huge prison complex was all contained inside a large casket.

But the Daleks captured the prison casket, and they hid it in the void between universes. It was their future, their survival — a vast army of Daleks waiting to emerge once the war was over.

TEST YOUR KNOWLEDGE

1. HOW MANY DALEKS CAN A DALEK SAUCER CARRY?
A. 20
B. 200
C. 2,000

2. WHICH DALEK SAUCER CARRIES THE EMPEROR DALEK?
A. The Dalek Flagship
B. The Primary Saucer
C. The one at the back on the left

3. WHAT DO THE EMPEROR'S GUARDS HAVE INSTEAD OF A SUCKER ARM?
A. A second, even more powerful eye
B. A second, even more powerful weapon
C. A cutting tool

4. WHO CREATED THE GENESIS ARK?
A. The Time Lords
B. The Daleks
C. The Mighty Jagrafess

5. WHAT WAS THE GENESIS ARK ORIGINALLY BUILT FOR?
A. To hold two of every species of life on Earth
B. It was a prison
C. To travel through the voids between universes

212 DALEK ENCOUNTERS

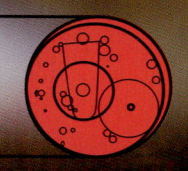

Apart from the Emperor's spaceship, and the Cult of Skaro, all the Daleks were destroyed in the Great Time War. Or so it seemed. In fact, one Dalek escaped — damaged and dying, it crashed through time and space to Earth. No one knew what it was, and eventually it was bought by Henry Van Statten, an incredibly rich collector. He kept it chained down in a cell and tried to learn its secrets. But when the Doctor and Rose arrived, the Dalek used energy from Rose to escape — energy she gained from her time travelling. It exterminated Van Statten's guards and repaired itself. But along with the energy it took from Rose it got something else. It got some of Rose's own personality and feelings. It began to question whether it should be killing all the time and who it really was…

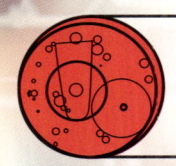

When the Doctor, Rose and Captain Jack were taken from the TARDIS and brought to the Game Station they didn't know the Daleks were waiting nearby, ready to invade. On the Game Station, the Doctor and his friends managed to escape being killed in deadly television shows. But Rose was transported through space to a Dalek ship. When the Doctor and Jack went to rescue her, they discovered that the Dalek Emperor had survived the Time War and created a new Dalek army ready to destroy Earth. There was a tremendous battle and the Doctor sent Rose home to her own time to keep her safe. But she managed to get back to him, and brought with her the terrible power of the Time Vortex, which she used to destroy the Daleks.

214

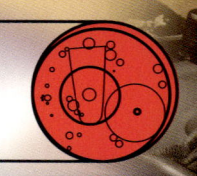

The Doctor and Rose thought that Earth was being invaded by the Cybermen coming through from a parallel world. Millions of Cybermen appeared on Earth — first as ghosts, then they became solid and real. They started to take over and convert people into more Cybermen. They were able to come through from the other world by following in the wake of a strange sphere, which everyone thought must be a Cyberman ship. But they were wrong — it was the Daleks!

The Cult of Skaro had survived the Great Time War by hiding in the void between universes, and now they were back. They brought with them the Genesis Ark, which they had stolen from the Time Lords. It looked just like a large casket, but like the TARDIS it was much bigger inside — and was hiding a whole army of Daleks.

The Daleks and the Cybermen had a tremendous battle, but the millions of Cybermen were no match for even the four Daleks in the sphere. The Daleks opened the Genesis Ark and hundreds more Daleks arrived, hovering over London.

With the help of Rose, the Doctor was able to open a gateway back into the Void and the Daleks and the Cybermen were dragged back in — away from Earth. The Doctor thought that was the end of the Daleks. But he was wrong! The Cult of Skaro had escaped to 1930s New York by performing an Emergency Temporal Shift. They were the last four Daleks in existence and they needed to evolve.

TEST YOUR KNOWLEDGE

1. WHAT WAS THE NAME OF THE COLLECTOR WHO KEPT A DALEK CHAINED IN A CELL?
A. Van de Graaf
B. Henry Van Statten
C. Harold Van Driver

2. WHO DID THE DALEK GET ENERGY FROM TO ESCAPE?
A. Captain Jack
B. The Doctor
C. Rose

3. WHAT WAS THE NAME OF THE SPACE STATION THE DOCTOR WAS TAKEN TO BEFORE HE DISCOVERED THE EMPEROR DALEK HAD SURVIVED?
A. The Game Station
B. Platform One
C. SkyLab Seven

4. WHAT DID PEOPLE THINK WAS INSIDE THE SPHERE THAT CAME FROM THE VOID BETWEEN UNIVERSES?
A. A parallel world
B. The Moxx of Balhoon
C. Cybermen

5. WHAT WAS REALLY INSIDE THE SPHERE?
A. Cybermen
B. Nothing at all
C. Daleks

TEST YOUR KNOWLEDGE

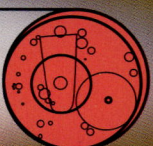

ANSWERS

Meet the Daleks
1 (b) 2 (c) 3 (b) 4 (a) 5 (c)

Dalek Allies
1 (a) 2 (c) 3 (b) 4 (b) 5 (a)

Dalek Enemies
1 (b) 2 (a) 3 (b) 4 (c) 5 (c)

History of the Daleks
1 (b) 2 (a) 3 (b) 4 (c) 5 (b)

Weapons and Technology
1 (c) 2 (a) 3 (b) 4 (a) 5 (b)

Dalek Adventures
1 (b) 2 (c) 3 (a) 4 (c) 5 (c)

DOCTOR·WHO

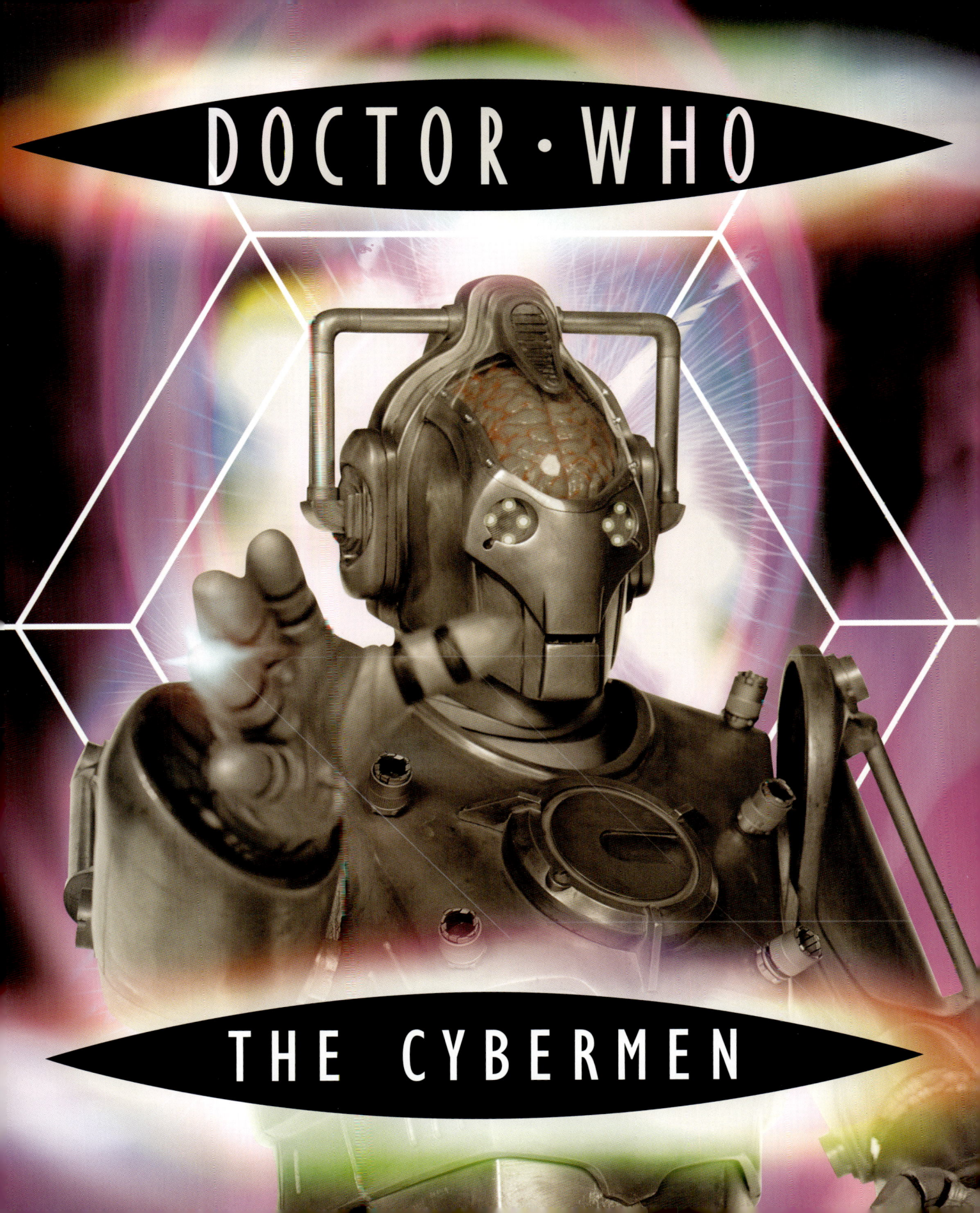

THE CYBERMEN

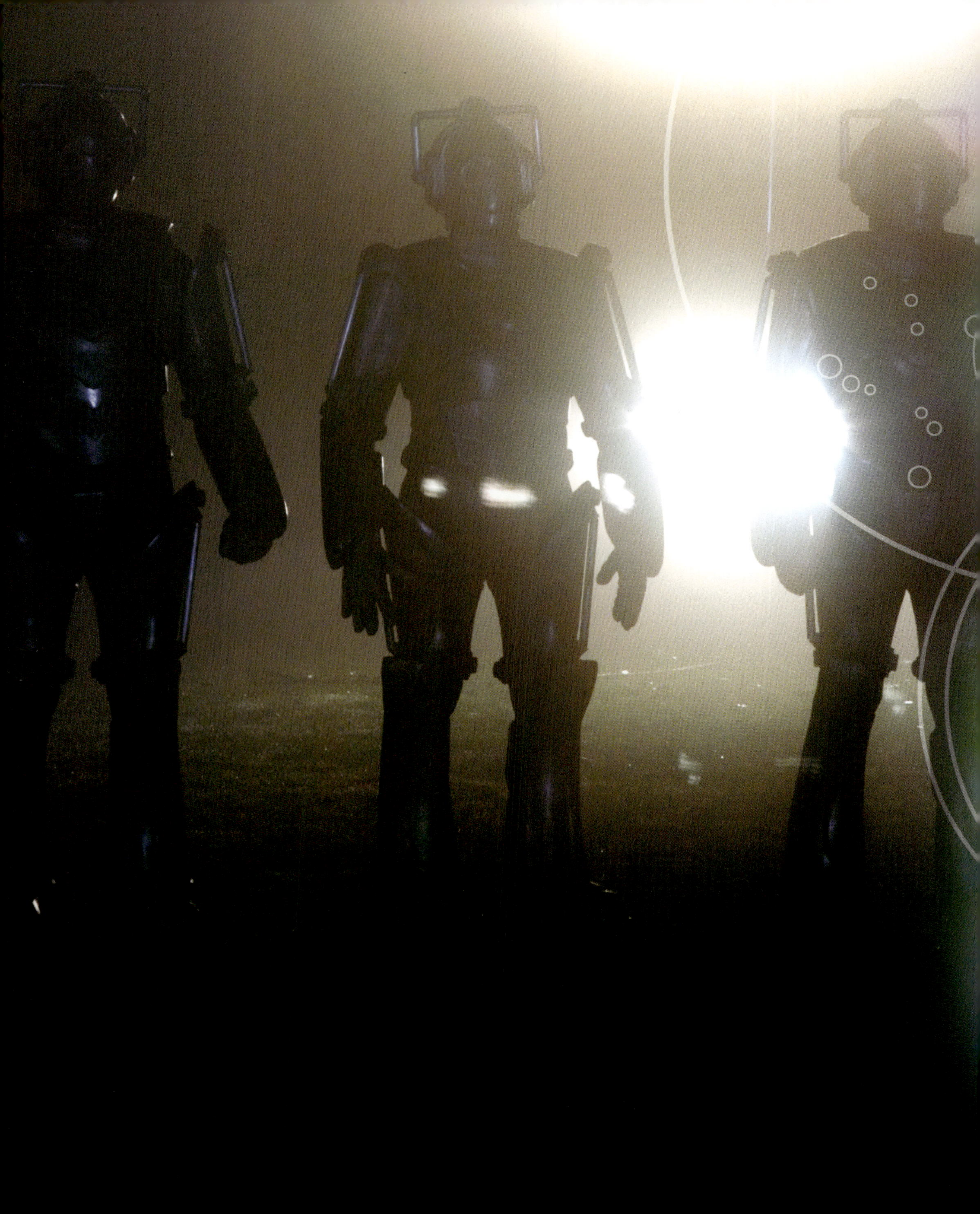

CONTENTS

The Cybermen
Meet the Cybermen..................220
Cyber Data..................222
Cyber Anatomy..................224
⬢ Test your Knowledge

Cyber Allies
John Lumic..................226
The Cyber Controller..................227
Controlled Humans..................228
The Army of Ghosts..................229
⬢ Test your Knowledge

Cyber Enemies
The Doctor..................230
The Preachers..................231
Pete Tyler..................232
The Daleks..................233
⬢ Test your Knowledge

Cyber Origins
The 'Other' Earth..................234
The Arrival of the Cybermen..................236
⬢ Test your Knowledge

Weapons and Technology
Cybus Industries..................238
Built-in Accessories..................240
⬢ Test your Knowledge

Cyber Encounters..................242
⬢ Test your Knowledge

Test your Knowledge Answers..................246

Going off the Rails..................31

MEET THE CYBERMEN

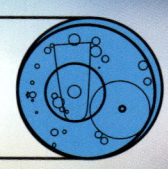

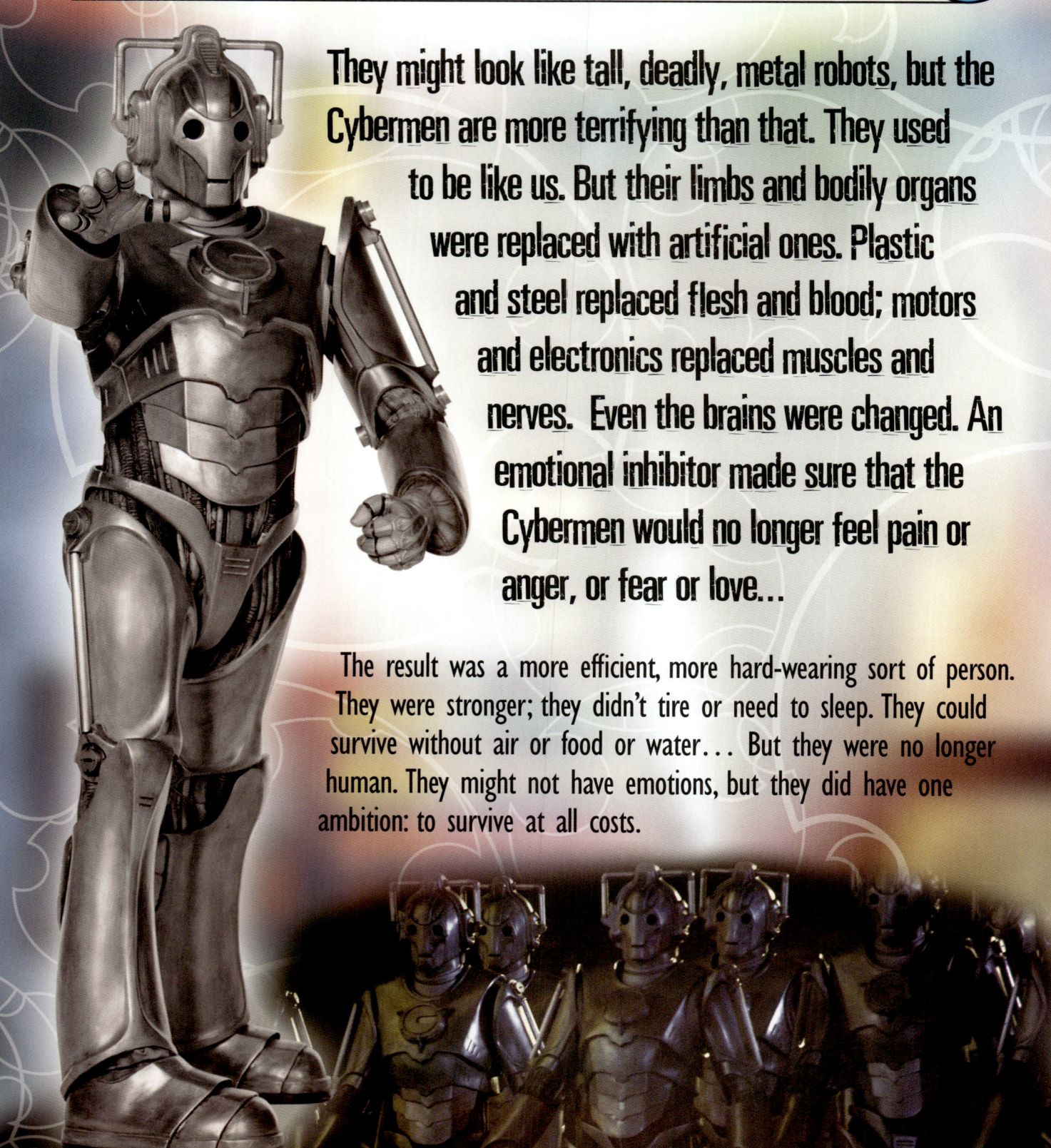

They might look like tall, deadly, metal robots, but the Cybermen are more terrifying than that. They used to be like us. But their limbs and bodily organs were replaced with artificial ones. Plastic and steel replaced flesh and blood; motors and electronics replaced muscles and nerves. Even the brains were changed. An emotional inhibitor made sure that the Cybermen would no longer feel pain or anger, or fear or love…

The result was a more efficient, more hard-wearing sort of person. They were stronger; they didn't tire or need to sleep. They could survive without air or food or water… But they were no longer human. They might not have emotions, but they did have one ambition: to survive at all costs.

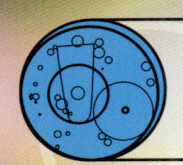

And so they converted more and more people into Cybermen, into bloodless, fleshless, soulless robots that used to be people. And deep inside, hidden away as if they are ashamed of it, there is still some flesh, some bone, some brain, some bits of humanity preserved amongst the plastic and metal. And perhaps, deep inside, there is also a memory of who they once were, and just possibly regret…

222 CYBER DATA

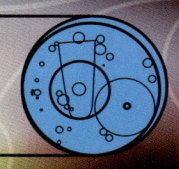

Name: Cybermen
Species: Adapted Human
Height: Over 2m (over 6'7")
Home planet: A parallel Earth
Weaponry: Inbuilt energy blaster
Protection: Metal armour
Invented by: John Lumic
Manufactured by: Cybus Industries
Construction: Plastic and steel
Leader: The Cyber Controller

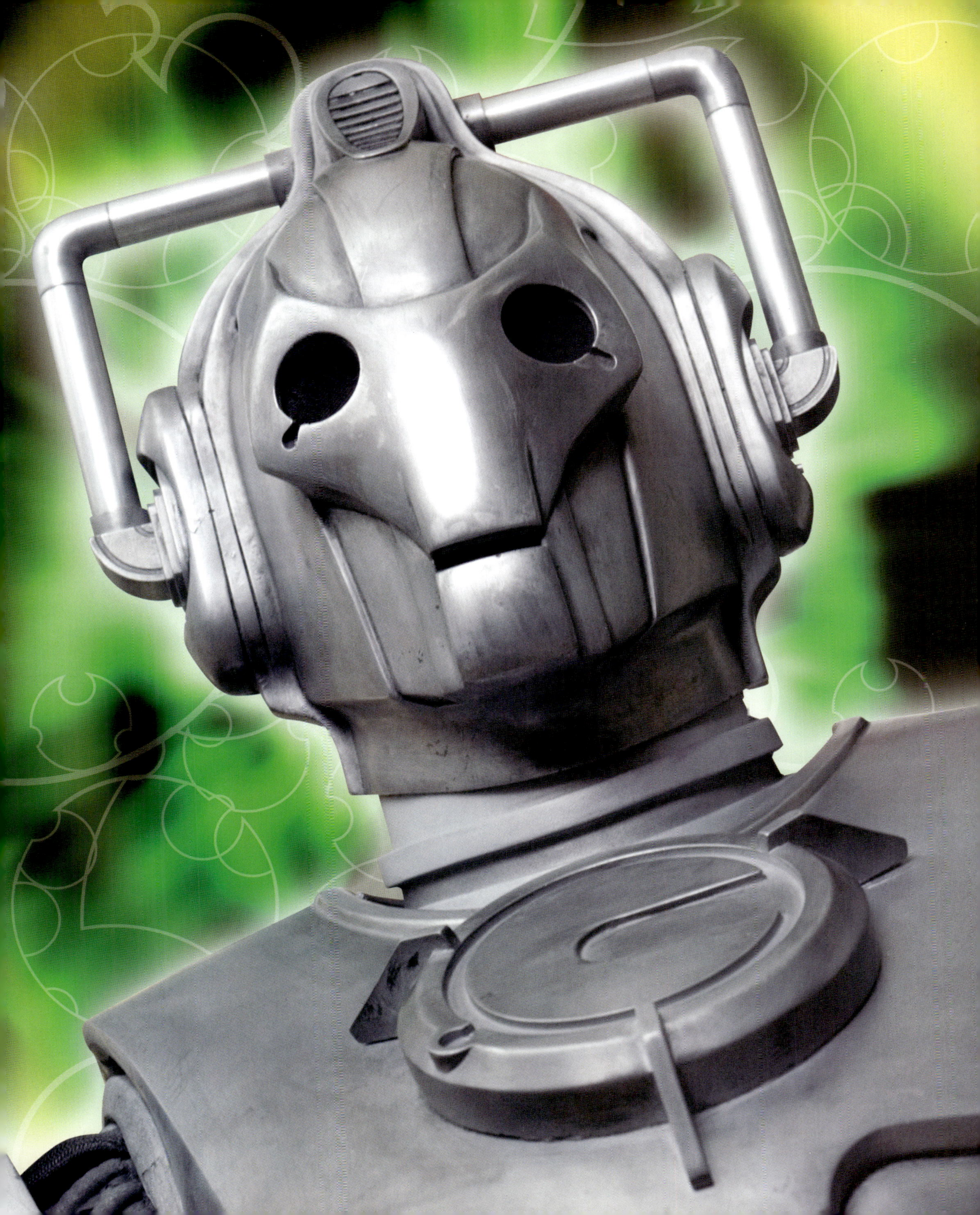

224 CYBER ANATOMY

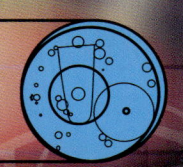

Over 2m tall

Powerful vision circuits

Electronically-generated voice

Chest unit replaces heart, lungs and other organs

Weaponry and other accessories are inbuilt

Plastic and steel replace flesh and bone

TEST YOUR KNOWLEDGE

1. WHO WERE THE CYBERMEN ORIGINALLY?
   A. Soldiers who lost a space war
   B. Ordinary people like us
   C. Robots from the planet Zark

2. WHAT WAS REMOVED FROM CYBERMEN'S BRAINS?
   A. Their memories
   B. All knowledge about racket sports
   C. Emotions like love and hate and fear

3. WHAT DO THE CYBERMEN'S CHEST UNITS REPLACE?
   A. Heart, lungs and other organs
   B. Identity cards
   C. Blood

4. WHAT IS THE NAME OF THE CYBERMEN'S LEADER?
   A. The Prime Cyberman
   B. The Cyber Controller
   C. Eric

5. WHERE DID THE CYBERMEN ORIGINATE?
   A. In the depths of the sea
   B. On planet Mars
   C. On another Earth similar to ours

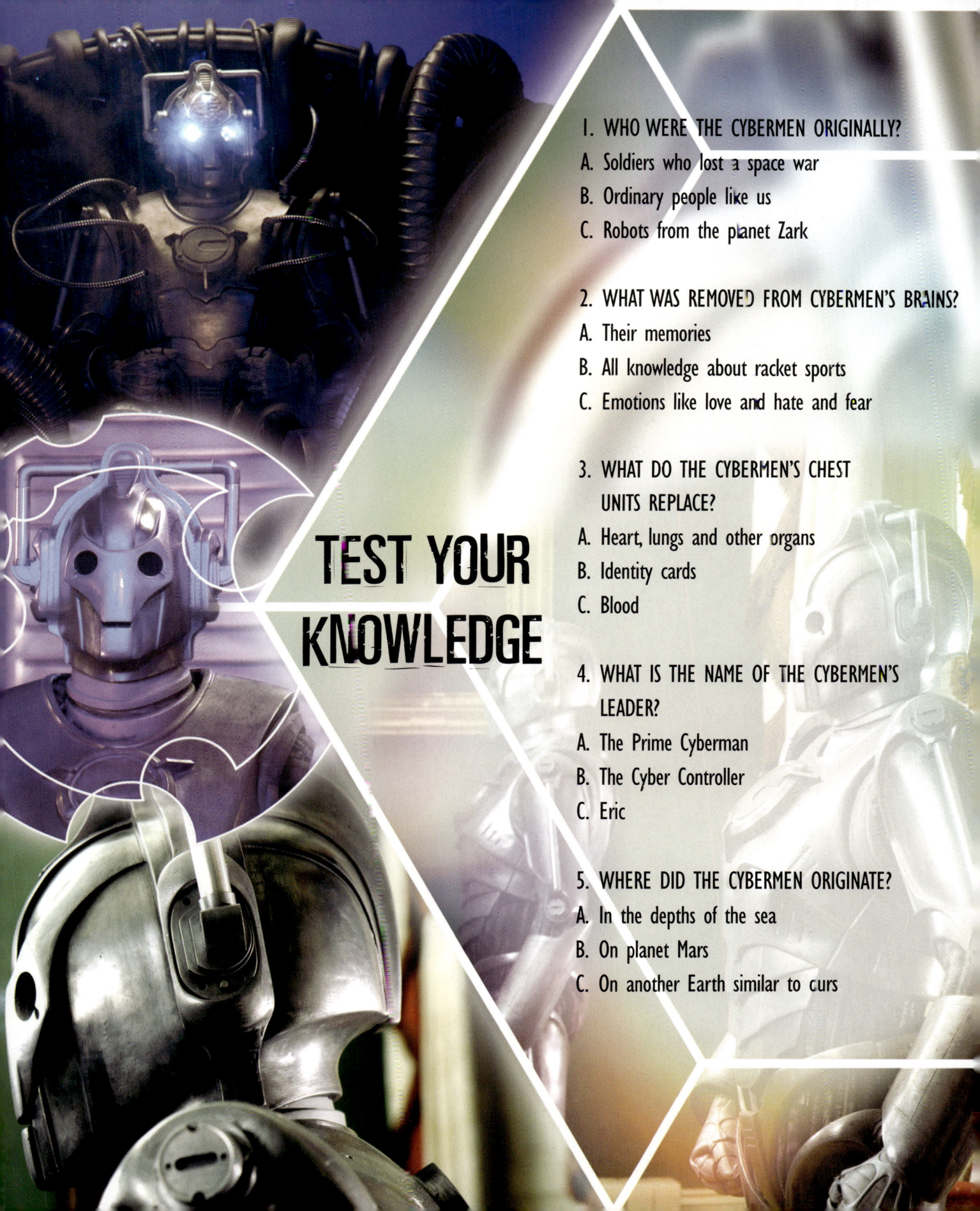

226 CYBER ALLIES

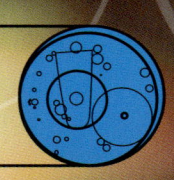

JOHN LUMIC

On another Earth, very like our own planet but in another universe running parallel to ours, a man called John Lumic invented the Cybermen. He saw Cybermen as an extension of our own evolution — an upgrade to humanity like computers and software programs get upgraded. He thought that turning people into Cybermen would be an *improvement*.

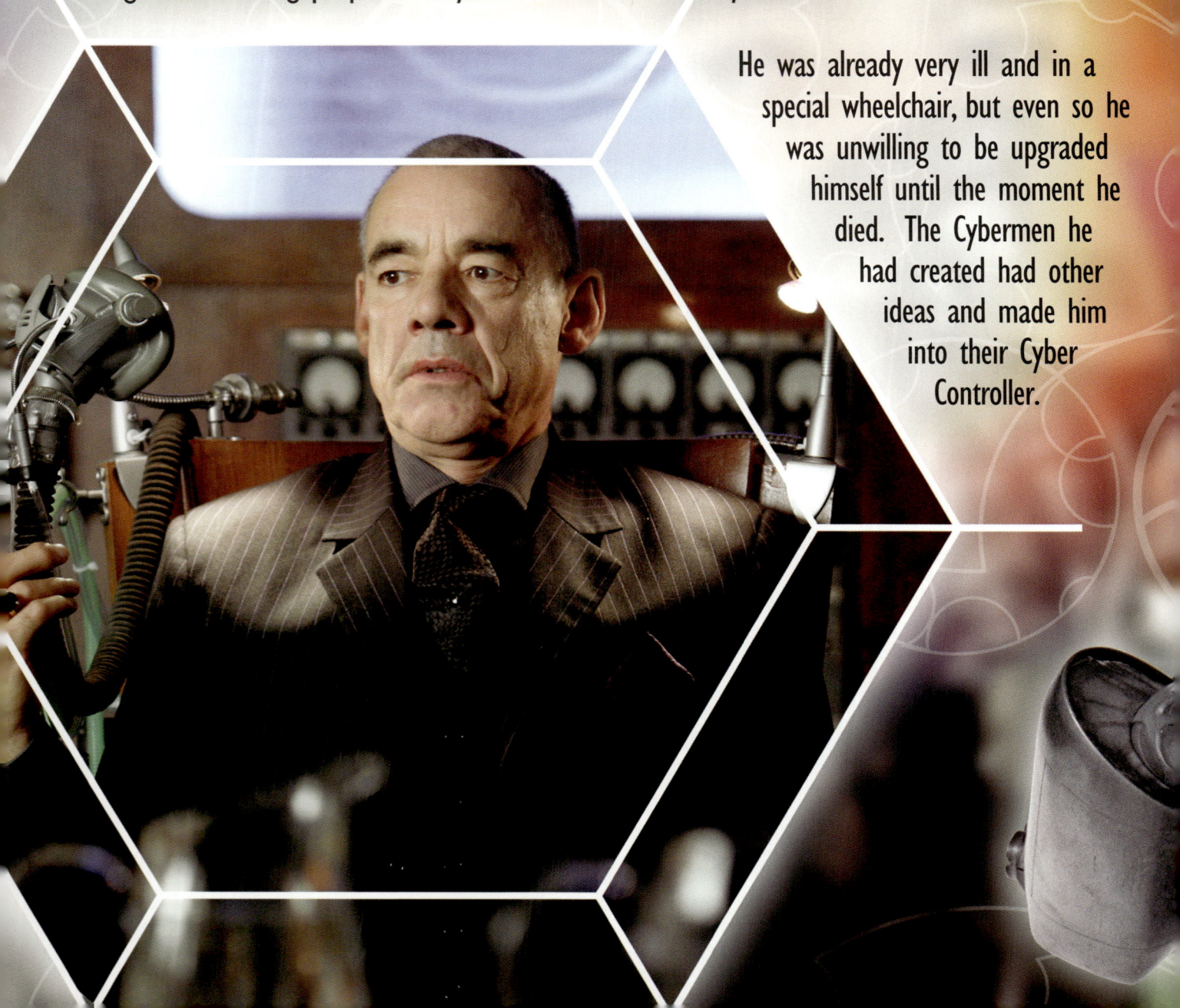

He was already very ill and in a special wheelchair, but even so he was unwilling to be upgraded himself until the moment he died. The Cybermen he had created had other ideas and made him into their Cyber Controller.

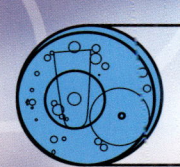

THE CYBER CONTROLLER

The Controller is the leader of the Cybermen. He used to be John Lumic, the man who created the Cybermen in the first place. The Controller is wired into a special throne and special pipes feed nutrient fluids and power into his body. When the Doctor, Rose and their friends destroyed the Cybermen, the Controller survived. He broke free of his throne and attacked them.

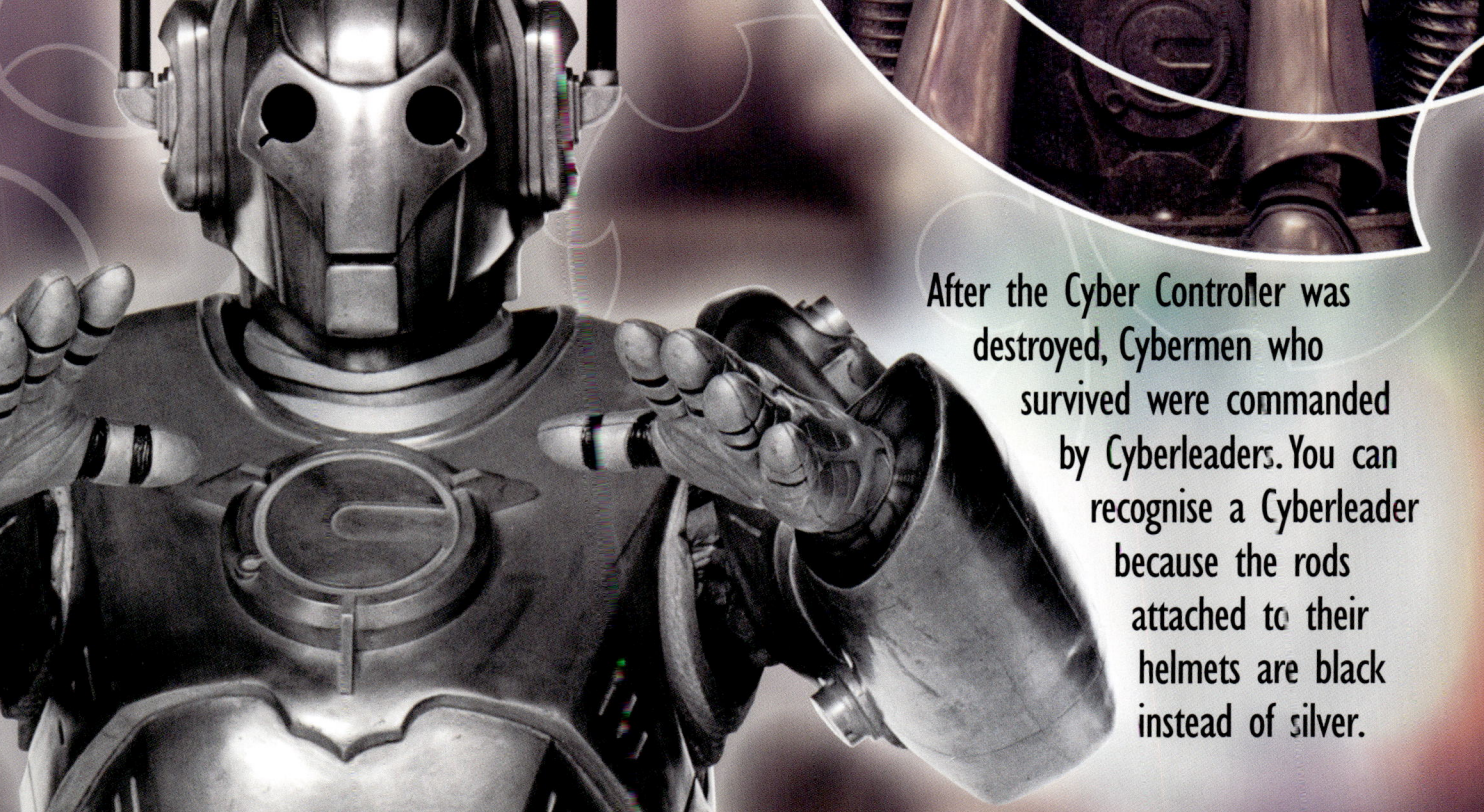

After the Cyber Controller was destroyed, Cybermen who survived were commanded by Cyberleaders. You can recognise a Cyberleader because the rods attached to their helmets are black instead of silver.

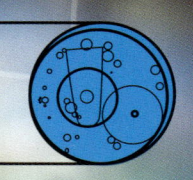

CONTROLLED HUMANS

The Cybermen can control humans who are not completely Cybermen using special headsets. These headsets look rather like the earpieces some people wear to use their mobile phones, and they feed Cyber instructions directly into the person's brain. The people taken over by the Cybermen no longer have any will power of their own, and are entirely controlled by the Cybermen.

Be careful when you see someone wearing one of these earpieces. Of course, they might just be using their mobile phone, but they *could* be a Cyberman agent!

THE ARMY OF GHOSTS

When ghostly figures first started to appear, there was panic. People were afraid of the faint, grey figures that appeared around the world. But after a while they decided that the ghosts meant them no harm. They thought that loved ones who had died were now coming back to visit their friends and relatives.

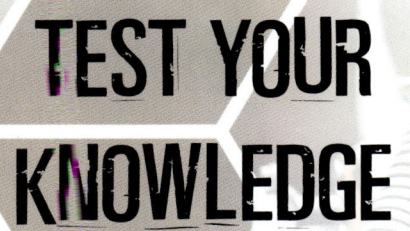

But that was not the case. The ghosts were the first hint that the Cybermen were coming. They had found a way through from another parallel world into our own universe. When at last they appeared fully, people realised their mistake. But by then it was too late — the Cybermen had already invaded. Millions of them were now on Earth, ready to turn us all into creatures like them: Cybermen.

TEST YOUR KNOWLEDGE

1. WHO CREATED THE CYBERMEN?
A. Dave Ross
B. John Lumic
C. Mickey Smith

2. WHAT DID THE CREATOR OF THE CYBERMEN BECOME?
A. The Cyber Controller
B. A Cyberleader
C. Very rich

3. HOW DO THE CYBERMEN CONTROL SOME HUMAN BEINGS?
A. Bribery
B. Through special earpieces
C. Threatening their friends

4. WHAT DID PEOPLE THINK THE ARMY OF GHOSTS WERE?
A. Invading Cybermen
B. Freak clouds
C. Ghosts of dead friends or relatives

5. WHAT WERE THE GHOSTS REALLY?
A. Invading Cybermen
B. Freak clouds
C. Ghosts of dead friends or relatives

230 CYBER ENEMIES

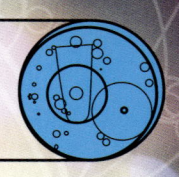

THE DOCTOR

The Doctor is the last of the Time Lords, a powerful race that had the secret of travel through time and space, but was destroyed in a Great Time War. The Doctor is the greatest enemy of the Cybermen and has defeated them in many times and places throughout his many lives.

The Doctor can change his appearance. When his body is worn out or damaged he can change into a new one. Travelling through space and time in his TARDIS and with the help of various companions, the Doctor fights against evil and injustice. He has met the Cybermen before, in our universe. So it was a big surprise for him to discover that Cybermen were being created on another version of Earth — a parallel world very like our own.

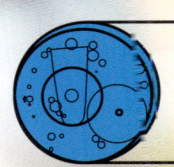

THE PREACHERS

The Preachers are opposed to the way the large corporation Cybus Industries is taking over the world and are determined to stop it. They are led by Ricky — a parallel version of Mickey Smith who lives in the other Earth. Mickey teamed up with the Preachers to help defeat Cybus and fight the Cybermen.

The other Preachers are Jake and Mrs Moore. They travel in a special van kitted out with equipment. The Preachers get their information about Cybus from a spy inside the company — they don't know who it really is, but the man calls himself 'Gemini'.

PETE TYLER

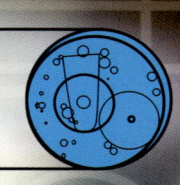

The Doctor's best friend and companion is Rose Tyler. Her dad died when she was a baby, but in the other world where the Cybermen were created, Rose's dad is still alive.

Pete Tyler works for John Lumic at Cybus Industries. But he is secretly sending out information about Lumic's plans, using the code name Gemini. When he finds he is broadcasting the information only to the Preachers he is disappointed. But they all work together — Pete, the Preachers, Rose, Mickey and the Doctor — and defeat the Cybermen.

When the Cybermen escape from Pete's world into our world, he follows to fight their evil wherever it appears.

THE DALEKS

Hated and feared throughout the whole universe, the Daleks are the most ruthless and evil creatures in all creation. They might look like robots, but inside that protective, armoured shell is a living creature. It was thought that they were all destroyed in a Great Time War against the Time Lords — the Doctor's people. But some survived.

The Cult of Skaro was a special group of Daleks that hid in the void between universes to wait for the Time War to end. Then they arrived on Earth, but their Void Ship left a trail that the Cybermen were able to follow to invade our world. While the Daleks and Cybermen fought a tremendous battle, the Doctor was able to defeat them both.

TEST YOUR KNOWLEDGE

1. WHAT WAS THE NAME OF ROSE'S DAD?
A. Pete Tyler
B. Mickey Smith
C. John Lumic

2. WHAT DID THE PEOPLE WHO OPPOSED CYBUS INDUSTRIES CALL THEMSELVES?
A. The Preachers
B. The Druids
C. The Gemini Brothers

3. WHAT WAS THE CODE NAME OF THE SPY AT CYBUS INDUSTRIES?
A. Capricorn
B. Gemini
C. TARDIS Timothy

4. WHAT DID THE PREACHERS TRAVEL IN?
A. A zeppelin
B. An armoured train
C. A special van

5. HOW DID THE CYBERMEN GET TO OUR WORLD?
A. Using a Cyber-transfer device
B. They followed the Dalek Void Ship
C. By zeppelin

CYBER ORIGINS

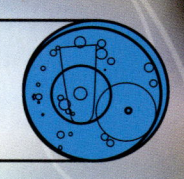

THE 'OTHER' EARTH

Rose and Mickey thought they were back in London when the TARDIS arrived on the other version of Earth. But soon they knew that the Doctor's TARDIS had brought them to another Earth — like our own world, but also very different. The London skyline was odd and there were large airships, zeppelins, in the sky over the city.

On this world, Rose had never been born, but her father was still alive. And Mickey was called Ricky. It was a strange moment when Mickey and Ricky met.

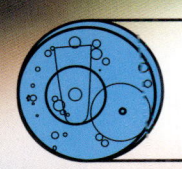

Ricky was the leader of the Preachers, a group of people trying to stop Cybus Industries from getting too powerful.

With communications technology further advanced on this other world than on our own, Cybus Industries was able to control people through special earpieces. People thought they were just getting the latest news, weather and sports information from the earpieces. But in fact Cybus was getting ready to take over. Even the Preachers did not know what Cybus was really doing.

They were taking homeless people off the streets and turning them into the first Cybermen. It was up to the Doctor and his friends, with help from the Preachers, to stop them…

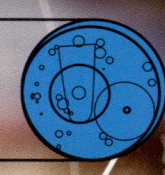

THE ARRIVAL OF THE CYBERMEN

Rose and the Doctor arrived back on Earth, and were introduced to a ghost! Rose's mum, Jackie, thought it was the ghost of her father. All over the world ghosts were appearing and people thought they were the spirits of their dead friends and relatives. At first people were scared and worried, but after a while they got used to the 'ghosts' being around and accepted they meant no harm.

But people were wrong. The faint cloudy shapes were not ghosts. They were the Cybermen breaking through into our world as they escaped from their own parallel Earth.

A secret group of scientists and soldiers called Torchwood was trying to find out more about the ghosts and actually bringing them through. The Cybermen took over some of the people at Torchwood and got them to open the doorway between the universes so they could come through properly.

People saw what was happening when the Cybermen became solid — it was an invasion. Millions of Cybermen arrived all over the world, and no one could stop them. No one except the Doctor and Rose.

TEST YOUR KNOWLEDGE

1. **WHEN THE TARDIS FIRST LANDED, WHERE DID ROSE AND MICKEY THINK THEY WERE?**
   A. In a parallel universe
   B. On our own Earth
   C. The planet Zark

2. **WHAT DID THE PREACHERS WANT TO DO?**
   A. Have parties and enjoy themselves
   B. Drive round very fast in their van
   C. Stop Cybus Industries getting too powerful

3. **WHAT DID PEOPLE THINK THE FAINT FIGURES WERE THAT APPEARED ROUND THE WORLD?**
   A. Ghosts
   B. The TARDIS
   C. Cybermen

4. **WHAT WERE THEY REALLY?**
   A. Ghosts
   B. The TARDIS
   C. Cybermen

5. **WHO WERE THE ONLY PEOPLE WHO COULD STOP THE CYBERMEN FROM INVADING?**
   A. The Preachers
   B. The Doctor and Rose
   C. Torchwood

WEAPONS AND TECHNOLOGY

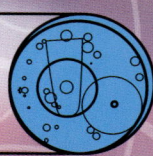

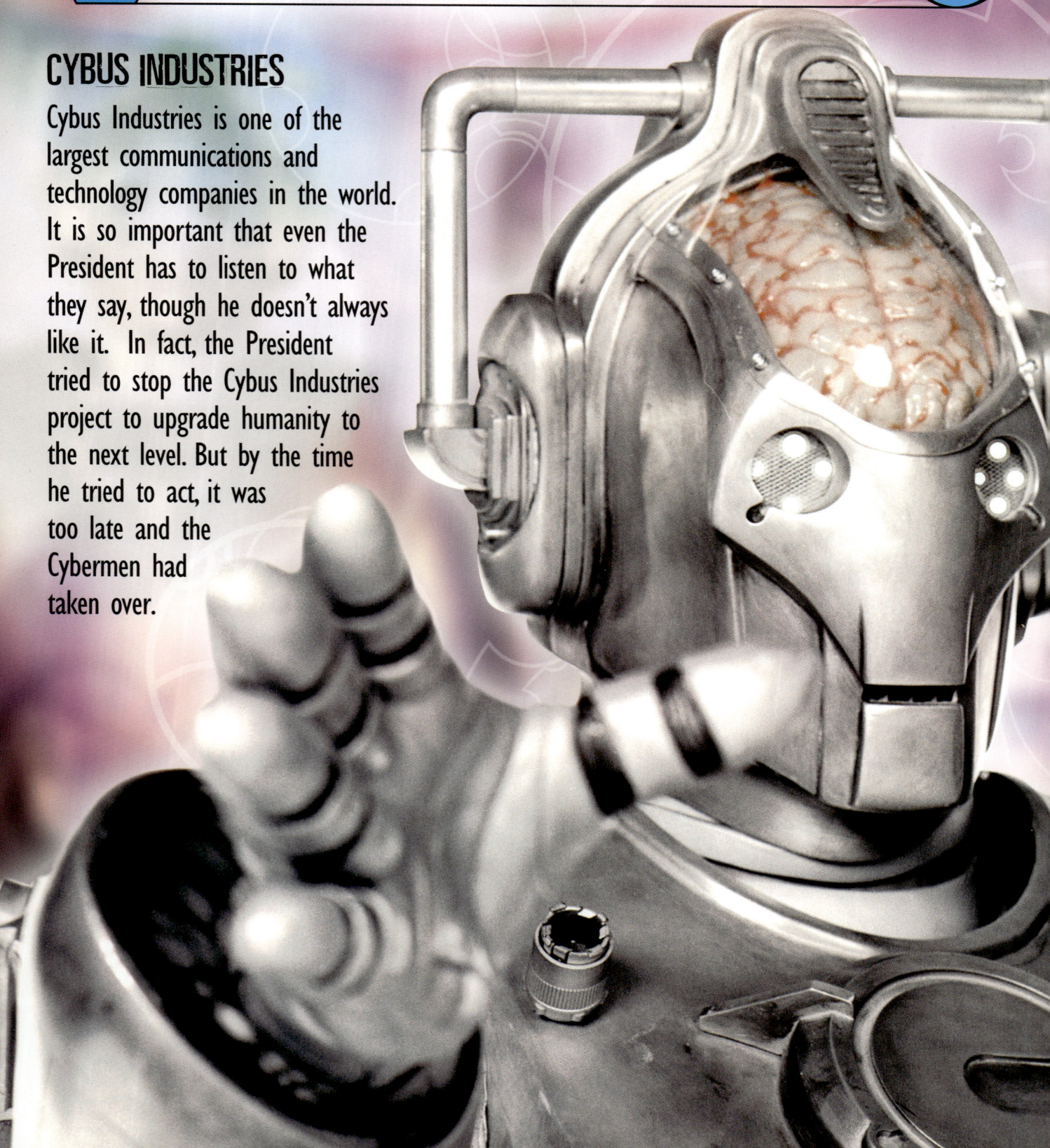

CYBUS INDUSTRIES

Cybus Industries is one of the largest communications and technology companies in the world. It is so important that even the President has to listen to what they say, though he doesn't always like it. In fact, the President tried to stop the Cybus Industries project to upgrade humanity to the next level. But by the time he tried to act, it was too late and the Cybermen had taken over.

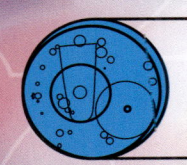

Cybus Industries also owns lots of other companies, such as International Electromatics. Together with these, Cybus provides information like news, weather, television and even winning lottery numbers. It also provides the technology so that people can receive that information. They get it sent directly to special earpieces that let them hear and see the broadcasts. The information is downloaded directly into people's brains.

But Cybus can control the earpieces, and use them to take people over. The affected people walk calmly, unthinking, into vast Cybus factories, where they are adapted and changed into more Cybermen.

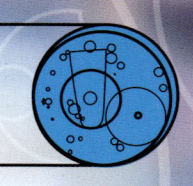

BUILT-IN ACCESSORIES

Designed by a technology company, the Cybermen have many accessories and functions that are built directly into them. The Cyberman's weaponry, for example, is part of the forearm. A high-energy blaster emerges from the arm and the Cyberman aims using a heads-up display in the eye circuits. This targeting system is linked directly to the Cyberman's arm to make sure that the gun is always on target.

As well as, or instead of, the standard weaponry, Cybermen may have other facilities built into the forearm. A Cyberman with an arm-mounted camera can broadcast the demands of its Cyberleader across a planet's own communications system by hacking into it.

TEST YOUR KNOWLEDGE

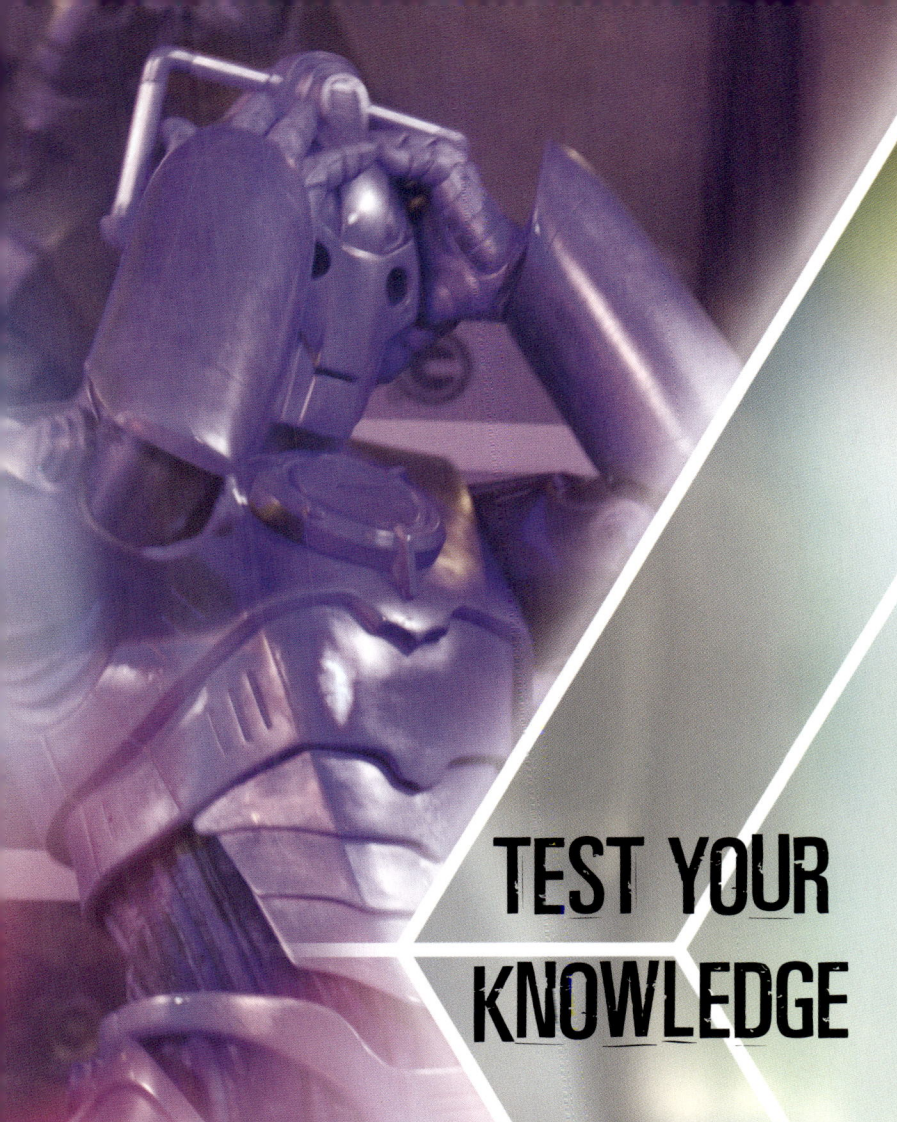

1. WHAT WAS THE NAME OF THE COMPANY THAT DEVELOPED THE CYBERMEN?
   A. International Electromatics
   B. Cybus Industries
   C. The British Broadcasting Corporation

2. HOW DID THEY BROADCAST INFORMATION TO PEOPLE?
   A. Through special earpieces
   B. Through x-ray spectacles
   C. Over the television

3. WHAT HAPPENS WHEN A CYBERLEADER IS DESTROYED?
   A. It explodes
   B. All the information it had is lost forever
   C. Its knowledge is downloaded into another Cyberman

4. WHERE DOES A CYBERMAN KEEP ITS WEAPONRY?
   A. In a holster at its side
   B. Inside the forearm
   C. In a locked cupboard

5. WHAT HAPPENS TO PEOPLE AT THE FACTORIES?
   A. They are turned into Cybermen
   B. They are given food and drink
   C. They get to see the latest news and weather

In addition to standard communications between Cybermen, they can also download information from one to another. In the event that a Cyberleader is destroyed, its entire data set and memory can be downloaded into another Cyberman. That Cyberman then becomes the Cyberleader — with all the experience, tactical expertise and knowledge of the original.

242 CYBER ENCOUNTERS

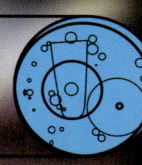

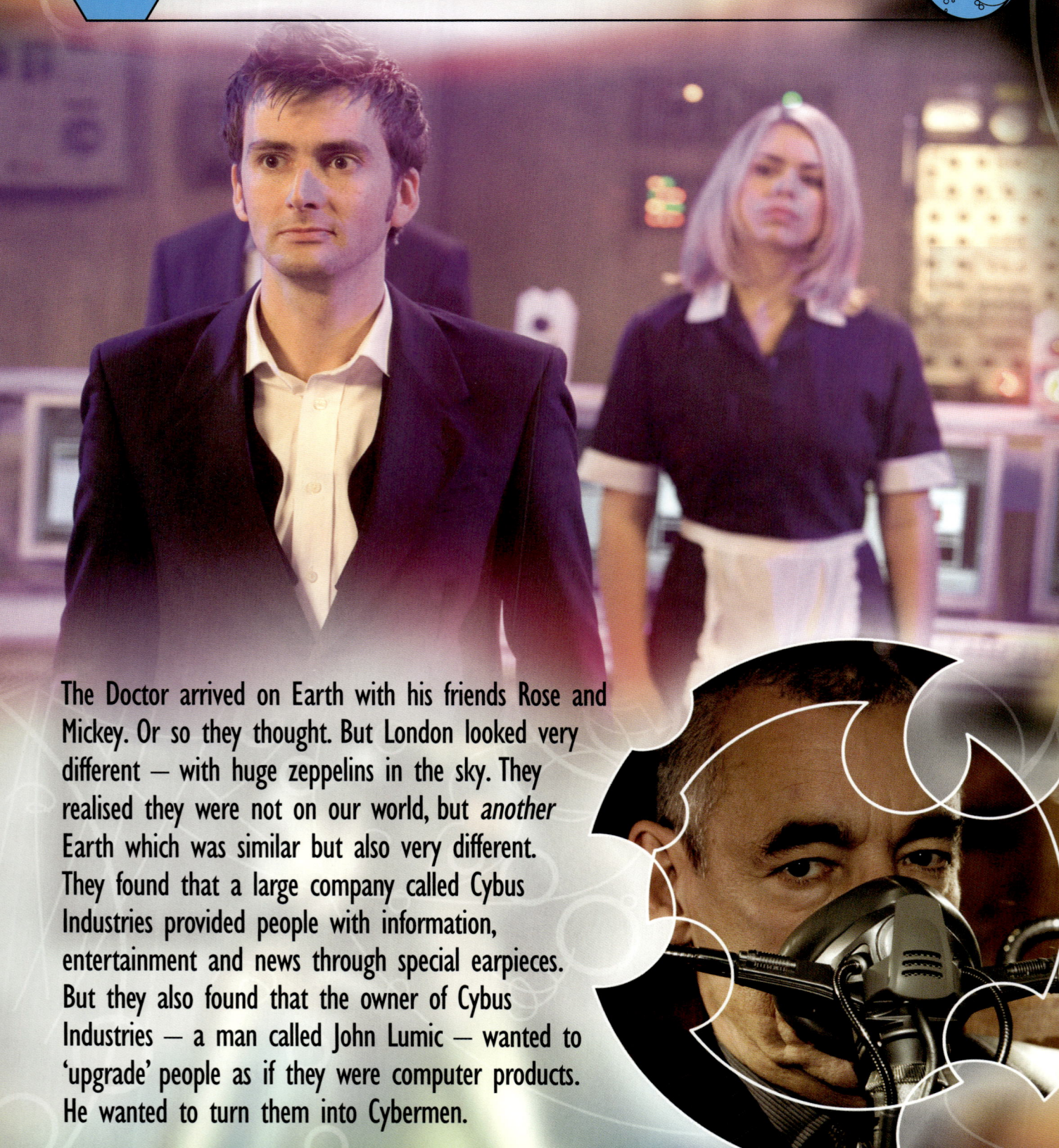

The Doctor arrived on Earth with his friends Rose and Mickey. Or so they thought. But London looked very different – with huge zeppelins in the sky. They realised they were not on our world, but *another* Earth which was similar but also very different. They found that a large company called Cybus Industries provided people with information, entertainment and news through special earpieces. But they also found that the owner of Cybus Industries – a man called John Lumic – wanted to 'upgrade' people as if they were computer products. He wanted to turn them into Cybermen.

243

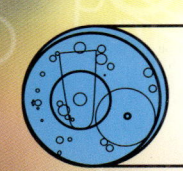

With the help of a group of people called the Preachers, who were opposed to what Cybus was trying to do, the Doctor and his friends managed to get into the factory where the Cybermen were being made. Mickey used Rose's mobile phone to jam the signal that blocked off the Cybermen's emotions. That meant that all the people who had been turned into Cybermen suddenly remembered who they had been and realised what had happened to them. The shock was so great that the Cybermen all died. All except John Lumic, who had been turned into the Cyber Controller. He tried to stop the Doctor, but he failed.

With the Cybermen defeated in London, Mickey and the Preachers were left to find out if there were more Cybus Industries factories in other cities, waiting to produce Cybermen…

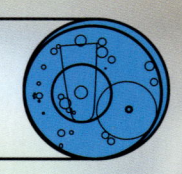

Mickey and the Preachers found that there were other Cybermen, and they were too late to stop them. But the Cybermen decided to escape from their world and found a way to get through the void between universes to reach our own Earth. They appeared only faintly at first — just vague outlines of figures which people thought were ghosts.

However, when scientists at a secret organisation called Torchwood interfered, the Cybermen were able to arrive fully in our world. Millions of Cybermen were invading and no one could stop them.

Then the Doctor and Rose realised it was even worse than that. The Cybermen had followed a strange sphere through the void — a Void Ship. When it opened, everyone expected there would be more Cybermen inside, but there weren't. The ship belonged to the Daleks, and Earth was being invaded not just by Cybermen, but by Daleks as well.

The Daleks and Cybermen fought but, even though there were millions of them, the Cybermen were no match for the Daleks. While the two evil races were battling it out, the Doctor and Rose managed to find a way to get rid of both the Cybermen and the Daleks and Earth was saved.

TEST YOUR KNOWLEDGE

1. WHAT DID JOHN LUMIC WANT TO DO TO PEOPLE?
A. Beam news directly into their brains
B. Send them into the void between universes
C. Upgrade them into Cybermen

2. WHAT DID THE DOCTOR AND HIS FRIENDS NOTICE WAS DIFFERENT ABOUT LONDON?
A. The river Thames was bright red
B. There were zeppelins in the sky
C. The streets were paved with gold

3. WHERE WERE PEOPLE TAKEN TO BE TURNED INTO CYBERMEN?
A. Cybus Industries factories
B. Pete Tyler's house
C. International Electromatics Headquarters

4. WHO INTERFERED AND MADE THINGS WORSE WHEN THE 'GHOSTS' ARRIVED?
A. The Doctor
B. Torchwood
C. The President

5. WHAT WAS INSIDE THE SPHERE-SHAPED VOID SHIP?
A. Cybermen
B. A caretaker called Colin
C. Daleks

TEST YOUR KNOWLEDGE

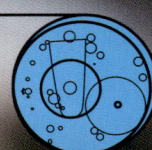

ANSWERS

Meet the Cybermen

1 (b) 2 (c) 3 (a) 4 (b) 5 (c)

Cyber Allies

1 (b) 2 (a) 3 (b) 4 (c) 5 (a)

Cyber Enemies

1 (a) 2 (a) 3 (b) 4 (c) 5 (b)

Cyber Origins

1 (b) 2 (c) 3 (a) 4 (c) 5 (b)

Weapons and Technology

1 (b) 2 (a) 3 (c) 4 (b) 5 (a)

Cyber Encounters

1 (c) 2 (b) 3 (a) 4 (b) 5 (c)

DOCTOR·WHO

MARTHA

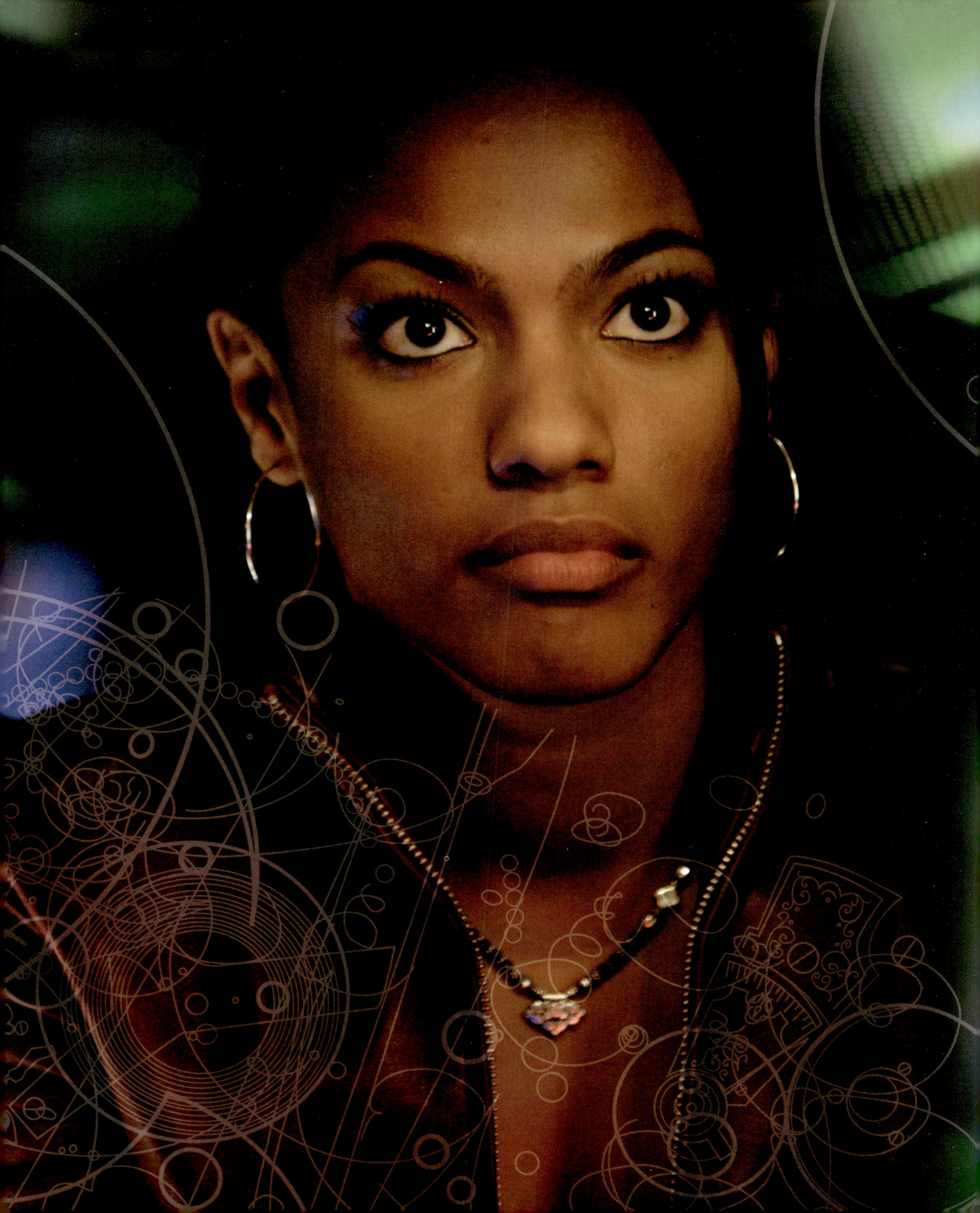

CONTENTS

Meet Martha
Introduction 250
Martha Data 252
Martha Anatomy 254
⬢ Test your knowledge

Friends and Family
The Doctor 256
Francine 257
Clive 257
Tish 258
Leo 258
Adeola 259
⬢ Test your knowledge

Enemies and Rivals
The Judoon 260
The Plasmavore 260
The Carrionites 261
The Daleks 261
The Family of Blood 262
The Weeping Angels 262
The Master 263
⬢ Test your knowledge

No place like home
Earth 264
Travels Through Time 266
⬢ Test your knowledge

Medical skills
Training 268
Essential Skills and Saving the World 269
Cardiopulmonary Resuscitation (CPR) 270
Concussion 271
⬢ Test your knowledge

Adventures at home 272
⬢ Test your knowledge

Test your knowledge Answers 276

250 MEET MARTHA

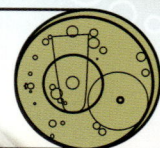

Like the rest of Earth, medical student Martha Jones knew that aliens existed. She'd heard about a spaceship flying into Big Ben, she had witnessed the sinister Sycorax invasion and she lost a cousin during the horrific Battle of Canary Wharf. But what she didn't know was that one day she would meet the man who saved the world on those, and many more, occasions.

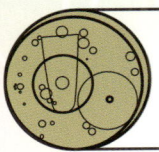

Martha met this man, the Doctor, while she was training to be a doctor herself at London's Royal Hope Hospital. Her life was safe and normal until then. She lived alone, she had exams coming up and she had a family that could, at times, go a bit mad.

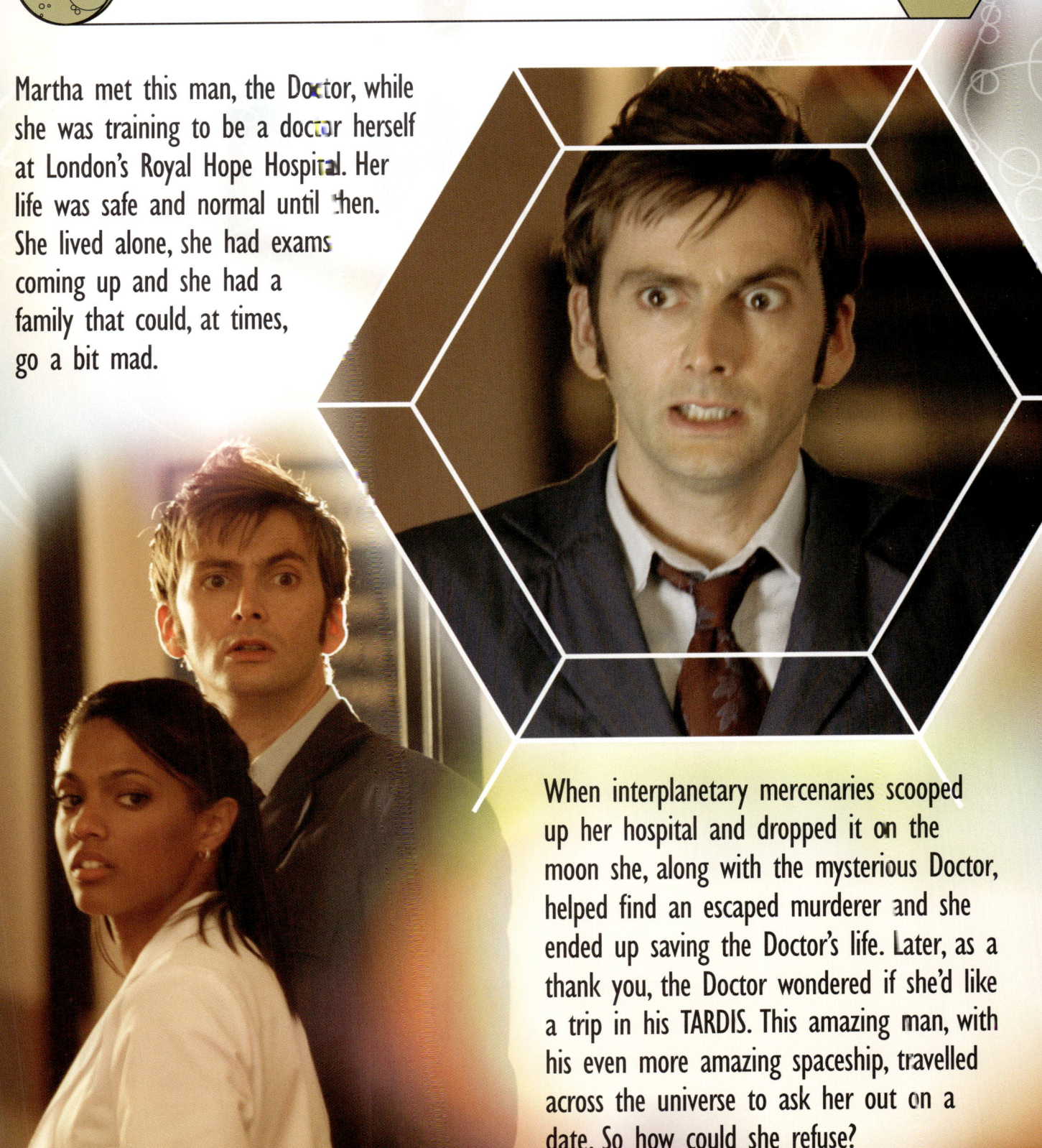

When interplanetary mercenaries scooped up her hospital and dropped it on the moon she, along with the mysterious Doctor, helped find an escaped murderer and she ended up saving the Doctor's life. Later, as a thank you, the Doctor wondered if she'd like a trip in his TARDIS. This amazing man, with his even more amazing spaceship, travelled across the universe to ask her out on a date. So how could she refuse?

252 MARTHA DATA

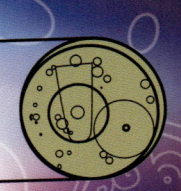

Name:	Martha Jones
Age:	23
Date of birth:	26 June 1983
Parents:	Clive and Francine Jones
Sister:	Tish Jones
Brother:	Leo Jones
Height:	1.58m (5'2")
Hair:	Black
Eyes:	Brown
Home:	London, England, UK, Earth
Species:	Human
Profession:	Medical student turned adventurer

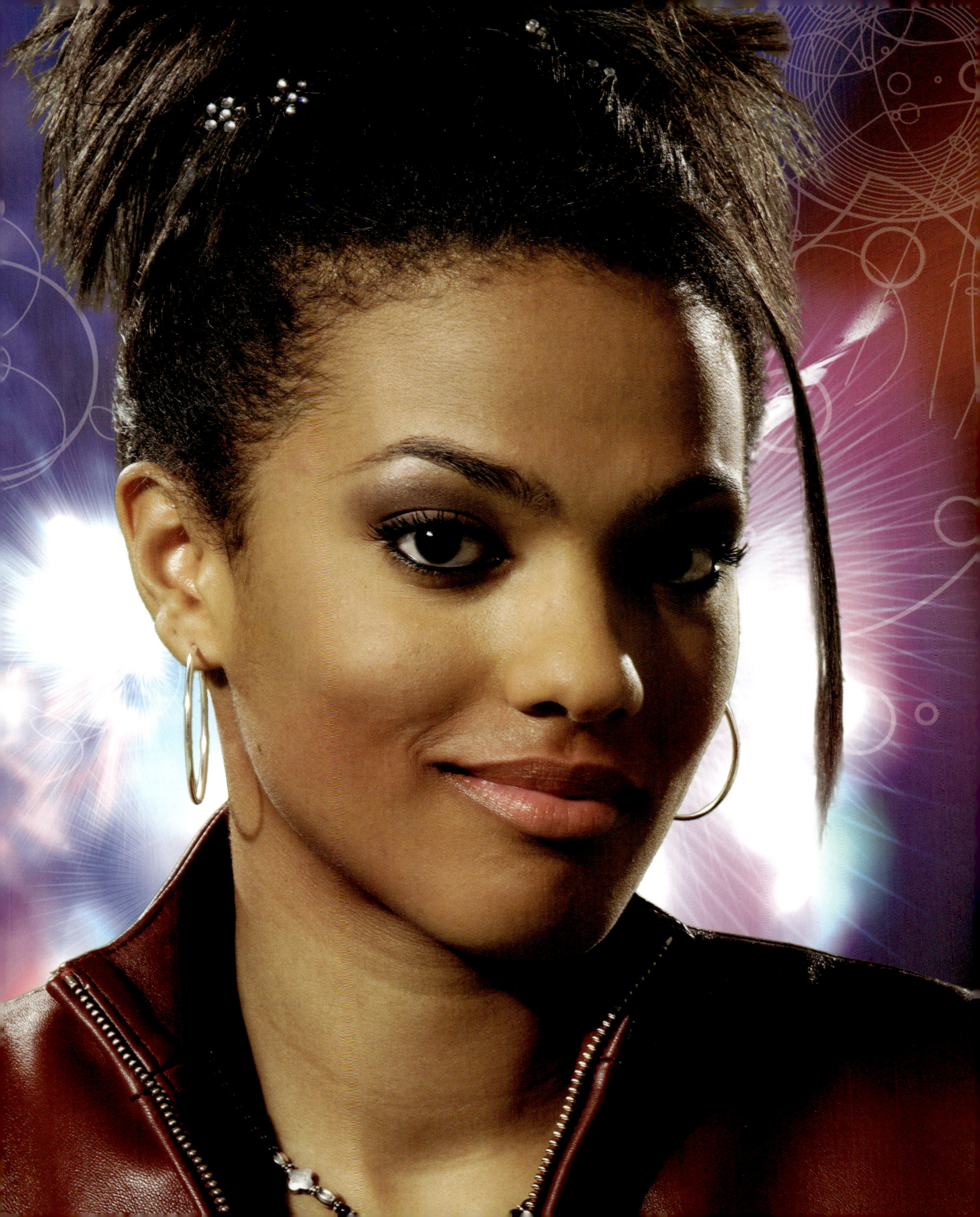

254 MARTHA ANATOMY

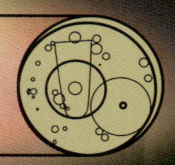

1.58m tall

Martha can't believe what she's seeing half the time!

The Doctor makes her smile

Dressed for a night out with her family

Martha looks similar to her cousin Adeola

TEST YOUR KNOWLEDGE

1. WHAT IS MARTHA TRAINING TO BE?
A. A librarian
B. A hairdresser
C. A doctor

2. WHAT ARE THE NAMES OF MARTHA'S PARENTS?
A. William and Sheila
B. Clive and Francine
C. Derek and Sue

3. WHAT WAS MARTHA'S COUSIN CALLED?
A. Adeola
B. Tish
C. Leo

4. WHICH HOSPITAL DID MARTHA WORK IN?
A. The St Martin's Free
B. The London City
C. The Royal Hope

5. HOW OLD IS MARTHA?
A. 18
B. 21
C. 23

256 FRIENDS AND FAMILY

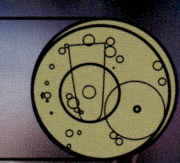

THE DOCTOR

When Martha met the Doctor for the first time, she thought he was an ordinary patient in the hospital — until she listened to his pulse and realised he had two hearts! The Doctor was impressed by Martha's calm reaction and curiosity when the hospital was scooped on to the Moon by the Judoon. The Doctor had been travelling alone for some time, so at first he was unsure about taking Martha with him. He invited her along for one trip in the TARDIS, but it soon became a whole series of dangerous and exciting adventures!

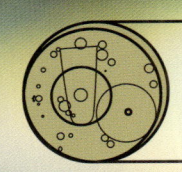

FRANCINE

Francine Jones is Martha's mum. A professional working woman, she has separated from Martha's dad, Clive. She has a good relationship with her three children, but she finds Clive quite difficult. At Leo's 21st birthday party, she insulted Clive's girlfriend by saying she looked orange. When she saw Martha the next day she thought her daughter was slightly different but couldn't work out why. And when she met the Doctor she had a feeling that his friendship with Martha could be dangerous!

CLIVE

Martha's dad, Clive Jones, is a successful and wealthy businessman. However, he does seem to be having a bit of a mid-life crisis. He drives a flashy sports car and his girlfriend, Annalise, is about the same age as Martha. He's a good dad, though, and his children all love him.

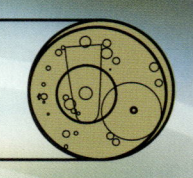

TISH

Tish, short for Letitia, is slightly older than Martha and relies on her to keep the peace between her argumentative family! When Martha and the hospital disappeared into thin air she really panicked. Tish worked for a short time as a senior PR assistant for Professor Lazarus. Although she's close to Martha, she's cross that every time she meets someone, Martha finds fault. She thinks the Doctor is a science geek, but she is probably a bit jealous of Martha's exciting new friend.

LEO

Leo is the youngest of the Jones family. He lives with his girlfriend, Shonara, and they have a baby, Keisha. His 21st birthday brought his whole family together - but soon pushed them all apart! After his dad's girlfriend stormed out of his party, the family all went home arguing - except Martha, who disappeared in time and space....

TORCHWOOD INSTITUTE

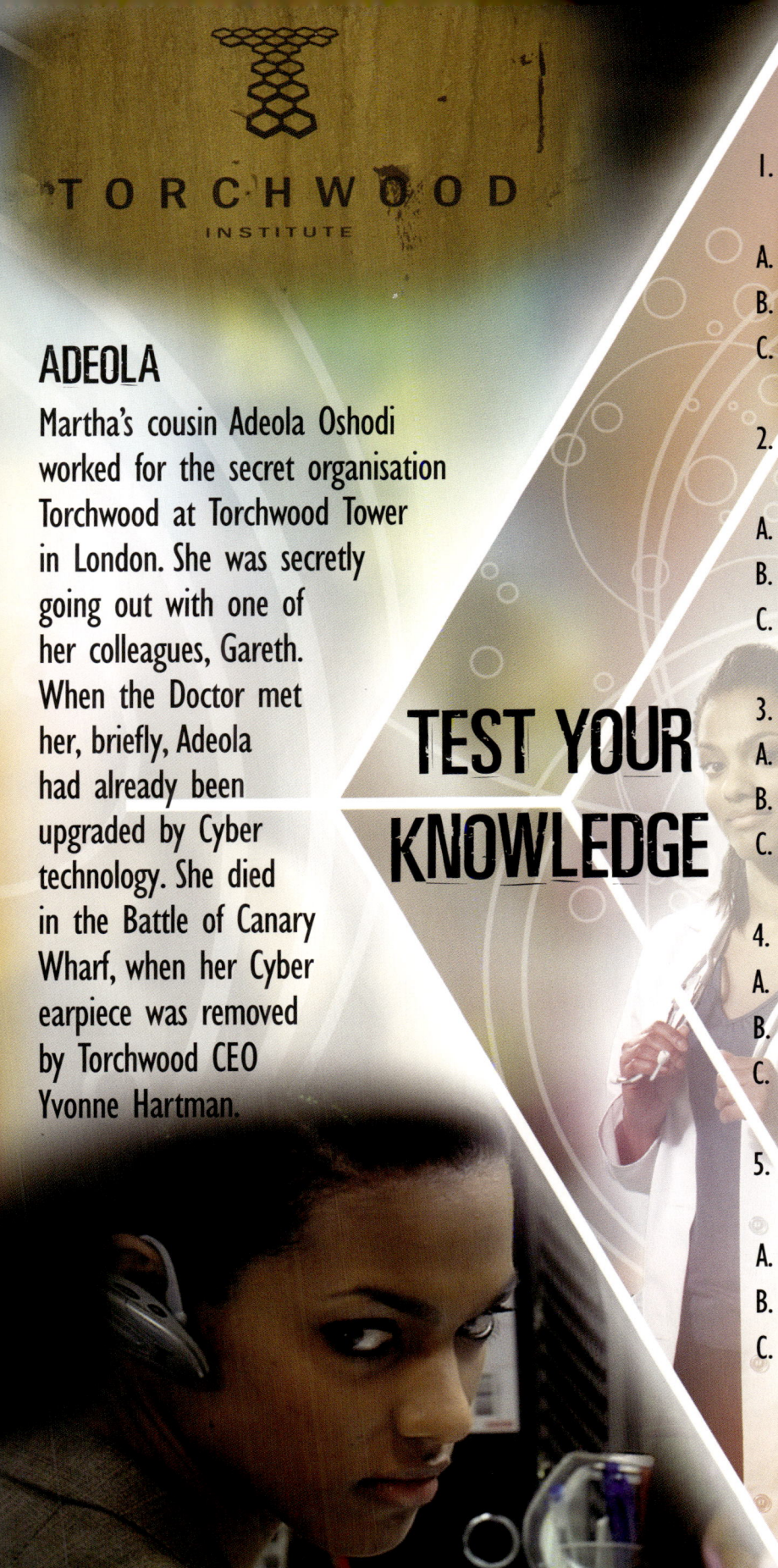

ADEOLA

Martha's cousin Adeola Oshodi worked for the secret organisation Torchwood at Torchwood Tower in London. She was secretly going out with one of her colleagues, Gareth. When the Doctor met her, briefly, Adeola had already been upgraded by Cyber technology. She died in the Battle of Canary Wharf, when her Cyber earpiece was removed by Torchwood CEO Yvonne Hartman.

TEST YOUR KNOWLEDGE

1. WHAT DID MARTHA NOTICE THAT WAS UNUSUAL ABOUT THE DOCTOR?
A. He had two hearts
B. His eyes were purple
C. He didn't have thumbs

2. HOW DID FRANCINE INSULT CLIVE'S GIRLFRIEND?
A. Said she's really stupid
B. Said she never listens
C. Said she looked orange

3. WHAT IS THE NAME OF CLIVE'S GIRLFRIEND?
A. Rose
B. Annalise
C. Jackie

4. WHO DID TISH WORK FOR?
A. The Judoon
B. Mother Doomfinger
C. Professor Lazarus

5. WHAT WERE THE JONES' CELEBRATING ON THE NIGHT MARTHA ENTERED THE TARDIS?
A. Clive and Annalise's engagement
B. Leo's 21st birthday
C. Martha passing her exams

ENEMIES AND RIVALS

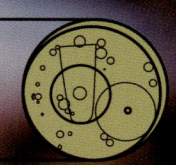

THE JUDOON

The Judoon were the first aliens Martha came face to face with. The brutish Judoon are a troop of space police in leather kilts and hefty boots. These interplanetary thugs were looking for an escaped Plasmavore, and they picked up Martha's hospital and everyone in it with an H_2O scoop. They placed it on to the neutral territory of the Moon when they thought they had found the missing alien.

THE PLASMAVORE

The sinister Florence Finnegan may look like an old lady in her seventies, but she is actually an escaped alien called a Plasmavore. She murdered the Child Princess of Padrivole Regency Nine and was hiding in a London hospital when Martha met her. A hospital, with all its blood banks, was the perfect place for a Plasmavore as they need blood to survive. She used a bendy straw to drain blood from her victims and had two slave drones called Slabs to help her.

THE CARRIONITES

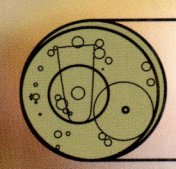

The Carrionites disappeared back at the dawn of the universe, banished into the Deep Darkness by the Eternals. Nobody knew if they were ever real or just a legend. They use shapes and words as power. When the Doctor and Martha arrived in London in 1599 they discovered that three Carrionites had managed to escape and, using the words of William Shakespeare, were about to free the rest of their race. Martha gave Shakespeare a new word from the Harry Potter novels to say, which expelled them from our world: 'Expelliarmus!'

THE DALEKS

The Daleks are one of the most evil races in the whole universe. But there aren't many left now. Four special Daleks, the Cult of Skaro, ended up in 1930s New York and continued with their mission to find new ways of killing enemies and staying alive. The Daleks stole more than a thousand humans and wiped their minds — ready to fill them with Dalek ideas and create a Human Dalek race.

THE FAMILY OF BLOOD

The Family of Blood are a nasty race of hunters with an amazing ability to sniff out anyone they want. When the Family's lifespans were running out they wanted the Doctor. They tracked him down across time and space, so the Doctor became human and then hid with Martha in a school in 1913 and waited for them to die. The Family of Blood travelled far and wide looking for him and eventually ended up at the school. By using molecular fringe animation to create animated scarecrows and taking over the bodies of some humans they managed to find the Doctor.

THE WEEPING ANGELS

The Weeping Angels look like ancient stone statues. They used to be known as the Lonely Assassins and no one knows where they come from. Thankfully, the Weeping Angels kill you quite nicely — as the Doctor and Martha found out. They simply zap you into the past and let you live out your lifespan until you die in your own past.

THE MASTER

The Master is a Time Lord like the Doctor. But unlike the Doctor he is after power and glory. Pretending to be Harold Saxon, the Master became Prime Minister of Britain and then took over the world, enslaving the human race. Martha spent a whole year travelling round the world finding a way to defeat the Master...

TEST YOUR KNOWLEDGE

1. HOW DID THE JUDOON PICK UP THE HOSPITAL?
   A. With a space spade
   B. With an H_2O scoop
   C. By hand

2. WHAT WAS THE NAME OF THE ESCAPED PLASMAVORE?
   A. Florence Nightingale
   B. Florence Fay
   C. Florence Finnegan

3. WHERE IN NEW NEW YORK COULD YOU FIND THE MACRA?
   A. Under the motorway
   B. In Pharmacytown
   C. By the hospital

4. WHO FIRST BANISHED THE CARRIONITES?
   A. The Doctor
   B. Martha Jones
   C. The Eternals

5. WHAT YEAR DID THE CULT OF SKARO ARRIVE IN NEW YORK?
   A. 1914
   B. 1930
   C. 2007

264 NO PLACE LIKE HOME

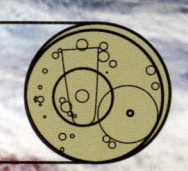

EARTH

Martha comes from the planet Earth, the third planet from the sun. Its one satellite, the Moon, was visited by Captain Neil Armstrong in 1969 and Martha's visited it too! She found herself there thanks to the Judoon. According to Galactic Law, the Judoon have got no jurisdiction over Earth, so they isolated a bit of the planet with an H_2O scoop and conducted their thuggish investigation from the Moon.

While everyone around her was screaming and afraid, Martha looked out in wonder at the Moon's surface and thought it was beautiful. In the distance she could see her home planet.

Home was a flat in London, although, when she started travelling with the Doctor, home became a blue police box called the TARDIS, which was bigger on the inside than the outside. The Doctor's TARDIS is an incredible spaceship that can travel anywhere in time and space. On her first trip, Martha wondered if the Doctor needed to pass a test to fly it and wanted to know what makes it travel in time. The Doctor refused to explain though, preferring to keep the mystery of his marvellous machine!

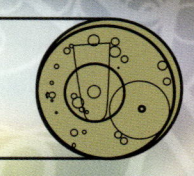

TRAVELS THROUGH TIME

Martha's first experience of time travel took her to her hometown of London — 400 years before she was born. She worried that she might change time by just being there, but with the help of the Doctor she soon got used to the idea of walking around in the past. While there she met the famous writer William Shakespeare, who really fancied her!

But one trip in time was not enough, so the Doctor took Martha into the far future. They landed in the year five billion and fifty-three — planet New Earth, the second home of mankind — fifty thousand light years away from Martha's home.

Later, Martha found herself stuck in history on a couple of occasions. To hide from aliens, she spent two months in Farringham School for Boys in Hereford in 1913, the year before the First World War. She became a maid in the school and was left to look after a human version of the Doctor. She didn't like the way women were treated back then.

Another time, she and the Doctor were thrown back into the past when they encountered a Weeping Angel. They found themselves trapped in 1969 and Martha had to get a job in a shop and support the Doctor while he worked out a clever way of getting the TARDIS back.

TEST YOUR KNOWLEDGE

1. WHAT PLANET DO THE JUDOON HAVE NO JURISDICTION OVER?
   A. The Moon
   B. Earth
   C. New Earth

2. WHICH FAMOUS WRITER FANCIED MARTHA?
   A. Charles Dickens
   B. Geoffrey Chaucer
   C. William Shakespeare

3. WHICH CITY DID MARTHA VISIT IN NOVEMBER 1930?
   A. New York
   B. New New York
   C. New Amsterdam

4. WHAT YEAR DID A WEEPING ANGEL SEND MARTHA AND THE DOCTOR BACK TO?
   A. 1913
   B. 1930
   C. 1969

5. WHERE WAS FARRINGHAM SCHOOL FOR BOYS?
   A. Devon
   B. Hereford
   C. London

Wherever, or whenever, they go, Martha is always amazed at what she sees. No two days are the same. Not many people get the chance to travel with the Doctor. She realises how lucky she is and loves every minute of it. But when they finally managed to defeat the Master, Martha had a very difficult decision to make. Should she stay at home with her family, or keep travelling with the Doctor?

MEDICAL SKILLS

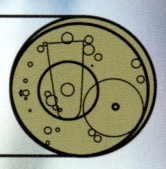

TRAINING

Martha Jones was a medical student training at the Royal Hope Hospital in London. Doctors have to train for several years. It's not an easy profession and to succeed as a doctor, students, like Martha, have to work incredibly hard and pass many exams.

Martha is nearing the end of her training - and the skills she has learned as a student come in very handy while she's travelling with the Doctor.

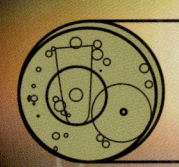

ESSENTIAL SKILLS

Martha has got the perfect character for being a doctor. She cares about people and always wants to help where she can. She is able to keep calm when others are panicking. While stuck on the Moon she continued to reassure patients that everything would be all right. She even promised the Doctor that she would get him back to Earth!

Not everyone she has met believes she could be a doctor. She had to prove she was training to be a doctor to a nurse Joan Redfern in 1913, so she described all the bones in the hand.

SAVING THE WORLD

With the Doctor and Captain Jack both held prisoner by the Master on his flying aircraft carrier, Valiant, it was up to Martha to save the world. She spent a year organising people and bringing them hope - and a way of defeating the Master once and for all.

CARDIOPULMONARY RESUSCITATION (CPR)

On many occasions Martha has had to use cardiopulmonary resuscitation (known as CPR) to help people breathe when they have fallen unconscious. This involves chest compressions and giving some of your own breath into a patient's lungs.

On the Moon, after the Doctor had been attacked by the Plasmavore, Martha did everything she could to save the Doctor. While oxygen was running out in the hospital, she gave her last bit of air to revive him.

In London, 1599, she tried to save Lynley when he was drowned by witchcraft. She later rescued the Doctor from a Carrionite attack by thumping his heart.

When Captain Jack Harkness was electrocuted she tried to revive him too — but thanks to his immortality, he managed to come back to life by himself.

CONCUSSION

Concussion is caused by an injury to the head and can be extremely serious. Martha is always quick to check people for it. When her brother Leo bumped his head, she got her mum to put an improvised ice pack on Leo's head and hold it down to reduce the swelling. And while the Doctor was stuck in a human body, he fell down some stairs and Martha was keen to know if the Matron had checked him for concussion.

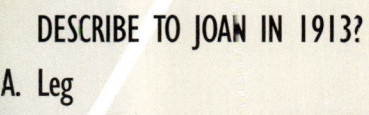

TEST YOUR KNOWLEDGE

1. WHAT BONES DID MARTHA DESCRIBE TO JOAN IN 1913?
   A. Leg
   B. Hand
   C. Neck

2. WHAT DOES CPR STAND FOR?
   A. Cardiopulmonary resuscitation
   B. Cardiopulmonary revival
   C. Cyberman resuscitation

3. WHY DID LEO NEED AN ICE PACK ON THIS HEAD?
   A. To reduce swelling
   B. He was warm
   C. He'd been electrocuted

4. WHAT HAPPENED TO LYNLEY?
   A. He had a headache
   B. He drowned
   C. He broke his leg

5. WHO ATTACKED THE DOCTOR ON THE MOON?
   A. A Cyberman
   B. A Dalek
   C. A Plasmavore

272 | ADVENTURES AT HOME

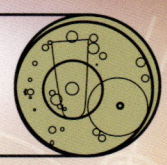

An ordinary day for Martha Jones turned into the most fantastic day of her life! In the Royal Hope Hospital everything was normal until rain started raining upwards and the entire hospital was kidnapped and transported to the Moon! Martha realised something was strange when she discovered she could still breathe and decided to trust the man who had checked into the hospital earlier that day. This man, the Doctor, later offered her one trip in his TARDIS.

Of course, one trip in the TARDIS is never enough! Martha went to the past twice and the far future before the TARDIS took her home. She arrived back on the morning after she had left, yet in that time Martha had met aliens, saved the world, and nearly kissed Shakespeare! While back home, she and the Doctor ended up going to a party for Professor Lazarus' new machine. Dormant genes in Lazarus's DNA reactivated something that evolution rejected millions of years ago and awoke a horrible creature. After this, Martha became a full-time traveller with the Doctor.

274

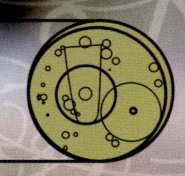

When the TARDIS arrived in Wester Drumlins House in present day Earth, it wasn't long before ancient creatures called Weeping Angels attacked the Doctor and Martha. The time travellers found themselves trapped in the past — in a time long before Martha was born!

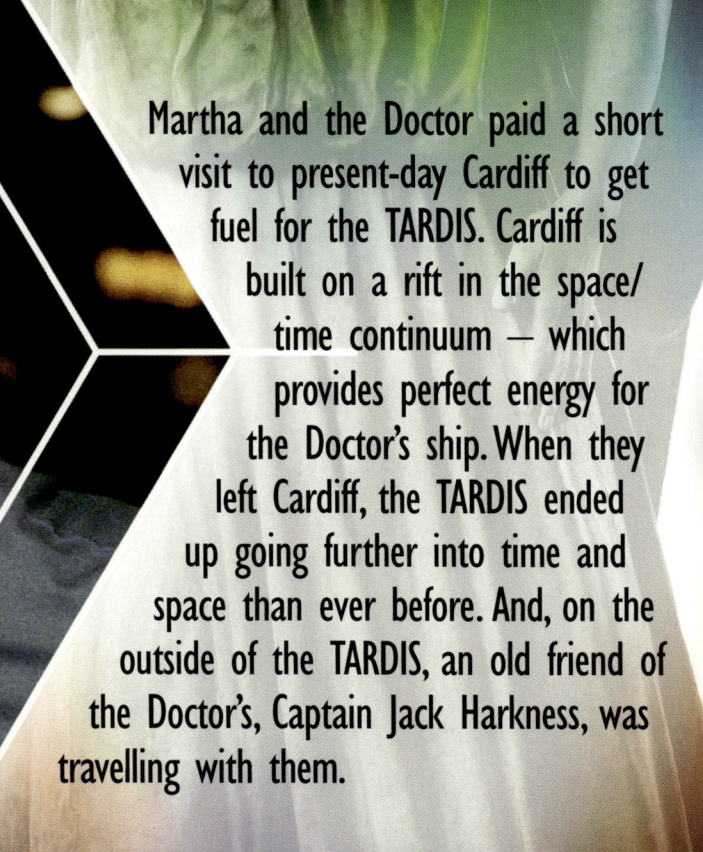

Martha and the Doctor paid a short visit to present-day Cardiff to get fuel for the TARDIS. Cardiff is built on a rift in the space/time continuum — which provides perfect energy for the Doctor's ship. When they left Cardiff, the TARDIS ended up going further into time and space than ever before. And, on the outside of the TARDIS, an old friend of the Doctor's, Captain Jack Harkness, was travelling with them.

When they returned to London, it was to find that the Doctor's oldest enemy – the Master – was now in charge. Hunted by the security services, Martha was about to start the most dangerous and exciting adventure of her life...

TEST YOUR KNOWLEDGE

1. WHEN MARTHA FIRST RETURNED HOME, HOW LONG HAD SHE BEEN AWAY?
A. One night
B. One year
C. 50 years

2. WHAT ATTACKED MARTHA AND THE DOCTOR AT WESTER DRUMLINS HOUSE?
A. The Ood
B. Weeping Willows
C. Weeping Angels

3. WHAT IS CARDIFF BUILT ON?
A. Water
B. A rift
C. A mountain

4. WHO JUMPED ON TO THE TARDIS WHEN THE DOCTOR AND MARTHA WERE IN CARDIFF?
A. Mickey Smith
B. Sarah Jane Smith
C. Captain Jack Harkness

5. AT WHOSE PARTY DID THE DOCTOR AND MARTHA MEET A HORRIFIC CREATURE?
A. Professor Lazarus'
B. Tish's
C. Jackie Tyler's 40th

TEST YOUR KNOWLEDGE

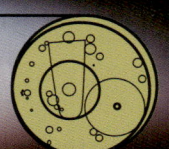

ANSWERS

Meet Martha
1 (c) 2 (b) 3 (a) 4 (c) 5 (c)

Friends and Family
1 (a) 2 (c) 3 (b) 4 (c) 5 (b)

Enemies and Rivals
1 (b) 2 (c) 3 (a) 4 (c) 5 (b)

No place like home
1 (b) 2 (c) 3 (a) 4 (c) 5 (b)

Medical skills
1 (b) 2 (a) 3 (a) 4 (b) 5 (c)

Adventures at home
1 (a) 2 (c) 3 (b) 4 (c) 5 (a)

DOCTOR·WHO

CAPTAIN JACK

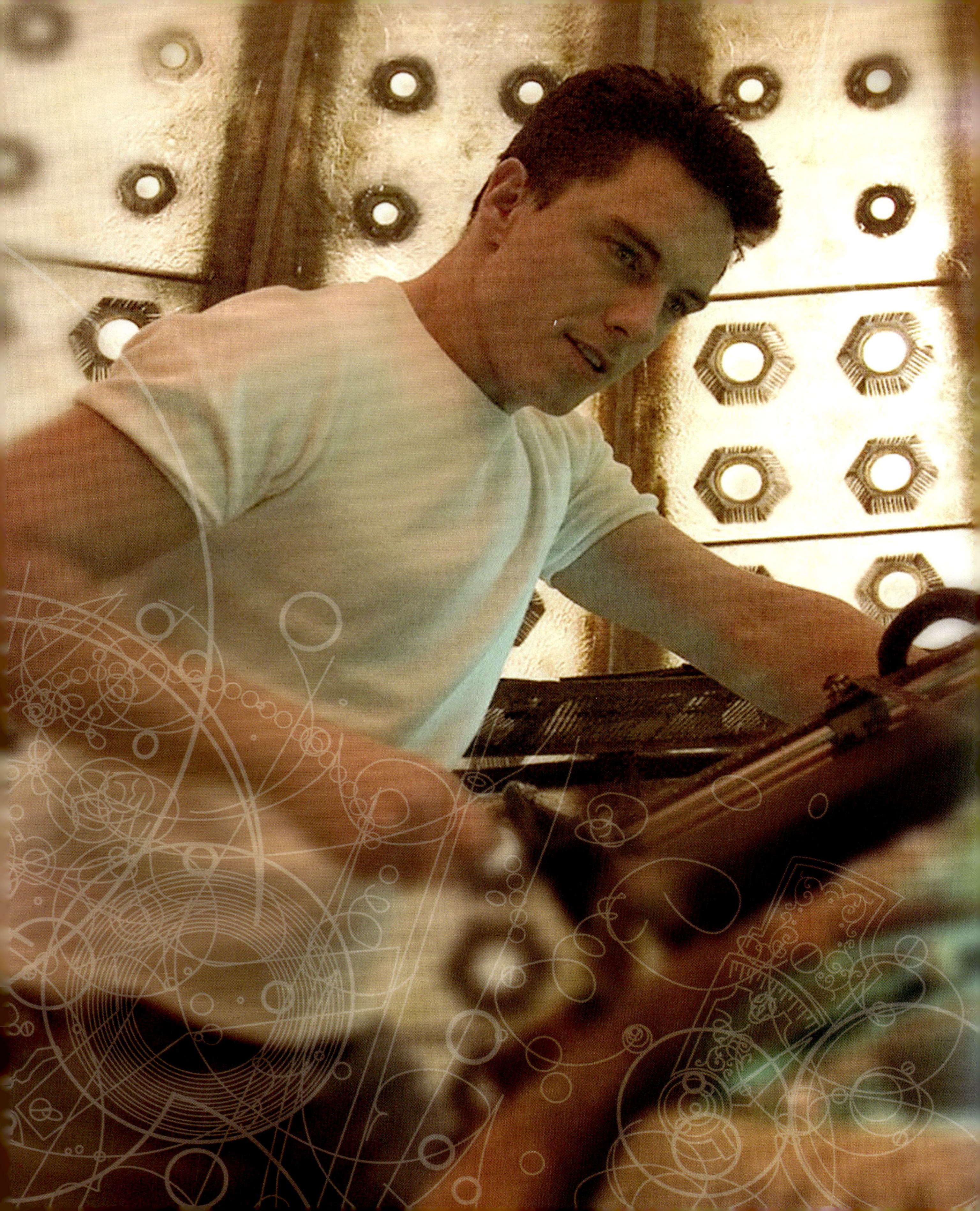

CONTENTS

Meet Captain Jack
Introduction..................................280
Captain Jack Data........................282
Captain Jack Anatomy..................284
◆ Test your knowledge

Captain Jack's Friends
The Doctor...................................286
Rose Tyler....................................287
Mickey Smith................................288
Martha Jones................................289
◆ Test your knowledge

Captain Jack's Enemies
The Empty Child..........................290
The Slitheen................................291
The Daleks...................................292
◆ Test your knowledge

The Lives and Times of Captain Jack
Mysterious Con Man.....................294
Reliving the Past..........................296
◆ Test your knowledge

Captain Jack's Capabilities
Invisible Spaceship.......................298
Vortex Manipulator and Handcuffs...299
Doctor Detector............................300
The Man Who Cannot Be Killed....301
◆ Test your knowledge

Further Adventures of Jack..........302
◆ Test your knowledge

Test your knowledge Answers........306

280 ⬡ MEET CAPTAIN JACK

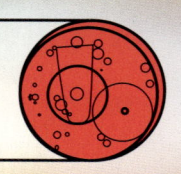

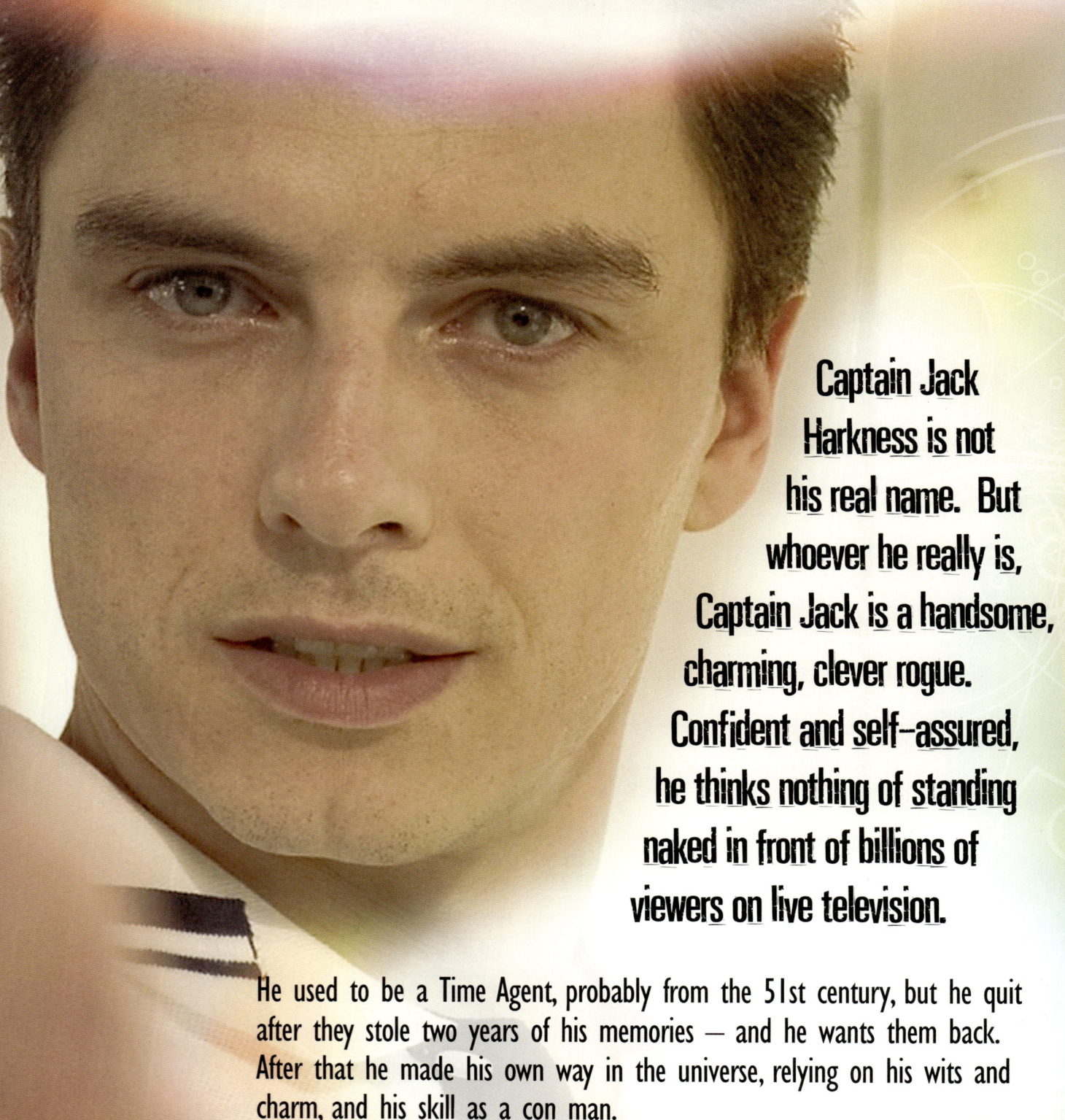

Captain Jack Harkness is not his real name. But whoever he really is, Captain Jack is a handsome, charming, clever rogue. Confident and self-assured, he thinks nothing of standing naked in front of billions of viewers on live television.

He used to be a Time Agent, probably from the 51st century, but he quit after they stole two years of his memories — and he wants them back. After that he made his own way in the universe, relying on his wits and charm, and his skill as a con man.

281

When the Doctor and Rose first met Captain Jack, his plan was to find some space junk, allow a Time Agent to track it to Earth and then convince the Agent it was valuable. Once Jack had a finder's fee, the junk would be destroyed by a German bomb, so the Agent would never discover it was a con.

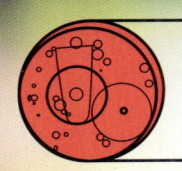

But after the Doctor and Rose saved him from his spaceship which was about to explode, Jack became something of a reformed character. He helped them sort out a Slitheen hiding in Cardiff, and organised the defence of the Game Station against an army of Daleks. But when he was exterminated, it seems his adventure may have just been beginning…

282 CAPTAIN JACK DATA

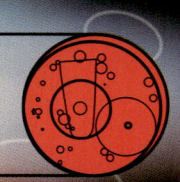

Name: Unknown
Alias: Captain Jack Harkness
Species: Unknown, possibly human
Height: 1.85m (6'1")
Hair: Dark
Eyes: Hazel
Age: Apparently about 35. Actually over 150.
Home Planet: Unknown, possibly Earth or one of its colonies.
Professions: Time Agent, Con Man, Investigator, Adventurer...

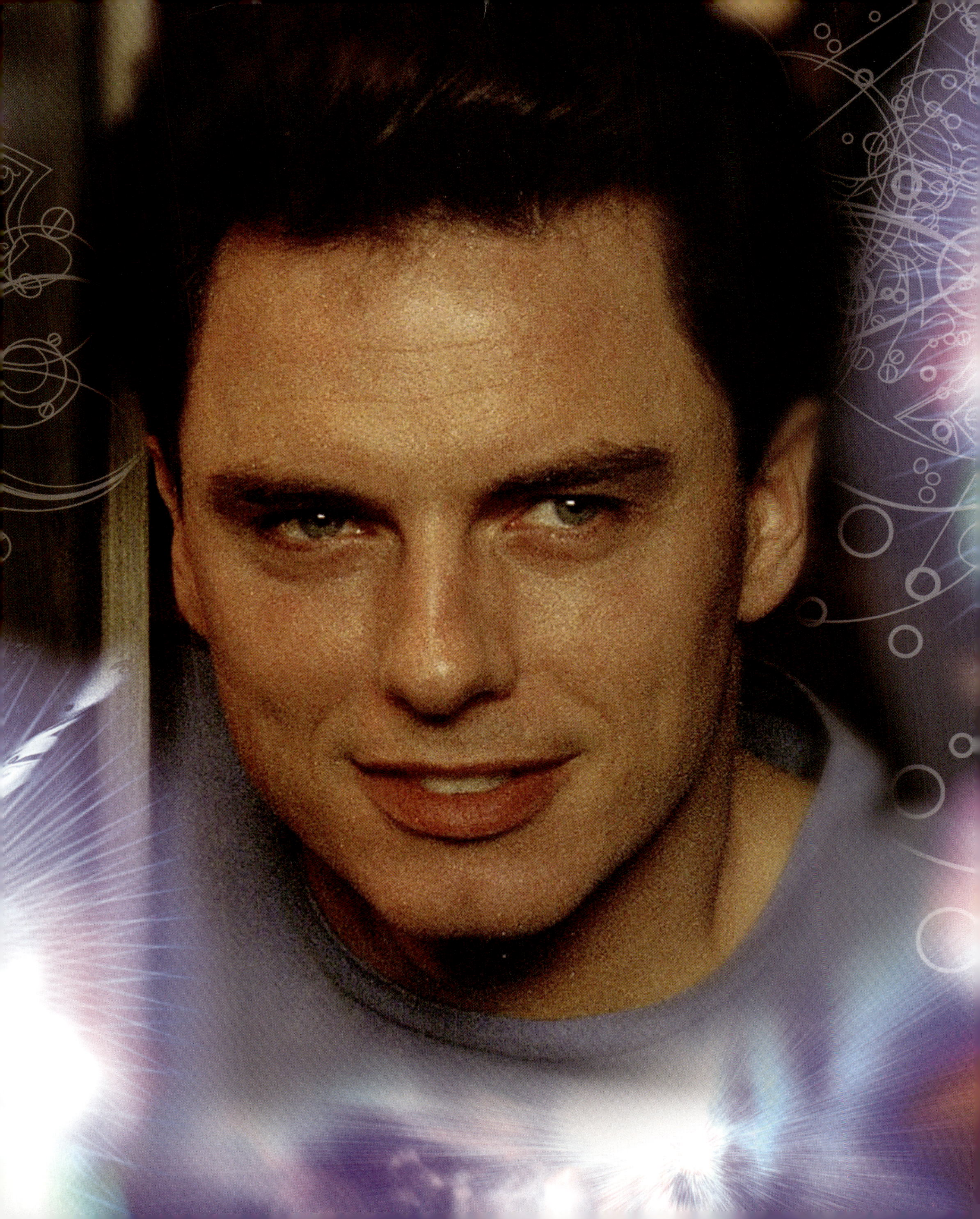

284 CAPTAIN JACK ANATOMY

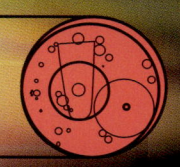

Tall and handsome — looking good for over 150 years old!

Often wears military great coat

Vortex Manipulator — enables Jack to survive in the Time Vortex

Even if Jack's heart stops, he doesn't die

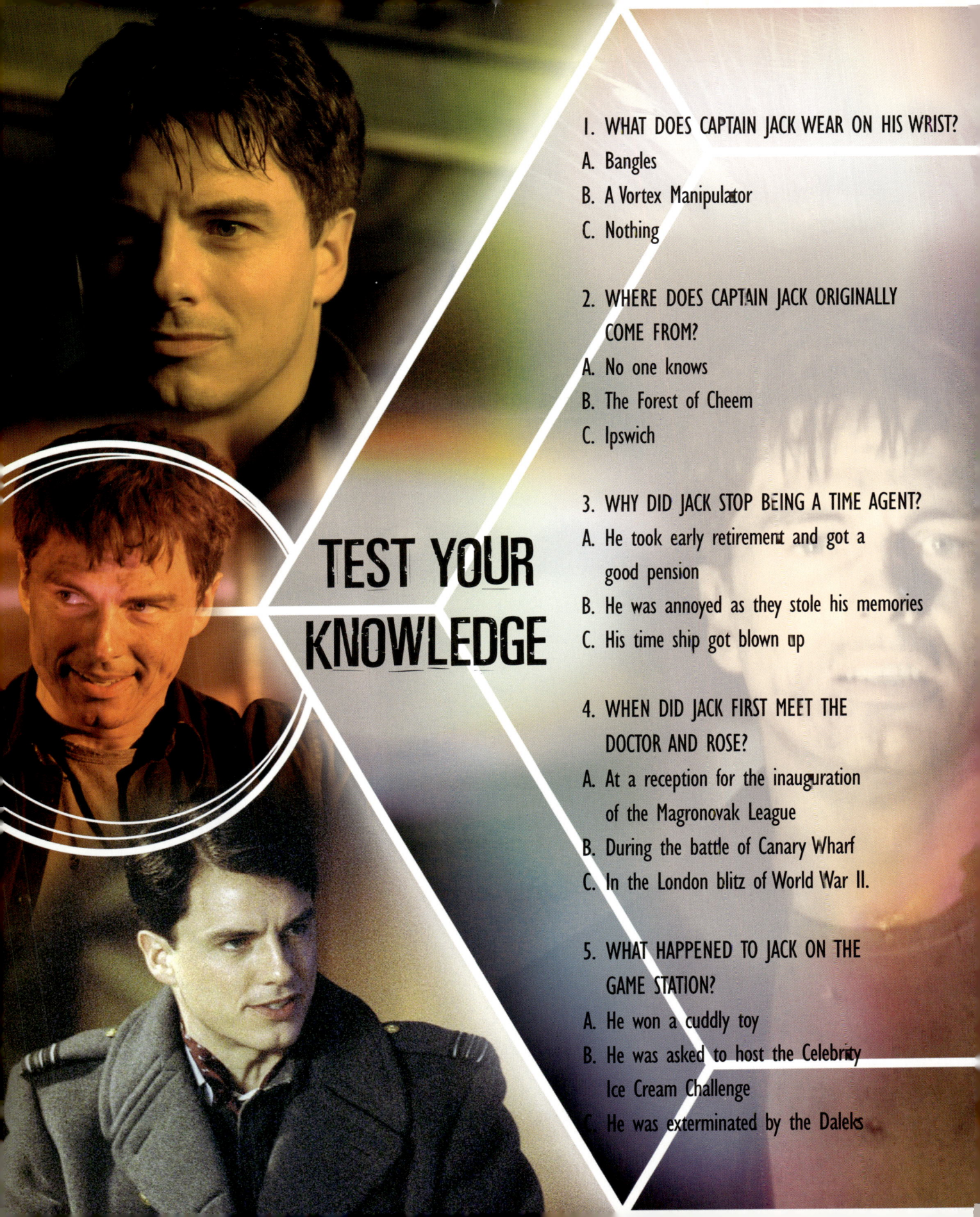

TEST YOUR KNOWLEDGE

1. WHAT DOES CAPTAIN JACK WEAR ON HIS WRIST?
A. Bangles
B. A Vortex Manipulator
C. Nothing

2. WHERE DOES CAPTAIN JACK ORIGINALLY COME FROM?
A. No one knows
B. The Forest of Cheem
C. Ipswich

3. WHY DID JACK STOP BEING A TIME AGENT?
A. He took early retirement and got a good pension
B. He was annoyed as they stole his memories
C. His time ship got blown up

4. WHEN DID JACK FIRST MEET THE DOCTOR AND ROSE?
A. At a reception for the inauguration of the Magronovak League
B. During the battle of Canary Wharf
C. In the London blitz of World War II.

5. WHAT HAPPENED TO JACK ON THE GAME STATION?
A. He won a cuddly toy
B. He was asked to host the Celebrity Ice Cream Challenge
C. He was exterminated by the Daleks

286 CAPTAIN JACK'S FRIENDS

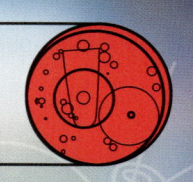

THE DOCTOR

When Jack first met the Doctor and Rose he thought they were Time Agents and tried to con them into buying a Chula Warship. But as they worked together to solve the mystery of the Empty Child they became friends. The Doctor is the last of the Time Lords, a powerful race who were destroyed in the Time War. A Time Lord can save himself from death by changing every cell in his body — this is called regeneration. After Jack was left behind on the Game Station, the Doctor was forced to regenerate — so when they meet again on the planet Malcassairo he doesn't appear to be the same man. But Jack knew it was the Doctor.

ROSE TYLER

Rose travelled with the Doctor when he first met Captain Jack. Rose and Captain Jack became good friends after he rescued her from hanging under a barrage balloon as the German air force arrived to attack London. They became such good friends that the Doctor even got a bit jealous.

When Jack was exterminated by the Daleks, Rose brought him back to life. Using the power of the Time Vortex she was able to save him, and now he cannot die! Jack remembers Rose fondly. When he found himself back on Earth in Rose's past, a couple of times in the 1990s he went back to the Powell Estate where she grew up. But he never spoke to her.

MICKEY SMITH

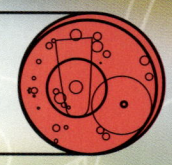

Mickey is a friend of Rose and the Doctor. He met Captain Jack in Cardiff when they landed the TARDIS there to refuel from a time rift. At first, Mickey didn't really like Captain Jack. He thought he was smarmy and too clever for his own good. Mickey was also jealous of how well he got on with the Doctor and especially with Rose. But they worked together to defeat a Slitheen who was hiding in Cardiff and planned to destroy the city.

MARTHA JONES

Martha was travelling with the Doctor when Captain Jack found him again. She was training to be a Doctor when her whole hospital was kidnapped and taken to the moon. The Doctor saved the day, and he and Martha became good friends. They have travelled back in time to meet Shakespeare, and into the far future together. Martha even looked after the Doctor when he had to live as a real human and lose his memory of who he really was. When Martha met Jack, they helped the Doctor to defeat one of his oldest enemies.

TEST YOUR KNOWLEDGE

1. HOW WERE THE TIME LORDS DESTROYED?
A. In the Great Time War
B. When their sun exploded
C. By accidentally eating a deadly poison

2. WHERE DID THE DOCTOR LEAVE CAPTAIN JACK?
A. In the TARDIS
B. At a large supermarket just outside Bristol
C. On the Game Station

3. WHAT WAS ROSE DOING WHEN JACK FIRST MET HER?
A. Emptying the TARDIS bins
B. Hanging from a barrage balloon
C. Fighting the Cybermen

4. WHAT DID MICKEY THINK OF CAPTAIN JACK?
A. He thought he was a police man
B. He thought he was smarmy and too clever for his own good.
C. He thought he'd like to hear all about Jack's adventures

5. WHAT DID MARTHA DO WHEN THE DOCTOR PRETENDED TO BE HUMAN?
A. She looked after him
B. She told him not to be so daft
C. She decided to go back home

290 CAPTAIN JACK'S ENEMIES

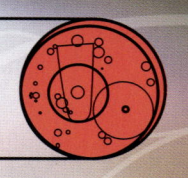

THE EMPTY CHILD

In the war-torn Britain of 1941, the children living on the streets (who should have been evacuated out of London) stole food from the houses of people sheltering from air raids. The other children regarded Nancy as their leader. But they were haunted by another child - a small boy wearing a gas mask, who was always asking for his mummy.

The mysterious child could project his voice through the TARDIS telephone, a radio and even a music box. Captain Jack didn't realise that it was all his fault because of the nanogenes in the Chula ambulance, but in the end the Doctor saved the day and everyone was all right.

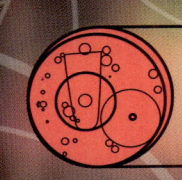

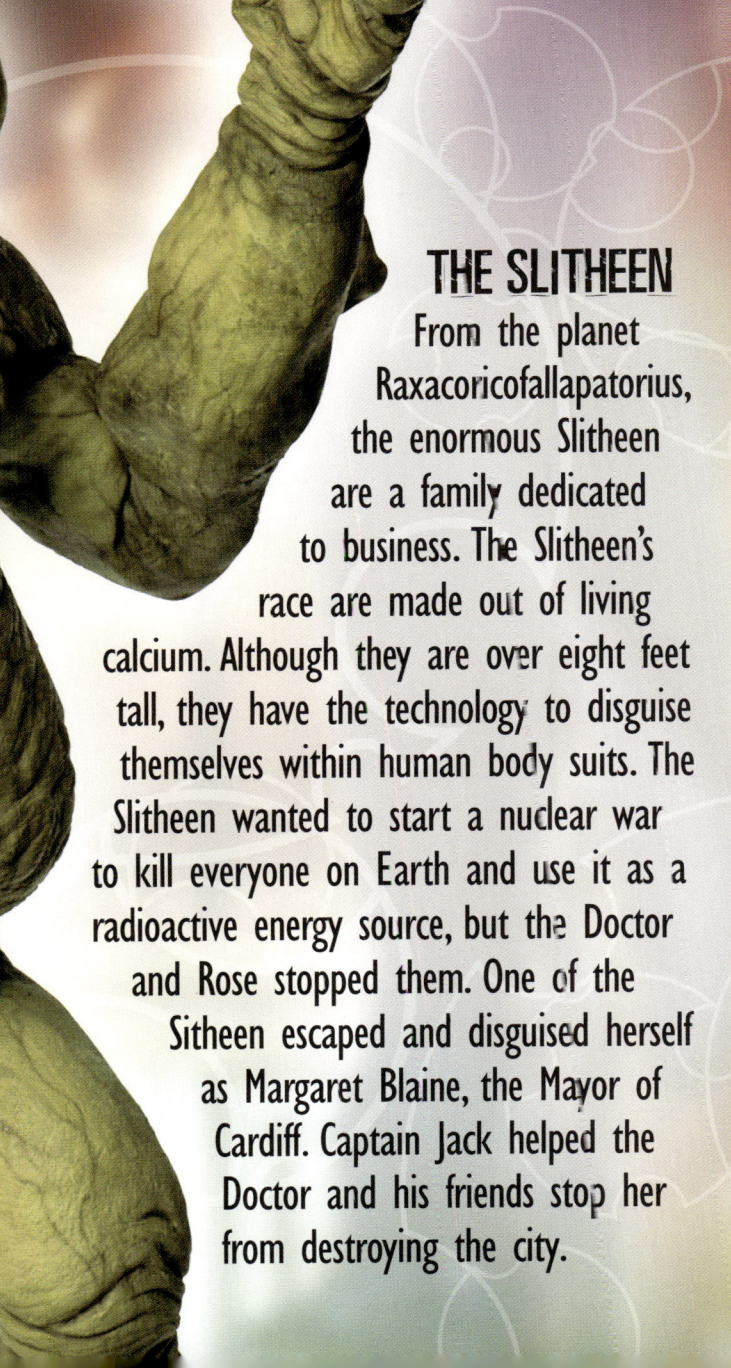

291

THE SLITHEEN

From the planet Raxacoricofallapatorius, the enormous Slitheen are a family dedicated to business. The Slitheen's race are made out of living calcium. Although they are over eight feet tall, they have the technology to disguise themselves within human body suits. The Slitheen wanted to start a nuclear war to kill everyone on Earth and use it as a radioactive energy source, but the Doctor and Rose stopped them. One of the Sitheen escaped and disguised herself as Margaret Blaine, the Mayor of Cardiff. Captain Jack helped the Doctor and his friends stop her from destroying the city.

THE DALEKS

Hated and feared throughout the whole universe, the Daleks are the most ruthless and evil creatures in all creation. They might look like robots, but inside that protective, armoured shell is a living creature.

The Daleks are so dangerous and evil that the Doctor's own people — the Time Lords — tried to go back to before their creation and stop them ever existing. As a result, the Daleks and the Time Lords have been the deadliest of enemies and fought a great Time War in which both sides seemed to be wiped out.

But the Daleks survived, and they are out to exterminate everyone and everything — especially their greatest enemy, the last of the Time Lords: the Doctor.

When the Dalek army attacked the Game Station, the Doctor put Captain Jack in charge of fighting against them. He managed to hold the Daleks back for a while — but then he was exterminated...

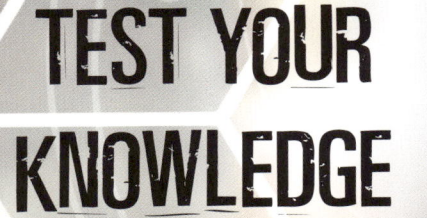

TEST YOUR KNOWLEDGE

1. WHAT YEAR DID CAPTAIN JACK MEET THE EMPTY CHILD?
   A. 1066
   B. 1941
   C. 5 billion

2. WHO WAS MARGARET BLAINE?
   A. The last survivor of the Great Time War
   B. A Time Agent who worked with Captain Jack
   C. A Slitheen pretending to be Mayor of Cardiff

3. WHAT IS INSIDE A DALEK'S PROTECTIVE CASING?
   A. A living Dalek creature
   B. Poisonous gas
   C. Baked beans

4. WHO FOUGHT AGAINST EACH OTHER IN THE GREAT TIME WAR?
   A. Earth and the Slitheen
   B. Daleks and Time Lords
   C. Arsenal and Chelsea

5. WHAT DID THE DALEKS DO TO CAPTAIN JACK?
   A. They exterminated him
   B. They took him out to a really good restaurant
   C. They questioned him about the Time Lords

294 THE LIVES AND TIMES OF JACK

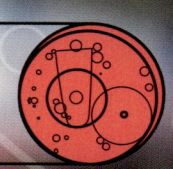

MYSTERIOUS CON MAN

When the Doctor and Rose first met Captain Jack Harkness he was in 1941, masquerading as an American volunteer in the RAF's 133 Squadron. Thinking the Doctor and Rose were Time Agents, he tried to sell them a Chula Warship. Only it wasn't actually a warship but an ambulance — Jack planned to blow it up before anyone found out. But the nanogenes — tiny little medical robots — from the ship had escaped and got out of control. They tried to turn everyone into a gas mask zombie. Luckily the Doctor was able to sort it all out and everyone was OK.

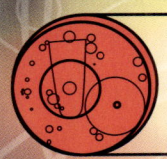

Jack risked his own life to stop a German bomb landing on the Chula Ship, and thought he was going to die when it exploded in his ship. But the Doctor and Rose arrived in the TARDIS and got him away to safety.

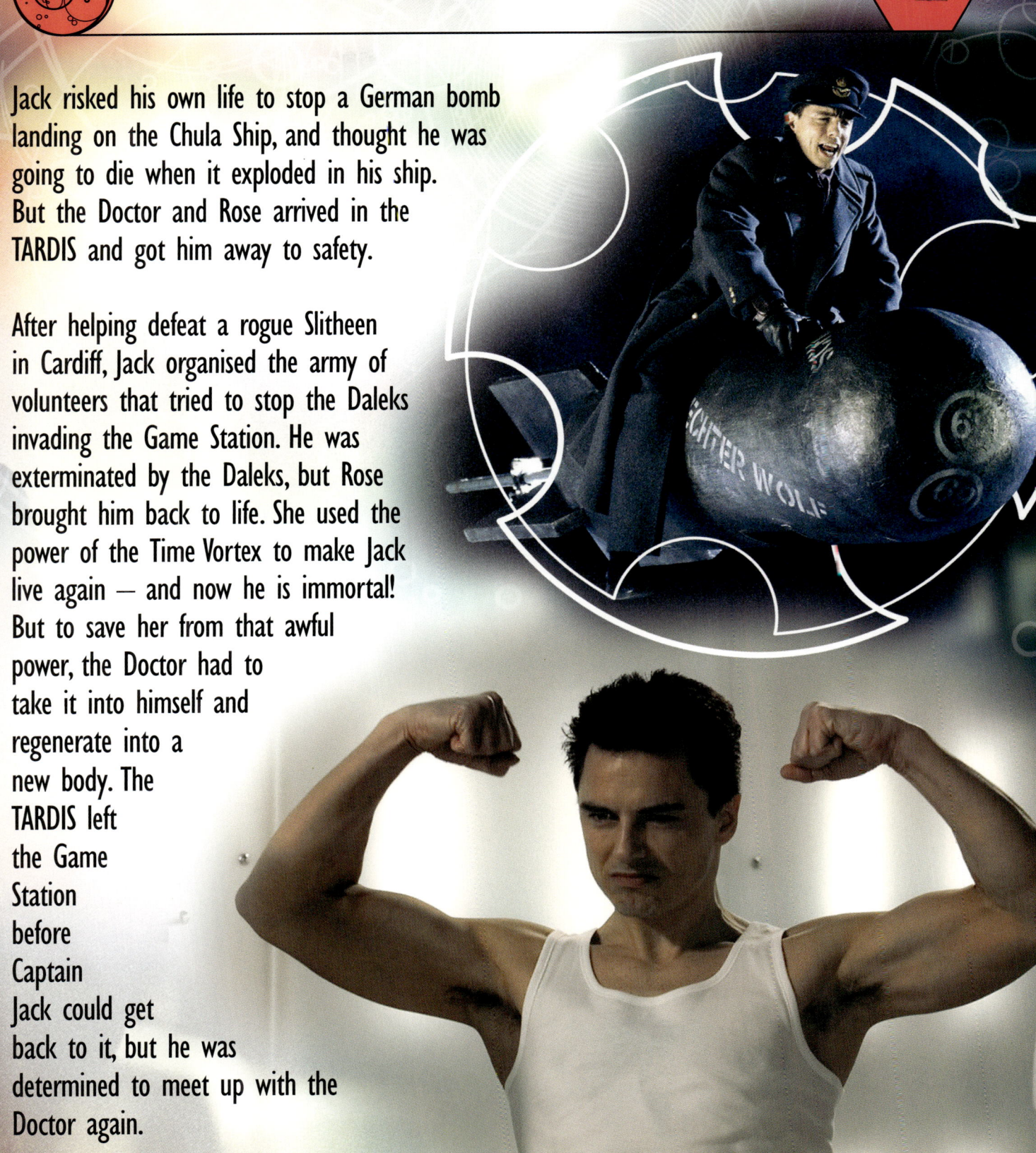

After helping defeat a rogue Slitheen in Cardiff, Jack organised the army of volunteers that tried to stop the Daleks invading the Game Station. He was exterminated by the Daleks, but Rose brought him back to life. She used the power of the Time Vortex to make Jack live again — and now he is immortal! But to save her from that awful power, the Doctor had to take it into himself and regenerate into a new body. The TARDIS left the Game Station before Captain Jack could get back to it, but he was determined to meet up with the Doctor again.

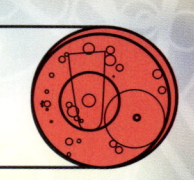

RELIVING THE PAST

Captain Jack used his Vortex manipulator to go back in time to look for the Doctor. He knew the Doctor would one day come to Cardiff to recharge the TARDIS using the time rift there, so that was where Jack planned to wait. He aimed for our time, but arrived in 1869. His Vortex Manipulator had burned out, so he had to wait over a hundred years for the Doctor.

In 1892, Captain Jack was on Ellis Island and got into a fight. He was shot through the heart — but he woke up again afterwards! Later he fell off a cliff, and one time he was trampled by horses. He died many times, during both world wars, and each time he came back from the dead. Having been saved by Rose, and given the power of the Time Vortex itself, Captain Jack was now indestructible.

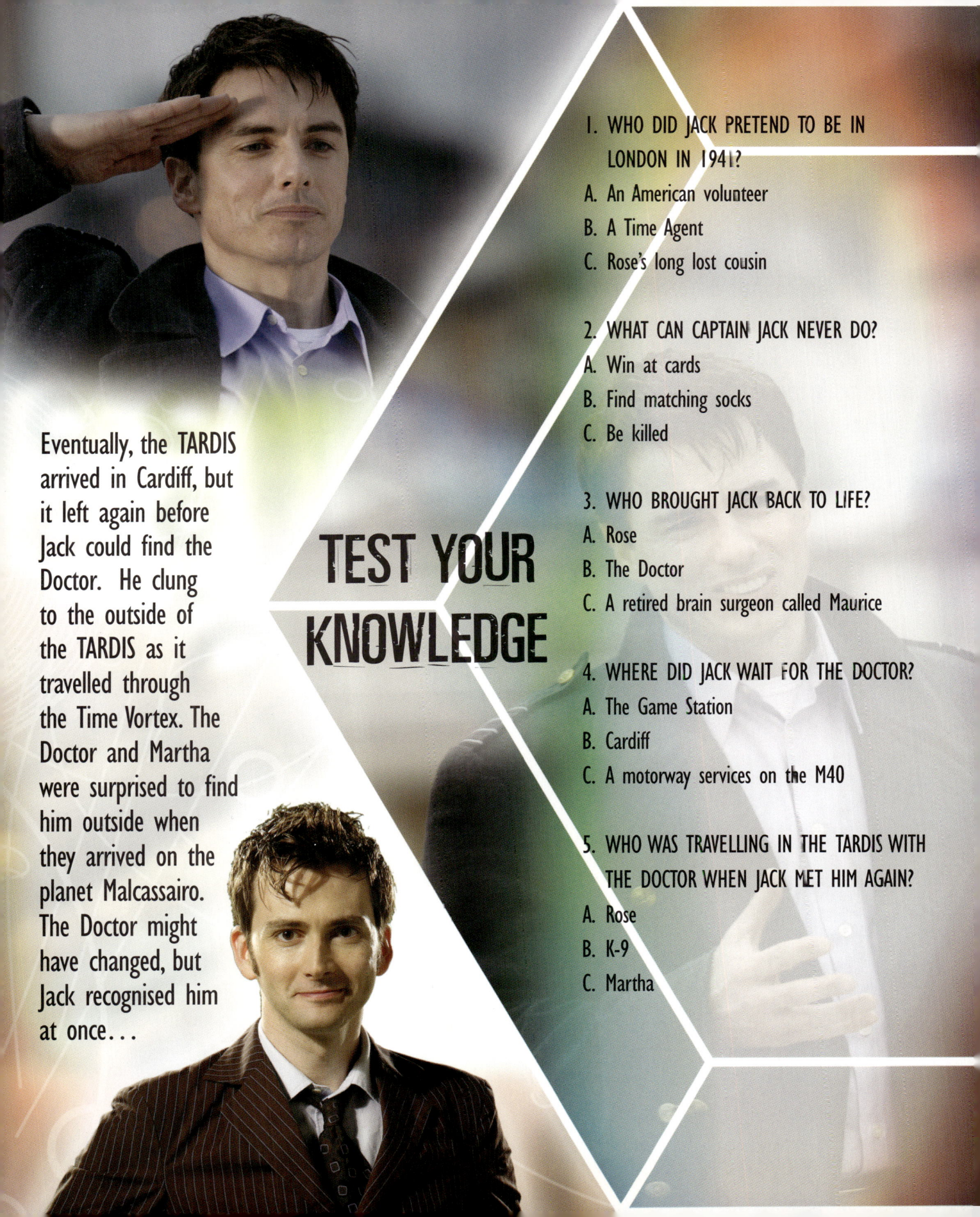

Eventually, the TARDIS arrived in Cardiff, but it left again before Jack could find the Doctor. He clung to the outside of the TARDIS as it travelled through the Time Vortex. The Doctor and Martha were surprised to find him outside when they arrived on the planet Malcassairo. The Doctor might have changed, but Jack recognised him at once…

TEST YOUR KNOWLEDGE

1. WHO DID JACK PRETEND TO BE IN LONDON IN 1941?
A. An American volunteer
B. A Time Agent
C. Rose's long lost cousin

2. WHAT CAN CAPTAIN JACK NEVER DO?
A. Win at cards
B. Find matching socks
C. Be killed

3. WHO BROUGHT JACK BACK TO LIFE?
A. Rose
B. The Doctor
C. A retired brain surgeon called Maurice

4. WHERE DID JACK WAIT FOR THE DOCTOR?
A. The Game Station
B. Cardiff
C. A motorway services on the M40

5. WHO WAS TRAVELLING IN THE TARDIS WITH THE DOCTOR WHEN JACK MET HIM AGAIN?
A. Rose
B. K-9
C. Martha

298 | JACK'S CAPABILITIES

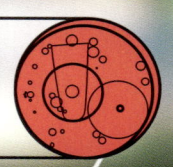

INVISIBLE SPACESHIP

When Jack first met the Doctor and Rose he had a spaceship that had active camouflage so it could become invisible. He had it tethered to Big Ben, so he wouldn't lose it! The ship's computer could make Jack's favourite cocktail, and he had a teleport back to the ship which was security-keyed to his molecular structure. Using the ship's om-com system he could transmit his voice to anything with a speaker.

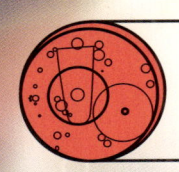

VORTEX MANIPULATOR

Captain Jack has a device on his wrist called a Vortex Manipulator. He's had it since he was a Time Agent, and it allows him to travel in time. Or rather, it did until it burned out. Its last working task was to take Jack from the Game Station in the far future to Earth in the 21st century. But he ended up stuck in 1869 instead.

The Doctor is not impressed with Jack's Vortex Manipulator. He said that comparing Jack's Manipulator to the TARDIS is like comparing a space hopper to a sports car!

HANDCUFFS

When the Doctor and his friends captured Blon Fel Fotch Pasameer-Day Slitheen, Jack lent the Doctor two rings that acted like handcuffs. The Doctor wore one, the Slitheen disguised as Margaret Blaine wore the other one. Then, if she then moved more than ten feet away from the Doctor she would have been electrocuted.

300

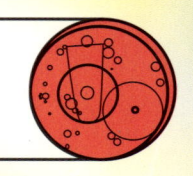

DOCTOR DETECTOR

Cardiff is a big place. Although Captain Jack knew that the Doctor would one day land the TARDIS over the Time Rift, he also wanted an early warning that the Doctor was on his way. He had missed several visits the Doctor made to Earth, so he wanted a way of knowing next time the Doctor was nearby.

On one visit, the Doctor defeated the Sycorax when they tried to invade Earth. He fought a duel against the Sycorax leader on the wing of their spaceship — the winner would decide the fate of the whole planet. The Doctor won, of course. But the Sycorax leader cut off the Doctor's hand! Luckily the Doctor had only just regenerated and so he was able to grow another one.

But the hand fell from the Sycorax ship and landed on top of a newsagent's shop in Dulwich, where Jack later found it. He kept it in a jar of special liquid — and if the liquid bubbled, that meant the Doctor was nearby.

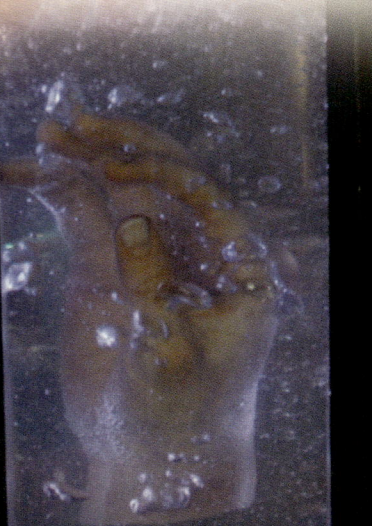

THE MAN WHO CANNOT BE KILLED

Jack's greatest ability is actually something he cannot do. Brought back from death by Rose Tyler using the power of the Time Vortex itself, Jack cannot be killed. He has survived being shot, falling off a cliff, trampled by horses…

So he was able to go into a room filled with deadly stet radiation to make sure Professor Yana's rocket could leave for Utopia — the radiation would kill anyone else, but not Jack. But it's a curse as well as a blessing — like the Doctor, Jack has seen friends grow old while he never changes…

TEST YOUR KNOWLEDGE

1. WHERE DID JACK WAIT FOR THE DOCTOR?
A. Cardiff
B. Manchester
C. Leeds

2. WHERE DID JACK LEAVE HIS INVISIBLE SPACESHIF?
A. In the Thames
B. Orbiting Asteroid Gamma Zed Nine Seven
C. Tethered to Big Ben

3. WHAT DOES THE DOCTOR THINK OF JACK'S VORTEX MANIPULATOR?
A. He thinks it's really neat and wants one himself
B. He thinks it is pretty rubbish compared to the TARDIS
C. He thinks it would be better if it was orange and purple

4. WHAT DOES JACK HAVE THAT TELLS HIM WHEN THE DOCTOR IS NEARBY?
A. A special pocket watch
B. A parrot called Montmorency
C. The Doctor's hand in a jar

5. WHY CAN'T JACK BE KILLED?
A. He has forgotten how to be
B. He was brought back to life by Rose
C. His mother was an immortal goddess

302 FURTHER ADVENTURES OF JACK

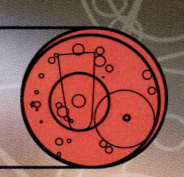

MEETING THE DOCTOR AGAIN

Captain Jack waited for over a hundred years for the Doctor to come back and find him. Just as he might have expected, Jack's reunion with the Doctor was not quiet and safe. On the planet Malcassairo, Captain Jack, the Doctor and Martha Jones found the last survivors of humanity trying to get to a new home — Utopia.

But, even though he didn't know it, Professor Yana — the only man who could save humanity — was actually the Doctor's oldest enemy. He was another Time Lord called the Master. With his memory restored, and determined to cause trouble, the Master stole the TARDIS and left Jack and his friends stranded and under attack by savages…

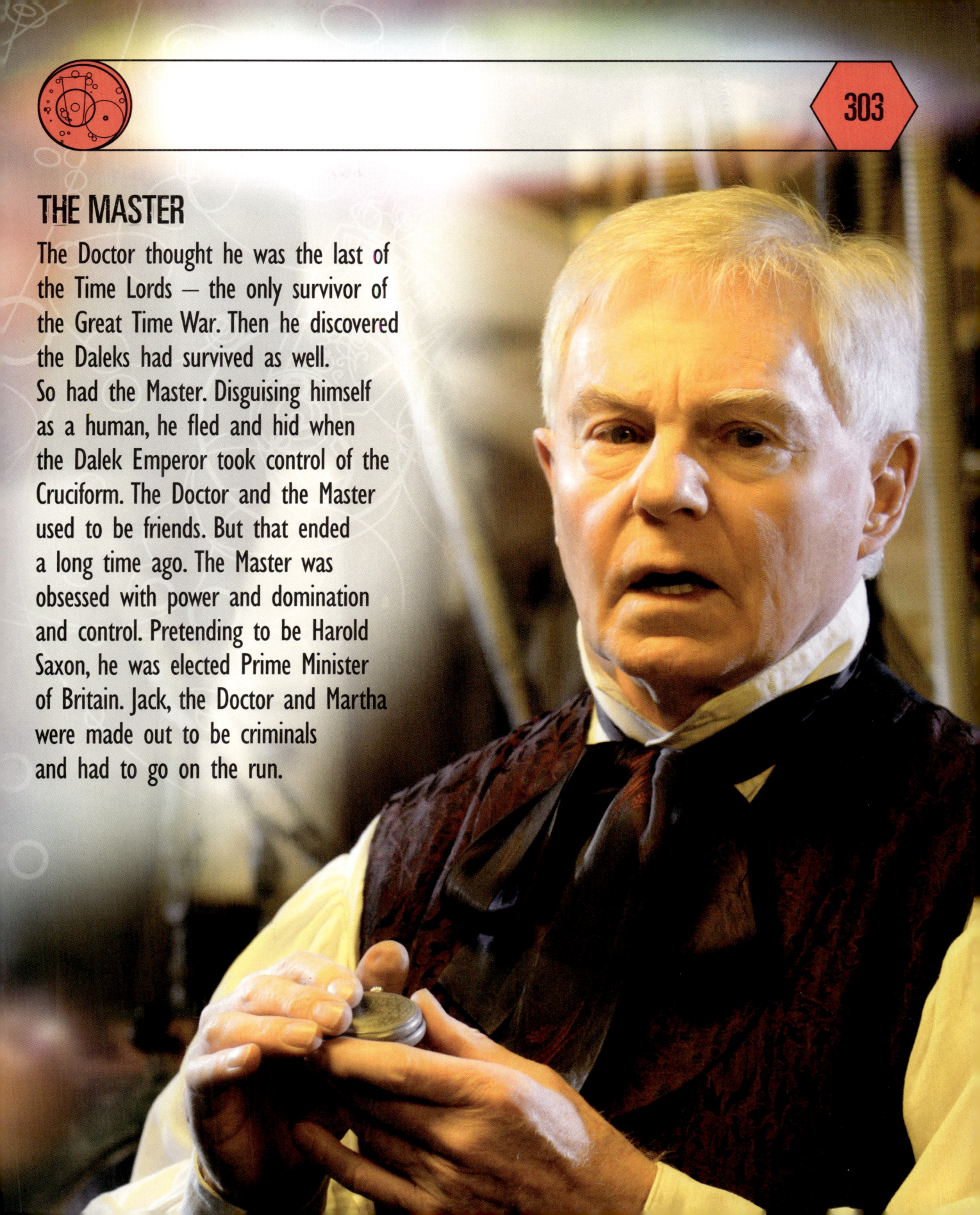

THE MASTER

The Doctor thought he was the last of the Time Lords — the only survivor of the Great Time War. Then he discovered the Daleks had survived as well. So had the Master. Disguising himself as a human, he fled and hid when the Dalek Emperor took control of the Cruciform. The Doctor and the Master used to be friends. But that ended a long time ago. The Master was obsessed with power and domination and control. Pretending to be Harold Saxon, he was elected Prime Minister of Britain. Jack, the Doctor and Martha were made out to be criminals and had to go on the run.

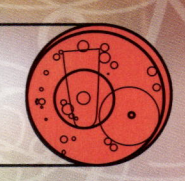

THE SPHERES

The Master claimed to have made contact with an alien race — metallic sphere creatures called the Toclafane. From the safety of the flying aircraft carrier Valiant, he brought six billion of the Spheres to invade Earth. Whole countries and continents of people were wiped out, and the survivors were enslaved. They were made to build great rocket ships that would wage war on the rest of the Universe. The Doctor and Jack were both held captive — only Martha could save the world.

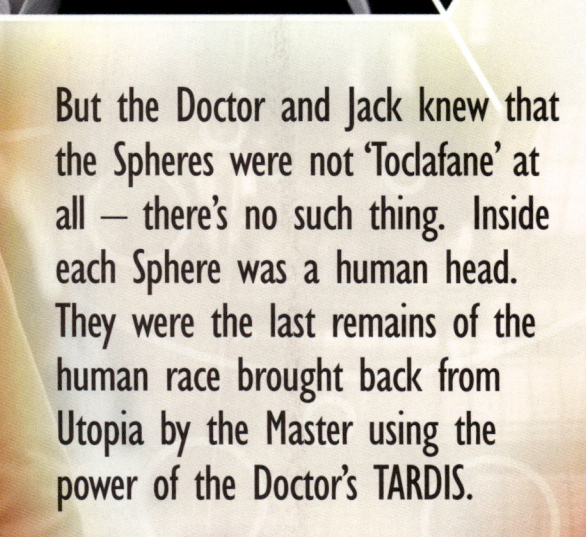

But the Doctor and Jack knew that the Spheres were not 'Toclafane' at all — there's no such thing. Inside each Sphere was a human head. They were the last remains of the human race brought back from Utopia by the Master using the power of the Doctor's TARDIS.

THE FUTURE?

With Jack's help, the Doctor and Martha finally defeated the Master. The invasion of the Spheres never happened and Earth was safe. But his experiences made Jack think about his responsibilities. While waiting for the Doctor he re-established Torchwood as a force for good, to combat alien invasion. He decided to go back and continue with this mission. He told the Doctor and Martha something that shocked them. Perhaps it is true, or maybe it is another of Jack's tall stories. He has realised that very slowly he is ageing, even though he cannot be killed. He wonders what will happen to him as he grows old with the universe. He remembers when he was the first Time Agent recruited from the Boeshane Peninsular — and how they nicknamed him the Face of Boe...

TEST YOUR KNOWLEDGE

1. WHAT WAS THE NAME OF THE NEW HOME FOR HUMANITY?
A. Toclafane
B. Malcassairo
C. Utopia

2. HOW DID THE MASTER HIDE AFTER THE TIME WAR?
A. Behind the sofa
B. He pretended to be human
C. He asked the Dalek Emperor for sanctuary

3. HOW DID THE DOCTOR KNOW THE MASTER?
A. They met on a bus
B. They are both Time Lords and used to be friends
C. They both arrived on the planet Malcassairo

4. WHAT WAS INSIDE EACH SPHERE?
A. A human head from the far future
B. Daleks
C. Nothing

5. WHAT LEGENDARY CREATURE MIGHT CAPTAIN JACK ONE DAY BECOME?
A. The Moxx of Balhoon
B. The Face of Boe
C. Emperor of the Daleks

TEST YOUR KNOWLEDGE

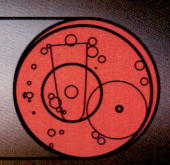

ANSWERS

Meet Captain Jack Harkness
1 (b) 2 (a) 3 (b) 4 (c) 5 (c)

Captain Jack's Friends
1 (a) 2 (c) 3 (b) 4 (b) 5 (a)

Captain Jack's Enemies
1 (b) 2 (c) 3 (a) 4 (b) 5 (a)

The Lives and Times of Jack
1 (a) 2 (c) 3 (a) 4 (b) 5 (c)

Jack's Capabilities
1 (a) 2 (c) 3 (b) 4 (c) 5 (b)

Further Adventures of Jack
1 (c) 2 (b) 3 (b) 4 (a) 5 (b)

DOCTOR·WHO

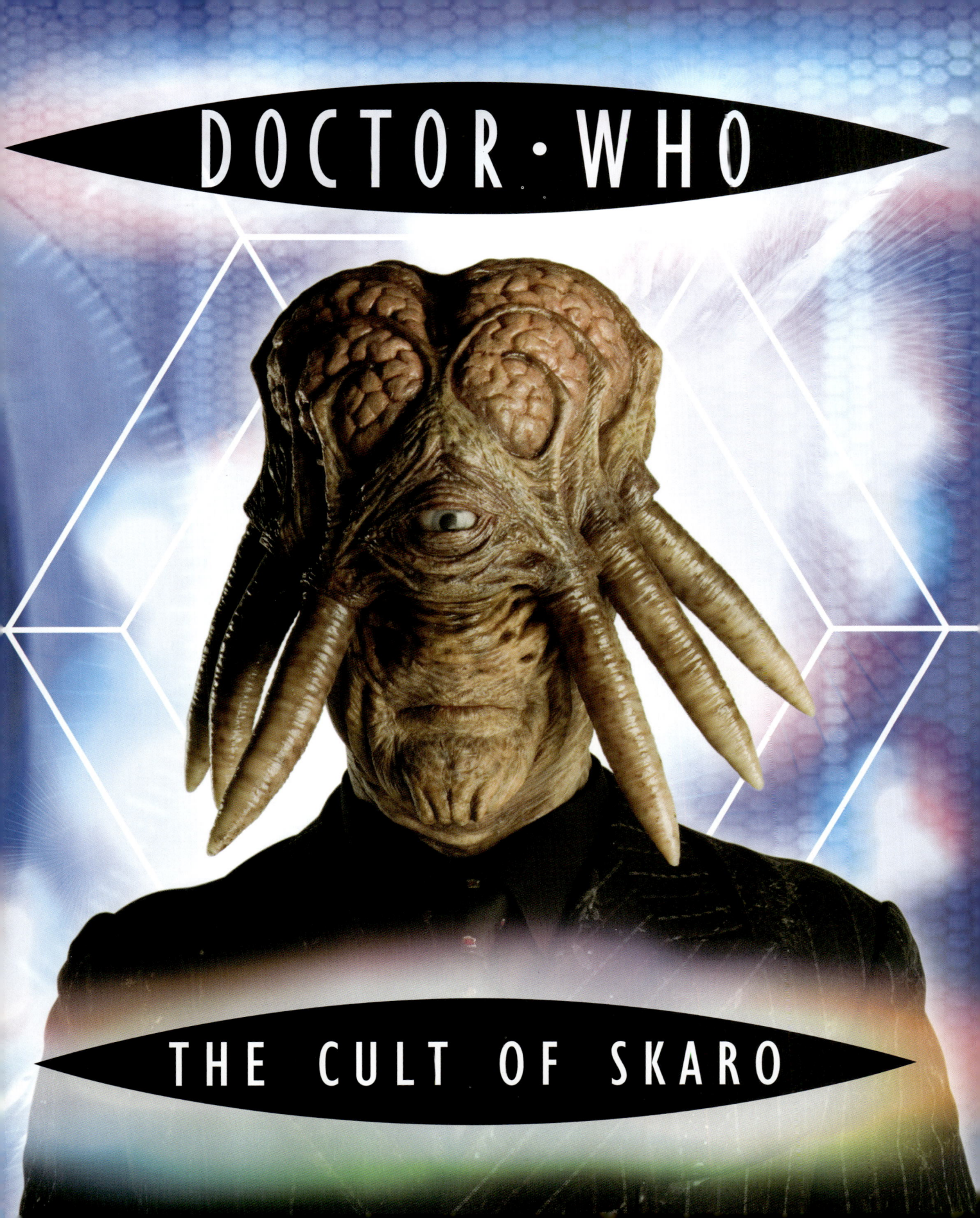

THE CULT OF SKARO

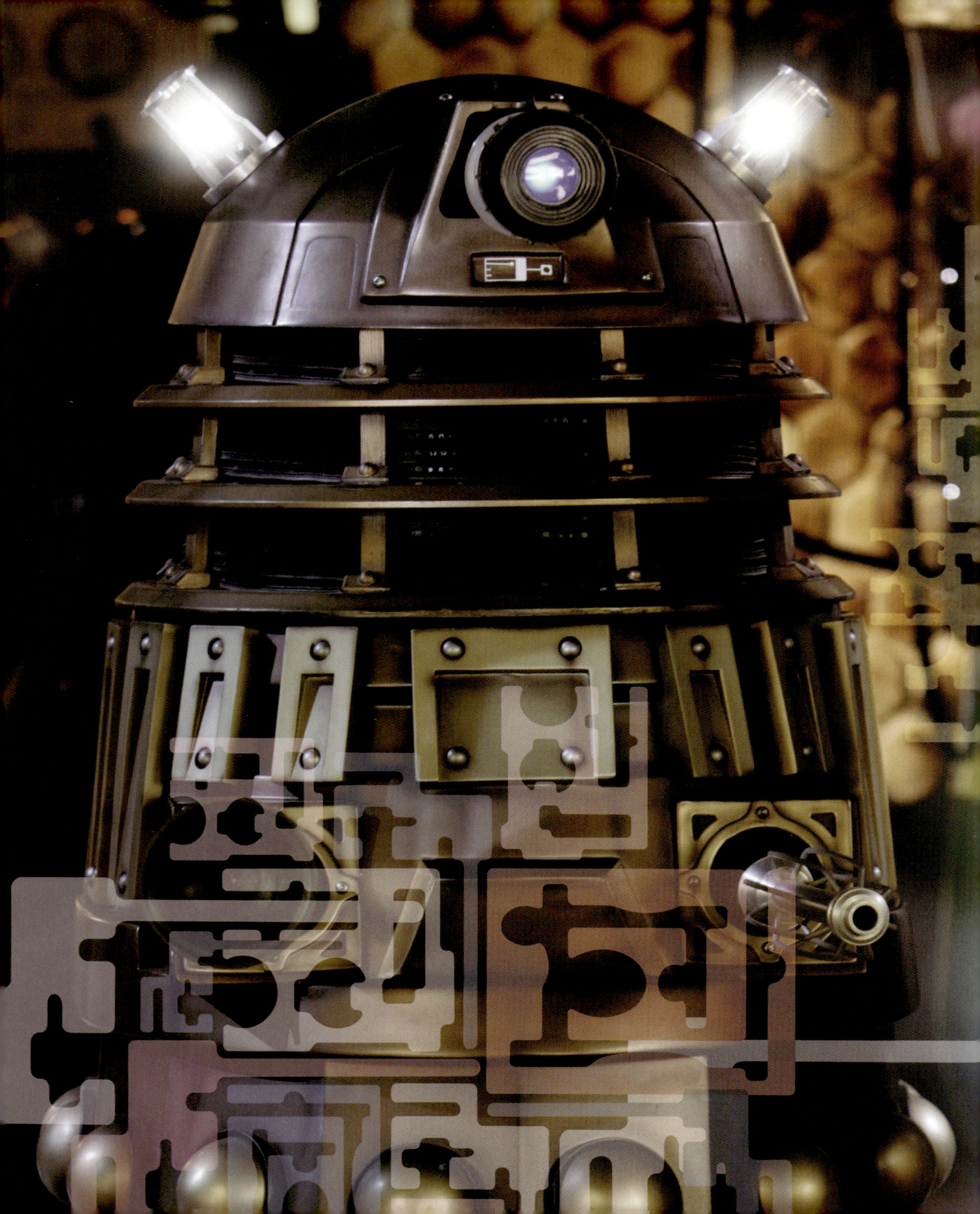

CONTENTS

Meet The Cult of Skaro

Introduction 310
Dalek Sec Data 312
Dalek Sec Hybrid Anatomy 314
◆ Test your knowledge

Cult of Skaro Allies

Emperor Dalek 316
The Daleks 317
Mr Diagoras 318
Pig Slaves 319
◆ Test your knowledge

Cult of Skaro Enemies

The Doctor 320
Martha 321
Tallulah and Laszlo 322
The Cybermen 323
◆ Test your knowledge

Cult of Skaro History

Origins 324
The Great Time War 325
Survivors 326
◆ Test your knowledge

Weapons and Technology

Transgenic Lab 328
Temporal Shift 329
The Void Ship and The Genesis Ark 330
Mind-Reading 331
◆ Test your knowledge

Cult of Skaro Adventures

The Battle of Canary Wharf 332
Daleks in Manhattan 334
◆ Test your knowledge

Test your knowledge Answers 336

310 MEET THE CULT OF SKARO

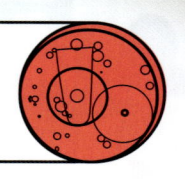

When the Great Time War with the Time Lords seemed inevitable, the Dalek Emperor set up The Cult of Skaro — a secret order of four Daleks whose job was to think the unthinkable and to dare to imagine. It was a plan so incredible that the Cult of Skaro became a myth — not even the Doctor was sure they really existed.

As important as the Dalek Emperor himself, the Cult of Skaro was made up of four Daleks who tried to think like the enemy, to get inside enemy minds and predict their strategies so as to give the Daleks an advantage in their wars.

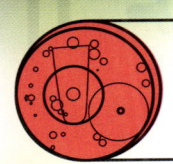

The Daleks in the Cult of Skaro even had names. They were called Thay, Sec, Jast, and Caan. They looked just like other Daleks — hideous mutated creatures living inside their armoured shells. Only Dalek Sec — leader of the Cult of Skaro was different. Sec had a distinctive black casing.

Their mission was to ensure the survival of the Dalek race at any cost, and they managed to survive the Great Time War. But even the other Daleks did not realize how far Dalek Sec was prepared to go to preserve the Daleks.

312 DALEK SEC DATA

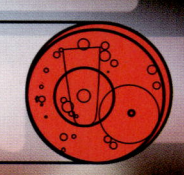

Name:	Dalek Sec
Title:	Leader of the Cult of Skaro
Height:	1.68m (5'6")
Home Planet:	Skaro (destroyed in the Great Time War)
Construction:	Metalert-enforced Dalekanium
Special abilities:	Mind-reading
Mode of transport:	Void ship/Temporal Shift
Mission:	To ensure the survival of the Dalek race

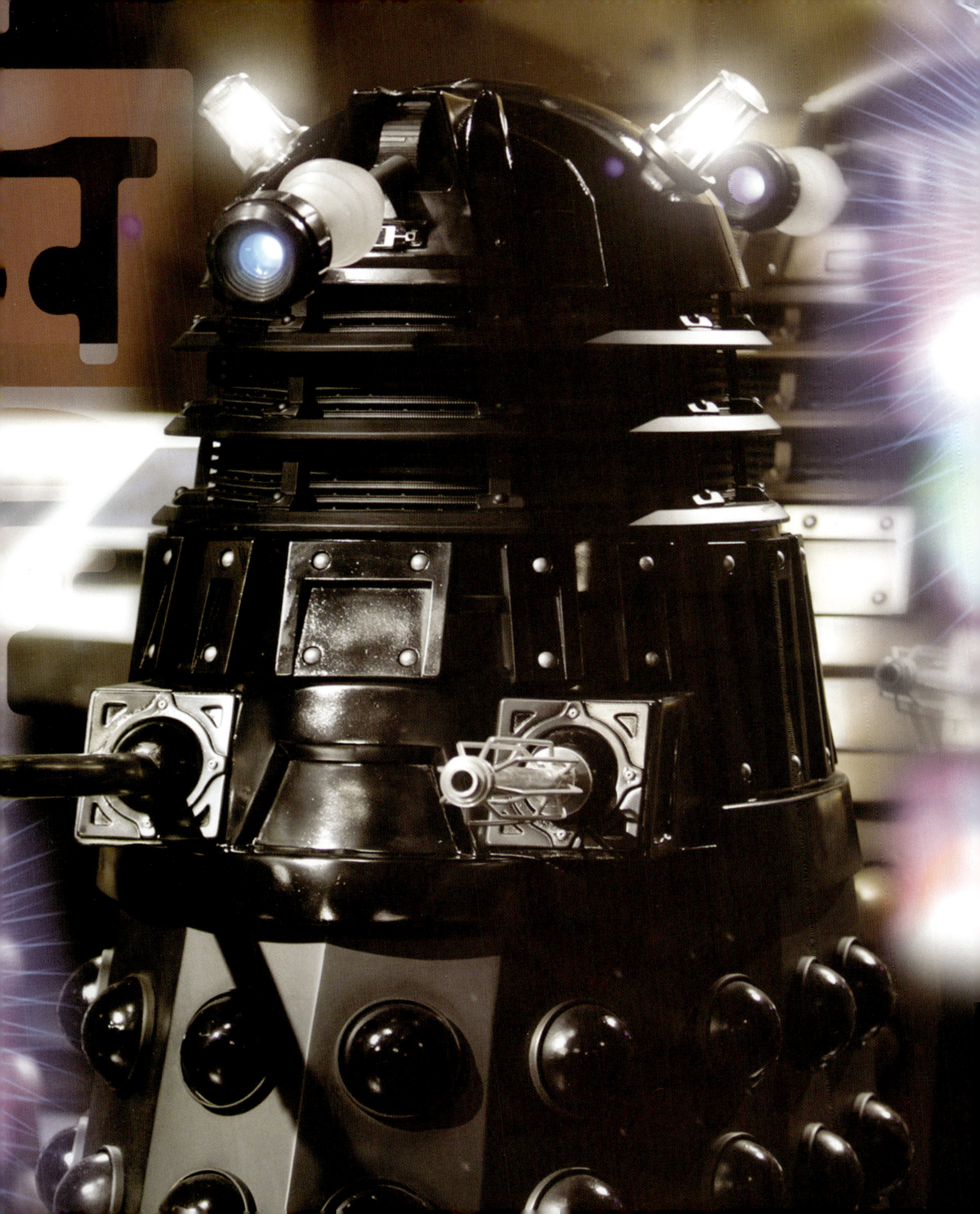

314 DALEK SEC HYBRID ANATOMY

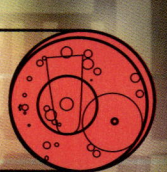

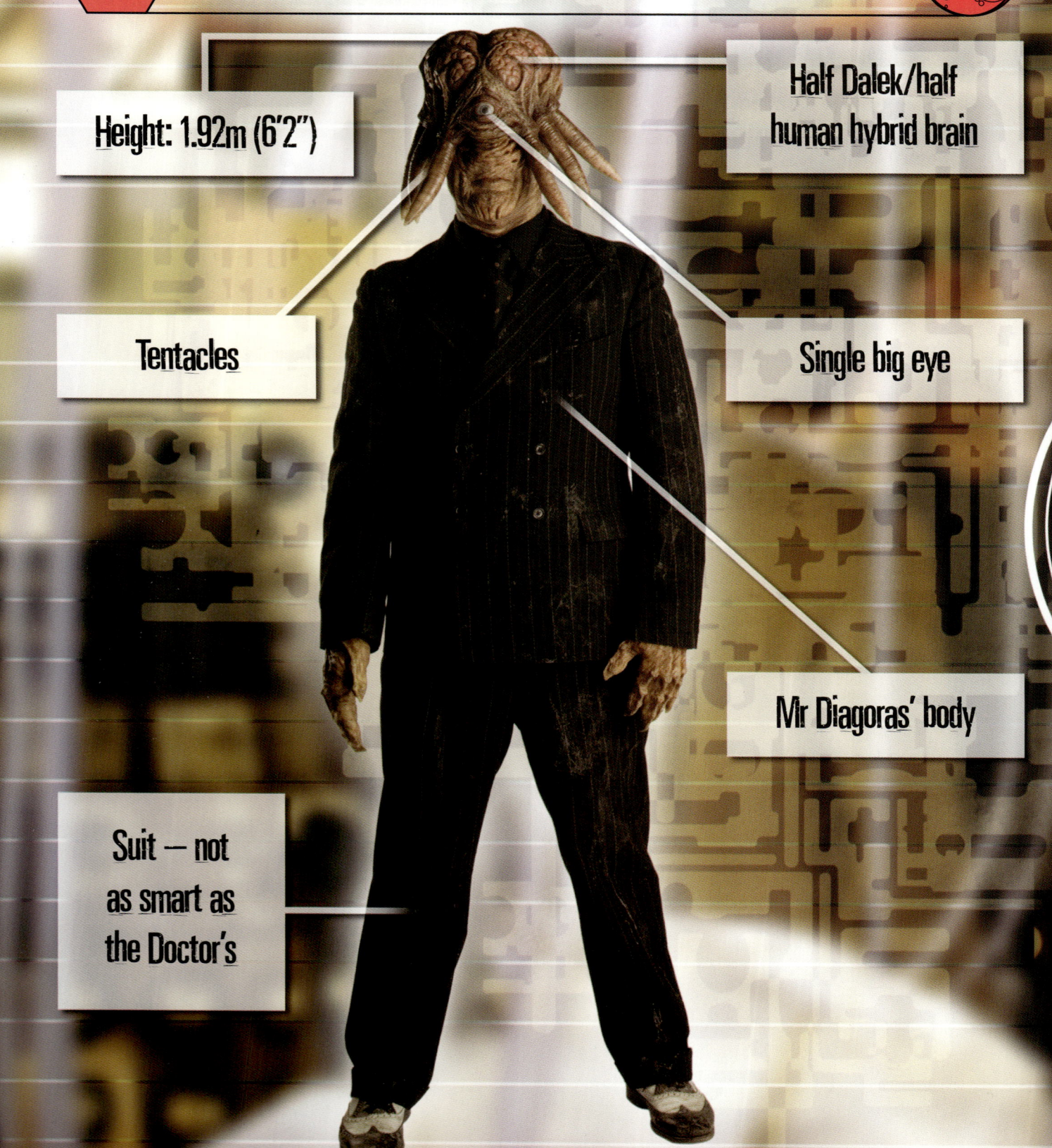

- Height: 1.92m (6'2")
- Tentacles
- Half Dalek/half human hybrid brain
- Single big eye
- Mr Diagoras' body
- Suit — not as smart as the Doctor's

TEST YOUR KNOWLEDGE

1. WHICH WAR DID THE CULT OF SKARO SURVIVE?
   A. World War II
   B. The Great Time War
   C. The War of the Worlds

2. HOW MANY DALEKS MAKE UP THE CULT OF SKARO?
   A. Three
   B. Five
   C. Four

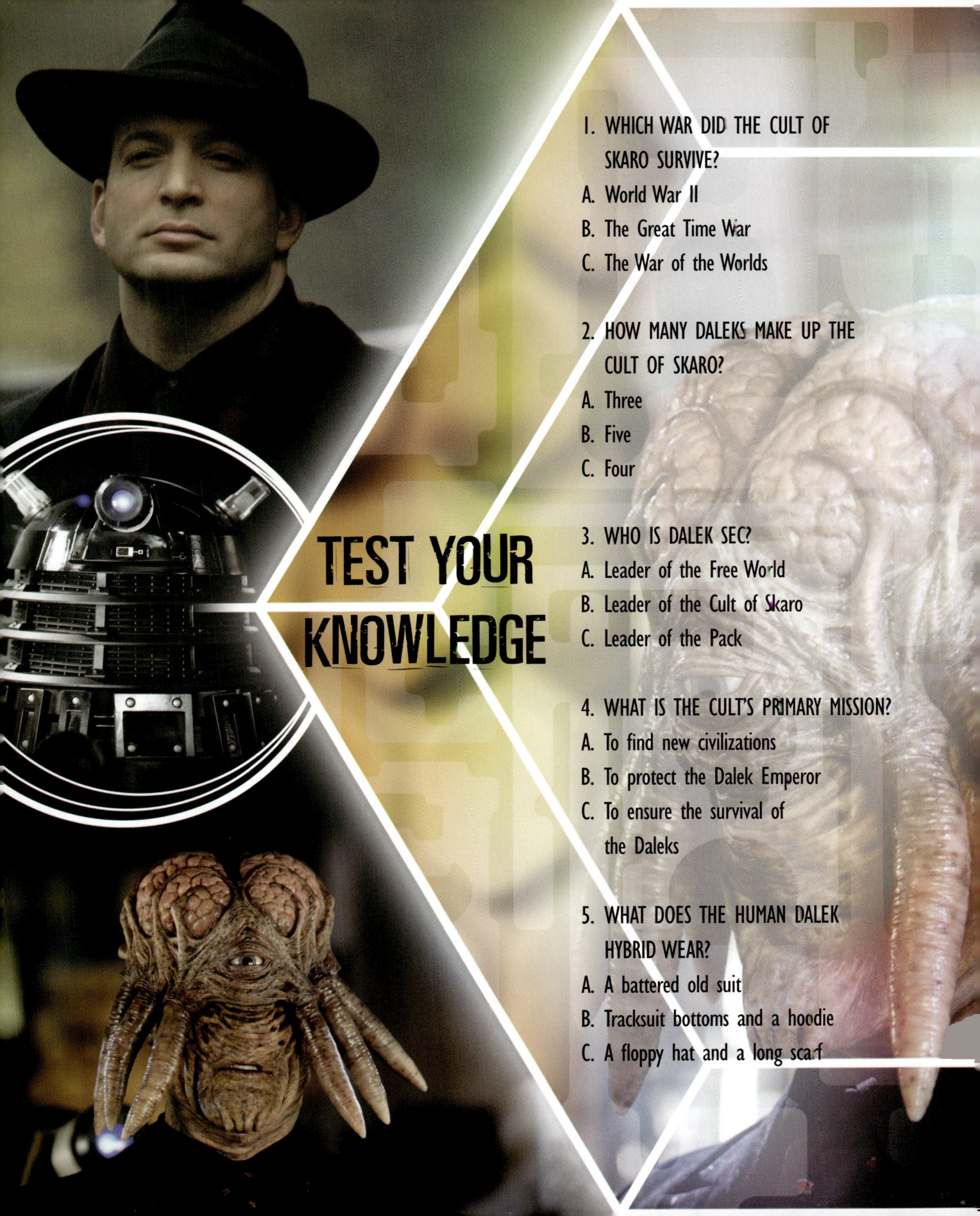

3. WHO IS DALEK SEC?
   A. Leader of the Free World
   B. Leader of the Cult of Skaro
   C. Leader of the Pack

4. WHAT IS THE CULT'S PRIMARY MISSION?
   A. To find new civilizations
   B. To protect the Dalek Emperor
   C. To ensure the survival of the Daleks

5. WHAT DOES THE HUMAN DALEK HYBRID WEAR?
   A. A battered old suit
   B. Tracksuit bottoms and a hoodie
   C. A floppy hat and a long scarf

316 CULT OF SKARO ALLIES

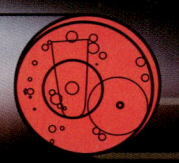

EMPEROR DALEK

The Cult of Skaro was set up by the Emperor Dalek and was allowed to carry out its work independent of the Emperor. While the Cult of Skaro devised a plan to make sure they survived the Great Time War, the Emperor led the Dalek armies against the Time Lords. Despite the millions of casualties on both sides, the Emperor survived, and slowly built up a new army of Daleks by converting humans kidnapped from a space station — the Game Station. But the Emperor did not know that he and his army were not the only Dalek survivors...

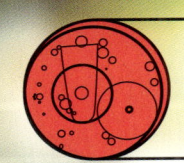

THE DALEKS

With the Emperor destroyed, it seemed as if the Daleks of the Cult of Skaro were the only Daleks still in existence. But they had rescued thousands of Dalek prisoners from the Time War, in the Time Lord prison they called the Genesis Ark.

These Daleks were released over London and joined the battle against the Cybermen over Canary Wharf. But they were sucked into the Void between universes by the Doctor and Rose.

After their escape to New York in 1930, the Cult of Skaro were forced to adopt a different plan to create more Daleks.

318

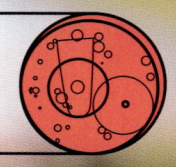

MR DIAGORAS

Believing themselves to be the last four Daleks in existence, the Cult of Skaro planned to evolve the Dalek race by bonding human and Dalek flesh.

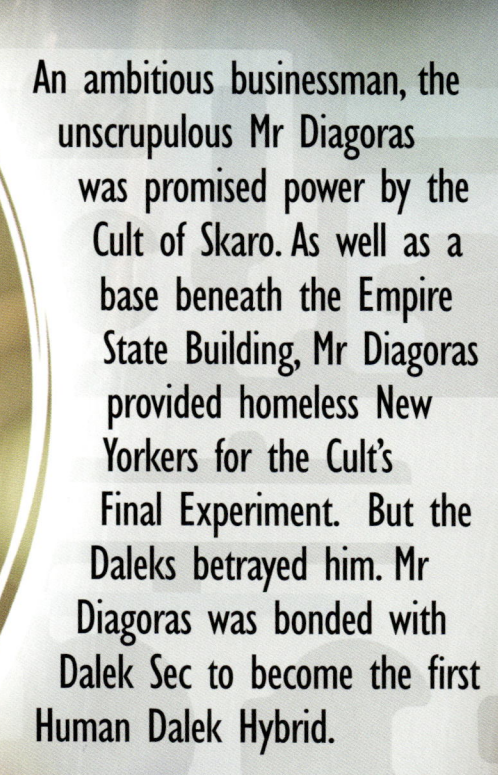

An ambitious businessman, the unscrupulous Mr Diagoras was promised power by the Cult of Skaro. As well as a base beneath the Empire State Building, Mr Diagoras provided homeless New Yorkers for the Cult's Final Experiment. But the Daleks betrayed him. Mr Diagoras was bonded with Dalek Sec to become the first Human Dalek Hybrid.

PIG SLAVES

The Cult of Skaro created an army of Pig Slaves out of homeless New Yorkers who were not considered clever enough to be used in the Final Experiment. Vicious and unthinking, the pig-faced creatures were trained to capture more humans, and to help the Daleks as they planned their Final Experiment.

Because of the way they were created, the Pig Slaves only lived for a few weeks — which suited their Dalek masters.

TEST YOUR KNOWLEDGE

1. WHO DESTROYED THE EMPEROR DALEK?
A. Rose Tyler
B. Martha Jones
C. The Doctor

2. WHAT WAS THE NAME OF THE CULT'S PROJECT?
A. The Human Slave Scheme
B. The Final Experiment
C. Mission Impossible

3. WHICH TWO CITIES DID THE CULT OF SKARO TRY TO TAKE OVER?
A. New York and Berlin
B. New York and London
C. London and Cardiff

4. WHAT AMERICAN LANDMARK WAS MR DIAGORAS IN CHARGE OF?
A. The Empire State Building
B. The Statue of Liberty
C. The Chrysler Building

5. HOW LONG DO PIG SLAVES LIVE?
A. About three days
B. About three months
C. About three weeks

320 CULT OF SKARO ENEMIES

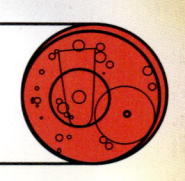

THE DOCTOR

The Doctor is the last of the Time Lords — the race that the Daleks fought in the Great Time War. He is their greatest enemy and has defeated them in many times and places. Every time he thinks he has won, they find a way to re-group and build an army once more. He lost his companion Rose in his last battle against the Cult of Skaro, and this made him even more determined to rid the universe of the Dalek threat.

The Doctor managed to prevent the Dalek's succeeding with their Final Experiment and the Daleks themselves destroyed the hybrid race they had created. But one Dalek, Dalek Caan, escaped. And he's out there, somewhere in the universe. Waiting and plotting against the Doctor.

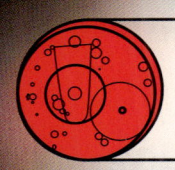

MARTHA JONES

Training to become a doctor, Martha Jones was more than a little surprised when her whole hospital was transported to the moon. But then she met the Doctor — and together they stood up to the alien Judoon and an evil Plasmavore.

In awe of the Time Lord, she managed to convince the lone traveller to take her "on the scenic route" back to her own time — with various exciting, and sometimes frightening, detours along the way. An intelligent woman, she is determined to prove herself to the Doctor. Her common sense and medical knowledge make her an ideal companion for the renegade Time Lord.

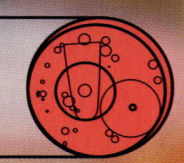

TALLULAH AND LASZLO

Laszlo was a stagehand at the Laurenzi Theatre when he was taken to the Daleks. He managed to escape before the process of turning him into a Pig Slave was completed, and returned to the theatre to see the woman he loved, Tallulah — a singer and dancer.

Together, Tallulah and Laszlo helped the Doctor and Martha defeat the Daleks' plans — Laszlo even managed to save the Doctor from a Dalek execution. After the Cult of Skaro was defeated and the threat was over, the Doctor was able to save Laszlo so that he and Tallulah could spend the rest of their lives together.

THE CYBERMEN

"Inferior species", "crude cybernetic constructs" — there's no doubt that the Cult of Skaro have little respect for their robotic enemies, the Cybermen. Despite both being ancient enemies of the Doctor, until recently, they had never encountered each other. The Battle of Canary Wharf saw the Daleks fight the Cybermen for the first time but there was only ever going to be one winner — the Doctor. Both races were sucked into the Void between universes, with only the Cult of Skaro managing to escape.

TEST YOUR KNOWLEDGE

1. WHO DID THE DOCTOR LOSE FIGHTING THE CULT OF SKARO?
A. K-9
B. Sarah Jane
C. Rose Tyler

2. WHAT WAS MARTHA JONES' JOB ON EARTH?
A. School teacher
B. Trainee doctor
C. Actress

3. WHERE DOES TALLULAH WORK?
A. The Laurenzi Theatre
B. The Globe
C. Tamworth Assembly Rooms

4. WHO CAPTURED LASZLO?
A. The Cybermen
B. The Pig Slaves
C. Dalek Caan

5. WHAT DID DALEK SEC CALL THE CYBERMEN?
A. "An inferior species"
B. "Jolly nice metal people"
C. "Hovering tin cans"

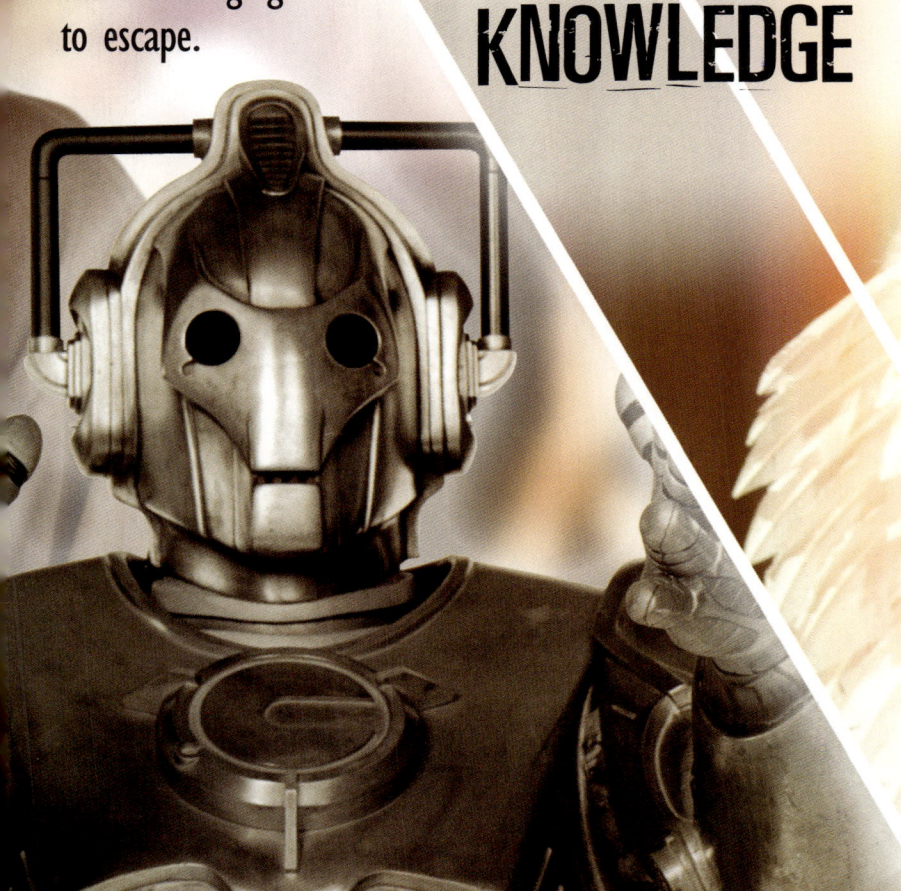

324 | CULT OF SKARO HISTORY

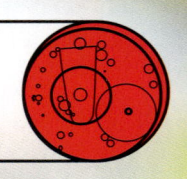

ORIGINS

The Cult of Skaro was set up by the Dalek Emperor as a secret order designed to think as their enemies think and devise new ways of keeping the Dalek race alive. The Emperor chose four Daleks to form the Cult, each of which had proven themselves to be outstanding in their fields - a Force Leader, a Commandant of a research facility, an Attack Squad Leader and a Commander.

The Dalek home planet, Skaro, was destroyed in the Great Time War, but the Cult of Skaro survived. The Doctor discovered that their fundamental DNA type is 467-989, but beyond that details of the mysterious Cult of Skaro are few and far between.

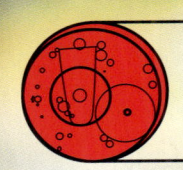

THE GREAT TIME WAR

The Daleks discovered that, long ago, the Time Lords of the planet Gallifrey had tried to prevent the Daleks ever existing. The Time Lords had sent the Doctor back in time to stop them being created. When they found out, the Daleks retaliated, and a full-scale war erupted within the Time Vortex and beyond that in the Ultimate Void.

Hiding in the Void between universes as the war raged, the Cult of Skaro waited and planned. They had with them a captured Time Lord prison — the Genesis Ark. When the Doctor defeated the Daleks who emerged from the Genesis Ark, the Daleks of the Cult of Skaro managed to escape using an emergency temporal shift to travel in time.

326

SURVIVORS

The shift took them to 1930s' New York, where they devised their most horrifying plan yet. With only four Daleks left, they had to find a way to ensure the future of their race. They created a way to bond with the very species that they have tried to destroy countless times - the human race. The Doctor managed to stop them once more, and destroy three members of the Cult. But the Dalek threat continues, as Dalek Caan survived.

TEST YOUR KNOWLEDGE

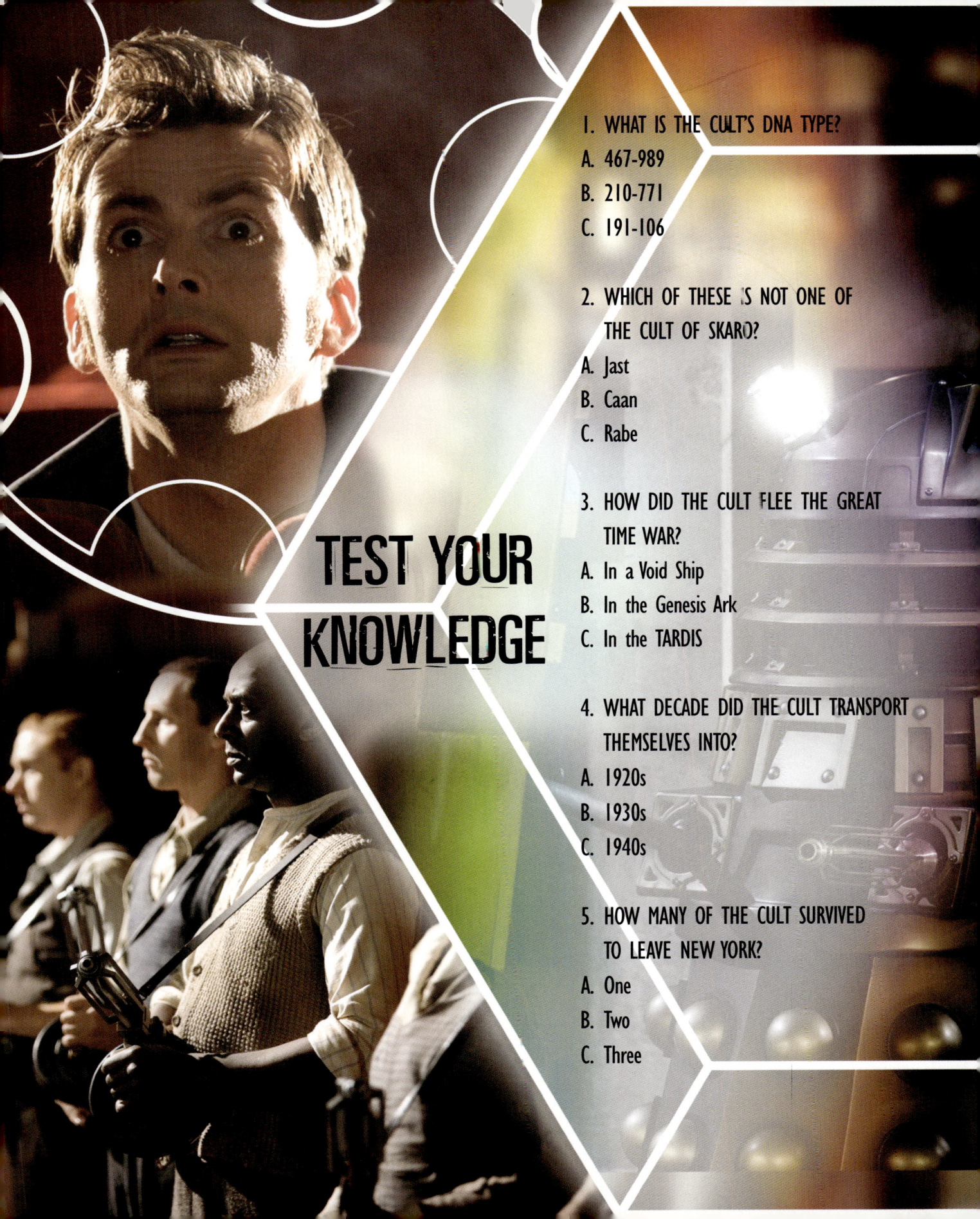

1. WHAT IS THE CULT'S DNA TYPE?
   A. 467-989
   B. 210-771
   C. 191-106

2. WHICH OF THESE IS NOT ONE OF THE CULT OF SKARO?
   A. Jast
   B. Caan
   C. Rabe

3. HOW DID THE CULT FLEE THE GREAT TIME WAR?
   A. In a Void Ship
   B. In the Genesis Ark
   C. In the TARDIS

4. WHAT DECADE DID THE CULT TRANSPORT THEMSELVES INTO?
   A. 1920s
   B. 1930s
   C. 1940s

5. HOW MANY OF THE CULT SURVIVED TO LEAVE NEW YORK?
   A. One
   B. Two
   C. Three

WEAPONS AND TECHNOLOGY

TRANSGENIC LAB

Hidden in the bowels of the Empire State Building, the Transgenic Lab represented the Cult of Skaro's best chance of survival.

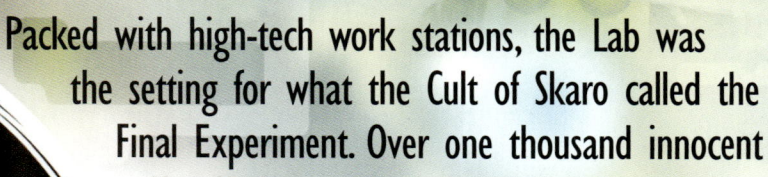

Packed with high-tech work stations, the Lab was the setting for what the Cult of Skaro called the Final Experiment. Over one thousand innocent New Yorkers with their minds wiped were placed on stretchers, silently waiting for their transformation into Human Dalek Hybrids.

Using liquid Chromatin Solution combined with powerful gamma rays from the Sun, the unconscious subjects had their DNA spliced with Dalek DNA, creating an entirely new race.

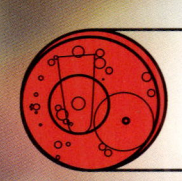

TEMPORAL SHIFT

In addition to their superior weaponry and powerful force field, the Daleks in the Cult of Skaro can also travel in time using a Temporal Shift. In an emergency, this can be used as a means of escape. But an Emergency Temporal Shift is unpredictable as the Dalek is unable to set specific coordinates.

When the Cult of Skaro escaped from the Battle of Canary Wharf, they ended up in New York in 1930. Dalek Caan again used an Emergency Temporal Shift to escape from the Doctor in New York — and he could have arrived at any point in Earth's history!

329

330

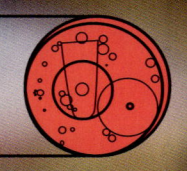

THE VOID SHIP AND THE GENESIS ARK

With the Great Time War between the Daleks and the Time Lords raging around them, the Cult of Skaro boarded a Void Ship and hid unnoticed in the space between dimensions.

They took with them an amazing piece of technology called the Genesis Ark. This Ark was actually a prison created by the Time Lords. Although it didn't appear to be very big, it was dimensionally transcendental, just like the TARDIS. It was much bigger on the inside and contained thousands of captured Daleks.

TEST YOUR KNOWLEDGE

1. **WHERE DID THE CULT OF SKARO CONDUCT THE FINAL EXPERIMENT?**
   A. The Transgenic Lab
   B. New Jersey
   C. Their home planet of Skaro

2. **WHAT WAS THE NAME OF THE LIQUID USED TO CREATE HUMAN DALEKS?**
   A. Gamma Solution
   B. Chromatin Solution
   C. Washing-up liquid

3. **HOW CAN THE CULT OF SKARO ESCAPE FROM DANGER?**
   A. By hiding behind the sofa
   B. By wearing a disguise
   C. By operating an Emergency Temporal Shift

4. **WHERE DID THE CULT HIDE WHEN THEY ESCAPED THE TIME WAR?**
   A. Under the sea
   B. Between dimensions
   C. A parallel world

5. **WHICH TIME LORD CREATION WAS STOLEN BY THE CULT OF SKARO?**
   A. The Genesis Ark
   B. Noah's Ark
   C. The Ark in Space

MIND-READING

The best way to think as your enemy does is to read their thoughts! The Cult of Skaro Daleks are capable of extracting human brainwaves.

They can also initiate an Intelligence Scan — something that came in very handy when deciding who would become a Pig Slave and who would become a Human Dalek. Only the cleverest humans were considered worthy of having their DNA spliced with the Daleks.

332 CULT OF SKARO ADVENTURES

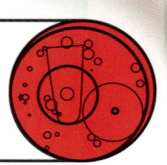

THE BATTLE OF CANARY WHARF

The Doctor thought that the Daleks had all been destroyed in the Great Time War - apart from the one which fell to Earth, that he met in Van Statten's museum. When the Cybermen came through to Earth from a parallel world, they were joined by a strange sphere. The sphere contained the four Daleks of the Cult of Skaro and the Genesis Ark. The Cult had hidden in the Void between universes, waiting for the right time to open the Ark and release the army of Daleks imprisoned inside.

333

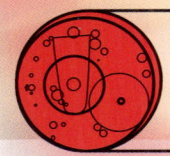

Both the Daleks and the Cybermen thought the Earth should be theirs. The Cybermen suggested an alliance of their forces, together they could upgrade the whole universe. But the Cult of Skaro knew the Cybermen were an inferior species and chose to destroy them instead. The Doctor defeated all of them by sending them back into the Void. Only the Cult of Skaro managed to escape.

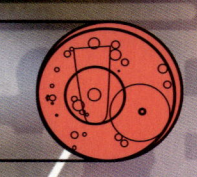

DALEKS IN MANHATTAN

Powerless after escaping the battle, the Cult of Skaro materialized in 1930s' New York. With the help of an army of Pig Slaves, the last of the Daleks collected as many people as possible to take part in the Final Experiment - making a new race of Human Daleks.

The leader of the Cult of Skaro, Sec, was genetically bonded with Mr Diagoras to form Human Dalek Sec. But with the human body came a more human away of thinking, and the other Daleks began to doubt Sec's ability to lead them. Daleks Thay, Jast and Caan rebelled against Sec, and he was destroyed, saving the Doctor from extermination.

To make their new race, the Cult of Skaro kidnapped over 1000 humans, performed genetic experiments on them, and used gamma radiation to bring them back to life as Human Daleks. But the Doctor got in the way of their experiment and part of his Time Lord DNA bonded with the Human Daleks. When the Daleks ordered their new race to destroy the Doctor, they refused and attacked the Cult of Skaro instead. Only Dalek Caan survived, performing an Emergency Temporal Shift to escape once again.

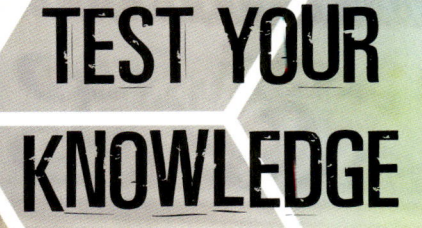

The last surviving member of the Cult of Skaro flew back into the Time War unprotected and rescued Davros from the jaws of the Nightmare Child. He saw time in all its majesty and promised Davros that the Daleks would be the masters of the universe. But instead Caan caused their destruction.

TEST YOUR KNOWLEDGE

1. WHERE WAS THE FIRST DALEK THAT THE DOCTOR MET AFTER THE GREAT TIME WAR?
   A. Van Statten's museum
   B. The Dalek planet, Skaro
   C. Shopping in the supermarket

2. WHAT DID THE CULT OF SKARO RELEASE FROM THE GENESIS ARK?
   A. The Genesis Device
   B. A Void Ship
   C. An army of Daleks

3. WHAT ANIMAL DO THE DALEK SLAVES LOOK LIKE?
   A. Bears
   B. Kangaroos
   C. Pigs

4. HOW MANY HUMANS DID THE CULT KIDNAP?
   A. More than 10
   B. Over 1,000
   C. Almost 10,000

5. WHOSE DNA GOT MIXED UP WITH THE HUMAN DALEKS?
   A. Martha's
   B. Tallulah's
   C. The Doctor's

336 TEST YOUR KNOWLEDGE

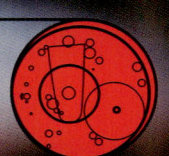

ANSWERS

Meet the Cult of Skaro
1 (b) 2 (c) 3 (b) 4 (c) 5 (a)

Cult of Skaro allies
1 (a) 2 (b) 3 (b) 4 (a) 5 (c)

Cult of Skaro Enemies
1 (c) 2 (b) 3 (a) 4 (b) 5 (a)

History of the Cult of Skaro
1 (a) 2 (c) 3 (a) 4 (b) 5 (a)

Weapons and technology
1 (a) 2 (b) 3 (c) 4 (b) 5 (a)

Adventures of the Cult of Skaro
1 (a) 2 (c) 3 (c) 4 (b) 5 (c)

DOCTOR·WHO

THE TARDIS

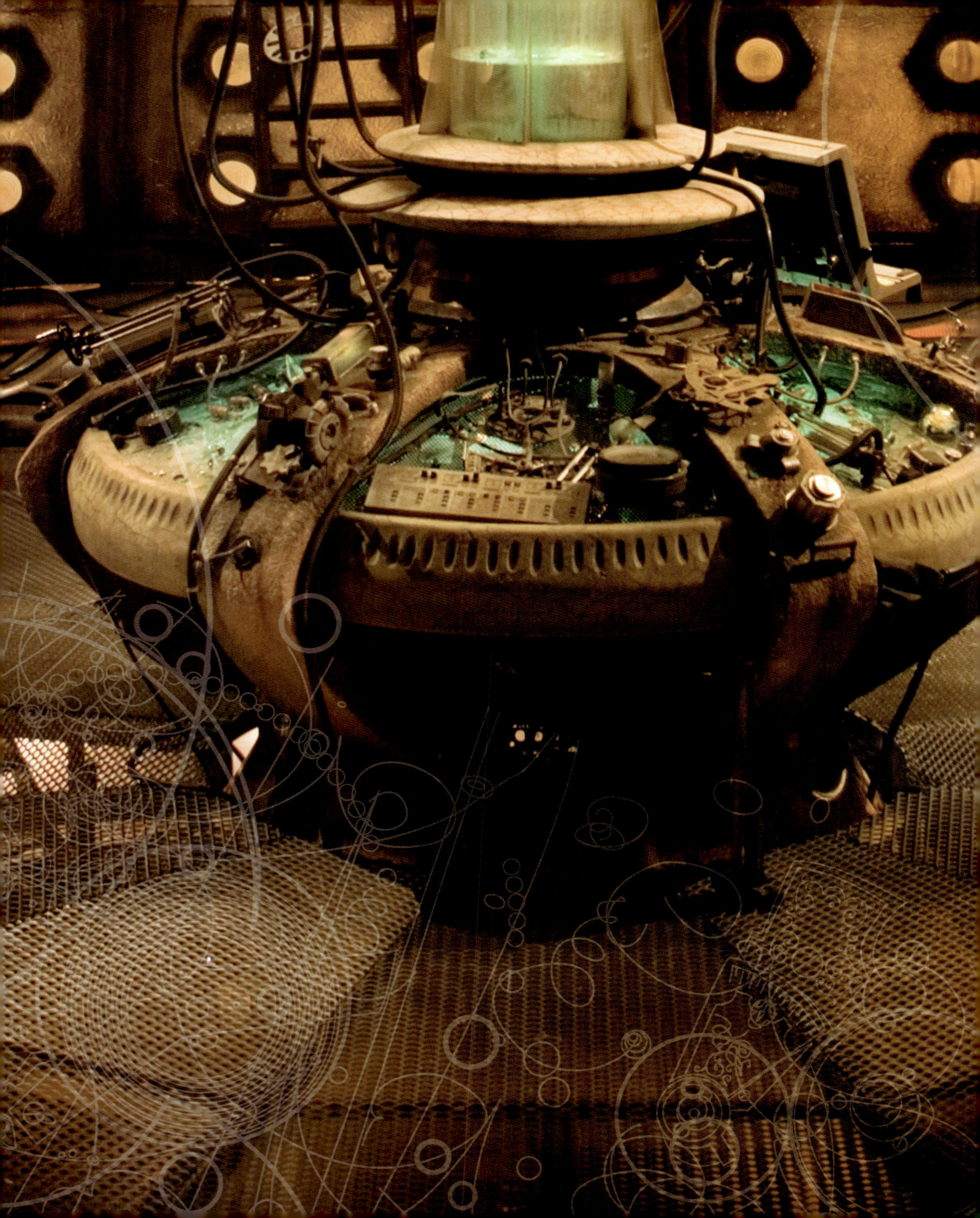

CONTENTS

Meet the TARDIS
Introduction 340
TARDIS Data 342
TARDIS Anatomy 344
◆ Test your knowledge

TARDIS Travellers
The Doctor 346
Martha 347
Donna 347
Captain Jack 348
Rose 349
◆ Test your knowledge

TARDIS Enemies
The Reapers 350
The Sycorax 350
The Daleks 351
The Family of Blood 352
The Weeping Angels 352
The Master 353
◆ Test your knowledge

TARDIS Origins
The Power of the Time Lords 354
The Heart of the TARDIS 355
Is the TARDIS alive? 356
The Last TARDIS? 357
◆ Test your knowledge

Transport and Technology
Time and Space Travel/Fuel 358
Dimensionally Transcendental 359
The Chameleon Circuit and Arch 360
Translation Circuit 361
◆ Test your knowledge

Adventures in Time and Space
The Parting of the Ways 362
The Runaway Bride 363
Human Nature/The Family of Blood 364
Utopia 365
◆ Test your knowledge

Test your knowledge Answers 366

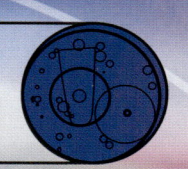

340 | MEET THE TARDIS

The TARDIS might look like an old police telephone box, but the unassuming blue wooden box hides so much more. It's a spaceship. It's a time machine. It's the Doctor's home and his best friend.

The initials stand for Time And Relative Dimension In Space. It can dematerialise in one place and materialise in any time or on any planet that the Doctor chooses. Sometimes, the TARDIS chooses for him and leads him into all kinds of adventures! The first thing the Doctor's companions notice about the TARDIS is that it's much bigger on the inside than the outside. It's because it uses amazing Time Lord technology that makes it dimensionally transcendental. It was quite a shock to Martha, but she soon got used to it and settled down for the ride of a lifetime.

The TARDIS contains any number of rooms and everything the Doctor might ever need is stored inside. When he regenerated into his tenth body, he searched through the vast wardrobe to find a suitable outfit for his new personality. This huge store of clothes is especially useful when visiting historical times, as it allows the Doctor and his companions to dress up and blend in with the locals, without attracting too much attention in their 21st century clothes! The Doctor even managed to produce a scooter from somewhere deep within the TARDIS, when he and Rose visited the 1950s.

342 TARDIS DATA

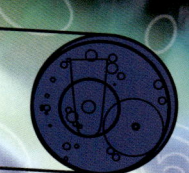

Name: TARDIS, which stands for Time And Relative Dimension in Space

Age: Over 900 years old, like the Doctor

Owner: The Doctor

Size: The TARDIS is bigger on the inside than the outside!

Current Appearance: 1950s police telephone box

POLICE PUBLIC CALL BOX
POLICE PUBLIC CALL BOX
POLICE TELEPHONE
FREE
FOR USE OF
PUBLIC
ADVICE & ASSISTANCE
OBTAINABLE IMMEDIATELY
OFFICER & CARS
RESPOND TO ALL CALLS
PULL TO OPEN

344 TARDIS ANATOMY

Glass column contains the Time Rotor, which lights up and moves when the TARDIS is in flight

TARDIS console

Emergency hammer

TEST YOUR KNOWLEDGE

1. WHAT DOES TARDIS STAND FOR?
   A. Take A Ride Down Inverness Street
   B. Time And Relative Dimension in Space
   C. Tell Aliens Rose Died in Scotland

2. HOW OLD IS THE TARDIS?
   A. Over 900 years
   B. 92 years
   C. It's brand new

3. WHERE IS THE TIME ROTOR?
   A. In the glass column on the console
   B. In the Doctor's pocket
   C. On Earth

4. WHAT DOES THE TARDIS LOOK LIKE?
   A. A police telephone box
   B. A large rock
   C. A sweet shop

5. WHAT DOES 'DIMENSIONALLY TRANSCENDENTAL MEAN?
   A. It's smaller on the inside
   B. It's bigger on the inside
   C. It's the same on the inside

Seats for bumpy rides

346 | TARDIS TRAVELLERS

THE DOCTOR

After the Doctor survived the Great Time War, the TARDIS was one of the few things that remained of his destroyed home planet, Gallifrey. The TARDIS is the Doctor's best friend - after all, they've been travelling together for hundreds of years. She has accompanied him through many adventures and several different bodies! The TARDIS is an important part of the Doctor's ability to regenerate and he couldn't survive without her. One of the worst moments of the Doctor's long life was watching the TARDIS doors close as his ancient enemy the Master stole her from him.

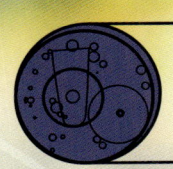

MARTHA

Martha's first impression of the TARDIS was just like every other human's who has entered it - she couldn't believe it was really bigger on the inside! She was surprised to see that the TARDIS has no crew and the Doctor travels alone. She soon got used to the idea though, and loves travelling through time and space with the Doctor.

DONNA

Donna was very surprised to find herself in the TARDIS! She'd been filled with Huon energy as part of an alien plot. The heart of the TARDIS also contains Huon Particles, and the two sets of Particles magnetised to pull Donna into the TARDIS. She thought she'd been abducted by a Martian, but the Doctor helped her escape from the real alien threat, the Empress of the Racnoss.

CAPTAIN JACK HARKNESS

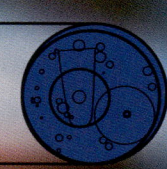

Captain Jack's travels in the TARDIS began when he met the Doctor during World War II and his own spaceship was destroyed. When Rose used the Time Vortex to bring him back to life after he was killed by the Daleks, he was left behind on the Game Station and thought he'd never see the Doctor again. The Time Vortex made Jack indestructible and he made his way back to Earth and waited over 100 years for the Doctor to return for him. When he finally heard the grinding of the ancient engines, he hitched a ride on the outside of the TARDIS to the year one hundred trillion - the end of the universe - and helped the Doctor and Martha to defeat the Master.

ROSE

Only Rose's connection to the TARDIS comes anywhere close to the Doctor's. When he thought her life was in danger on the Game Station, he used the TARDIS to send her home. But Rose couldn't leave him and she forced the TARDIS console open. The Time Vortex inside flowed into her, taking her back to the Doctor and allowing her to see all of time and space. She destroyed the Daleks and their Emperor. But the energy of the Vortex was killing her, so the Doctor took it into himself to save her, which caused him to regenerate.

TEST YOUR KNOWLEDGE

1. WHO STOLE THE TARDIS FROM THE DOCTOR?
A. Martha
B. Captain Jack
C. The Master

2. WHEN DID CAPTAIN JACK MEET THE DOCTOR?
A. During World War II
B. Last Tuesday
C. Christmas Day

3. WHICH PART OF THE TARDIS DID ROSE BREAK OPEN?
A. The doors
B. The console
C. The telephone

4. WHAT PULLED DONNA INTO THE TARDIS?
A. Huon particles
B. The Doctor
C. Martians

5. WHAT COULDN'T THE DOCTOR DO WITHOUT THE TARDIS?
A. Cook
B. Survive
C. Knit

350 TARDIS ENEMIES

THE REAPERS

When Rose created a paradox in time by going into the past and saving her dad's life, the TARDIS suffered. The Doctor opened the doors to discover it had turned into an empty wooden box. Only when Pete Tyler died as he should have, did the TARDIS return to normal.

THE SYCORAX

While the Tenth Doctor was recovering from his regeneration, the Sycorax teleported the TARDIS, along with Rose and members of the British government on to their ship. The TARDIS protected the unconscious Doctor from the alien invaders, but its translation circuits couldn't operate while the Doctor slept.

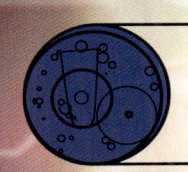

THE DALEKS

Any enemy of the Doctor's is an enemy of the TARDIS, and the Daleks are one of his greatest foes. He's come up against them many times, but it's not often they actually make it inside the TARDIS! When the Daleks captured Rose on the Game Station, Captain Jack and the Doctor were so quick to rush to her rescue that they materialised the TARDIS around a Dalek, as well as Rose. Jack destroyed the lone Dalek with his defabricator and they used the Slitheen extrapolator to protect themselves and the TARDIS from the remaining Daleks. Rose was able to use the powers of the heart of the TARDIS to destroy the Daleks and their Emperor.

THE FAMILY OF BLOOD

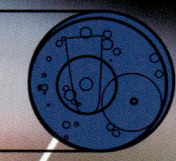

The Family of Blood used a stolen Time Agent's Vortex Manipulator to track the Doctor and his TARDIS through time and space. The Doctor was able to put the TARDIS on emergency power to hide itself from them, while he hid his own identity in a Time Lord pocket watch. The Family wanted his Gallifreyan life force to help them live forever.

THE WEEPING ANGELS

The Weeping Angels sent the Doctor and Martha back into the past, then stole his TARDIS. They wanted to feast on the time energy inside, but they couldn't open the doors without the key. Sally Sparrow helped to return the TARDIS to the Doctor and turn the Angels to stone, before they could do any damage.

THE MASTER

The Doctor thought his oldest enemy, the Master, had died in the Great Time War along with the rest of the Time Lords. When the Face of Boe said to him "You are not alone.", the last thing the Doctor expected was that the Master had survived. He was living in the far distant future, using the Time Lord technique of hiding his alien identity in a very special pocket watch. He was unaware of his true identity until the Doctor arrived. The Master once had a TARDIS of his own, but had to steal the Doctor's to escape from the planet Malcassairo.

TEST YOUR KNOWLEDGE

1. WHICH REGENERATION OF THE DOCTOR'S MET THE SYCORAX?
   A. Eighth
   B. Ninth
   C. Tenth

2. WHAT DIDN'T WORK WHEN THE DOCTOR WAS UNCONSCIOUS?
   A. Chameleon circuit
   B. Translation circuit
   C. Sonic screwdriver

3. WHAT DID ROSE USE TO DEFEAT THE DALEKS?
   A. The Time Vortex
   B. Sonic screwdriver
   C. Persuasion

4. WHO SAVED THE TARDIS FROM THE WEEPING ANGELS?
   A. Rose
   B. Martha
   C. Sally Sparrow

5. WHERE WAS THE MASTER'S IDENTITY HIDDEN?
   A. The TARDIS
   B. A pocket watch
   C. Down the back of the sofa

354 TARDIS ORIGINS

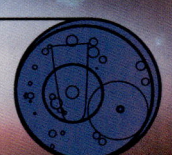

THE POWER OF THE TIME LORDS

Centuries ago, during what the Time Lords call 'The Old Time', Rassilon, their greatest leader, discovered the secret of space-time travel. But to make it a reality he needed a huge source of power. He worked with a stellar engineer called Omega to try to harness the energy of a black hole. Omega used a stellar manipulator sometimes known as The Hand of Omega to turn the black hole into a source of unimaginable power.

Omega was lost in the resulting supernova, but Rassilon managed to control the nucleus of the black hole. Each TARDIS carried a direct link to this power source, which Rassilon called The Eye of Harmony.

THE HEART OF THE TARDIS

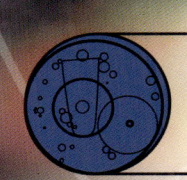

The Doctor's TARDIS is actually a Type 40 TT Capsule. The central column of the TARDIS main console, sometimes referred to as the Time Rotor, is the very heart of the machine. The main energy source for the TARDIS is under that column, and held in check by it. When the column moves, it proves the extent of the power thrust. If the column were to come out of the console completely, the power would be free to escape. As Rose discovered — the power at the heart of the TARDIS is the tremendous, deadly power of the Time Vortex itself.

IS THE TARDIS ALIVE?

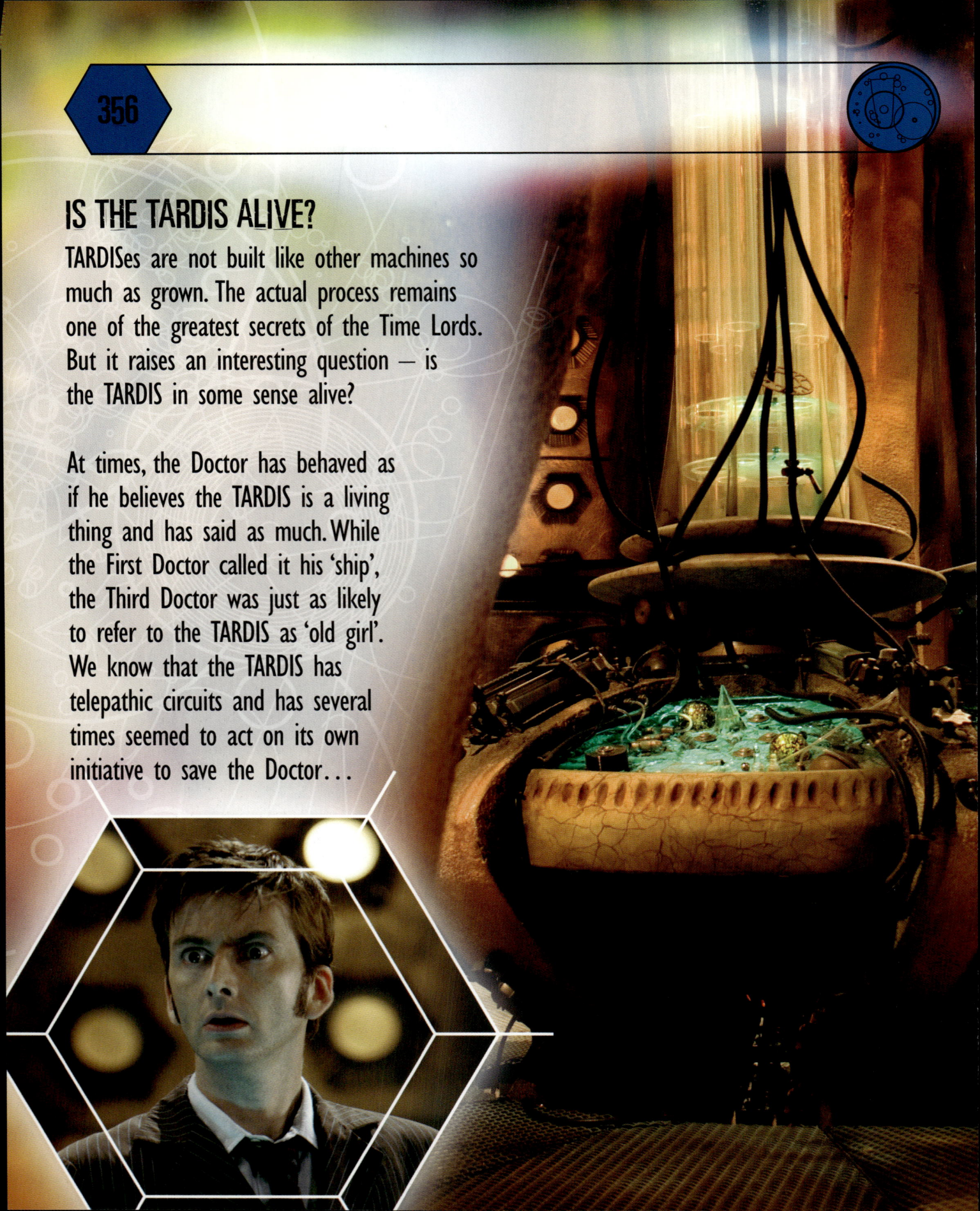

TARDISes are not built like other machines so much as grown. The actual process remains one of the greatest secrets of the Time Lords. But it raises an interesting question — is the TARDIS in some sense alive?

At times, the Doctor has behaved as if he believes the TARDIS is a living thing and has said as much. While the First Doctor called it his 'ship', the Third Doctor was just as likely to refer to the TARDIS as 'old girl'. We know that the TARDIS has telepathic circuits and has several times seemed to act on its own initiative to save the Doctor…

THE LAST TARDIS?

If the Doctor is the last of the Time Lords, is his TARDIS the last of their time machines? The Doctor has met other rogue Time Lords with stolen TARDISes over the years. A strange meddling monk hoping to help King Harold win the battle of Hastings had a TARDIS that looked identical inside to the Doctor's. The amoral Time Lady the Rani also had her own TARDIS.

Like the Doctor, the Master survived the Great Time War, though he seems not to have saved his TARDIS. Over the years he has acquired several — all of them more advanced than the Doctor's. Perhaps somewhere he has another, hidden away and waiting…

TEST YOUR KNOWLEDGE

1. WHO WAS THE GREATEST LEADER OF THE TIME LORDS?
   A. The Master
   B. Rassilon
   C. Omega

2. WHAT POWER LIES AT THE HEART OF THE TARDIS?
   A. The Time Vortex
   B. The Time Battery
   C. The Rassilon Reactor

3. HOW ARE TARDISES GROWN?
   A. In an allotment
   B. It's a secret
   C. Under water

4. WHAT DID THE THIRD DOCTOR CALL THE TARDIS?
   A. Boris
   B. His ship
   C. Old girl

5. WHAT TYPE OF SHIP IS THE TARDIS?
   A. A Type 19 Rocket
   B. A Type 33 Saucer
   C. A Type 40 TT Capsule

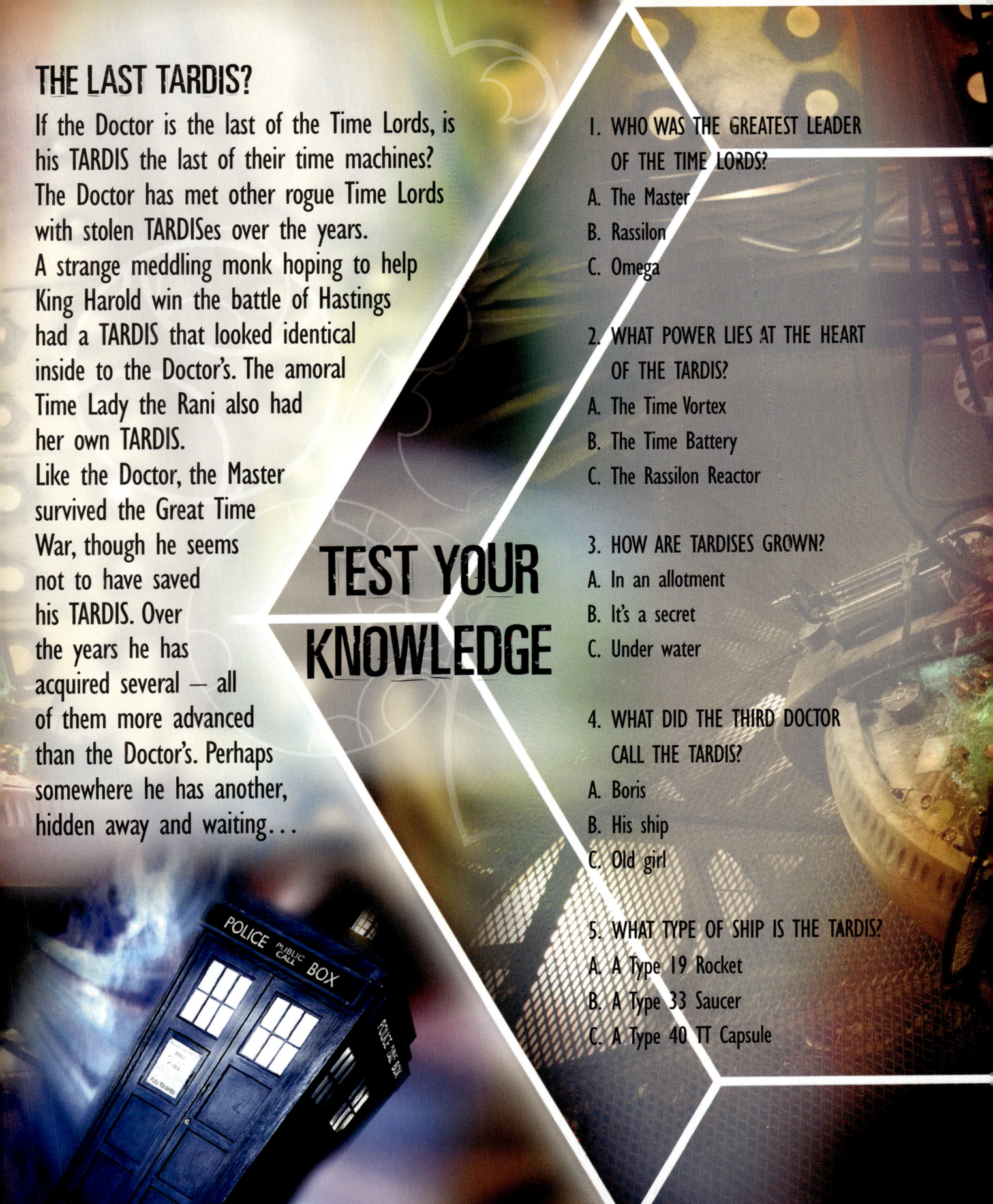

TRANSPORT AND TECHNOLOGY

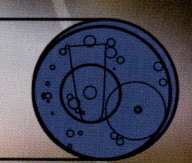

TIME AND SPACE TRAVEL

In theory, the Doctor can programme the flight computer with coordinates and travel to anywhere or anywhen in time and space. Often though, the TARDIS decides for him and takes the Doctor and his companions to wherever they can be the most useful! It usually travels through the Vortex, dematerialising from one place, and materialising in another, but it can also fly conventionally, such as when the Doctor rescued Donna from the Santa Robot taxi driver.

FUEL

Power for the TARDIS comes from the Artron energy in the Eye of Harmony, an artificial black hole created by the Time Lords. However, the Doctor can also park the TARDIS on rifts in time, like the one in Cardiff, to allow it to soak up the radiation.

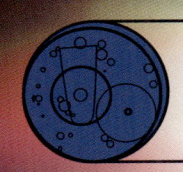

DIMENSIONALLY TRANSCENDENTAL

The Time Lords developed an incredible technology which allowed them to make things that are much bigger on the inside than they appear on the outside. The inside and the outside somehow exist in two different dimensions, that are connected at the entrance to the TARDIS. This technology was also used to create the Genesis Ark, a capsule that was used to imprison thousands of Daleks during the Great Time War. Even the Doctor's pockets are bigger on the inside!

CHAMELEON CIRCUIT

One of the key features of any TARDIS is its chameleon circuit, which allows it to change shape to blend in to its surroundings wherever it lands. The chameleon circuit on the Doctor's TARDIS has been broken for a long time, trapping it in its disguise as a 1950s police box. The Doctor could fix it if he wanted to, but he's become quite attached to the old blue box.

CHAMELEON ARCH

The chameleon arch allows the Doctor to rewrite every cell in his body, so he can become whoever, or whatever, he wants to be. He used it to disguise himself as a human when hiding from the Family of Blood.

TRANSLATION CIRCUIT

The TARDIS is telepathic and has a translation circuit. It gets into the head of anyone who travels in it, translating alien languages and writing into the traveller's own language. It allows the Doctor and his companions to understand each other and everyone they meet. The translation circuit rarely fails, but it was unable to translate the writing of the Beast on Krop Tor, as it was more ancient than even the TARDIS itself.

TEST YOUR KNOWLEDGE

1. WHO DID CAPTAIN JACK GET THE EXTRAPOLATOR FROM?
A. The Gelth
B. The Weeping Angels
C. The Slitheen

2. WHAT ALLOWS THE TARDIS TO CHANGE ITS APPEARANCE?
A. Chameleon circuit
B. Spider circuit
C. Hummingbird circuit

3. WHO WAS THE DOCTOR HIDING FROM WHEN HE BECAME HUMAN?
A. The Family of Blood
B. Martha
C. Professor Yana

4. WHAT IS THE EYE OF HARMONY?
A. A telescope
B. An artificial black hole
C. A jewel

5. WHERE DID THE DOCTOR MEET THE BEAST?
A. Krop Tor
B. The supermarket
C. New York

362 ADVENTURES IN TIME AND SPACE

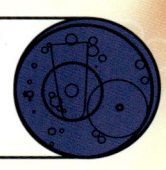

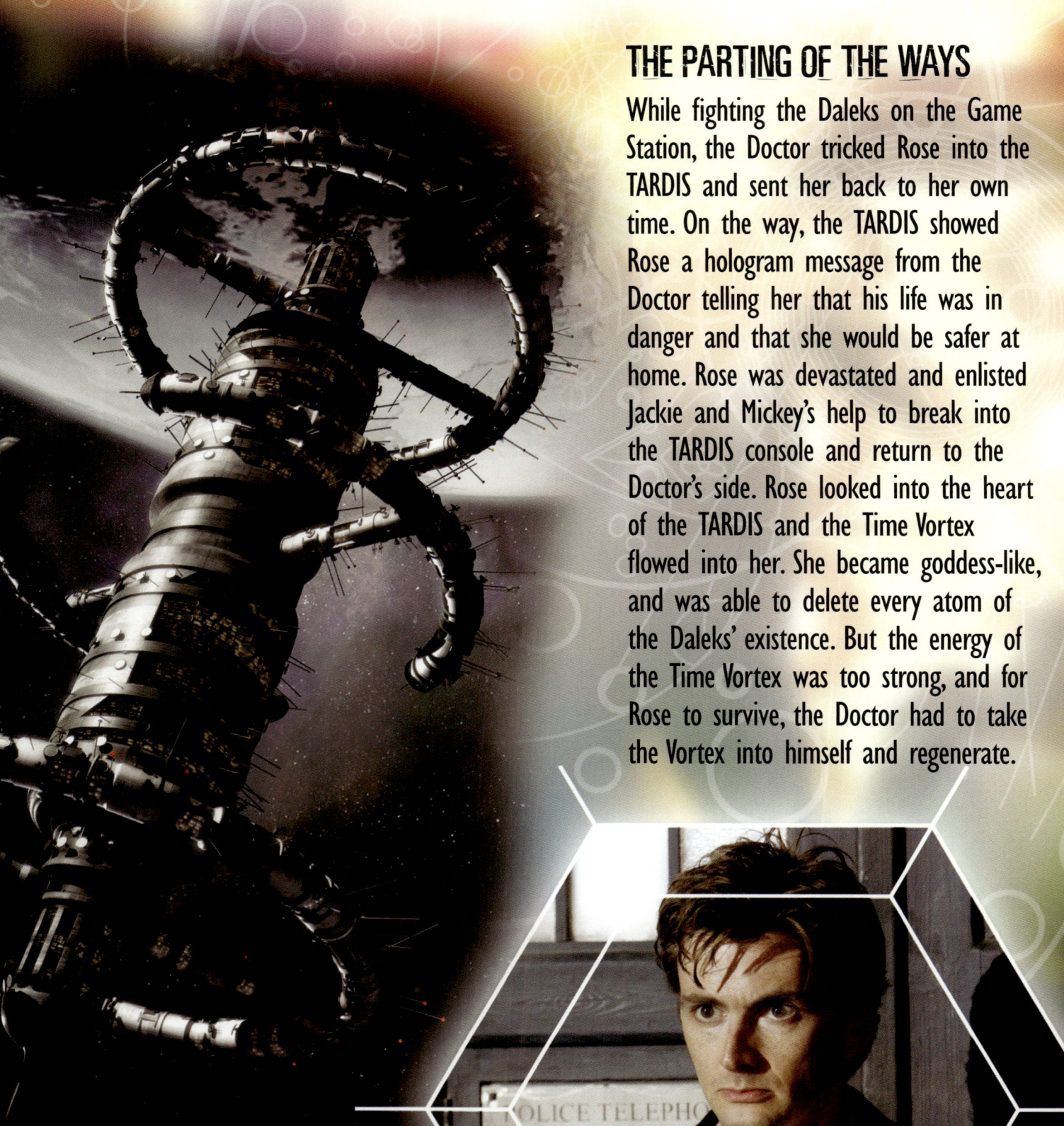

THE PARTING OF THE WAYS

While fighting the Daleks on the Game Station, the Doctor tricked Rose into the TARDIS and sent her back to her own time. On the way, the TARDIS showed Rose a hologram message from the Doctor telling her that his life was in danger and that she would be safer at home. Rose was devastated and enlisted Jackie and Mickey's help to break into the TARDIS console and return to the Doctor's side. Rose looked into the heart of the TARDIS and the Time Vortex flowed into her. She became goddess-like, and was able to delete every atom of the Daleks' existence. But the energy of the Time Vortex was too strong, and for Rose to survive, the Doctor had to take the Vortex into himself and regenerate.

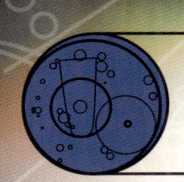

THE RUNAWAY BRIDE

Travelling alone, the Doctor was just as surprised as Donna when she suddenly materialised inside the TARDIS. Donna thought she was being abducted, but the TARDIS was saving her from being part of an alien plot. She had been fed with Huon Particles which magnetised with those in the heart of the TARDIS and pulled her into it. The Empress of the Racnoss wanted to use her as a key to unlock a ship full of young Racnoss hidden at the Earth's core. The Doctor was able to use the Empress' own weapons against her. He flooded her lair and destroyed her plans for world domination.

HUMAN NATURE/THE FAMILY OF BLOOD

When the Family of Blood chased the Doctor across the universe, he used the chameleon arch to turn himself into a human and become a schoolteacher called John Smith. The TARDIS created a whole new life for him and remained hidden in a barn near the school, while Martha became a maid who watched over the Doctor. He left her a message in the TARDIS, with instructions on what to do while the alien part of him was gone. When the Family caught up with them, Martha had to force John Smith to face up to who he really was, and the Doctor returned to defeat them.

UTOPIA

The TARDIS flew all the way to the end of the universe to try and shake off a hitch-hiker that was clinging to the outside - Captain Jack. The Doctor had been avoiding him since Rose brought him back to life. On the planet Macassairo, Professor Yana was trying to perfect the technology to send the surviving members of the human race to a place called Utopia. The Doctor was horrified when he realised Professor Yana was actually his ancient enemy, the Master. The Master stole the TARDIS and left the Doctor stranded in a dying universe..

TEST YOUR KNOWLEDGE

1. WHERE DID THE DOCTOR SEND ROSE IN THE TARDIS?
A. Home
B. New Earth
C. Brighton

2. WHAT HAD DONNA BEEN FED WITH?
A. Chips
B. Huon Particles
C. Banana milkshake

3. WHO HITCH-HIKED ON THE SIDE OF THE TARDIS?
A. The Master
B. Rose
C. Captain Jack

4. WHAT DID MARTHA WORK AS WHILE THE DOCTOR WAS HUMAN?
A. A doctor
B. A writer
C. A maid

5. WHERE WAS PROFESSOR YANA TRYING TO SEND PEOPLE?
A. Utopia
B. Malcassairo
C. Krop Tor

TEST YOUR KNOWLEDGE

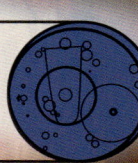

ANSWERS

Meet the TARDIS
1 (b) 2 (a) 3 (a) 4 (a) 5 (b)

TARDIS Travellers
1 (c) 2 (a) 3 (b) 4 (a) 5 (b)

TARDIS Enemies
1 (c) 2 (b) 3 (a) 4 (c) 5 (b)

TARDIS Origins
1 (b) 2 (a) 3 (b) 4 (c) 5 (c)

Transport and Technology
1 (c) 2 (a) 3 (a) 4 (b) 5 (a)

Adventures in Time and Space
1 (a) 2 (b) 3 (c) 4 (c) 5 (a)

DOCTOR·WHO

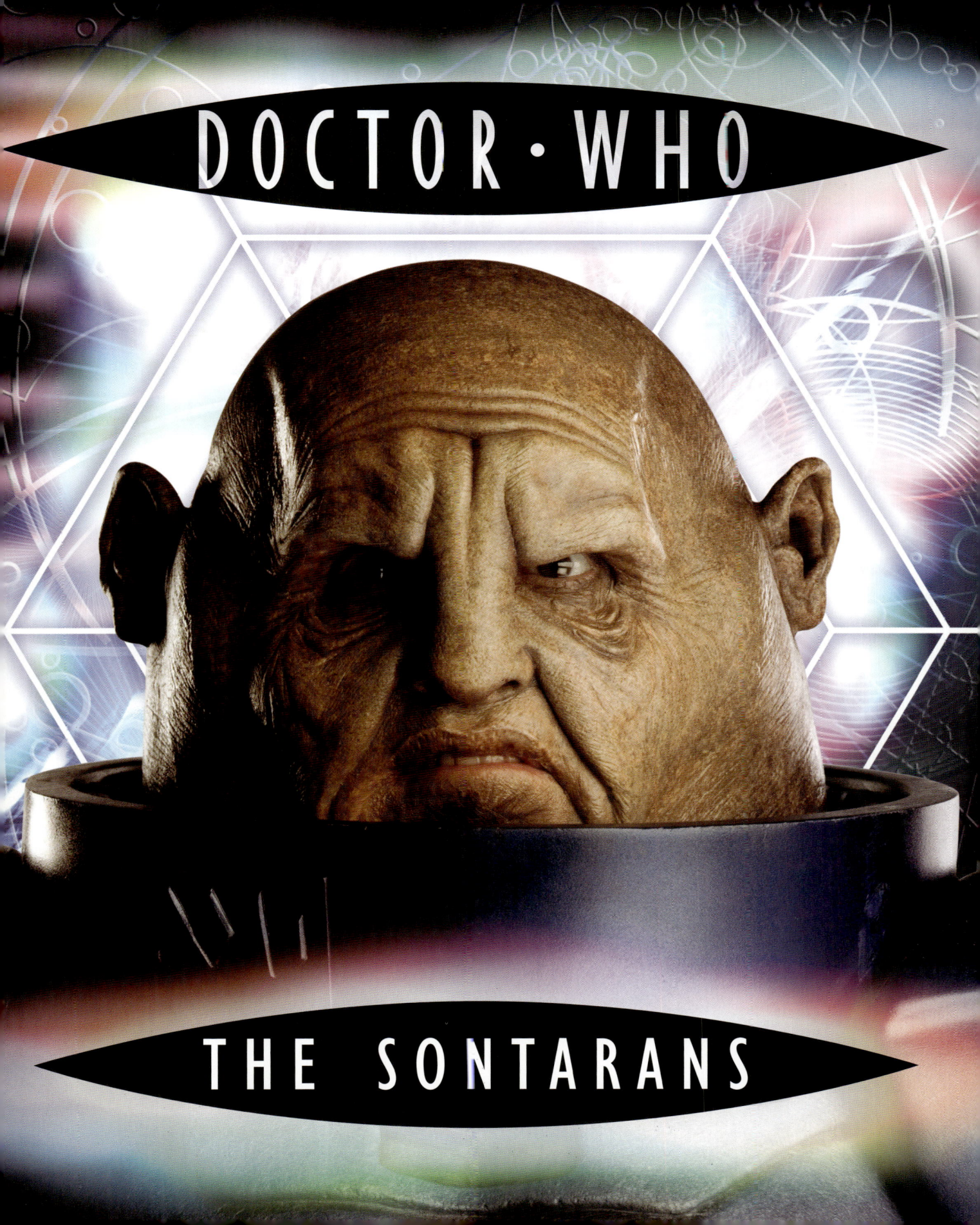

THE SONTARANS

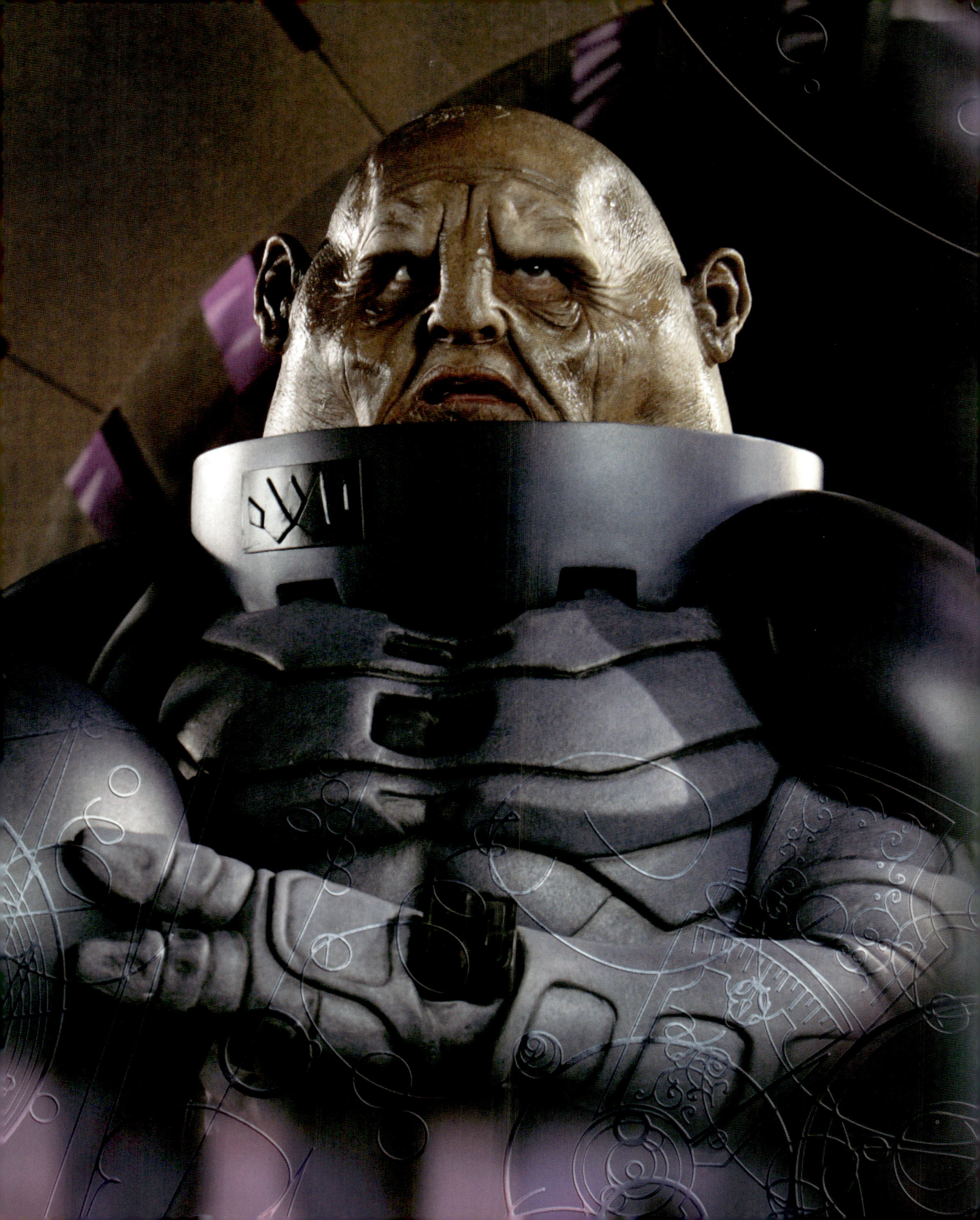

CONTENTS

The Sontarans
Meet the Sontarans..................370
Sontaran Data..........................372
Sontaran Anatomy....................374
⬢ Test your knowledge

Sontarans and their Allies
General Staal............................376
Commander Skorr & Lieutenant Skree......377
Other Sontarans........................378
Luke Rattigan............................379
⬢ Test your knowledge

The Rutans
The War....................................380
Earth..381

Other Sontaran Enemies
The Doctor................................382
Donna Noble.............................383
⬢ Test your knowledge

Defending Earth
Martha Jones............................384
UNIT..385

Attacking Earth
ATMOS......................................386
⬢ Test your knowledge

Weapons and Technology
Clones......................................388
Sontaran Warships....................390
Sontaran Scoutships.................391
⬢ Test your knowledge

Sontaran Strategies
Previous Strategies...................392
The ATMOS Strategy.................394
⬢ Test your knowledge

Test your knowledge Answers.................396

370 | MEET THE SONTARANS

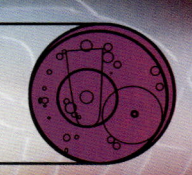

They might look like dumpy potato-heads, but the Sontarans are a brutal race of warriors dedicated to warfare. They have been at war with the Rutans for thousands of years, neither side gaining a lasting advantage in the struggle. But the Sontarans will attack anyone if they think they can gain an advantage in the Sontaran-Rutan war.

The Sontarans come from the high-gravity planet, Sontar. They reproduce by cloning - at a rate of a million every four minutes in great muster parades. They are all identical in appearance.

Despite their ruthlessness and brutality, the Sontarans have a keen sense of honour. Nothing makes a Sontaran more angry than to suggest he is without honour, or that he has failed in his mission.

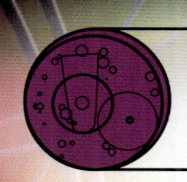

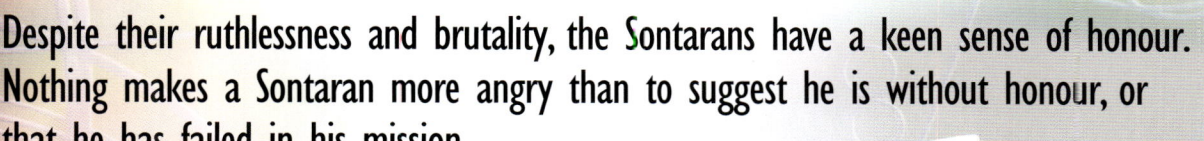

They even see their greatest weakness as a strength because a Sontaran can only be stunned by a blow to the probic vent. Since the probic vent is a small hole at the back of the neck, the Sontarans believe this means they must always face their enemies.

They might not have defeated the Rutans yet, but the Sontarans are formidable adversaries and amongst the most feared warrior races of the Universe.

372 SONTARAN DATA

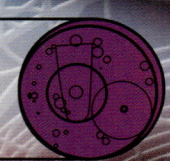

Name: Sontaran
Species: Cloned warrior
Height: 1.6m (5'6")
Home Planet: Sontar
Weaponry: A choice of deadly guns and artillery
Protection: Battle armour
Communication: Universal translation device
Weakness: Probic vent (at the back of the neck) is very sensitive
Greatest Enemies: The Rutan Host and the Doctor
Battle Cry: Sontar-ha! Sontar-ha! Sontar-ha!

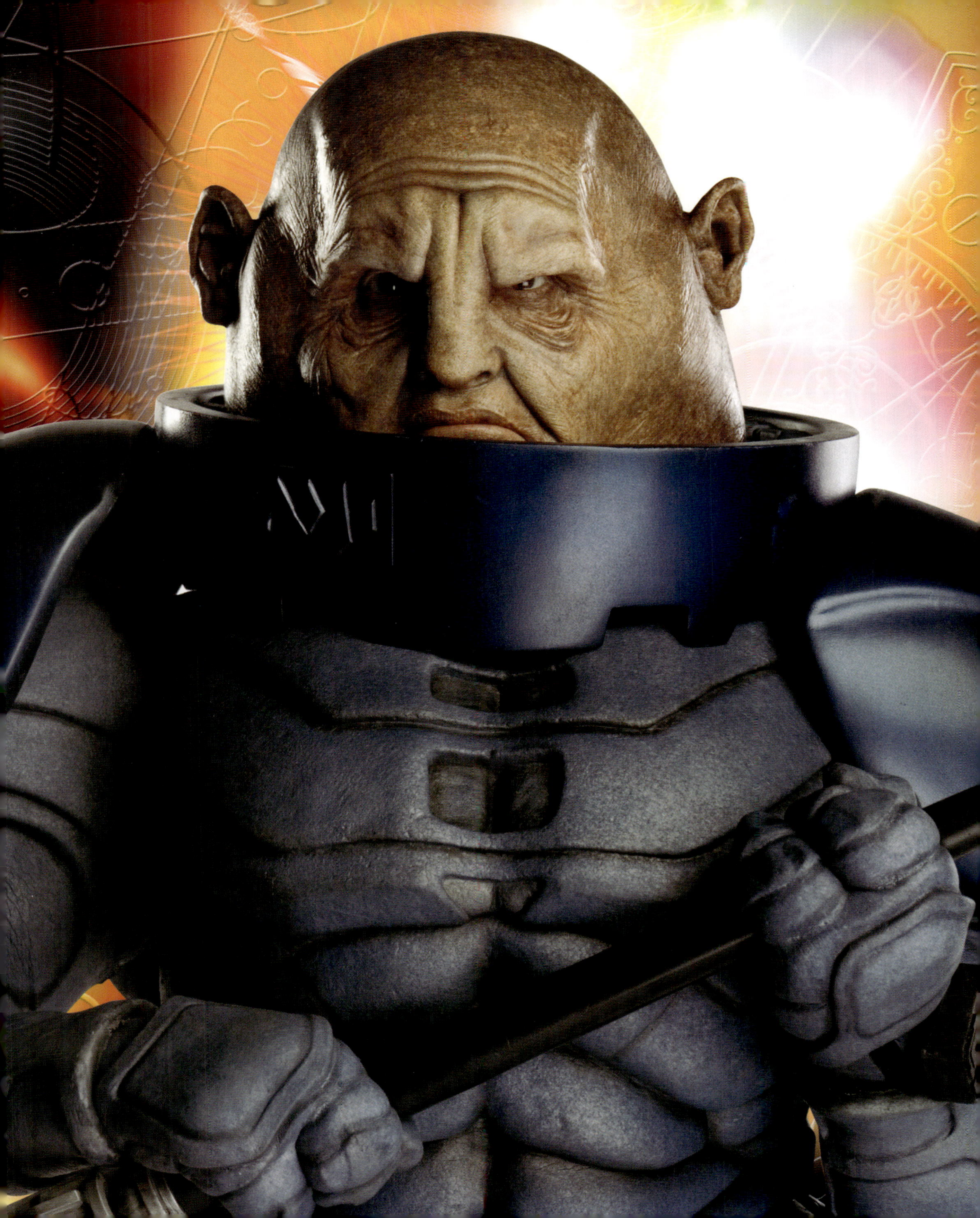

374 SONTARAN ANATOMY

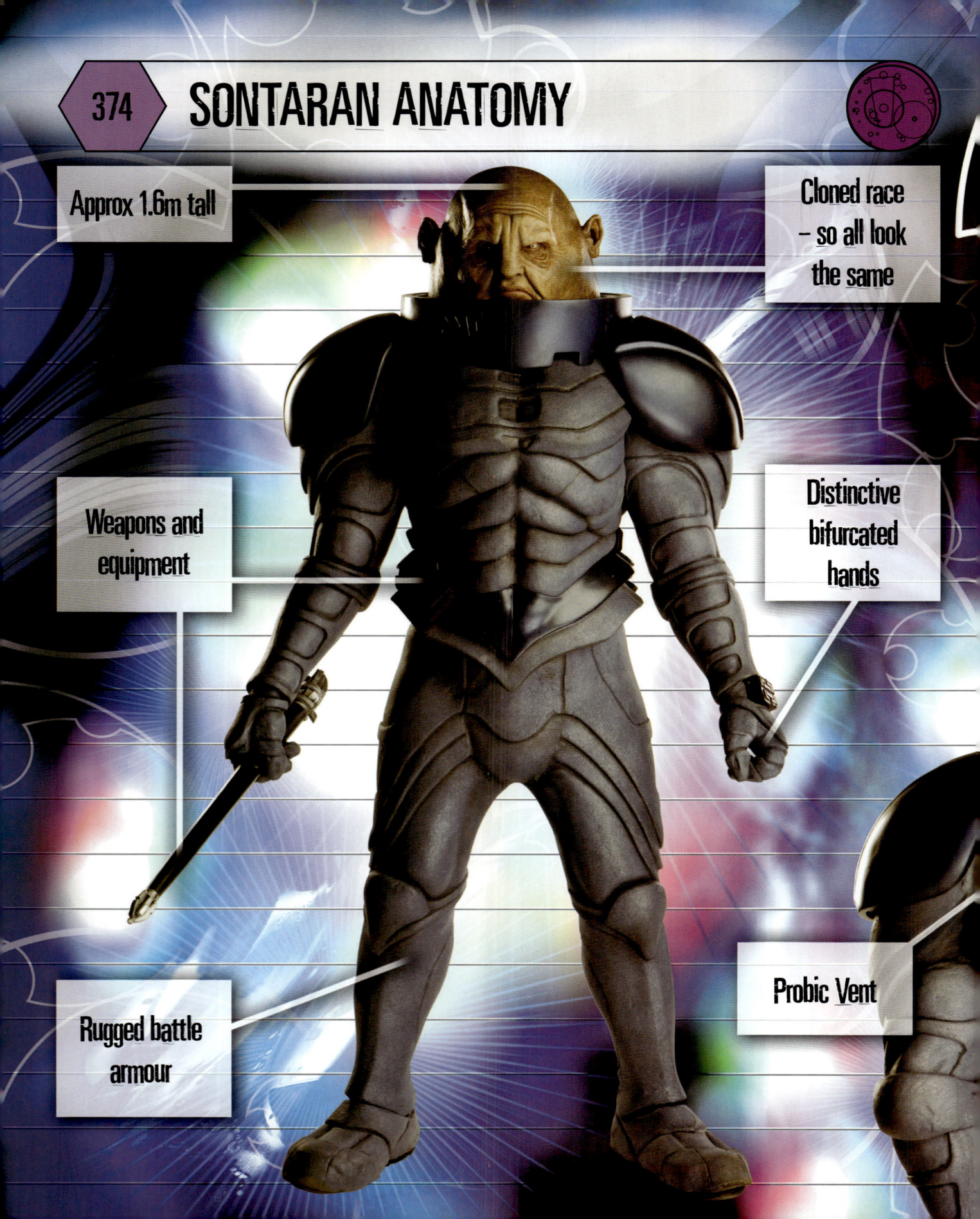

Approx 1.6m tall

Cloned race – so all look the same

Weapons and equipment

Distinctive bifurcated hands

Rugged battle armour

Probic Vent

TEST YOUR KNOWLEDGE

1. WHAT ARE THE SONTARANS?
A. Mutated potatoes
B. A brutal race of warriors
C. Fashion designers to galactic royalty

2. WHAT IS THE NAME OF THE SONTARAN HOME PLANET?
A. Sontar
B. Muster-Parade
C. Flim Flam Alpha

3. WHAT IS THE SONTARAN WEAK POINT?
A. The top of the head
B. The bifurcated hand
C. The probic vent

4. WITH WHICH RACE ARE THE SONTARANS AT WAR?
A. The Mega-Ostriches of Bangle 5
B. The Rutans
C. The Bifurcates

5. WHAT IS THE SONTARAN BATTLE CRY?
A. We're gonna win the cup!
B. They look like blobs of jelly, but don't put them in your trifle. If you meet a Rutan scout, shoot him with your rifle.
C. Sontar-ha! Sontar-ha! Sontar-ha!

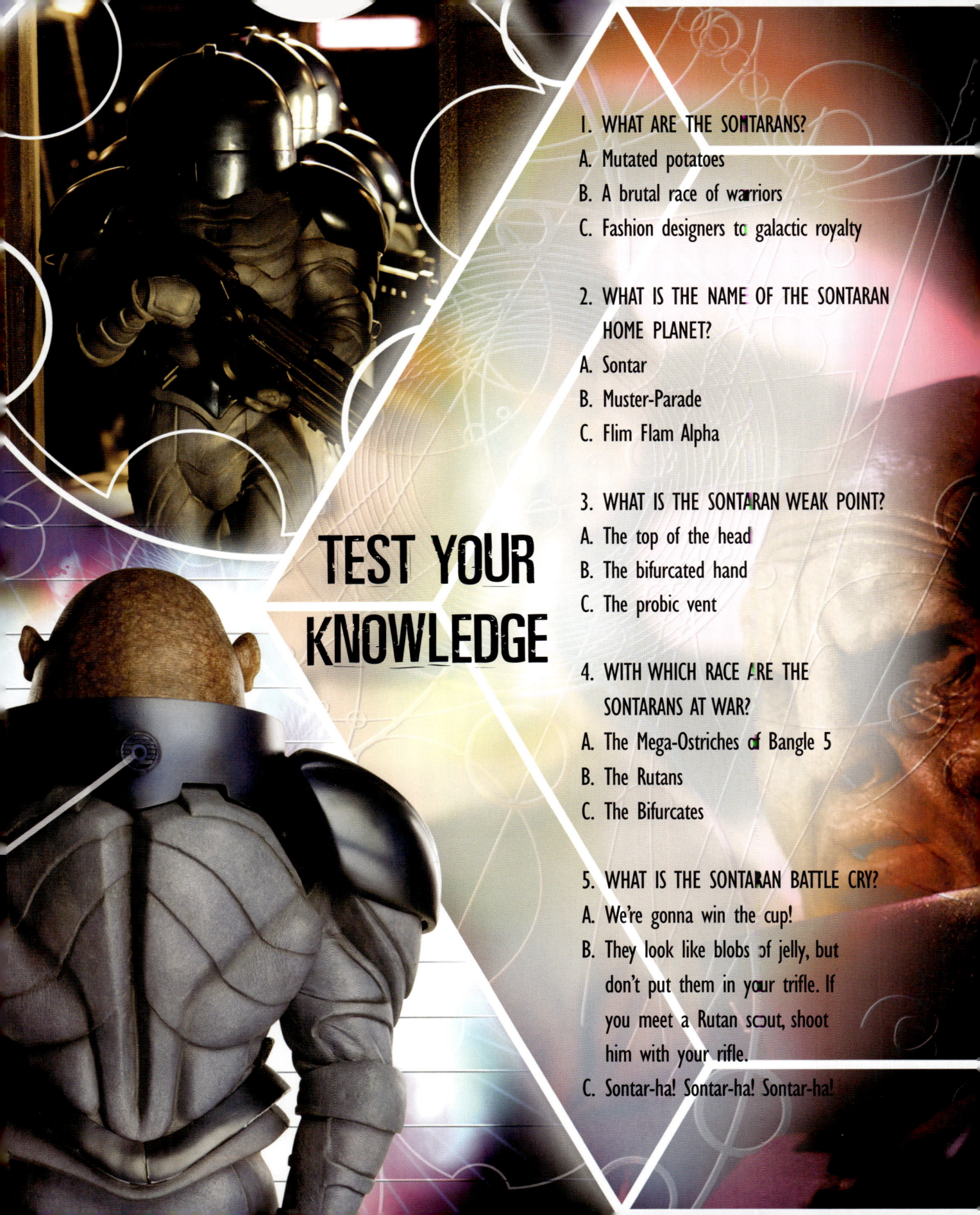

376 SONTARANS AND THEIR ALLIES

GENERAL STAAL

Like all Sontarans, General Staal of the Tenth Sontaran Battle Fleet was a dedicated soldier. Bred to be a Sontaran commander, he had highly-developed strategic skills, a keen sense of honour and a lust for glory. General Staal was put in charge of the Sontaran attempt to turn Earth into a Clone World in the early 21st century by Sontaran High Command.

Victorious in all his previous campaigns and battles, the General was known as Staal the Undefeated. But he was killed when the attempt to take over Earth failed and his warship was blown up.

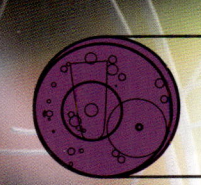

COMMANDER SKORR

Commander Skorr reported directly to General Staal and was second in command of the Tenth Sontaran Battle fleet. Known as Skorr the Bloodbringer, he was every bit as ruthless and determined as his commanding officer.

General Staal entrusted the vital raid on the ATMOS Factory to Commander Skorr. But Skorr was ultimately defeated and shot down by Colonel Mace of UNIT.

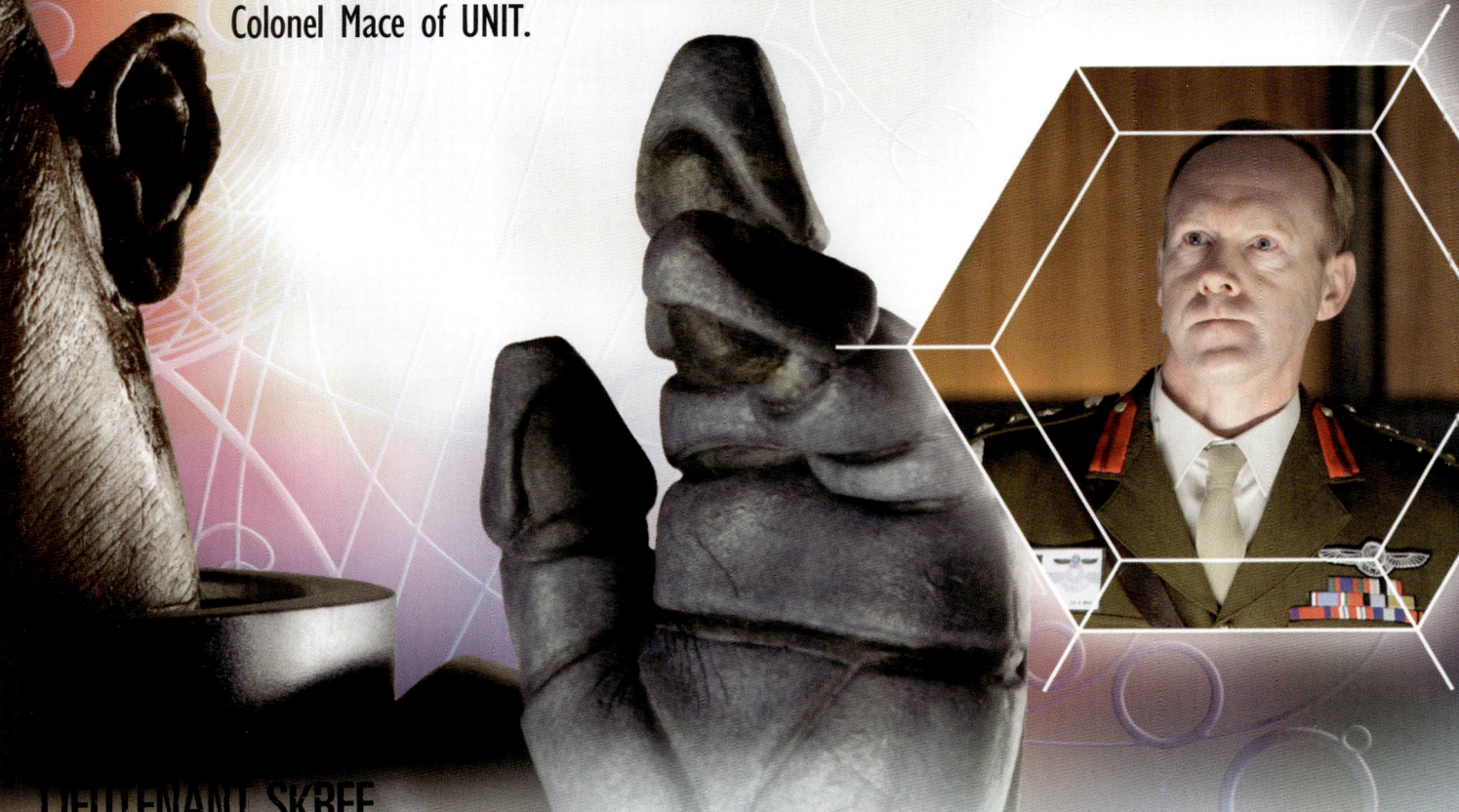

LIEUTENANT SKREE

In command of the day-to-day running of General Staal's flagship, Lieutenant Skree remained loyal to his general - and to the Sontaran code of war — right to his death when the flagship was destroyed.

As well as coordinating the attack on the ATMOS Factory, he was responsible for planning the weapons strike that would destroy all life on Earth.

OTHER SONTARANS

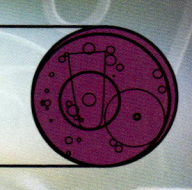

Although he knew about them, it was not until his third incarnation that the Doctor first met a Sontaran. Commander Linx of the Fifth Sontaran Army Space Fleet was stranded in medieval Britain, offering modern weapons to a robber baron in exchange for help repairing his ship.

The Fourth Doctor managed to stop a Sontaran invasion when he defeated Field Major Styre in single combat on a fire-blasted Earth of the future. Later, he defeated a Sontaran invasion of the Time Lord home planet Gallifrey led by Commander Stor of the elite SSSS — the Sontaran Special Space Service.

Then the Sixth Doctor and the Second Doctor joined forces against Group Marshal Stike of the Ninth Sontaran Battle Group and his adjutant Varl in 20th-century Spain...

LUKE RATTIGAN

Teenage technology genius Luke Rattigan invented the Fountain Six Search Engine when he was just 12 years old. He became a millionaire almost overnight as a result, and later opened the Rattigan Academy — a private school educating hand-picked students from all over the world.

But Rattigan was in league with the Sontarans. In return for his help producing and distributing the ATMOS system, he thought the Sontarans would take him and his gifted students to a new planet to start a new Earth...

But the Sontarans just used Rattigan, with no intention of helping him. Betrayed and disillusioned, Rattigan destroyed the Sontaran warship, killing General Staal and ending the Sontaran threat to Earth.

TEST YOUR KNOWLEDGE

1. WHICH FLEET DID GENERAL STAAL COMMAND?
   A. The Fleet Air Arm
   B. The Admiral Ofta Fleet
   C. The Tenth Sontaran Battle Fleet

2. WHICH SONTARAN LED THE ATTACK ON THE ATMOS FACTORY?
   A. Commander Skorr
   B. Lieutenant Scale
   C. Sergeant Screem

3. WHO WAS THE FIRST SONTARAN THE DOCTOR MET?
   A. Field Major Stike
   B. Commander Linx
   C. General Staal

4. WHAT DID LUKE RATTIGAN INVENT WHEN HE WAS 12?
   A. The Fountain Six Search Engine
   B. The steam engine
   C. Sliced bread

5. WHAT DID LUKE RATTIGAN SET UP FOR GIFTED CHILDREN?
   A. A bump-and-bounce play area in Liverpool
   B. The Rattigan Academy
   C. Toy soldiers

380 THE RUTANS

THE WAR

From the cold, icy planet of Ruta 3, the Rutans evolved in the sea before adapting to land. They look like large, glowing green jellyfish with tentacles that can give a massive electric shock — enough to kill. The Rutans are the sworn enemies of the Sontarans, and the Rutan Empire has been at war with the Sontarans for thousands of years.

The Rutans developed a metamorphosis technique that allowed them to take on the appearance of other creatures with which they had come into contact.

EARTH

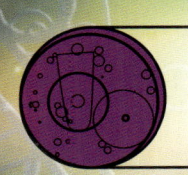

Although Commander Linx was ambushed by a squadron of Rutan fighters close to Earth in medieval times, it wasn't until centuries later that the planet's strategic position became important. A Rutan expedition to Earth in the early 20th century concluded the planet was too dangerous to attack, after the Doctor destroyed the Rutans that attacked the Fang Rock lighthouse.

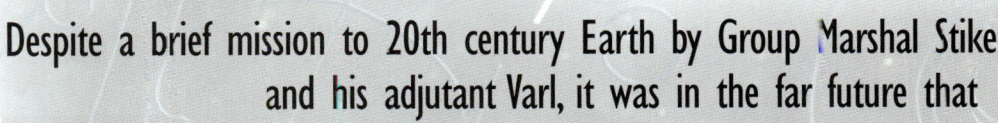

Despite a brief mission to 20th century Earth by Group Marshal Stike and his adjutant Varl, it was in the far future that the Sontarans assessed Earth as a military target. They also experimented on humans to see if they were fit for war. They concluded that it was not in their interests to attack — again, after the Doctor intervened.

With the help of UNIT and his friends Donna and Martha, the Doctor defeated a Sontaran attempt to turn Earth into a clone world…

382 OTHER SONTARAN ENEMIES

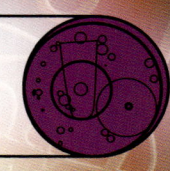

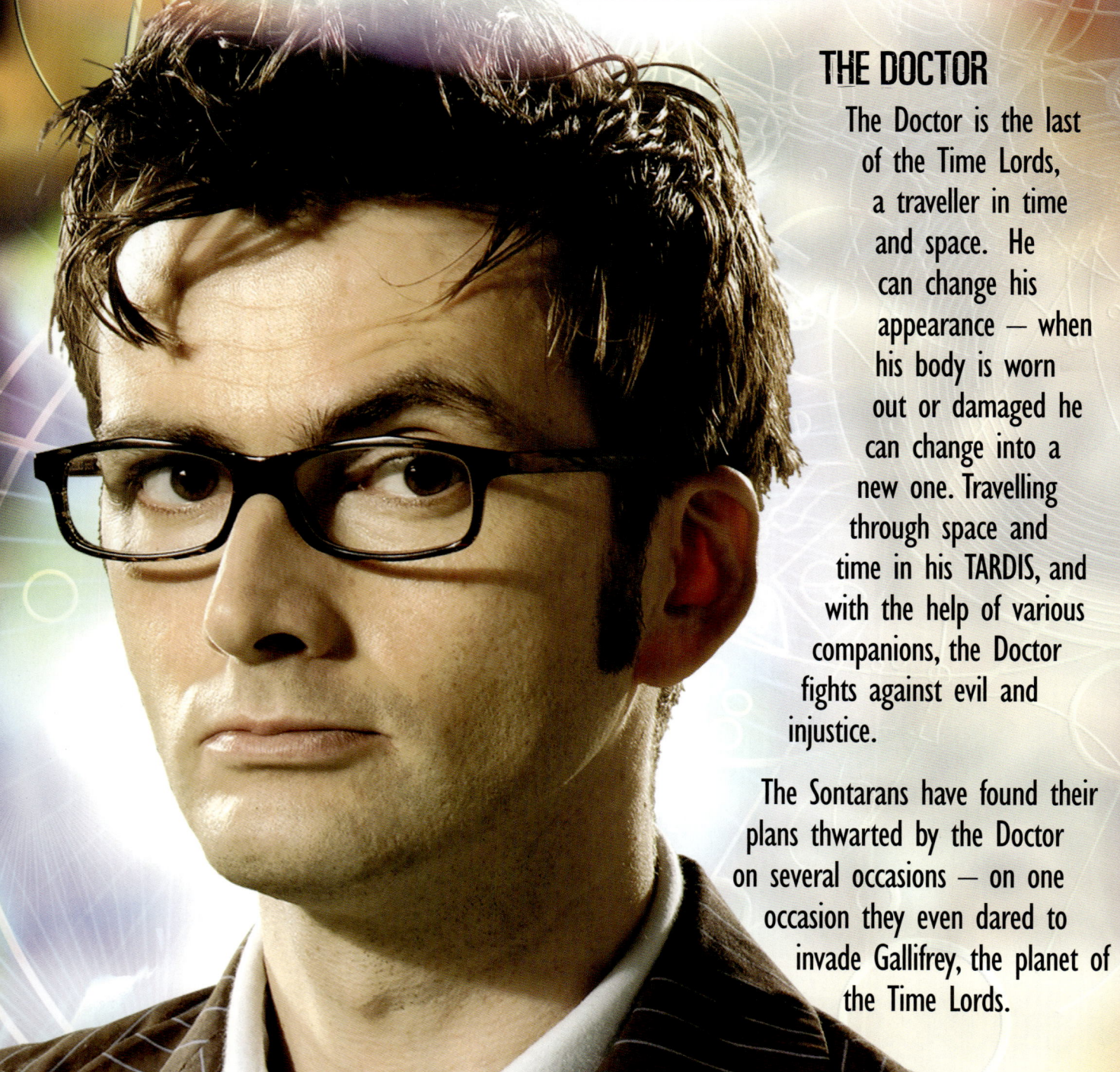

THE DOCTOR

The Doctor is the last of the Time Lords, a traveller in time and space. He can change his appearance — when his body is worn out or damaged he can change into a new one. Travelling through space and time in his TARDIS, and with the help of various companions, the Doctor fights against evil and injustice.

The Sontarans have found their plans thwarted by the Doctor on several occasions — on one occasion they even dared to invade Gallifrey, the planet of the Time Lords.

DONNA NOBLE

Donna first met the Doctor when she found herself mysteriously transported from her own wedding into the TARDIS. After a hectic adventure, Donna turned down the Doctor's offer to travel with him.

But she came to regret this decision, and when she and the Doctor met up again, Donna accepted the renewed offer of a trip in the TARDIS. After travelling to Pompeii in the past and the Ood Sphere in the future, Donna came home to discover that present day Earth can be just as dangerous. With the help of Martha Jones and UNIT, Donna and the Doctor managed to stop the Sontarans turning Earth into a clone world.

TEST YOUR KNOWLEDGE

1. WHAT PLANET DO THE RUTANS COME FROM?
A. Bandraginus 5
B. Ruta 3
C. Chelsea Nil

2. WHY DID THE SONTARANS AND RUTANS BECOME INTERESTED IN EARTH?
A. Because they thought humans were weak
B. Because they wanted to steal the world's supply of chocolate
C. Because of its strategic position

3. WHERE WAS THE LIGHTHOUSE THE RUTAN SCOUT ATTACKED?
A. Fang Rock
B. Tooth Cove
C. Dentures Alley

4. WHO DEFEATED THE SONTARANS WHEN THEY INVADED GALLIFREY?
A. The Master
B. Montmorency Peskerville
C. The Doctor

5. WHERE WAS DONNA WHEN SHE WAS TRANSPORTED TO THE TARDIS?
A. At her own wedding
B. At her own christening
C. At the supermarket

384 | DEFENDING EARTH

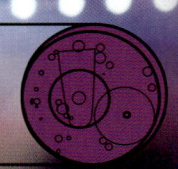

MARTHA JONES

Martha Jones used to travel with the Doctor. She left him to stay with her family after she helped the Doctor and Captain Jack Harkness defeat the Master. When the Doctor and Donna meet her again, Martha is working with UNIT to investigate the ATMOS system.

Although she saw incredible things and faced many dangers when she was with the Doctor, nothing quite prepares Martha for meeting herself. The Sontarans create a clone copy of Martha who infiltrates UNIT and betrays them. The real Martha remains in a coma while the clone is at large. But the clone dies when the Doctor revives the real Martha.

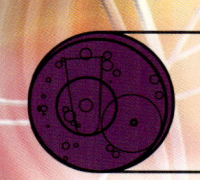

UNIT

The Doctor has worked with UNIT — which stands for UNified Intelligence Taskforce — many times over many years. UNIT is a worldwide force that deals with alien incursions and other extraordinary threats to Earth.

UNIT's Operation Blue Sky is a raid on the ATMOS Factory, led by Colonel Mace. But they are almost too late to stop the Sontaran stratagem. The UNIT force manages to avoid the worst effects of the ATMOS gas by blowing it away using the massive engines of its flying aircraft carrier Valiant. Colonel Mace and his troops then fight off the Sontaran invaders, giving the Doctor time to defeat the Sontarans.

386 ATTACKING EARTH

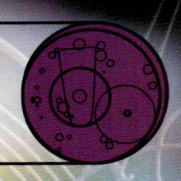

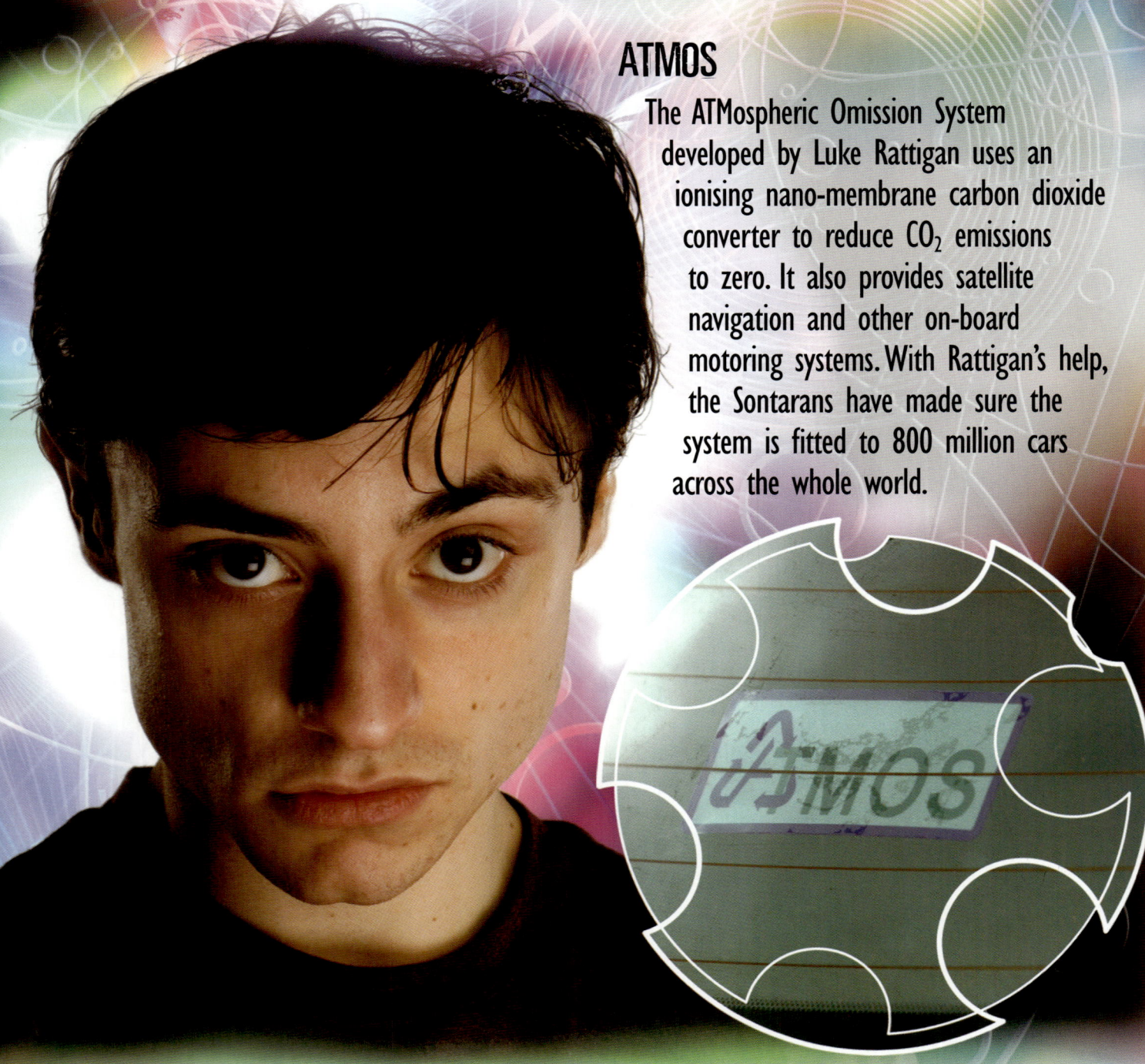

ATMOS

The ATMospheric Omission System developed by Luke Rattigan uses an ionising nano-membrane carbon dioxide converter to reduce CO_2 emissions to zero. It also provides satellite navigation and other on-board motoring systems. With Rattigan's help, the Sontarans have made sure the system is fitted to 800 million cars across the whole world.

UNIT becomes suspicious when over fifty people die at the exact same time under the same circumstances all across the world. The Doctor realises that ATMOS uses advanced alien technology.

In fact, ATMOS is a Sontaran weapon. When activated, it emits a gas called Caesofine Concentrate from the cars' exhausts. One part Probic 5 to two parts Bosteen, the gas is a clonefeed. It will change Earth's atmosphere so it is suitable for the Sontarans to clone billions of troops. But the gas is poisonous and will also make it uninhabitable for humans.

Luckily, the gas is volatile and the Doctor is able to burn it off, thwarting the Sontarans' plans.

TEST YOUR KNOWLEDGE

1. WHO IS MARTHA JONES HELPING?
   A. OFSTED
   B. GPO
   C. UNIT

2. WHAT DOES UNIT STAND FOR?
   A. UNified Intelligence Taskforce
   B. Understand No Imagined Threat
   C. Undermine Nasties In Time

3. WHAT IS ATMOS FITTED TO?
   A. Trains
   B. Cars
   C. Bicycles

4. WHO HELPED THE SONTARANS WITH ATMOS?
   A. Martha Jones
   B. Queen Victoria
   C. Luke Rattigan

5. WHAT DOES THE CAESOFINE CONCENTRATE GAS DO?
   A. Turns Earth into a Sontaran clone world
   B. Cuts carbon dioxide emissions
   C. Performs conjuring tricks in the village hall

WEAPONS AND TECHNOLOGY

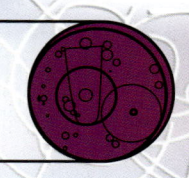

CLONES

The Sontarans are a race of clones. They can create a million more Sontarans every four minutes in huge Muster Parades on dedicated clone worlds. With such vast numbers of troops available so quickly, they can sustain huge losses in battle against their sworn enemies — the Rutans.

As well as cloning themselves, the Sontarans can also create clones of other species. To create a clone of an individual human, they need access to the original person. They clone several UNIT soldiers to defend vital areas of the ATMOS Factory and spy on UNIT. They also clone Martha Jones.

389

When they cloned her, they kept the real Martha in a coma while the clone infiltrated UNIT and sabotaged Earth's counter-attack against the invading Sontarans. But the Doctor knew at once that the fake Martha was a clone. As well as reduced iris contraction in her eyes, and slight differences in her hair, he can detect a distinctive smell.

Clone Martha has been 'programmed' to help the Sontarans, but as she dies, she gains enough of her original personality and feelings to give the real Martha and the Doctor vital information about the Sontaran plans — information that enables the Doctor to work out what they are up to and defeat them.

SONTARAN WARSHIPS

A race that lives for war has many terrible weapons at its disposal. None of these have more firepower than the fearsome Sontaran warships. Huge, majestic, and lethal, Sontaran warships are armed with a variety of weapons, including enough missiles to destroy entire planets. They go into battle in a distinctive arrow-shaped formation.

General Staal's flagship has teleport ability — a direct link to locations like the Rattigan Academy as well as remote systems that Staal uses to bring the TARDIS on-board.

The ship is destroyed when Luke Rattigan operates the Doctor's atmospheric converter, recalibrated so it will ignite the air in the Sontaran ship. As the ship burns, its missiles explode and the Sontaran invasion force is completely destroyed.

SONTARAN SCOUTSHIPS

A Sontaran warship is equipped with scoutships that can detach from the main craft for short range expeditions. The Sontaran scoutship is spherical, spinning its way through space.

The Sontarans also use scoutships for clandestine operations as they are small enough to avoid Rutan — and other — detection systems. Incredibly powerful for their size, they can also be used to spearhead attacks on stationary targets like spacestations. Some more advanced scoutships can be placed in 'clear' when they have landed — making them invisible.

TEST YOUR KNOWLEDGE

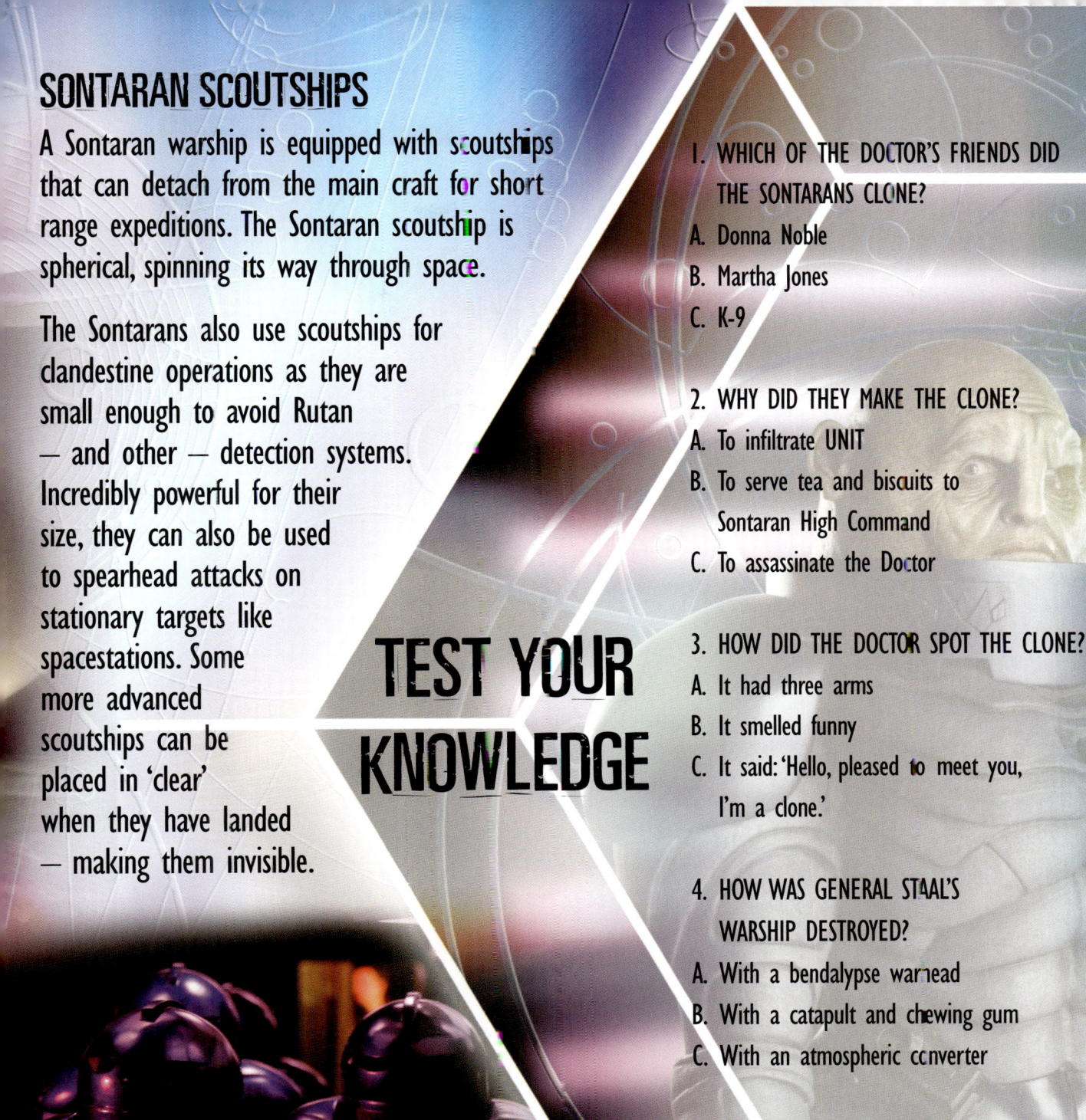

1. WHICH OF THE DOCTOR'S FRIENDS DID THE SONTARANS CLONE?
A. Donna Noble
B. Martha Jones
C. K-9

2. WHY DID THEY MAKE THE CLONE?
A. To infiltrate UNIT
B. To serve tea and biscuits to Sontaran High Command
C. To assassinate the Doctor

3. HOW DID THE DOCTOR SPOT THE CLONE?
A. It had three arms
B. It smelled funny
C. It said: 'Hello, pleased to meet you, I'm a clone.'

4. HOW WAS GENERAL STAAL'S WARSHIP DESTROYED?
A. With a bendalypse warhead
B. With a catapult and chewing gum
C. With an atmospheric converter

5. WHAT SHAPE IS A SONTARAN SCOUTSHIP?
A. Arrow-shaped
B. A cube
C. A sphere

392 SONTARAN STRATEGIES

PREVIOUS STRATEGIES

The Doctor encountered the Sontarans several times before he foiled their attempt to turn Earth into a Sontaran Clone World.

The Second Doctor had to be rescued by his own Sixth incarnation when he was kidnapped by the Sontaran Group Marshal Stike and held prisoner in Spain. Stike hoped to learn the secret of time travel from the Doctor.

In fact the Sontarans soon obtained limited time travel ability. The Third Doctor was called in by UNIT to investigate when key scientists went missing. Helped — for the first time — by journalist Sarah Jane Smith, he discovered the scientists were in Medieval England. Sontaran Commander Linx was using an Osmic Projector to kidnap scientists from the future to help repair his damaged ship.

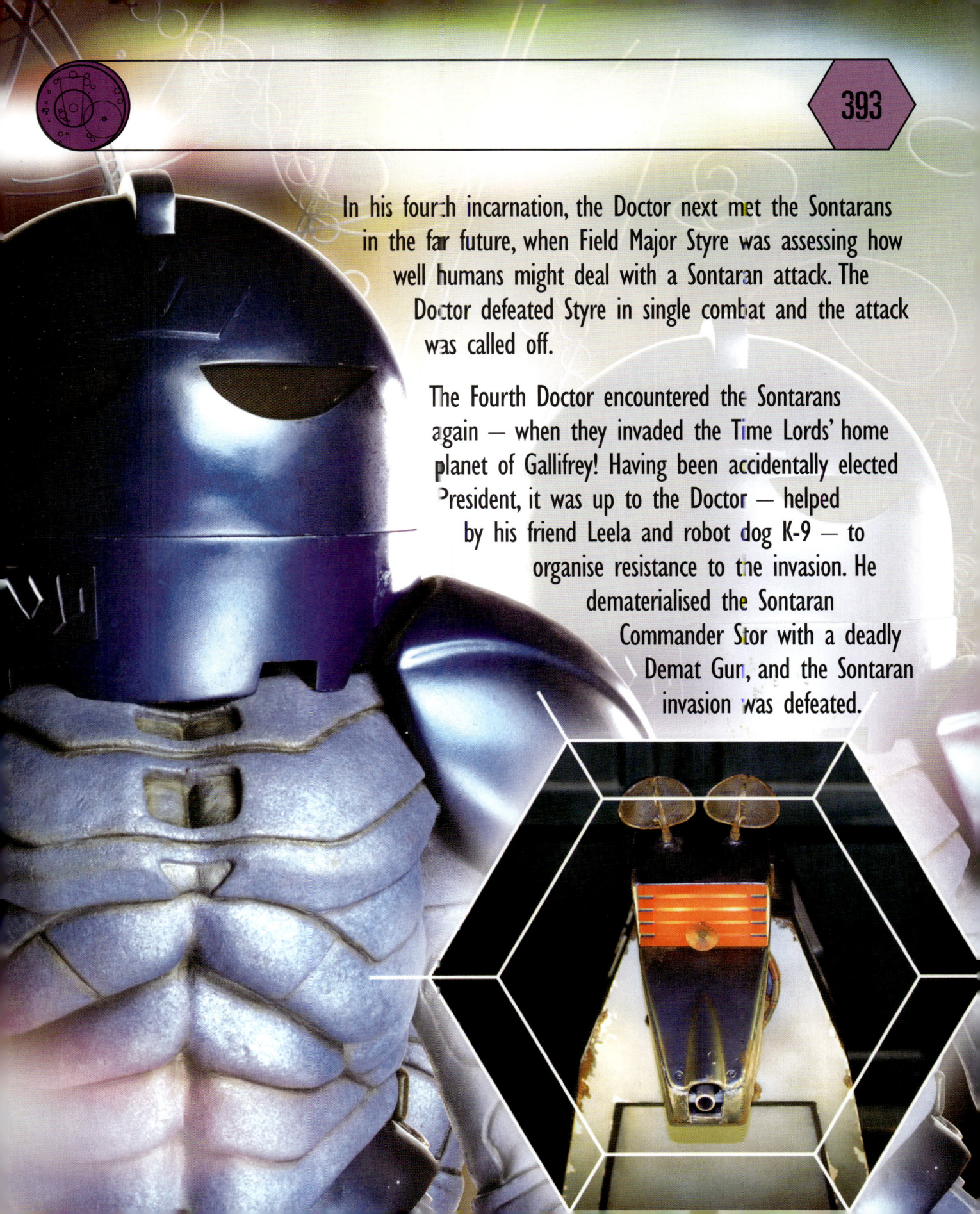

In his fourth incarnation, the Doctor next met the Sontarans in the far future, when Field Major Styre was assessing how well humans might deal with a Sontaran attack. The Doctor defeated Styre in single combat and the attack was called off.

The Fourth Doctor encountered the Sontarans again — when they invaded the Time Lords' home planet of Gallifrey! Having been accidentally elected President, it was up to the Doctor — helped by his friend Leela and robot dog K-9 — to organise resistance to the invasion. He dematerialised the Sontaran Commander Stor with a deadly Demat Gun, and the Sontaran invasion was defeated.

THE ATMOS STRATEGY

Again, UNIT was involved from the outset in foiling the Sontaran ATMOS Strategem. Suspicious of a series of identical deaths caused by the ATMOS system installed in cars across the world, UNIT raided the Atmos factory.

The Doctor and Donna teamed up with UNIT and the Doctor's friend Martha Jones to discover the involvement of the Sontarans, led by General Staal. Despite UNIT soldiers being hypnotised and Martha Jones being replaced by a Sontaran clone, the Doctor and Donna were able to discover the truth of the Sontaran plan.

The Sontarans were going to use the ATMOS system installed in millions of cars to emit a gas that would suffocate all humans. But the gas would create the ideal conditions for Earth to become a Clone World — where the Sontarans could create millions of cloned troops to battle their ancient enemy, the Rutans.

While UNIT battled bravely against Sontaran shock troops, the Doctor managed to create an Atmospheric Converter to burn off the deadly gas. With the help of Luke Rattigan — the inventor of ATMOS who had been betrayed by his Sontaran allies — the Doctor used the Converter to destroy the Sontaran Warship in orbit above Earth.

TEST YOUR KNOWLEDGE

1. WHAT WAS THE NAME OF THE SONTARAN STRANDED IN MEDIEVAL ENGLAND?
A. Larynx
B. Linx
C. Legolas

2. WHO HELPED THE DOCTOR DEFEAT THE SONTARAN INVASION OF GALLIFREY?
A. Sarah Jane Smith
B. Luke Rattigan
C. Leela and K-9

3. WHO WAS THE LEADER OF THE SONTARAN ATTEMPT TO TURN EARTH INTO A CLONE WORLD?
A. General Staal
B. General Stores
C. General Knowledge

4. WHAT DID THE DOCTOR USE TO GET RID OF THE POISONOUS ATMOS GAS?
A. A huge vacuum cleaner
B. A trained hamster called Ferdinand
C. An Atmospheric Converter

5. WHO DID THE SONTARANS CLONE?
A. K-9 and Leela
B. Martha Jones
C. Alvin and the Chipmunks

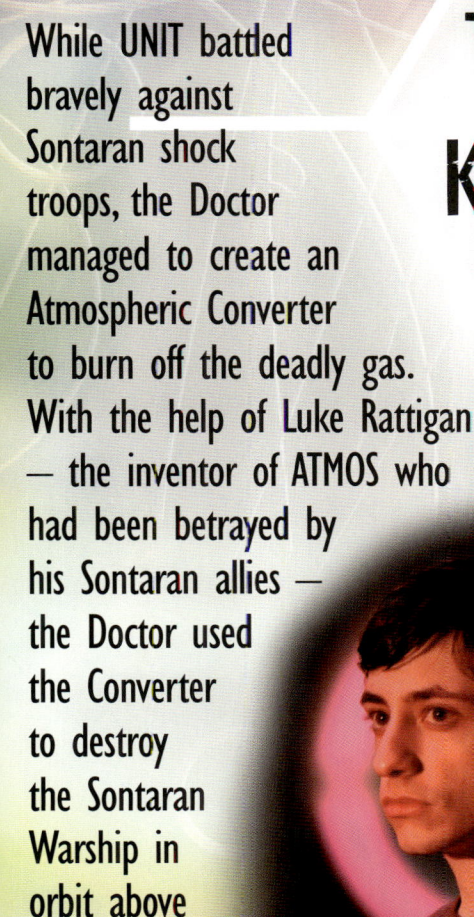

TEST YOUR KNOWLEDGE

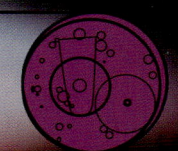

ANSWERS

The Sontarans
1 (b) 2 (a) 3 (c) 4 (b) 5 (c)

Sontarans and their Allies
1 (c) 2 (a) 3 (b) 4 (a) 5 (b)

The Rutans & Other Sontaran Enemies
1 (b) 2 (c) 3 (a) 4 (c) 5 (a)

Defending Earth & Attacking Earth
1 (c) 2 (a) 3 (b) 4 (c) 5 (a)

Weapons and Technology
1 (b) 2 (a) 3 (b) 4 (c) 5 (c)

Sontaran Strategies
1 (b) 2 (c) 3 (a) 4 (c) 5 (b)

DOCTOR·WHO

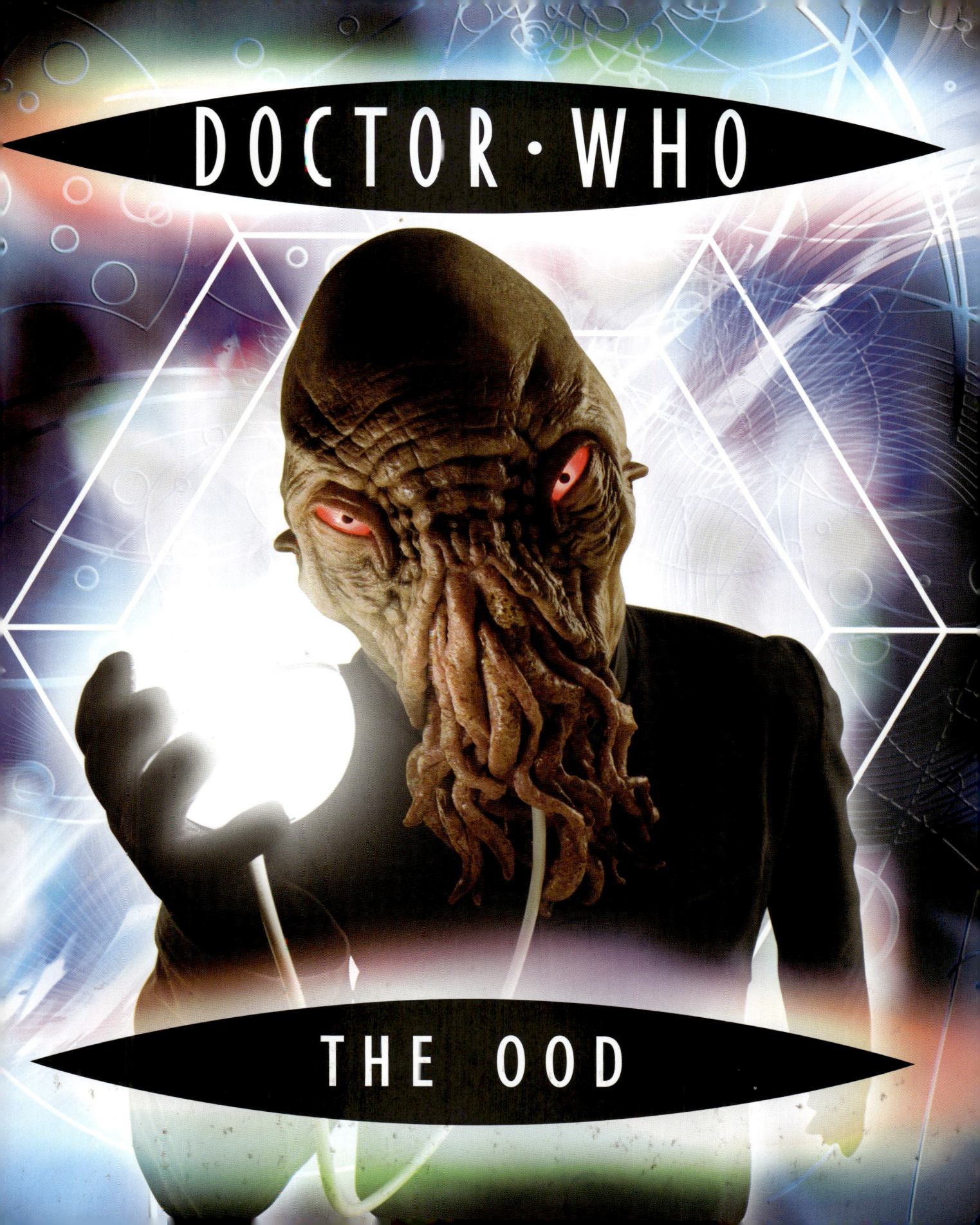

THE OOD

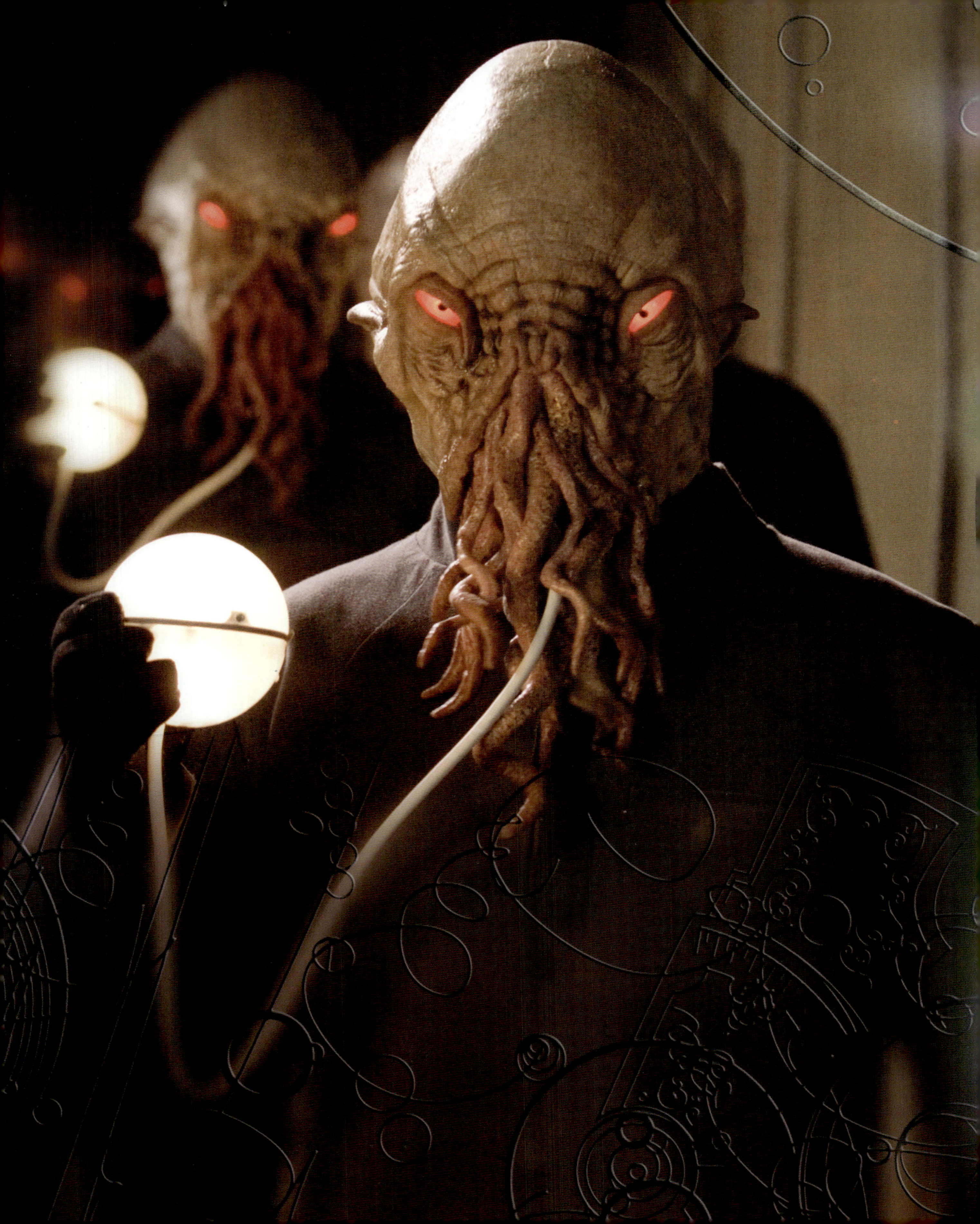

CONTENTS

Meet the Ood
Introduction..400
Ood Data..402
Ood Anatomy...404
◆ Test your knowledge

Oodkind
Ood...406
Natural Ood...407
Ood Sigma...408
The Ood Brain...409
◆ Test your knowledge

Ood Friends and Enemies
The Doctor, Rose, Donna............................410
Sanctuary Base Six......................................411
The Beast..411
Klineman Halpen...412
Friends of the Ood......................................413
◆ Test your knowledge

Background
Ood-Sphere...414
Krop Tor..415
Red-Eye...416

Telepathy...416
The Circle..417
◆ Test your knowledge

Converting the Ood
Ood Conversion...418
Ood Operations...419
Translator Ball...420
Warehouse Fifteen......................................421
◆ Test your knowledge

Ood Encounters
On Krop Tor...422
On the Planet of the Ood............................424
◆ Test your knowledge

Test your knowledge Answers.....................426

400 MEET THE OOD

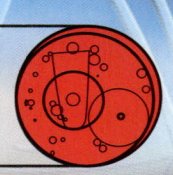

In the 42nd century, the Second Great and Bountiful Human Empire spans three galaxies, and the Ood live only to serve people.

At first glance, the Ood look quite terrifying. They have fleshy tentacles in place of a nose and mouth. However, this race of mildly telepathic creatures is completely harmless, unless they become infected.

401

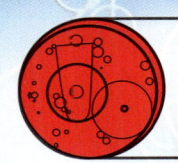

Humans believe that all Ood want to do is serve people. By the year 4126, at least fifty per cent of all homes across Galactic Central have an Ood to carry out all their menial tasks. Most people don't think it's cruel to own an Ood because if they don't receive any orders the creatures just pine and eventually die.

The Ood don't have individual names, just numbers, but humans like to think of Ood as trusted friends. Unfortunately, the problem with the Ood is that, being telepathic, they are prone to being taken over by creatures with stronger minds. And that's when the trouble begins.

402 — OOD DATA

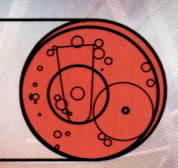

Name: Ood
Species: Oodkind
Height: 1.83m (6ft)
Home Planet: Ood-Sphere in the Horsehead Nebula
Skin: Pale, with fleshy red tentacles
Weapons: Translator ball can electrocute victims
Strengths: They do the jobs humans love to hate
Weaknesses: When given no orders, they die
Look out for: Red-Eyed Ood — they're dangerous!

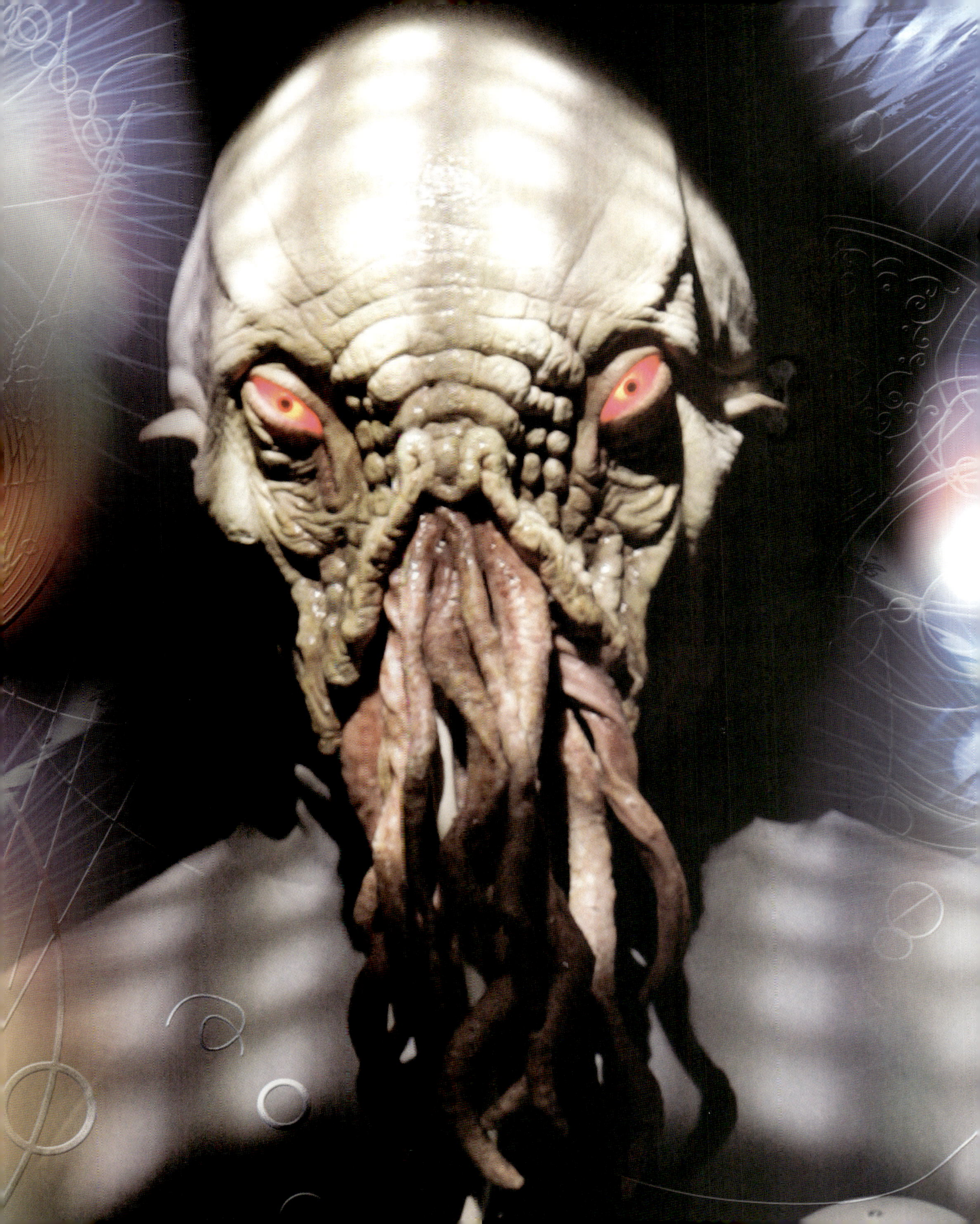

404 OOD ANATOMY

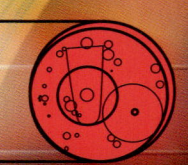

Eyes — when possessed, Ood eyes turn red signifying danger!

Fleshy tentacles

Code sewn on to tunic to identify Ood

Simple grey tunic, worn by nearly all converted Ood

Telepathic signals from brain

Pale skin, with purple blood beneath

Translator ball — when not translating it can be used as an energy weapon

TEST YOUR KNOWLEDGE

1. WHAT DO OOD HAVE INSTEAD OF A MOUTH AND NOSE?
   A. A beak
   B. Strange symbols
   C. Fleshy tentacles

2. WHAT COLOUR DO AN OOD'S EYES TURN WHEN POSSESSED?
   A. Purple
   B. Red
   C. White

3. WHAT HAPPENS IF AN OOD RECEIVES NO ORDERS?
   A. It pines and dies
   B. It dances and sings
   C. It finds another owner

4. HOW MANY HOMES ACROSS GALACTIC CENTRAL HAVE AT LEAST ONE OOD?
   A. Ten per cent
   B. Fifty per cent
   C. One hundred per cent

5. IN THE 42ND CENTURY, WHAT EMPIRE SPANS THREE GALAXIES?
   A. The Empire of the Ood
   B. The Second Great and Bountiful Human Empire
   C. The Roman Empire

406 OODKIND

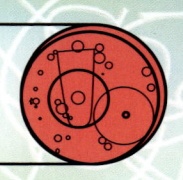

Ood

Humans don't just breed Ood, they convert them into slaves. Their Hind-Brain is cut off and replaced by a translator ball. In this way, a workforce of Ood who want to serve is created.

Ood come with a standard translator setting, but can be adapted to a variety of different styles, including one with a female voice or a comedy classic setting for humour. Ood are used across the galaxy as servants to carry out all the jobs humans don't want to do. They are considered better than robots because they don't need technical support or software upgrades. An Ood is for life.

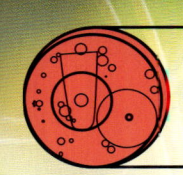

NATURAL OOD

In their natural state, Ood used to roam around happily on the ice plains of the Ood-Sphere. Natural Ood sing to each other telepathically, and the songs are beautiful. They are quite different from the processed Ood that end up serving humans.

Born with a Hind-Brain that contains their memories and emotions, they hold it out in front of them in their hands like some kind of offering. Donna thought that a creature born with a brain in its hands would have to trust anyone it meets.

408

OOD SIGMA

Ood Sigma is the personal assistant to Halpen, the Chief Executive of Ood Operations on the Ood's home planet. Ood Sigma wears a special grey suit with a Greek Sigma on the pocket. Halpen thinks of him as his faithful servant, but Ood Sigma is secretly turning the power-hungry Chief Exec into Oodkind, with the fake hair tonic in his hip flask.

THE OOD BRAIN

Centuries before Ood Operations started processing Ood, the Ood Brain was found beneath the Northern Glacier on the Ood-Sphere. The brain is the telepathic centre of Oodkind and connects the creatures with a beautiful song.

An Ood is unable to survive with a separate forebrain and Hind-Brain because they would constantly be at war with themselves, so the Ood Brain brings them together. A massive pulsating brain, the captured Ood Brain fills an entire warehouse on the Ood-Sphere. Oodkind needs the Ood Brain to survive — if it dies, so do the Ood creatures.

TEST YOUR KNOWLEDGE

1. WHAT ARE OOD BORN WITH IN THEIR HANDS?
   A. A handbag
   B. A translator ball
   C. A Hind-Brain

2. WHAT IS THE DESIGNATION OF HALPEN'S PERSONAL OOD?
   A. Ood Jeeves
   B. Ood Sigma
   C. Ood Brabinger

3. WHY ARE OOD CONSIDERED BETTER THAN ROBOTS?
   A. They don't talk back
   B. They don't need software upgrades or maintenance
   C. They can do two things at once

4. WHERE WAS THE OOD BRAIN ORIGINALLY FOUND?
   A. Beneath the Northern Glacier on the Ood-Sphere
   B. On Krop Tor, near a black hole
   C. Warehouse Fifteen on the Ood-Sphere

5. WHAT HAPPENS IF THE OOD BRAIN DIES?
   A. The Ood are free
   B. The Ood sing
   C. The Ood die too

410 OOD FRIENDS AND ENEMIES

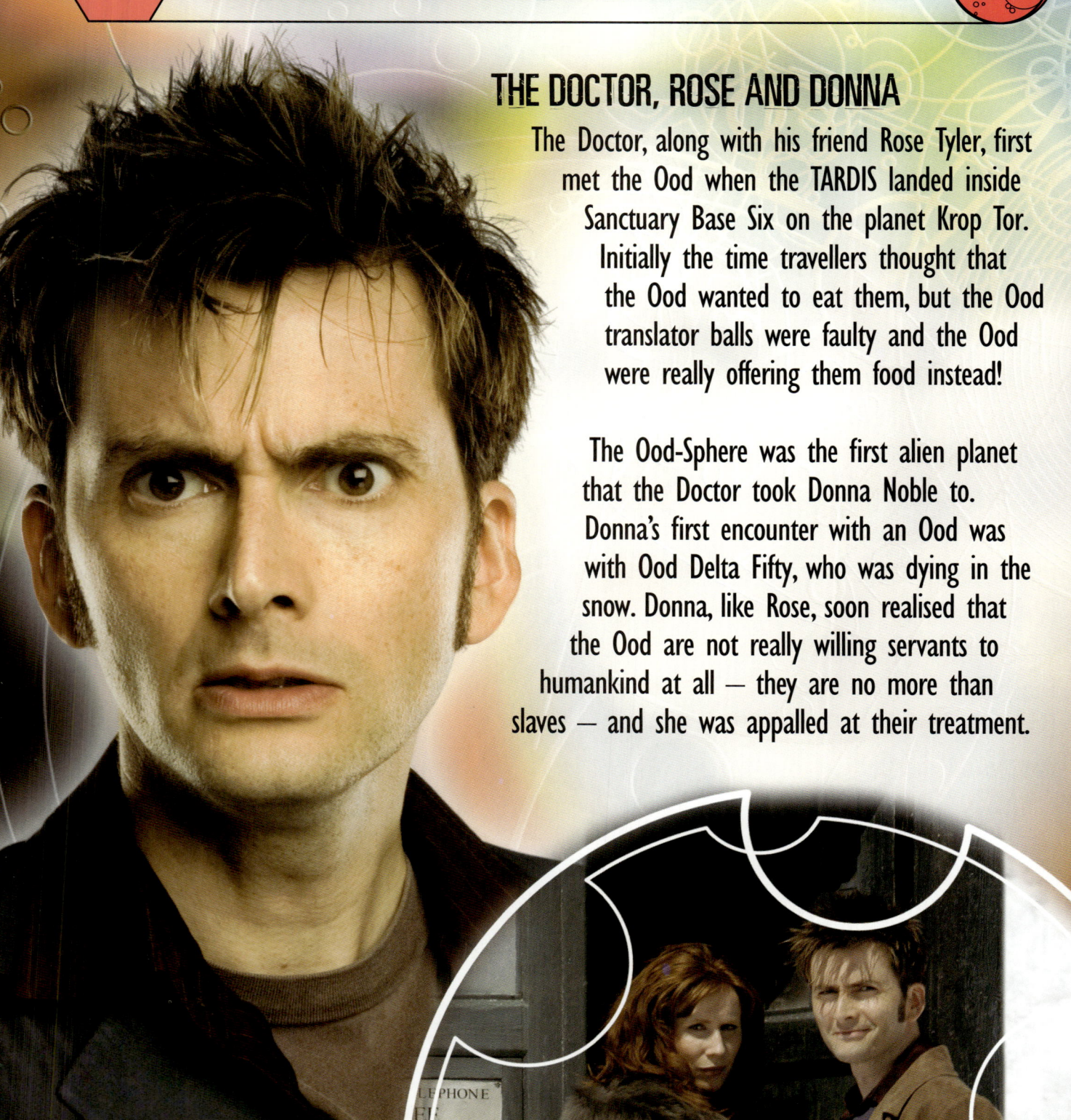

THE DOCTOR, ROSE AND DONNA

The Doctor, along with his friend Rose Tyler, first met the Ood when the TARDIS landed inside Sanctuary Base Six on the planet Krop Tor. Initially the time travellers thought that the Ood wanted to eat them, but the Ood translator balls were faulty and the Ood were really offering them food instead!

The Ood-Sphere was the first alien planet that the Doctor took Donna Noble to. Donna's first encounter with an Ood was with Ood Delta Fifty, who was dying in the snow. Donna, like Rose, soon realised that the Ood are not really willing servants to humankind at all — they are no more than slaves — and she was appalled at their treatment.

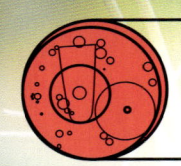

SANCTUARY BASE SIX

The small human crew of Sanctuary Base Six on Krop Tor used a group of fifty Ood to help them drill down into the depths of the planet, as well as cooking and looking after them. Their computer didn't even register Ood as proper life forms. When a hidden creature called the Beast awoke, the Ood were taken over by him and suddenly became his legion. They attempted to kill the crew one by one.

THE BEAST

Chained deep beneath the planet Krop Tor, the Disciples of Light had enslaved the massive Beast millions of years ago. The creature possessed one of the crew, Toby Zed, and then used the Ood in his attempt to escape from the pit. When possessed by the Beast, the Ood's eyes glowed bright red.

412

KLINEMAN HALPEN

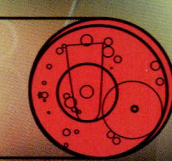

Klineman Halpen was the Chief Executive of Ood Operations on the Ood-Sphere. When sales of Ood began to slow, Halpen reduced the price to fifty credits and expected the Ood conversion to be doubled. Halpen's father took him to the warehouse containing the Ood Brain when he was only six years old, and he always knew the horrific truth about how the Natural Ood were converted into slaves. Halpen believed the Doctor and Donna to be Friends of the Ood activists and was eventually turned into an Ood himself by Ood Sigma.

FRIENDS OF THE OOD

The Friends of the Ood, or FOTO, are a group of people who think that the Ood are treated badly and should be free. Head of Ood Management, Doctor Ryder, secretly worked for FOTO. It took him ten years to get inside Ood Operations. When he did, he was able to lower the barrier that prevented the Ood from connecting with each other, allowing some of the Ood to break free. This eventually brought about the destruction of Ood Operations, although Ryder was killed by Halpen in the process.

TEST YOUR KNOWLEDGE

1. WHICH OF THE DOCTOR'S COMPANIONS HAVE MET THE OOD?
A. Donna and Martha
B. Martha and Rose
C. Rose and Donna

2. HOW MANY OOD WERE ON KROP TOR?
A. Fifty
B. Five hundred
C. Five thousand

3. WHAT HAPPENED TO THE FIRST OOD DONNA MET?
A. It tried to feed her
B. It died in the snow
C. It asked her to marry it

4. WHAT DOES FOTO STAND FOR?
A. Foes of the Ood
B. Family of the Ood
C. Friends of the Ood

5. WHAT WAS KLINEMAN HALPEN'S JOB?
A. Head of Ood Management
B. A Disciple of Light
C. Chief Executive of Ood Operations

414 BACKGROUND

OOD-SPHERE

A planet in the Horsehead Nebula, the distant world of Ood-Sphere is a cold, windswept place with ice plains covered in snow. This breathtaking world is the home planet of the Ood and the Ood Brain. The Doctor visited this solar system years ago, when he landed on the nearby planet Sense-Sphere.

KROP TOR

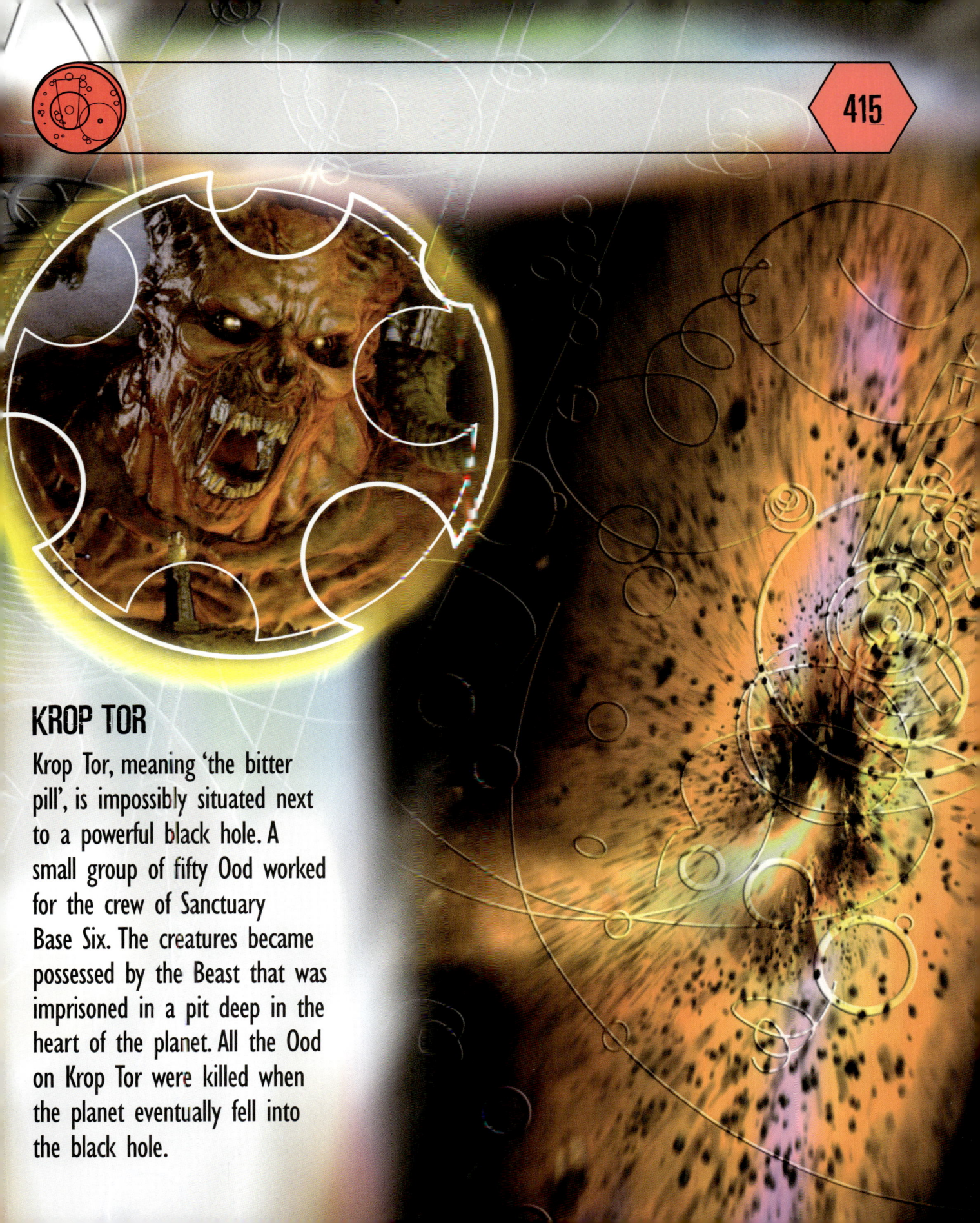

Krop Tor, meaning 'the bitter pill', is impossibly situated next to a powerful black hole. A small group of fifty Ood worked for the crew of Sanctuary Base Six. The creatures became possessed by the Beast that was imprisoned in a pit deep in the heart of the planet. All the Ood on Krop Tor were killed when the planet eventually fell into the black hole.

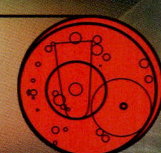

RED-EYE

An immediate warning that an Ood has become infected and is dangerous is when it develops something called Red-Eye. When the creatures' eyes glow bright red, the Ood become uncharacteristically savage, will disobey orders and may even attempt to kill.

On Krop Tor, this was a sign that the Beast had possessed them. When the Doctor and Donna met them on the Ood-Sphere, it showed that the Ood were trying to finally break free.

TELEPATHY

Ood are able to communicate with each other telepathically, which means they can hear each other in their minds. On Krop Tor, one of the crew, Danny Bartok, monitored their telepathic field. It was usually rated at Basic 5.

When the Ood were disturbed by the Beast the telepathic field rose to Basic 30, which was the equivalent of them screaming and shouting silently inside their heads, and it eventually rose to Basic 100. Danny thought this was impossible, as technically it meant they should have been dead.

Danny eventually managed to send out a telepathic flare to Basic Zero, which caused the possessed Ood to collapse.

THE CIRCLE

When the Doctor and Donna met a dying Ood on the ice plains of the Ood's home planet, the creature said that 'the circle must be broken'. Later, when Donna was trapped with Red-Eyed Ood they mentioned that the circle must be broken so that they could sing.

The circle literally referred to the pylons surrounding the Ood Brain, which dampened the telepathic field. When the circle was finally broken, the Ood could communicate with each other freely again. Oodkind contacted each other across the galaxy requesting that the Ood all come home — as they were free at last.

TEST YOUR KNOWLEDGE

1. WHAT PLANET IS THE OOD-SPHERE NEAR?
A. Earth
B. Horsehead
C. Sense-Sphere

2. WHAT DOES KROP TOR MEAN?
A. The oncoming storm
B. The bitter pill
C. The circle must be broken

3. WHAT HAPPENED WHEN DANNY BARTOK SENT OUT A TELEPATHIC FLARE?
A. The Ood became possessed by the Beast
B. The Ood collapsed
C. The Ood died

4. WHAT DID A DYING OOD SAY TO THE DOCTOR AND DONNA?
A. You are not alone
B. She is not dead
C. The circle must be broken

5. WHAT WAS THE CIRCLE?
A. The barrier around the Ood Brain
B. A song the Ood sang
C. Where the Beast was trapped

418 — CONVERTING THE OOD

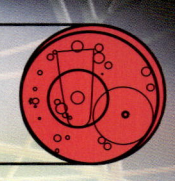

OOD CONVERSION

The Doctor thought that a species born to serve could never evolve. He realised that Ood Operations was doing something to create creatures with no concept of freedom and a desire to obey.

He soon discovered the horrible truth — Ood Operations was ripping out the Ood's Hind-Brain and then replacing it with a translator ball to create the perfect servant.

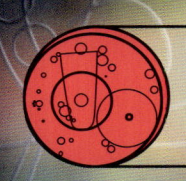

OOD OPERATIONS

Based on the Ood-Sphere, Ood Operations, also known affectionately as Double O, was the main headquarters for the conversion of Natural Ood into Oodkind ready to be sold. Converted Ood were kept in containers, ready to be flown out by rocket to the three galaxies.

Ood Operations were looking to expand into new territories before the Ood managed to break the circle and Ood Operations was closed down.

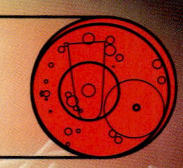

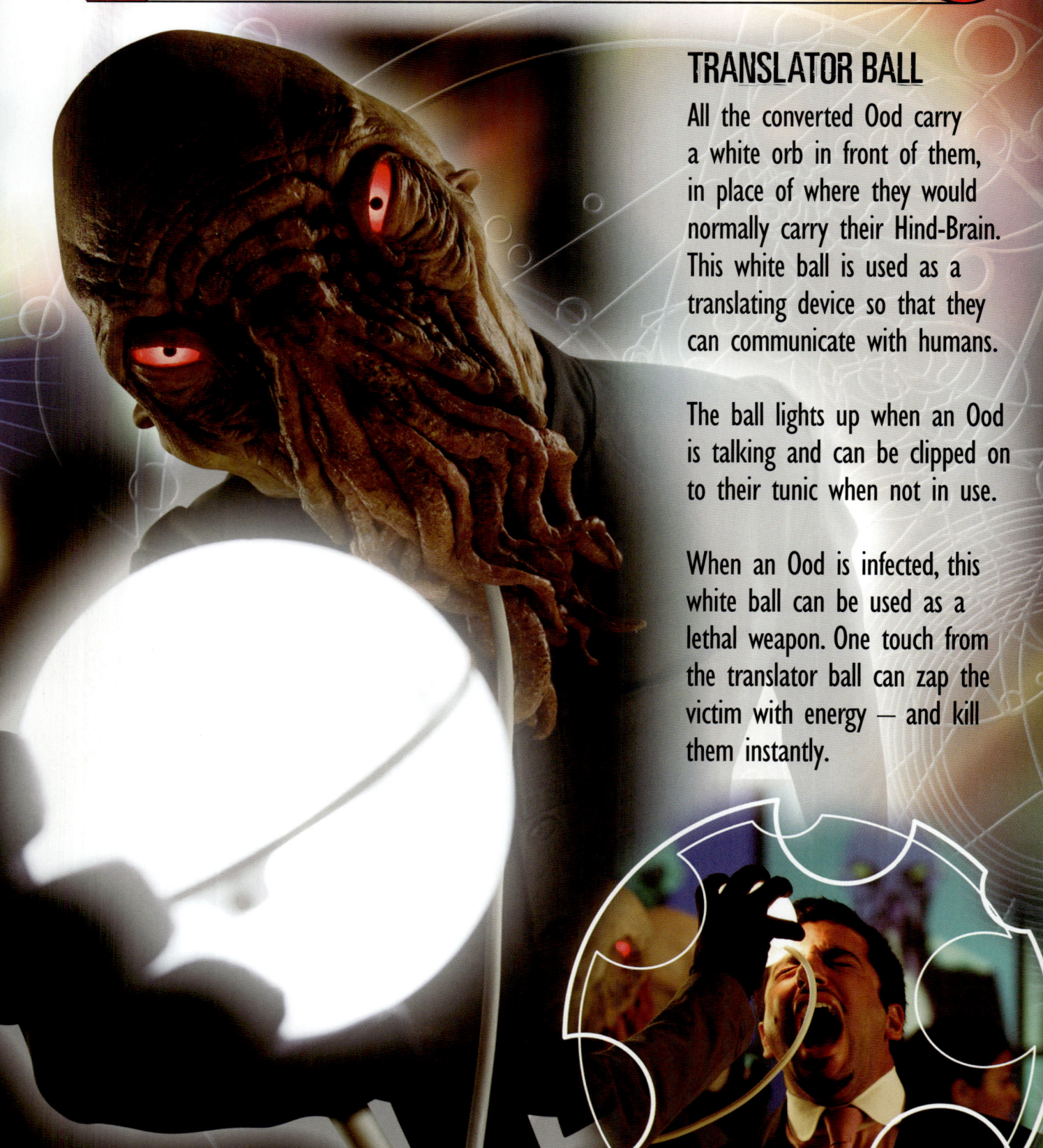

TRANSLATOR BALL

All the converted Ood carry a white orb in front of them, in place of where they would normally carry their Hind-Brain. This white ball is used as a translating device so that they can communicate with humans.

The ball lights up when an Ood is talking and can be clipped on to their tunic when not in use.

When an Ood is infected, this white ball can be used as a lethal weapon. One touch from the translator ball can zap the victim with energy — and kill them instantly.

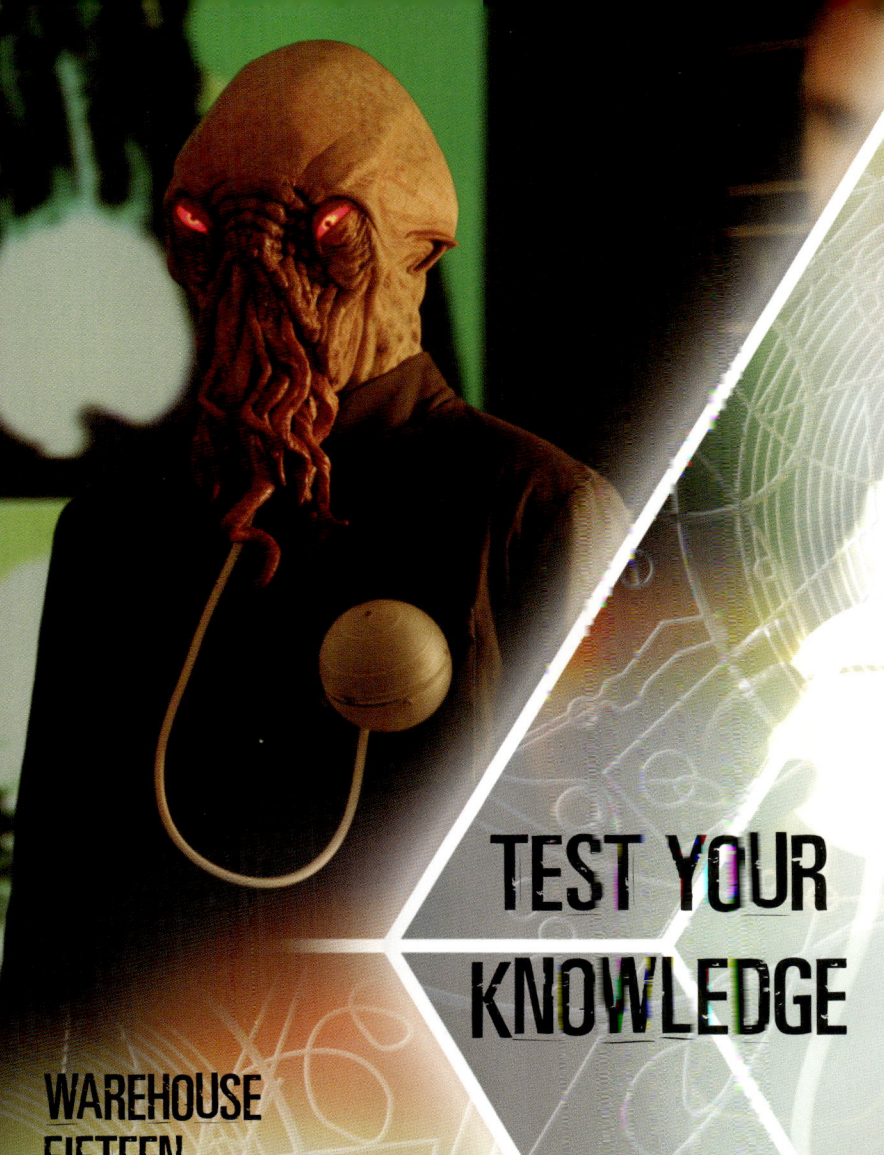

WAREHOUSE FIFTEEN

One of the giant warehouses belonging to Ood Operations was called Warehouse Fifteen. Inside this warehouse Ood Operations kept the gigantic pulsating Ood Brain captive. Using a circle of pylons around the creature, the company was able to stop the Ood from communicating with each other and have complete control over them.

TEST YOUR KNOWLEDGE

1. WHAT IS OOD OPERATIONS ALSO KNOWN AS?
   A. The House of Ood
   B. Double O
   C. Ood Shop

2. WHAT HAPPENS TO THE TRANSLATOR BALL WHEN THE OOD ARE COMMUNICATING?
   A. Nothing
   B. It glows red
   C. It glows white

3. WHERE WAS THE OOD BRAIN HELD CAPTIVE?
   A. In a pit on Krop Tor
   B. Under an ice plain on the Ood-Sphere
   C. In Warehouse Fifteen

4. WHAT ELSE CAN THE TRANSLATOR BALL DO?
   A. Wash clothes
   B. Write
   C. Kill

5. WHEN NOT IN USE, WHERE DOES THE TRANSLATOR BALL GO?
   A. It is clipped to the Ood's tunic
   B. It can be detached
   C. In the Ood's pocket

422 OOD ENCOUNTERS

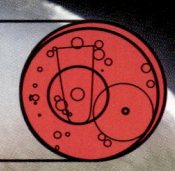

ON KROP TOR

There was a group of fifty Ood serving the humans on Krop Tor, a planet that was impossibly orbiting a black hole.

These Ood were just innocent creatures, unprepared for what happened to them. Their daily routine involved serving the small crew on Sanctuary Base Six and responding to their every command. They cooked, they maintained the base and they even helped to mine — basically they worked as slaves. The crew relied on the creatures, like so many humans across the galaxy. And because Ood pine and die if not given orders, the crew didn't think there was anything wrong in using the Ood to do everything for them.

423

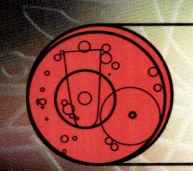

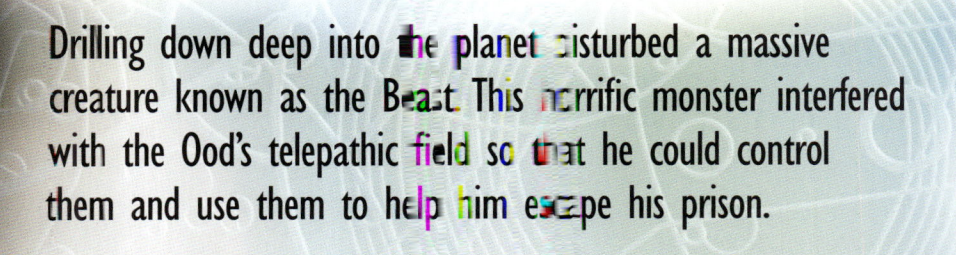

Drilling down deep into the planet disturbed a massive creature known as the Beast. This horrific monster interfered with the Ood's telepathic field so that he could control them and use them to help him escape his prison.

One of the Ood told Rose that 'The Beast and his armies shall rise from the pit to make war against God.' Immediately it corrected itself and said that it hoped she would enjoy her meal.

Later, with the Doctor trapped in the pit deep beneath the planet, Rose was left on the base to join the crew in the fight against the infected Ood. The possessed Ood attacked the crew and even killed some of them using their translator balls as weapons. Eventually Danny Bartok was able to send out a telepathic flare which made the Ood collapse and stopped them attacking. Krop Tor, along with all the Ood, was destroyed when it was sucked into the black hole.

The crew who escaped recorded the Ood deaths in a final report, awarding them honours for their services.

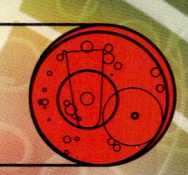

ON THE PLANET OF THE OOD

After she was reunited with the Doctor, Donna's first intergalactic trip was to the home planet of the Ood, a snowy planet in the Horsehead Nebula called the Ood-Sphere.

On this planet, the Doctor discovered the real reason behind the Ood's willingness to serve humans. It wasn't instinct that made them serve at all — they were being turned into slaves and were part of a profitable business. For many years, Ood Operations had been converting the creatures to sell across three galaxies. An operation removed the Ood's Hind-Brain and added a translator ball in its place.

Unknown to the Chief Executive of Ood Operations, Friends of the Ood had managed to infiltrate the company and help the Ood from the inside.

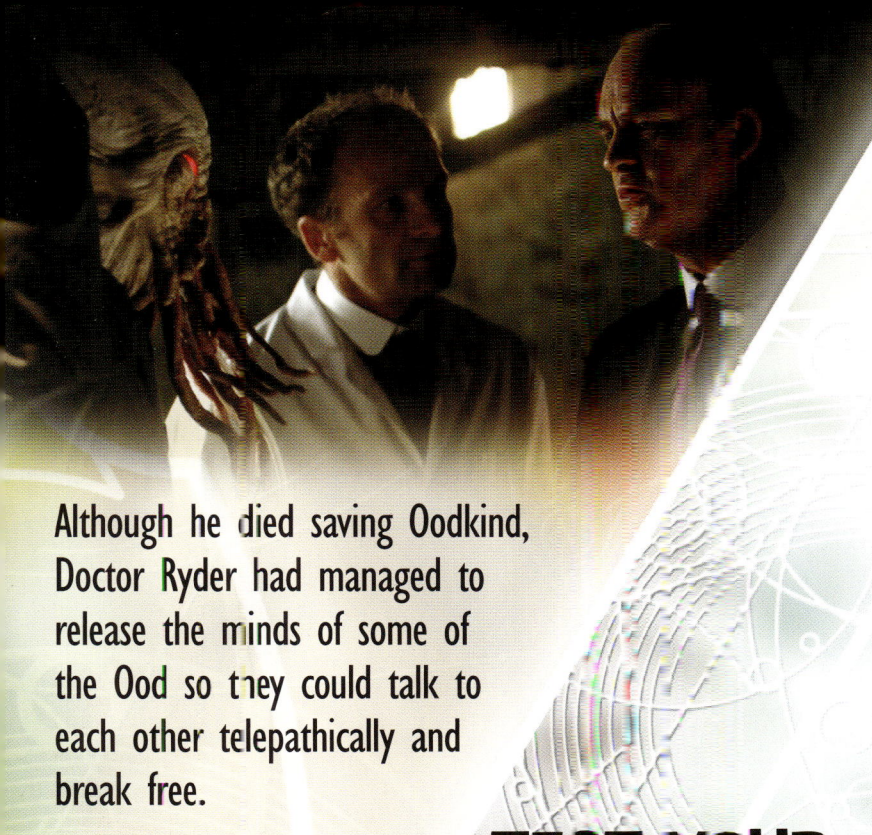

Although he died saving Oodkind, Doctor Ryder had managed to release the minds of some of the Ood so they could talk to each other telepathically and break free.

With help from the Doctor and Donna Oodkind had been set free. The beautiful song of the freed Ood called enslaved Ood across the galaxy back to their home. As the Doctor and Donna left in the TARDIS, the Ood said that they would never forget them.

TEST YOUR KNOWLEDGE

1. ON KROP TOR, WHAT DID THE OOD INTEND TO SAY TO ROSE?
   A. It wanted her to know she would leave the Doctor
   B. It wanted her to run away
   C. It hoped she enjoyed her meal

2. WHAT WAS IMPOSSIBLE ABOUT KROP TOR?
   A. It looked exactly like Earth
   B. It was orbiting a black hole
   C. Donna and Rose have both been there

3. WHAT DID THE CREW OF SANCTUARY BASE SIX THINK ABOUT HAVING OOD WITH THEM?
   A. They thought it was completely normal
   B. They were all Friends of the Ood and didn't like it
   C. They never trusted them

4. WHAT DID OOD OPERATIONS DO?
   A. Upgraded Ood to Cybermen
   B. Saved Ood
   C. Converted Ood into slaves they could sell

5. WHAT DID THE OOD SAY WHEN THE DOCTOR AND DONNA LEFT THE OOD-SPHERE?
   A. Never come back!
   B. They would never forget them
   C. They all wanted to travel in the TARDIS too

TEST YOUR KNOWLEDGE

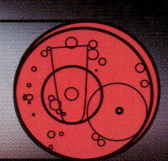

ANSWERS

Meet the Ood
1 (c) 2 (b) 3 (a) 4 (b) 5 (b)

Oodkind
1 (c) 2 (b) 3 (b) 4 (a) 5 (c)

Ood Friends and Enemies
1 (c) 2 (a) 3 (b) 4 (c) 5 (c)

Background
1 (c) 2 (b) 3 (b) 4 (c) 5 (a)

Converting the Ood
1 (b) 2 (c) 3 (c) 4 (c) 5 (a)

Ood Encounters
1 (c) 2 (b) 3 (a) 4 (c) 5 (b)

DOCTOR·WHO

THE MASTER

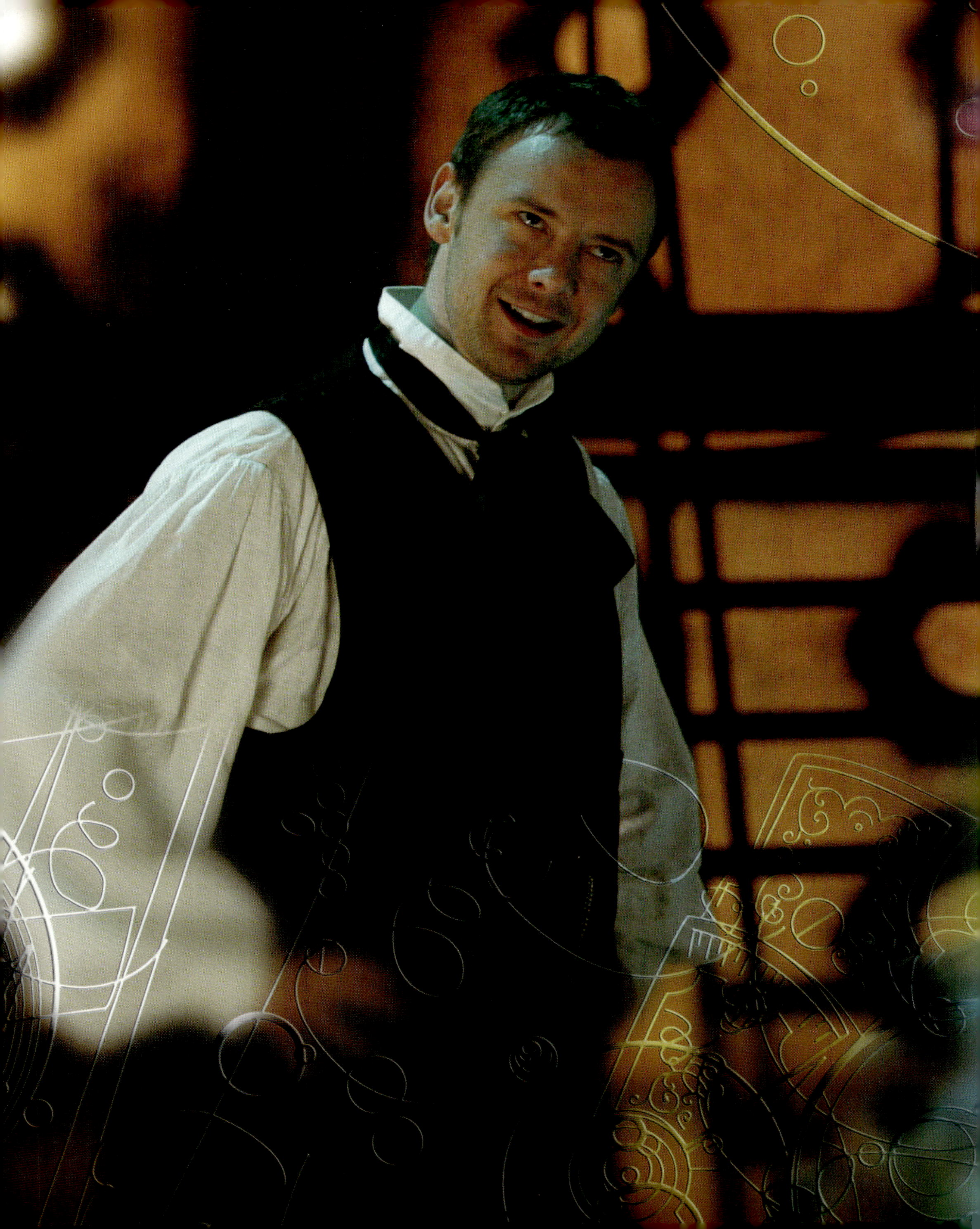

CONTENTS

Meet The Master
Introduction.................................430
Master Data................................432
The Master Anatomy....................434
⬢ Test your knowledge

The Master's Aliases and Friends
Professor Yana...........................436
Chantho.....................................437
Harry Saxon...............................438
Lucy Saxon.................................438
Toclafane....................................439
⬢ Test your knowledge

The Master's Enemies
The Doctor..................................440
Martha Jones..............................441
Captain Jack Harkness................442
The Jones Family........................443
⬢ Test your knowledge

The Past Master
The Past Master..........................444
Life on Malcassairo....................446
⬢ Test your knowledge

The Master's Technology
Fob Watch..................................448
Laser screwdriver.......................448
Aircraft Carrier Valiant................449
Archangel Communications Network..........449
The TARDIS................................450
⬢ Test your knowledge

The Master on Earth........452
⬢ Test your knowledge

Test your knowledge Answers....................456

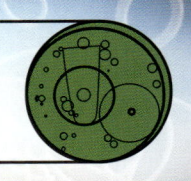

430 MEET THE MASTER

The Master — a fitting title for one of the most ruthless people to ever exist. A renegade Time Lord, the Master's sole mission in the Universe was to destroy and conquer. Charming yet totally insane, the Doctor's oldest and deadliest enemy was capable of destroying worlds on a whim.

The Doctor went to school with the Master and the two used to be close friends. But while the Doctor used his powers for good, his childhood companion used his for evil after, at the age of eight, he looking into the Untempered Schism, a rip in the fabric of reality, which sent him mad.

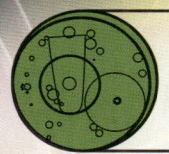

Brought back to life to fight the Daleks in the Time War, the Master ran away when the Daleks took control of the Cruciform - hiding at the end of the Universe because he was so scared.

It was here that the Doctor discovered his old friend - disguised as Professor Yana on the planet Malcassairo. After he escaped in the Doctor's TARDIS, the Master quickly took control of the Earth, hypnotising the population and preparing to wage war on the rest of the Universe. Then the Doctor arrived…

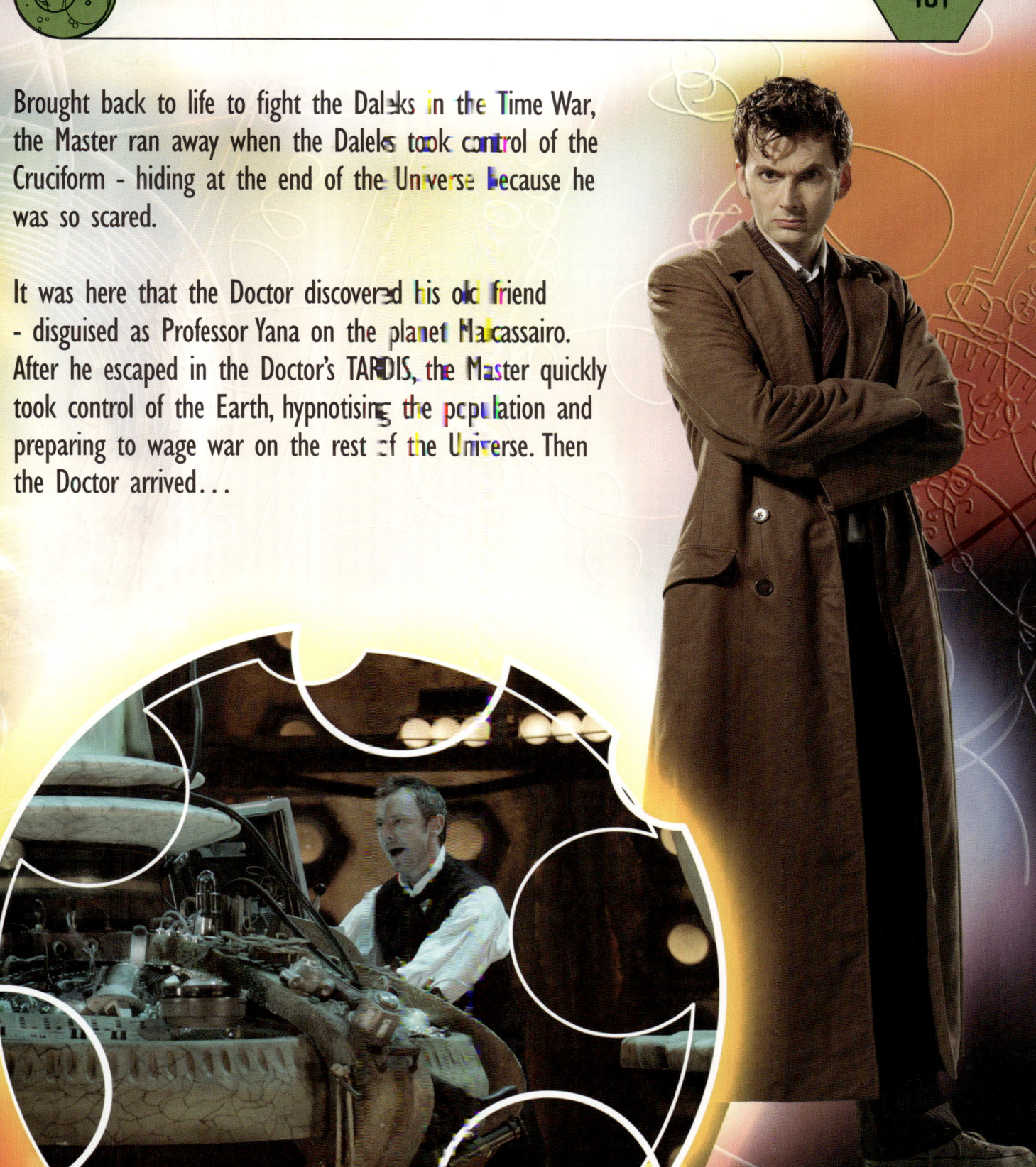

432 | MASTER DATA

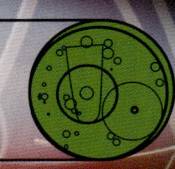

Name: Master
Alias: Professor Yana
Prime Minister Harry Saxon
Species: Time Lord
Age: Unknown
Height: 1.78m (5'10")
Hair colour: White/brown
Eye colour: Brown
Home Planet: Gallifrey
Profession: Time Lord, Prime Minister,

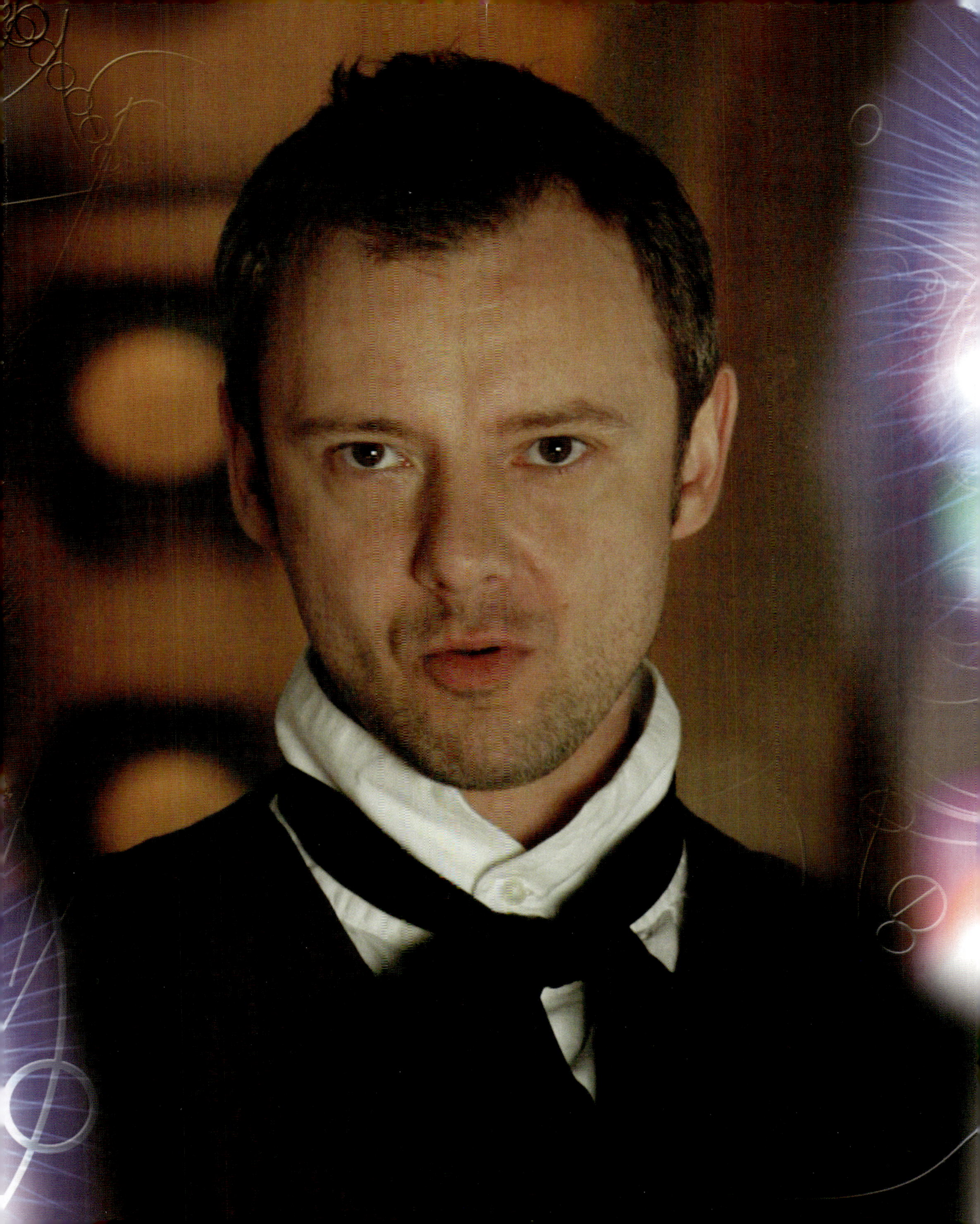

434 THE MASTER ANATOMY

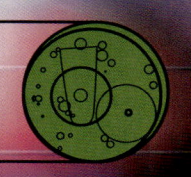

PROFESSOR YANA

- Grey hair — about 70 years old
- Constantly hears drumming

HAROLD SAXON

- Two hearts — just like the Doctor
- Fob watch — contains the Master's Time Lord essence

TEST YOUR KNOWLEDGE

1. WHAT SENT THE MASTER INSANE?
   A. The Untempered Schism
   B. The Time War
   C. The Doctor

2. WHERE DOES THE MASTER ORIGINALLY COME FROM?
   A. Earth
   B. Gallifrey
   C. Skaro

3. WHO WAS THE MASTER DISGUISED AS ON MALCASSAIRO?
   A. Professor Yana
   B. Professor Tremas
   C. Professor Plum

4. WHY DID THE MASTER RUN AWAY FROM THE TIME WAR?
   A. He didn't want to fight
   B. He was scared
   C. He was attacked by the Dalek Emperor

5. WHAT ITEM CONTAINED THE MASTER'S TIME LORD ESSENCE?
   A. A wallet
   B. A suitcase
   C. A fob watch

LazLabs logo on his ring

Laser screwdriver — who'd have sonic?

436 THE MASTER'S ALIASES & FRIENDS

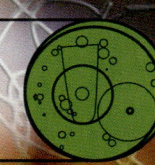

PROFESSOR YANA

Unknown even to himself, Professor Yana held a dark, murderous secret. He was actually the Master — one of only two Time Lords left alive following the Great Time War. The only signs of his previous life were a fob watch and the constant sound of drumming, which Yana had heard his entire life.

Hidden at the end of the dying Universe, the Professor helped to build a rocket which would send the last of the human race to Utopia so they could start again. However, once Martha had drawn his attention to his unopened fob watch, the kindly Professor Yana would never be seen again.

437

CHANTHO

The last of the insectoid species the Malmooth, Chantho had been a faithful companion to Professor Yana for seventeen years. Hard-working and intelligent, Chantho was also very polite – starting every sentence with "Chan" and finishing it with "tho" because to do otherwise would have been like swearing!

During their time together, Chantho fell in love with the Professor – something that Martha could understand as she felt the same way about the Doctor. Despite this, Chantho was forced to shoot him after he opened his fob watch and turned into the Master. Chantho was also the first victim of the Master as she was electrocuted by the heartless Time Lord.

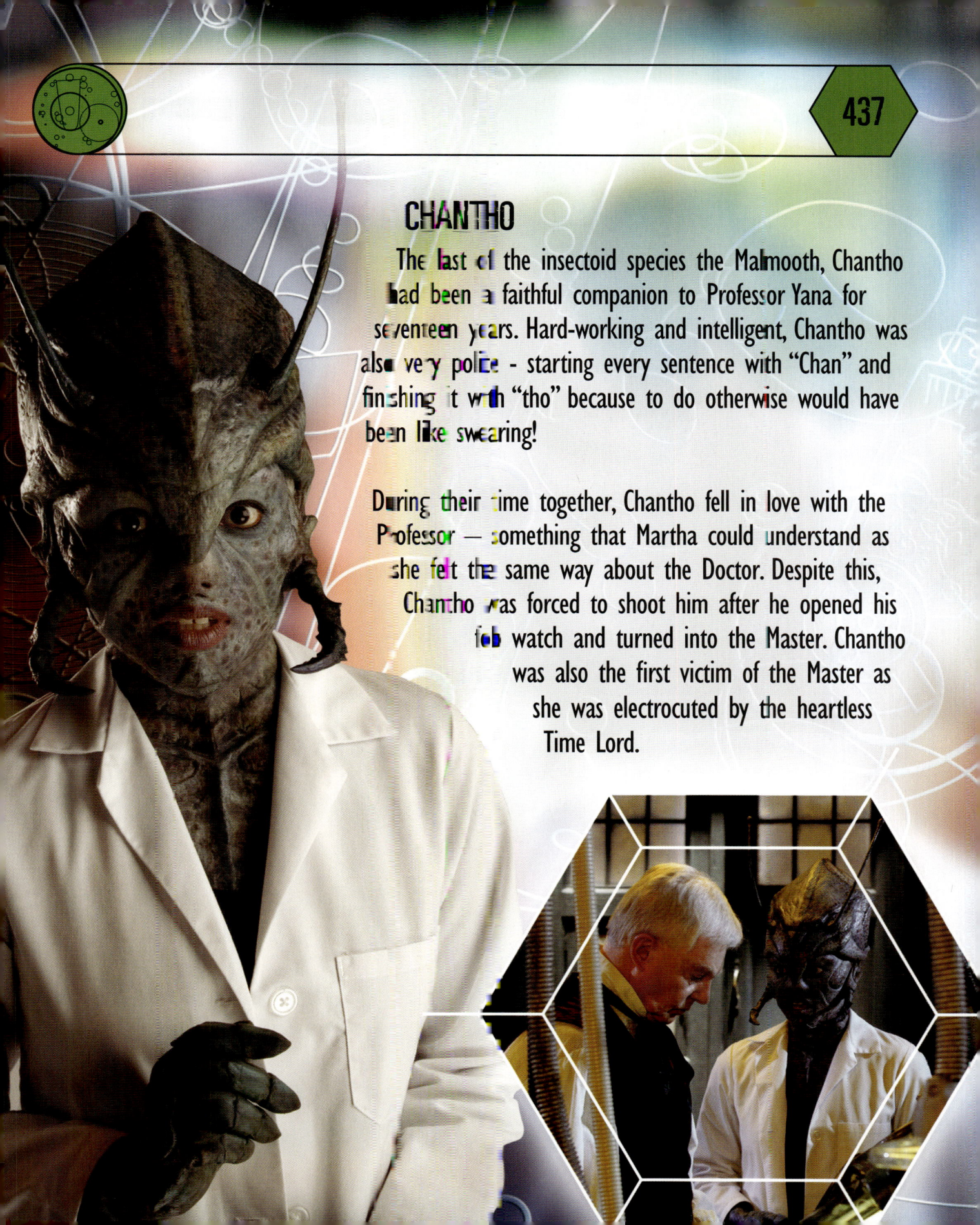

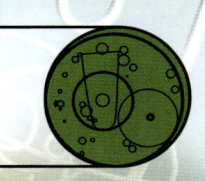

HARRY SAXON

Harry Saxon went to Cambridge University before entering the Ministry of Defence and rising quickly through government to become the Prime Minister of the United Kingdom. With McFly and Sharon Osbourne on his side, the "man of the people" was elected to office by a 98% landslide.

Little did the British public know that Saxon was actually the diabolical Master, who had regenerated into a new, younger body after being shot by Chantho. With a new alias in place, the Master took control of planet Earth and later enslaved the world's population.

LUCY SAXON

Lucy Saxon met the Master when she was working at the publishing house which released Harold Saxon's autobiography. Seduced by his power, charm and good looks, Lucy married the Master and became both his wife and, at first, his most loyal supporter. However, after suffering a year of bullying from the evil Time Lord, she shot and killed him. Lucy Saxon's current whereabouts are unknown...

TOCLAFANE

Named after the Gallifreyan equivalent of the 'bogeyman', the Toclafane were the Master's foot soldiers in his attempt to take over Earth. The sphere-shaped creatures are perfect killing machines that, on the Master's orders, wiped out one tenth of the population using concentrated rays of energy.

Martha discovered that the Toclafane were the last members of the human race from the year 100 trillion. In order to survive the end of the Universe, they had placed all that remained of their flesh into metallic spheres which were then transported to modern day Earth with the help of the Master's Paradox Machine.

TEST YOUR KNOWLEDGE

1. HOW MANY TIME LORDS SURVIVED THE TIME WAR?
   A. Three
   B. Two
   C. None

2. WHO SHOT PROFESSOR YANA?
   A. The Doctor
   B. Martha
   C. Chantho

3. WHERE DID HARRY SAXON GO TO UNIVERSITY?
   A. Cambridge
   B. Oxford
   C. Hull

4. WHICH CELEBRITIES SUPPORTED HARRY SAXON?
   A. McFly and Sharon Osbourne
   B. Girls Aloud and Ozzy Osbourne
   C. Justin Timberlake and Kelly Osbourne

5. WHAT DOES THE NAME 'TOCLAFANE' REFER TO?
   A. Candyman
   B. Bogeyman
   C. Spider-Man

440 THE MASTER'S ENEMIES

THE DOCTOR

Although they were the only two Time Lords left in existence, there was no love lost between the Master and the Doctor. While the Doctor spent his many lives trying to help the human race, the Master spent his trying to destroy them.

Their latest encounter saw the Master imprison the Doctor for a whole year – using his laser screwdriver to age the Doctor by nine hundred years and temporarily remove his ability to regenerate. Despite this, the Doctor forgave his old friend for everything that he had done.

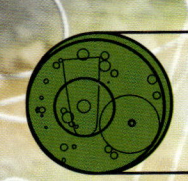

MARTHA JONES

Martha had enjoyed many adventures with the Doctor before they met the Master. She recognized Professor Yana's fob watch after seeing the Doctor use a similar device to hide from the Family of Blood during one of their previous adventures.

Martha travelled telling everyone about her friend the Doctor, who was the only person able to stop Earth from being destroyed by the Master.

After helping to save the planet from the power hungry Time Lord, brave Martha Jones decided to stay with her family rather than continue travelling with the Doctor — leaving him her mobile phone just in case she needs him in the future.

442

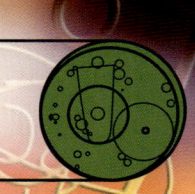

CAPTAIN JACK HARKNESS

Captain Jack is an absolute hero who cannot die. He has been shot through the heart, electrocuted, poisoned and even hit by a javelin, but he has still made it past his 150th birthday!

After tracking down the Doctor and hitching a ride on the side of his TARDIS, Jack arrived on Malcassairo and used his Vortex Manipulator to allow the Time Lord and Martha to escape the dying planet. After going on the run, the three time travellers were captured by the Master, who chained Jack up in the bowels of the aircraft carrier Valiant.

Once released, the former Time Agent helped the Doctor defeat the Master and went back to his day job — defending Earth against alien threats.

THE JONES FAMILY

Martha's parents and sister were all enslaved by the Master, who used them to lure the Doctor and Martha aboard the Valiant.

Martha's sister Tish was twice employed by the Master — once as an assistant at the government-funded LazLabs and once when he was posing as Prime Minister Harry Saxon.

After being told that the Doctor was dangerous by one of Saxon's helpers, Martha's mother Francine agreed to help the Master find her daughter, only for her plan to be foiled by her ex-husband, Clive, who stopped his daughter walking into the Master's trap.

With Tish, Francine and Clive working as slaves on-board the Valiant, Martha was determined to defeat the Master and set her family free.

TEST YOUR KNOWLEDGE

1. HOW LONG WAS THE DOCTOR IMPRISONED FOR?
A. One week
B. One month
C. One year

2. HOW DID CAPTAIN JACK ESCAPE FROM MALCASSAIRO?
A. He used his Vortex Manipulator
B. He hitchhiked
C. He used the TARDIS

3. WHO CANNOT DIE?
A. Tish Jones
B. Captain Jack
C. Lucy Saxon

4. WHICH FAMILY DID THE DOCTOR HIDE FROM?
A. The Partridge Family
B. Sly and the Family Stone
C. The Family of Blood

5. WHERE DID TISH JONES WORK?
A. The local chip shop
B. LazLabs
C. Woolworths

444 THE PAST MASTER

Insane since childhood, the Master spent his life searching for power, happy to crush anyone foolish enough to stand in his way.

The young Time Lord went mad after staring into the Untempered Schism on his home planet of Gallifrey — the Shining World of the Seven Systems. When they looked into the Schism, Gallifreyans could see the entire Time Vortex — an amazing sight that could both inspire and terrify.

While the Doctor was scared by what he saw and ran away, the Master was sent insane — constantly hearing drums which he saw as a call to war.

445

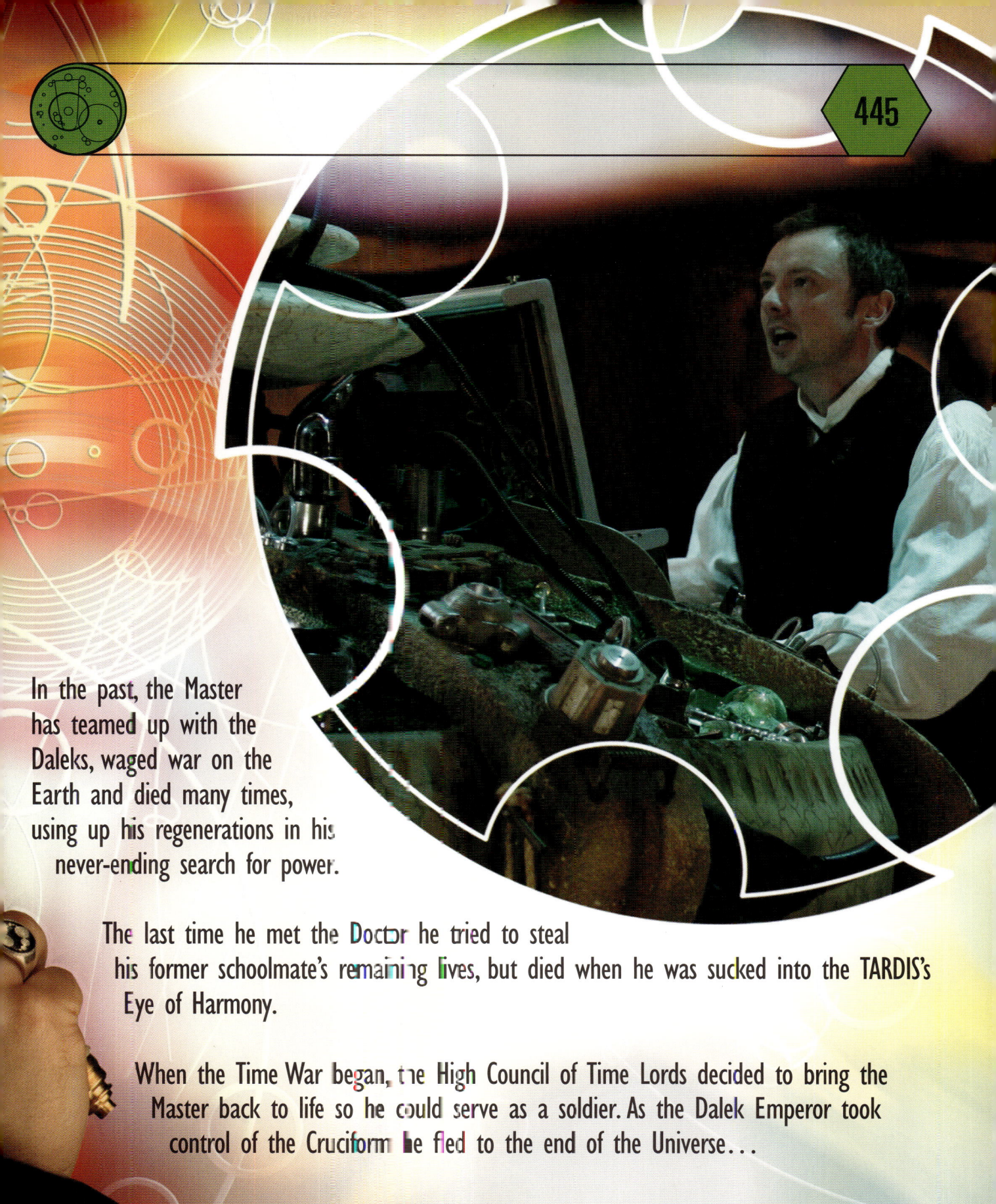

In the past, the Master has teamed up with the Daleks, waged war on the Earth and died many times, using up his regenerations in his never-ending search for power.

The last time he met the Doctor he tried to steal his former schoolmate's remaining lives, but died when he was sucked into the TARDIS's Eye of Harmony.

When the Time War began, the High Council of Time Lords decided to bring the Master back to life so he could serve as a soldier. As the Dalek Emperor took control of the Cruciform he fled to the end of the Universe…

LIFE ON MALCASSAIRO

When he ran away from the Time War, the Master turned himself into a human and hid his old Time Lord self inside a fob watch. He ended up in the Isop Galaxy where he was found naked on the coast of the Silver Devastation, with only his watch and the constant sound of drumming hinting at his past life.

When the Doctor, Martha and Captain Jack arrived on Malcassairo, the Master had been living there as Professor Yana — an elderly genius who was trying to help the last of humankind to escape the end of the Universe in a big rocket.

Yana intended to direct the rocket to a place deep in space called Utopia, but he couldn't figure out how to launch the ship. With the Doctor's help the Professor managed to find a way to engage the rocket's engines and send it beyond the stars.

The Doctor's admiration for the "magnificent" Yana quickly turned into fear when Martha told him about the Professor's fob watch. Although he thought that he was the only Time Lord left, the Doctor was scared that the watch might contain one of his deadliest enemies – the Master.

Sadly, he was right…

TEST YOUR KNOWLEDGE

1. HOW ELSE WAS GALLIFREY KNOWN?
A. The Shining World of the Seven Systems
B. The Red Planet
C. The Third Planet from the Sun

2. WHO DID THE MASTER ONCE TEAM UP WITH?
A. The Cybermen
B. The Daleks
C. The Ood

3. HOW DID THE MASTER DIE WHEN HE LAST MET THE DOCTOR?
A. He was electrocuted
B. He fell into the TARDIS' Eye of Harmony
C. He choked on a chicken bone

4. WHERE WAS THE MASTER FOUND AFTER HE FLED THE TIME WAR?
A. Saturn
B. Behind a sofa
C. The coast of the Silver Devastation

5. WHERE DID PROFESSOR YANA WANT TO SEND THE LAST OF HUMANKIND?
A. Utopia
B. Raxacoricofallapatorius
C. Coventry

448 THE MASTER'S TECHNOLOGY

FOB WATCH

Professor Yana's fob watch contained the Master's DNA, which was released when the Professor opened the "broken" timepiece. It may have looked simple, but the watch actually contained advanced Time Lord technology.

In order to avoid being found by the Time Lords, the Master used a Chameleon Arch to turn himself into a human and stored all of his memories in the watch. A perception filter was then added to it, which meant that the Professor did not realize that the fob watch contained his old self — the Master.

LASER SCREWDRIVER

While the Doctor rarely leaves the TARDIS without his trusty sonic screwdriver, the Master would be helpless without his laser screwdriver. The Doctor never uses his screwdriver to hurt or kill, but the Master's was used for the complete opposite purpose. As well as having a built-in laser beam that can kill people on the spot, it also contained a Hypersonic Sound Wave Manipulator which the Master used to age the Doctor by nine hundred years. The screwdriver's isomorphic controls meant that it could only be used by the Master.

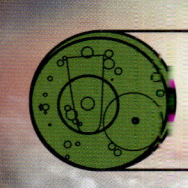

AIRCRAFT CARRIER VALIANT

During his time as Harry Saxon, the Master was employed by the Ministry of Defence. He helped to design and create the aircraft carrier Valiant — an enormous airborne ship which was supposed to protect the skies of planet Earth from alien invaders.

However, the Master took control of the Valiant — murdering the President of America and using the Toclafane to overpower the UNIT soldiers that controlled the ship. From the Valiant, the Master and Lucy Saxon watched the world below them burn as the Toclafane carried out the evil Time Lord's every command.

ARCHANGEL COMMUNICATIONS NETWORK

Fifteen satellites spread throughout space allowed the Master to gain control of Britain and then the world. The Archangel communications network used the sound of drums — a low-level signal that pulsed through mobile phones - to tell people to vote Harry Saxon for Prime Minister. After the Master came to power, it also kept the public scared of the renegade Time Lord. However the Doctor used the power of the network to free himself from the Master's clutches and become strong again.

450

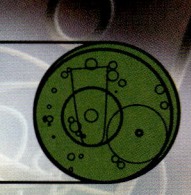

THE TARDIS

Stranded at the end of the Universe, the Master stole the Doctor's TARDIS to escape - leaving the Doctor, Captain Jack and Martha in the depths of space. However, just before the TARDIS dematerialized, the Doctor used his sonic screwdriver to jam its console so that it could only travel between the last two places it had been — Earth in the twenty-first century and Malacassairo in 100 trillion.

When the Doctor finally located his TARDIS on the Aircraft Carrier Valiant, he was horrified to find that the Master had turned his home into a Paradox Machine. The Time Lord had spent the previous eighteen months working in the TARDIS — pulling it apart and rebuilding it to fit in with his evil plan.

During this time, the Master also made allies of the last humans alive — the Toclafane - that he brought back to Earth via the Paradox Machine he constructed within the TARDIS.

The Paradox Machine allowed the Toclafane to murder millions of innocent humans. Without the machine, they would have been unable to kill their ancestors as they would have also wiped themselves out as a result.

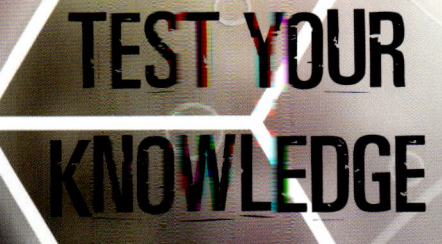

TEST YOUR KNOWLEDGE

1. WHAT DID THE MASTER USE TO BECOME HUMAN?
A. A Chameleon Arch
B. A laser screwdriver
C. A golden arch

2. HOW MANY YEARS DID THE MASTER AGE THE DOCTOR BY?
A. Nine
B. Nine hundred
C. Nine thousand

3. WHO DID THE MASTER MURDER ON-BOARD THE VALIANT?
A. The President of the United States
B. The President of India
C. The President of the Republic of Azerbaijan

4. WHAT ALLOWED THE TOCLAFANE TO MURDER THEIR ANCESTORS?
A. A Silver Machine
B. A Paradox Machine
C. A machine gun

5. WHO DESTROYED THE PARADOX MACHINE?
A. Martha
B. The Doctor
C. Captain Jack

Once Captain Jack destroyed the Paradox Machine, time reversed to heal itself and the Toclafane were returned to the year 100 trillion.

452 THE MASTER ON EARTH

With the TARDIS' controls disabled by the Doctor, the Master arrived in Britain in 2007 with a new body and created a new alias — Harold Saxon.

The Master began working at the Ministry of Defence where he set up the Archangel Communications Network which controlled the thoughts of the general public.

After being voted in as Prime Minister, he arranged a meeting with the American President where the Toclafane would be revealed live to the world on television. Upon their arrival, the "alien beings" murdered President Winters leaving the Master in control of the world…with the Toclafane by his side.

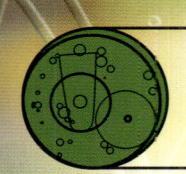

The Doctor, Martha and Captain Jack followed the Master to London using Jack's Vortex Manipulator. They went on the run as soon as they arrived, after the Master named them public enemy number one and tried to blow them up.

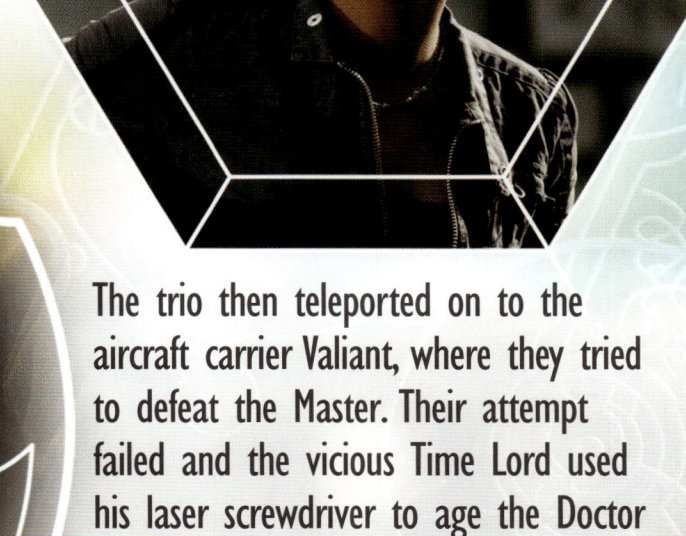

The trio then teleported on to the aircraft carrier Valiant, where they tried to defeat the Master. Their attempt failed and the vicious Time Lord used his laser screwdriver to age the Doctor by one hundred years.

While the Master was distracted, Martha used the Vortex Manipulator to teleport away from the Valiant, just as the Toclafane were ordered to wipe out one tenth of Earth's population by the ruthless Time Lord.

454

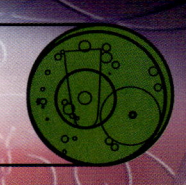

For the next year, the Master kept the Doctor and Captain Jack as his prisoners on-board the Valiant, while his human slaves were ordered to build 200,000 rockets on Earth below. He also found time to have his face carved into the rock of Mount Rushmore!

As the Master prepared to wage war on the rest of the Universe, Martha Jones was busy trying to save the world by travelling from town to town telling people about the man she loved, the only man who could defeat the Master - the Doctor.

After twelve months, Martha deliberately allowed herself to be caught by the Master who took her back to the Valiant in order to kill her in front of the Doctor. But then something amazing happened...

Everyone on Earth chanted the Doctor's name.

The world - united by Martha's stories of the Doctor — used the power of the Archangel Network to psychically connect with the Time Lord and free him from the Master's power.

Once the Doctor had overpowered his old enemy he decided to look after him — keeping him with him in his TARDIS. But before the two could leave together, the Master was shot by his wife, Lucy Saxon.

But rather than regenerate and spend the rest of his life with the Doctor, the Master decided to die instead — leaving the Doctor as the only Time Lord in existence once more...

However, as the Master's body was laid to rest, his LazLabs ring was taken from the embers by an unknown woman's hand...

TEST YOUR KNOWLEDGE

1. WHAT WAS THE MASTER'S COMMUNICATIONS NETWORK CALLED?
A. Dark Angel
B. Archangel
C. Angel Communications

2. WHAT WAS THE AMERICAN PRESIDENT CALLED?
A. President Winters
B. President Summers
C. President Springs

3. HOW MANY ROCKETS WERE BUILT ON EARTH?
A. 200
B. 2000
C. 200,000

4. WHAT DID THE MASTER HAVE HIS FACE CARVED INTO?
A. A block of ice
B. A block of wood
C. Mount Rushmore

5. WHO SHOT THE MASTER?
A. Martha Jones
B. Lucy Saxon
C. The Doctor

456 TEST YOUR KNOWLEDGE

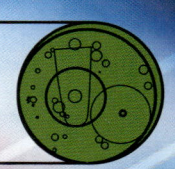

ANSWERS

Meet the Master
1 (a) 2 (b) 3 (a) 4 (b) 5 (c)

The Master's Aliases and Friends
1 (b) 2 (c) 3 (a) 4 (a) 5 (b)

The Master's Enemies
1 (c) 2 (a) 3 (b) 4 (c) 5 (b)

The Past Master
1 (a) 2 (b) 3 (b) 4 (c) 5 (a)

The Master's Technology
1 (a) 2 (b) 3 (a) 4 (b) 5 (c)

The Master on Earth
1 (b) 2 (a) 3 (c) 4 (c) 5 (b)

DOCTOR·WHO

DONNA

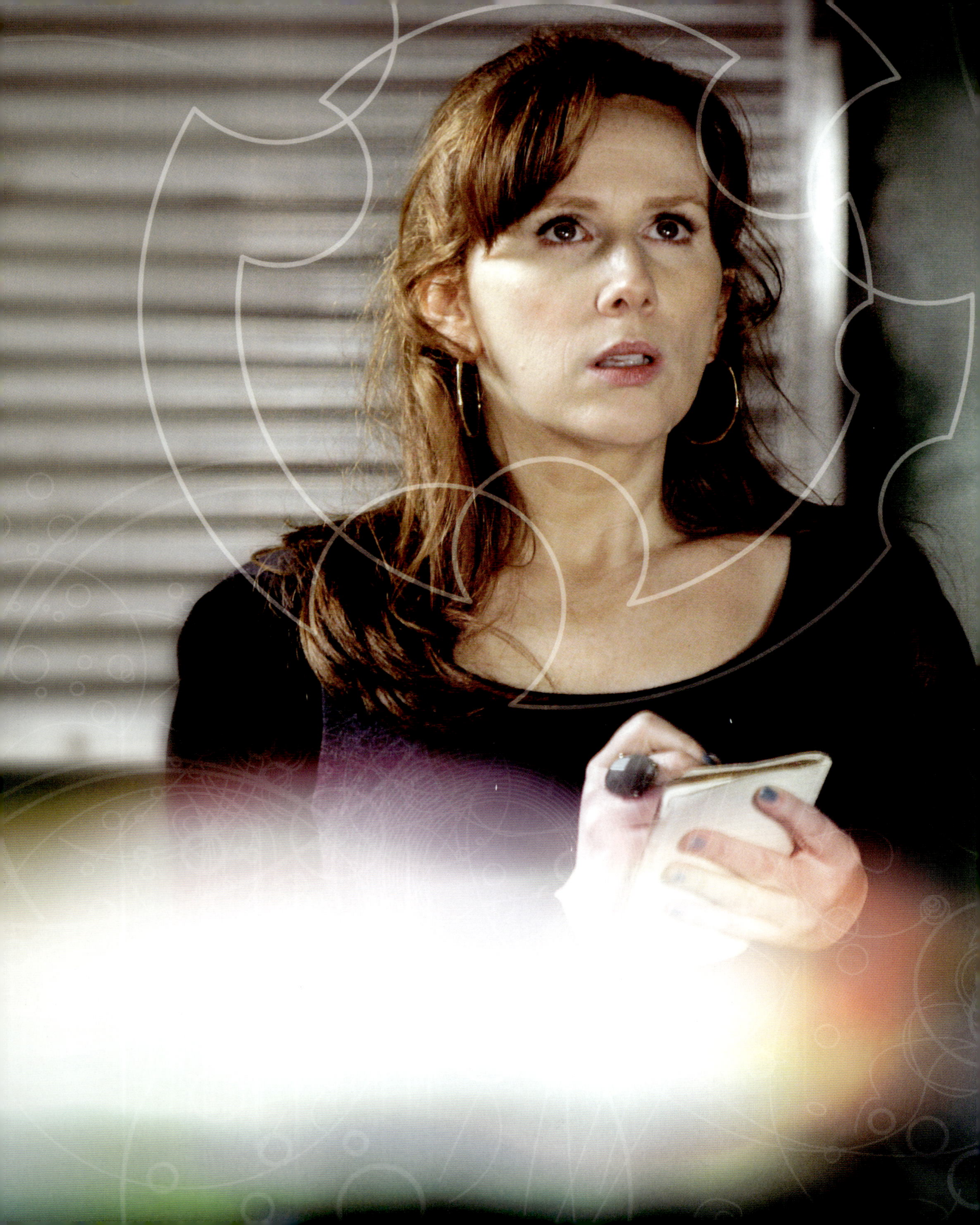

CONTENTS

Meet Donna
Introduction..................... 460
Donna Data....................... 462
Donna Anatomy................. 464
◆ Test your Knowledge

Friends and Family
The Doctor........................ 466
Sylvia and Geoff................ 467
Wilf................................... 468
Lance Bennett.................... 469
◆ Test your Knowledge

Enemies and Rivals
The Empress of the Racnoss..... 470
Matron Cofelia................... 470
The Pyrovile...................... 471
The Sontarans.................... 471
The Vespiform................... 472
The Vashta Nerada............. 472
The Daleks........................ 473
◆ Test your Knowledge

Adventures
In the present.................... 474
In the past......................... 475
In the future...................... 476
◆ Test your Knowledge

Parallel Worlds
The Library....................... 478
Turn Left.......................... 480
◆ Test your Knowledge

The DoctorDonna
Biological metacrisis.......... 482
Defeating the Daleks.......... 484
◆ Test your Knowledge

Test your Knowledge Answers....... 486

460 MEET DONNA NOBLE

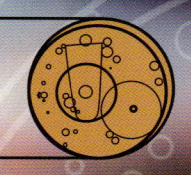

Before she crossed paths with the Doctor, Donna Noble was just an ordinary temp from Chiswick. She worked as a secretary for a security firm called H.C. Clements. Nothing exciting had ever happened in her humdrum life. She managed to miss both the Sycorax Invasion and the Battle at Canary Wharf. So it came as a massive shock when Donna was whisked into the TARDIS on her wedding day!

To say that she wasn't happy about it is a bit of an understatement. Donna was furious! She had been seconds away from becoming Mrs Lance Bennett and was convinced her nemesis Nerys had plotted her kidnapping.

But it was far more sinister that that. Donna was the key in an alien plot. Her fiancé had secretly been dosing her with deadly Huon particles so that the Empress of the Racnoss could use her to release her starving babies from the centre of the Earth.

461

Together, the Doctor and Donna foiled the Empress's plans and saved the planet from being devoured. The Doctor invited her to travel with him but she declined. Later, Donna realised what an amazing opportunity she'd let slip through her fingers and when they met again, she jumped at the chance of becoming the Doctor's companion.

462 DONNA DATA

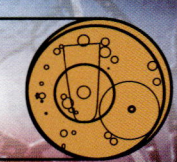

Name: Donna Noble
Parents: Sylvia and Geoff Noble
Grandfather: Wilfred Mott
Height: 1.73m (5'8")
Hair: Red
Eyes: Green
Home planet: Earth
Home Address: Chiswick, London, UK
Species: Human
Profession: Temp turned adventurer

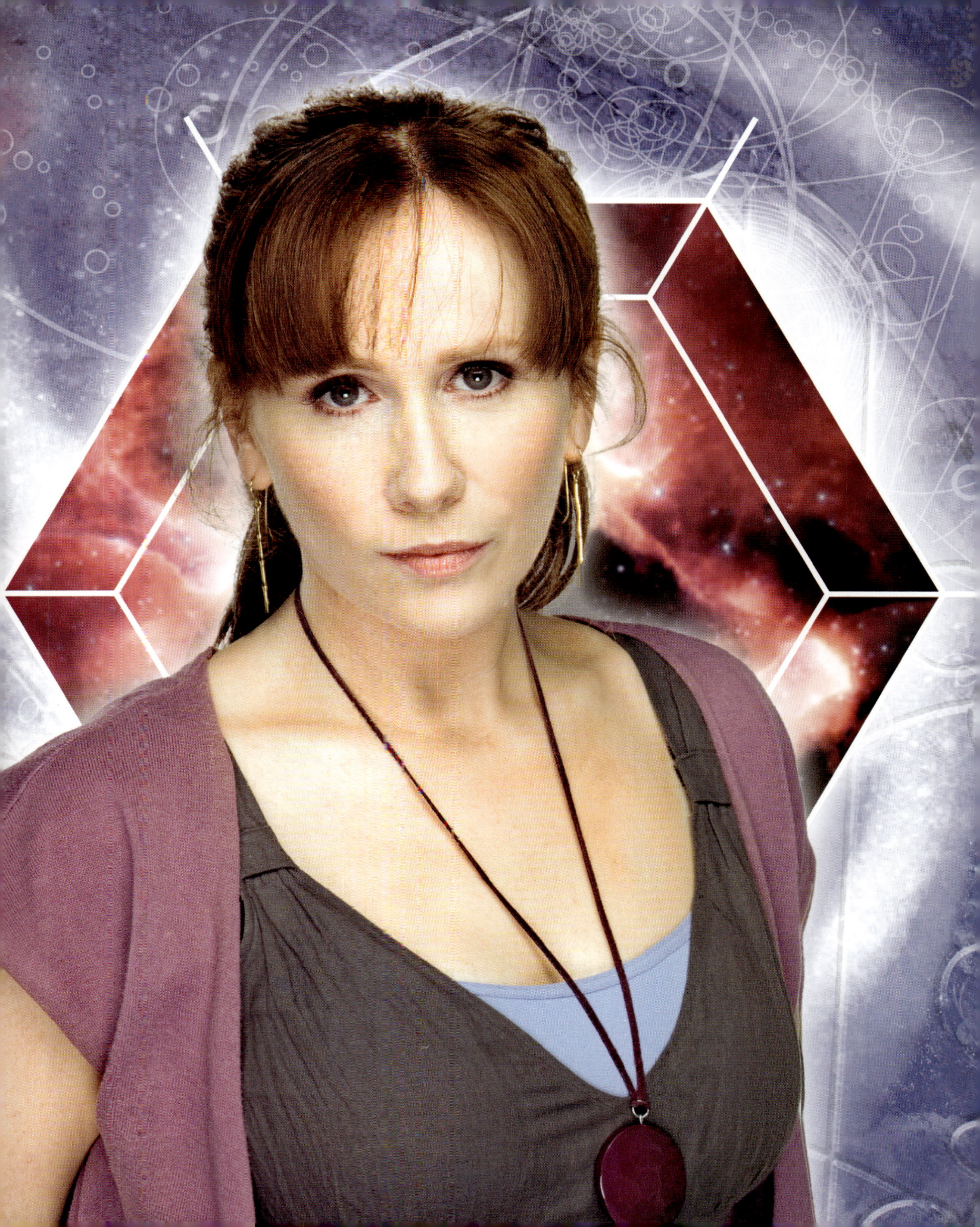

464 DONNA ANATOMY

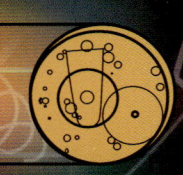

Not one for keeping quiet, Donna always says what she thinks

1.73m tall (5'8")

Favourite word: 'Oi!'

Serious pair of lungs. Good for shouting!

Fast fingers. Donna can type 100 words a minute

For all her fiery temper, Donna has a huge heart

Donna took clothes for every possible occasion

Trainers — essential footwear for keeping up with the Doctor!

TEST YOUR KNOWLEDGE

1. WHICH COMPANY DID DONNA WORK FOR?
A. H.C. Cement
B. Adipose Industries
C. H.C. Clements

2. WHAT'S DONNA'S GRANDDAD CALLED?
A. Boe
B. Wilf
C. Alf

3. WHAT WAS DONNA ABOUT TO DO WHEN SHE APPEARED IN THE TARDIS?
A. Put the kettle on
B. Get married
C. Go ten-pin bowling

4. WHO DOES DONNA THINKS PAID TO KIDNAP HER?
A. The Slitheen
B. Lance
C. Nerys

5. LANCE DOSES DONNA WITH…
A. Huon particles
B. Chocolate
C. Racnoss dust

466 FRIENDS AND FAMILY

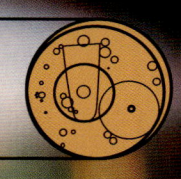

THE DOCTOR

Donna's best friend in the whole universe is a Time Lord called the Doctor. He comes from the planet Gallifrey and is over 900 years old. When Donna first met the Doctor she was convinced he was just a 'stupid Martian' and did her best to escape him. But she soon came to realise how incredible he was. And by simply being with him, the Doctor showed Donna that she was brilliant too.

Together they travelled through time and space, saving planets, rescuing civilisations and defeating monsters. But most of all, they had fun! Donna wanted to travel with the Doctor forever, but it wasn't to be. It broke the Doctor's heart leaving his best friend behind.

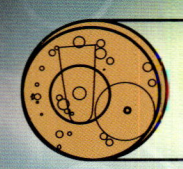

SYLVIA

Tall, blonde and with a tongue twice as sharp as her daughter's, Sylvia Noble is in many ways Donna's harshest critic. When Donna vanished on her wedding day, her mum thought she was just showing off. But deep down she's fiercely protective of her only child. Donna never told her mum that she was travelling with the Doctor, which was probably for the best as Sylvia thought the Doctor was trouble!

GEOFF

Donna's dad Geoff was a kind and patient man, who started out working on a market stall with Sylvia. He did his best to comfort his wife during their daughter's disastrous wedding day. But sadly he passed away not long afterwards.

468

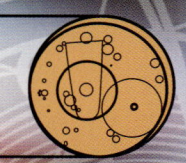

WILF

When Donna's granddad Wilfred Mott wasn't manning his newspaper stall, he spent most of his time up in his allotment, gazing at the stars and dreaming of the day mankind would explore the far corners of the universe. Little could he guess that his own granddaughter would be the one to do it!

Spanish flu forced Wilf to miss Donna's wedding, but the following Christmas he met the Doctor when he teleported to Earth from the Titanic. Wilf was one of the few people brave enough to stay in London after the Sycorax scares of the previous year.

Donna and Wilf share a special bond. He's her greatest supporter and the only person she confided in about the Doctor.

LANCE BENNETT

When the head of HR offered to make Donna coffee on her first day at H.C. Clements she couldn't believe her luck. Lance Bennett seemed too good to be true. They dated for just six months before he agreed to marry her. But Donna was too wrapped up in her fiancé to see he was a fraud. Lance had been slowly poisoning her with Huon particles on the Empress of the Racnoss's orders. Donna was devastated by Lance's betrayal. But his scheming didn't pay off as the monstrous Empress fed him to her starving children.

TEST YOUR KNOWLEDGE

1. WHEN THEY FIRST MET, DONNA THOUGHT THE DOCTOR WAS A...
A. Stupid Martian
B. Bonkers Brazilian
C. Lunatic Gallifreyan

2. WHAT PLANET IS THE DOCTOR FROM?
A. Sontar
B. Gallifrey
C. Clom

3. WHEN DONNA VANISHED FROM THE CHURCH, SYLVIA THOUGHT...
A. She'd gone shopping
B. She needed the loo
C. She was showing off

4. WHAT STOPPED WILF FROM ATTENDING DONNA'S WEDDING?
A. The World Cup final
B. Spanish flu
C. An astronomy convention

5. LANCE SECRETLY SERVED...
A. The Daleks
B. The Cybermen
C. The Empress of the Racnoss

470 ENEMIES AND RIVALS

THE EMPRESS OF THE RACNOSS

This vicious eight-legged creepy crawly originated in the Dark Times, billions of years ago. Her race devoured whole planets but was hunted to extinction by the Fledgling Empires. The Empress hid in hibernation at the edge of the universe but awoke when Torchwood drilled into the centre of Earth, disturbing her frozen offspring. Her attempts to free them were thwarted by Donna and the Doctor, and her Webstar was later blown up.

MATRON COFELIA

Donna first met this outer-space supernanny when she was investigating Adipose Industries. Matron Cofelia was posing as a human named Miss Foster in order to market a miracle diet pill. But secretly she was creating a new generation of fat monsters out of human flab. Once the Doctor reported her crime, the Adiposian First Family dropped her like a hot potato and flew their babies home.

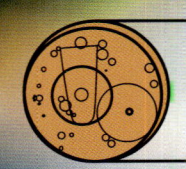

THE PYROVILE

Donna and the Doctor came dangerously close to being scorched by these fire-breathing magma monsters in Pompeii in 79AD. The Pyrovile had fallen to Earth after their planet was stolen by the Daleks. They seeded themselves into the lungs of humans and were using volcanic power to turn them into stone. In order to save the world, the Doctor and Donna were forced to blow up Vesuvius, destroying the Pyrovile but also Pompeii.

THE SONTARANS

These ugly soldiers live for the glory of battle. They had been locked in war against the Rutans for thousands of years and needed new soldiers. So they tried to change our planet into a clone world. But they didn't realise Earth had a secret weapon — Donna Noble! While on their ship, she clobbered a Sontaran and deadlocked open their teleports, giving the Doctor the opportunity to foil their evil plan.

472

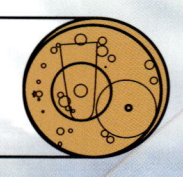

THE VESPIFORM

The Vespiform are giant alien wasps with hives in the Silfrax galaxy. Donna narrowly escaped being stung by one at a garden party in 1926. The Vespiform was disguised in human form as the Reverend Golightly, and was killing off the guests in the style of an Agatha Christie novel. But his mind was linked to the Firestone necklace and when Donna chucked it in a lake, the Vespiform drowned.

THE VASHTA NERADA

The Vashta Nerada are the piranhas of the air. Shadows that melt the flesh, lurking in the dark, waiting to gobble up anyone foolish enough to step out of the light. They originated in forests, but when the trees were turned into books, they hatched in the largest library in the universe and began attacking visitors. They can devour an entire person in a second.

THE DALEKS

The Daleks are the Doctor's deadliest enemy. When Davros was rescued from the Time War, he created a new empire of Daleks, each one grown from cells from his own body. On Davros's orders, the Daleks snatched Earth and 26 other planets out of time and space to build the Reality Bomb — a weapon so powerful it could reduce the universe to dust, leaving the Daleks to rule supreme. All of the Children of Time rallied together to defeat them.

TEST YOUR KNOWLEDGE

1. WHAT HUMAN NAME DID MATRON COFELIA USE?
A. Nerys
B. Miss Hartigan
C. Miss Foster

2. WHO HAVE THE SONTARANS BEEN FIGHTING FOR THOUSANDS OF YEARS?
A. The Time Lords
B. The Rutans
C. The Cybermen

3. WHERE DO THE VESPIFORM HAVE THEIR HIVES?
A. Bognor Regis
B. The Medusa Cascade
C. The Silfrax galaxy

4. WHAT DO THE VASHTA NERADA LIKE DOING?
A. Eating people
B. Reading books
C. Yodelling

5. WHOSE IDEA WAS THE REALITY BOMB?
A. Donna's
B. Davros's
C. The Supreme Dalek's

ADVENTURES

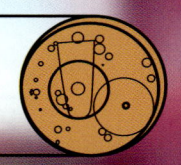

IN THE PRESENT

After the Racnoss ruined her wedding day, Donna went on a two-week holiday to Egypt looking for adventure. But she soon found life without the Doctor was deathly dull. He'd opened her eyes to the universe and she wanted to see more. She began investigating alien conspiracy theories, hoping it would lead her back to the Doctor. Her determination paid off and she was reunited with the Doctor at Adipose Industries.

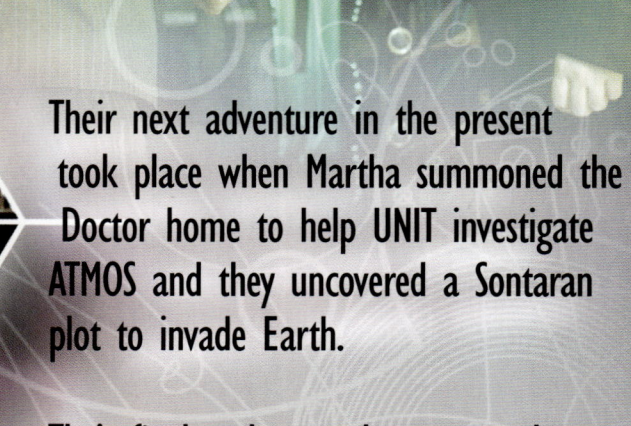

Their next adventure in the present took place when Martha summoned the Doctor home to help UNIT investigate ATMOS and they uncovered a Sontaran plot to invade Earth.

Their final and most dangerous adventure on present-day Earth involved the Daleks and all the Children of Time. Together they stopped the stars from blinking out.

IN THE PAST

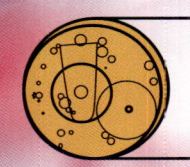

While fighting the Racnoss, the Doctor took Donna back 4.6 billion years to the creation of Earth. She was the first human to ever witness it and although at the time she said she just wanted to see her bed, the sheer beauty of it took her breath away.

Their next trip to the past saw her speaking Latin in Pompeii in 79AD. Donna wanted to warn everyone about the eruption of Vesuvius but she soon came to realise that some things are fixed points in history and can't be changed.

In 1926 Donna helped crime-writer Agatha Christie solve a murder mystery and saved the Doctor's life with a kiss.

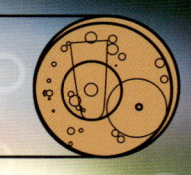

IN THE FUTURE

Having only ever gone on package holidays, Donna was so excited when the Doctor set the TARDIS controls to random and it landed on her first alien planet in the year 4126. Then she found it was absolutely freezing, inhabited by rabid Ood, and mankind had turned into cruel slave traders. She seriously considered going home!

Her next trip to the future was to planet Messaline in 6012 with the Doctor and Martha. They got dragged into a bitter war between a fish-like race called the Hath and the humans. When a machine created the Doctor's daughter, Donna named her Jenny and helped him see that she was more than just an echo of a Time Lord.

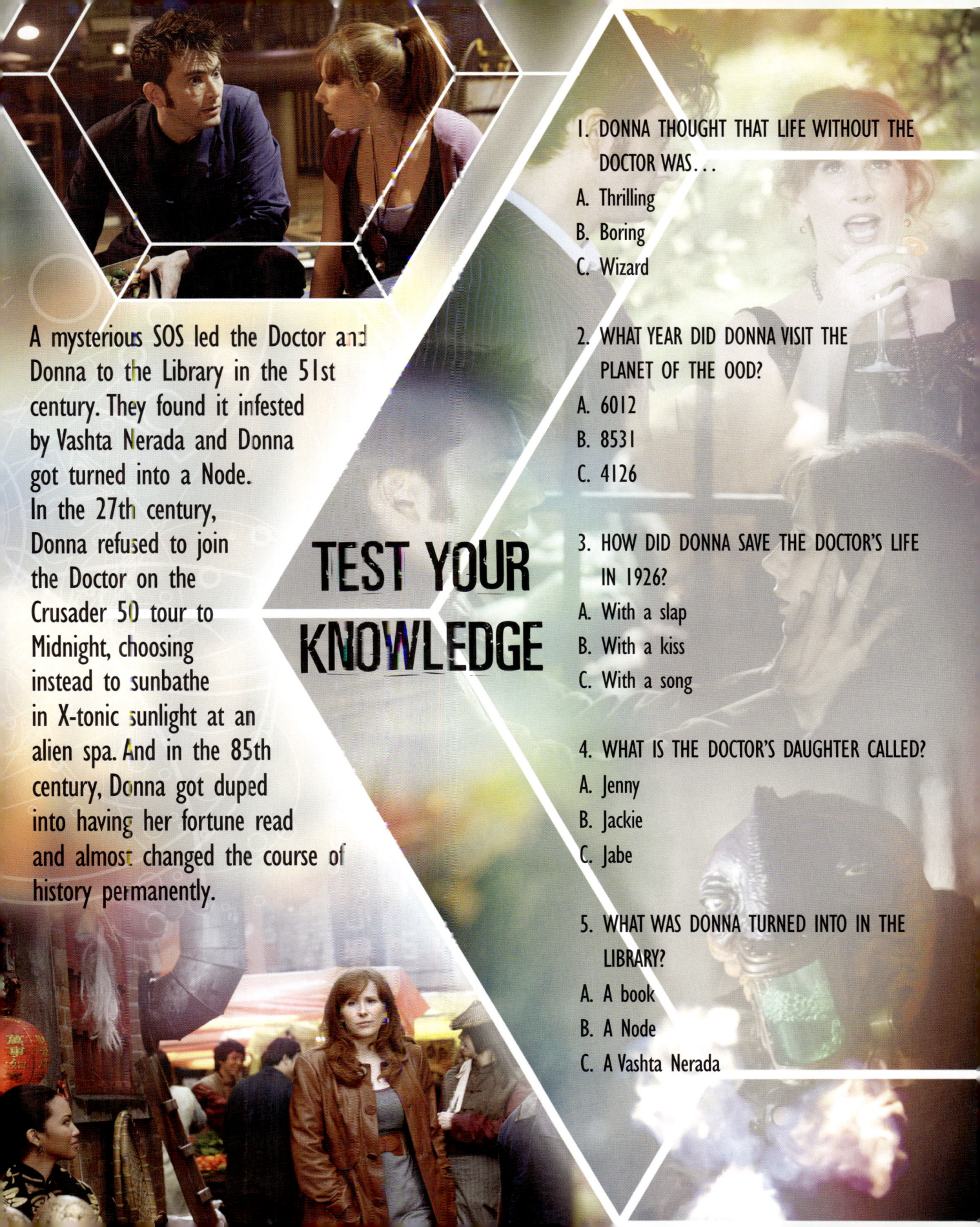

A mysterious SOS led the Doctor and Donna to the Library in the 51st century. They found it infested by Vashta Nerada and Donna got turned into a Node. In the 27th century, Donna refused to join the Doctor on the Crusader 50 tour to Midnight, choosing instead to sunbathe in X-tonic sunlight at an alien spa. And in the 85th century, Donna got duped into having her fortune read and almost changed the course of history permanently.

TEST YOUR KNOWLEDGE

1. DONNA THOUGHT THAT LIFE WITHOUT THE DOCTOR WAS…
A. Thrilling
B. Boring
C. Wizard

2. WHAT YEAR DID DONNA VISIT THE PLANET OF THE OOD?
A. 6012
B. 8531
C. 4126

3. HOW DID DONNA SAVE THE DOCTOR'S LIFE IN 1926?
A. With a slap
B. With a kiss
C. With a song

4. WHAT IS THE DOCTOR'S DAUGHTER CALLED?
A. Jenny
B. Jackie
C. Jabe

5. WHAT WAS DONNA TURNED INTO IN THE LIBRARY?
A. A book
B. A Node
C. A Vashta Nerada

478 PARALLEL WORLDS

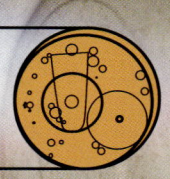

THE LIBRARY

Great big parallel worlds had a habit of forming around Donna Noble. It was as if reality itself was bending around her. When the Vashta Nerada attacked in the Library, the Doctor tried to teleport Donna back to the safety of the TARDIS. But CAL, the little girl whose mind was wired up to the Library's computer, saved Donna to her data core. Her face appeared on a Node and her mind got sucked into cyberspace.

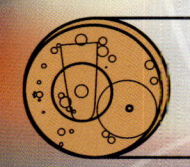

In Donna's virtual world, Dr Moon wiped her memory of the Doctor and seven years passed in the blink of an eye. Donna married a sweet, stammering man called Lee McAvoy and they had two children together — Ella and Joshua. But none of it was real. Donna's children were never alive. Once she knew the truth, they vanished. When she returned to the Library, she thought her husband was only virtual too and left before he had a chance to call her name.

480

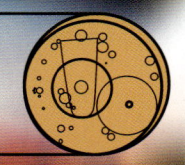

TURN LEFT

A second alternate reality was created around Donna by the Time Beetle — one of the Trickster's Brigade. It jumped on Donna's back in the Fortune Teller's tent on Shan Shen and rewrote history. By forcing Donna to turn right instead of left at a crucial point in her past, she never met the Doctor and he died fighting the Racnoss.

Without him, there was no one to stop the Plasmavore, Matron Cofelia, the Sontarans, and the Titanic from crashing into London. The Noble family became refugees and Earth descended into chaos.

But a mysterious blonde woman knew that none of these terrible events were meant to happen. Rose Tyler had been pulled across from another parallel world because a far greater danger was coming, one that would affect every world – the Daleks. And both Donna and the Doctor were needed to defeat them. So she sent Donna back in time to undo the Time Beetle's evil work and give the Doctor an urgent message: Bad Wolf.

TEST YOUR KNOWLEDGE

1. WHO DO THE TIME BEETLE AND THE FORTUNE TELLER WORK FOR?
A. Davros
B. Rose
C. The Trickster

2. WHAT WAS DONNA DOING WHEN CAL SAVED HER?
A. Ironing
B. Teleporting
C. Running

3. WHAT DID LEE MCAVOY SUFFER FROM?
A. A limp
B. Hiccups
C. A stammer

4. WHAT DID THE FORTUNE TELLER FORCE DONNA TO DO?
A. Turn left
B. Turn right
C. Turn into a beetle

5. WHAT URGENT MESSAGE DID ROSE GIVE TO DONNA FOR THE DOCTOR?
A. Bad Wolf
B. The Daleks are coming
C. You are not alone

482 THE DOCTORDONNA

BIOLOGICAL METACRISIS

The Doctor was seconds away from being reunited with Rose when a Dalek exterminated him. But instead of changing bodies, he regenerated just enough to heal himself and poured all his excess energy into his handy spare hand.

Later, when the TARDIS was about to be torn apart by Z-Neutrino energy in the core of the Dalek Crucible, Donna touched the Doctor's spare hand and caused a two-way biological metacrisis. A second part-human Doctor grew out of the hand and Donna became part Time Lord — the DoctorDonna of Ood Sigma's prophesy.

It became clear that something had been binding the Doctor and Donna together for a long time. He met her once, then he met her grandfather, then he met her again. She even parked her car in the same street that he left the TARDIS. It was no coincidence. It was the work of Dalek Caan.

When the last of the Cult of Skaro flew unprotected into the Time War he saw time in its infinite complexity. It drove Caan crazy, but it also gave him the power to control the Time Lines. He saw all the terrible deeds the Daleks had done and decided it had to stop. So he made sure Donna would be in the right place at the right time so she could destroy them once and for all.

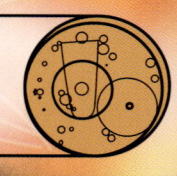

DEFEATING THE DALEKS

Just when Davros thought he'd won and the end of the universe had come, the DoctorDonna stopped the Reality Bomb with the flick of a switch. The Doctor was gobsmacked. Donna couldn't even change a plug and here she was disarming the most powerful weapon ever created! She was brilliant!

The DoctorDonnna and the two Doctors sent the stolen planets home and the Dalek empire was destroyed. But her genius had come at a terrible price. All that Time Lord knowledge was killing her. Dalek Caan had predicted everlasting death for the Doctor's most faithful companion and he was right. The DoctorDonna was doomed to die.

Tragically, the only way the Doctor could save Donna was to wipe her mind of every trace of him and their wonderful adventures together. He took her back to Chiswick and made Wilf and Sylvia promise never to tell her. If she remembered even for a second she'd burn up.

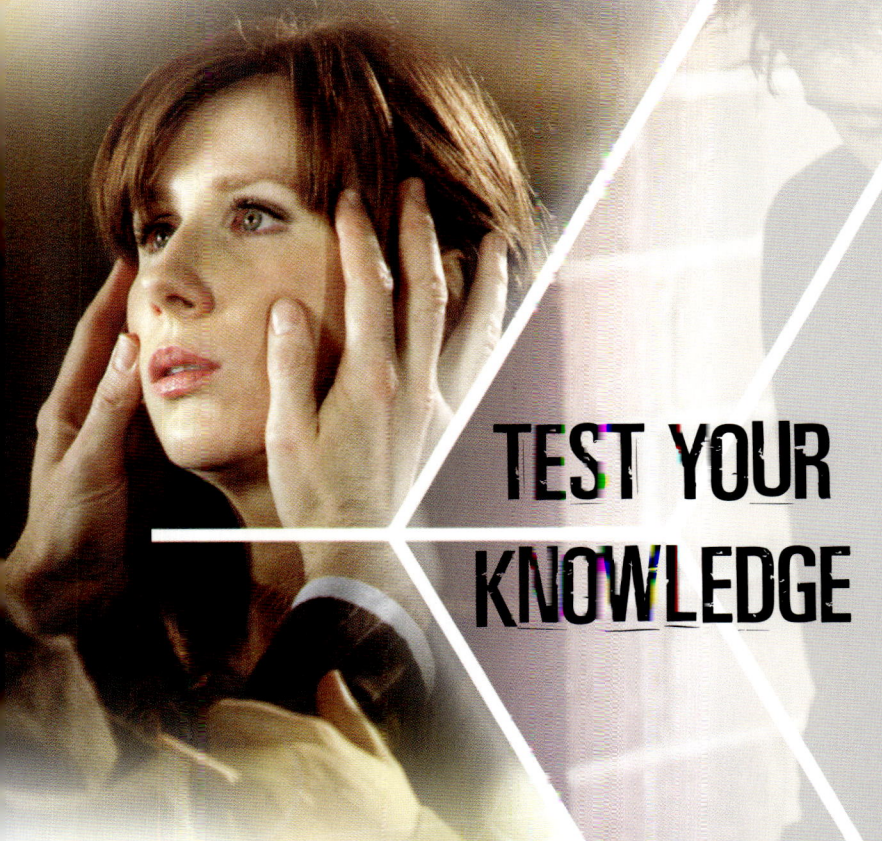

TEST YOUR KNOWLEDGE

1. WHERE DID THE DOCTOR PUT THE EXCESS ENERGY FROM HIS REGENERATION??
   A. In a suitcase
   B. In his spare hand
   C. In his sonic screwdriver

2. WHAT IS THE DALEK SHIP CALLED?
   A. The Destroyer
   B. The TARDIS
   C. The Crucible

3. WHO WAS CONTROLLING THE TIME LINES?
   A. Dalek Caan
   B. Donna
   C. Davros

4. WHAT WEAPON DID THE DOCTORDONNA STOP FROM DETONATING?
   A. The Warp Star
   B. The Reality Bomb
   C. The Osterhagen missile

5. WHAT WILL HAPPEN IF DONNA EVER REMEMBERS THE DOCTOR?
   A. She'll get sucked back in time
   B. She'll vanish
   C. She'll burn up

But thanks to Donna Noble there are worlds out there safe in the sky. People are singing songs about her a thousand million light years away. For one shining moment Donna Noble, the super-temp from Chiswick, was the most important person in the whole universe. And even though she can never remember, the rest of the universe will never forget her bravery and her sacrifice.

TEST YOUR KNOWLEDGE

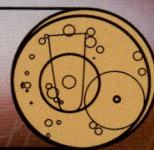

ANSWERS

Meet Donna
1(c) 2(b) 3(b) 4(c) 5(a)

Friends and Family
1(a) 2(b) 3(c) 4(b) 5(c)

Enemies and Rivals
1(c) 2(b) 3(c) 4(a) 5(b)

Adventures
1(b) 2(c) 3(b) 4(a) 5(b)

Parallel Worlds
1(c) 2(b) 3(c) 4(b) 5(a)

The DoctorDonna
1(b) 2(c) 3(a) 4(b) 5(c)

DOCTOR · WHO

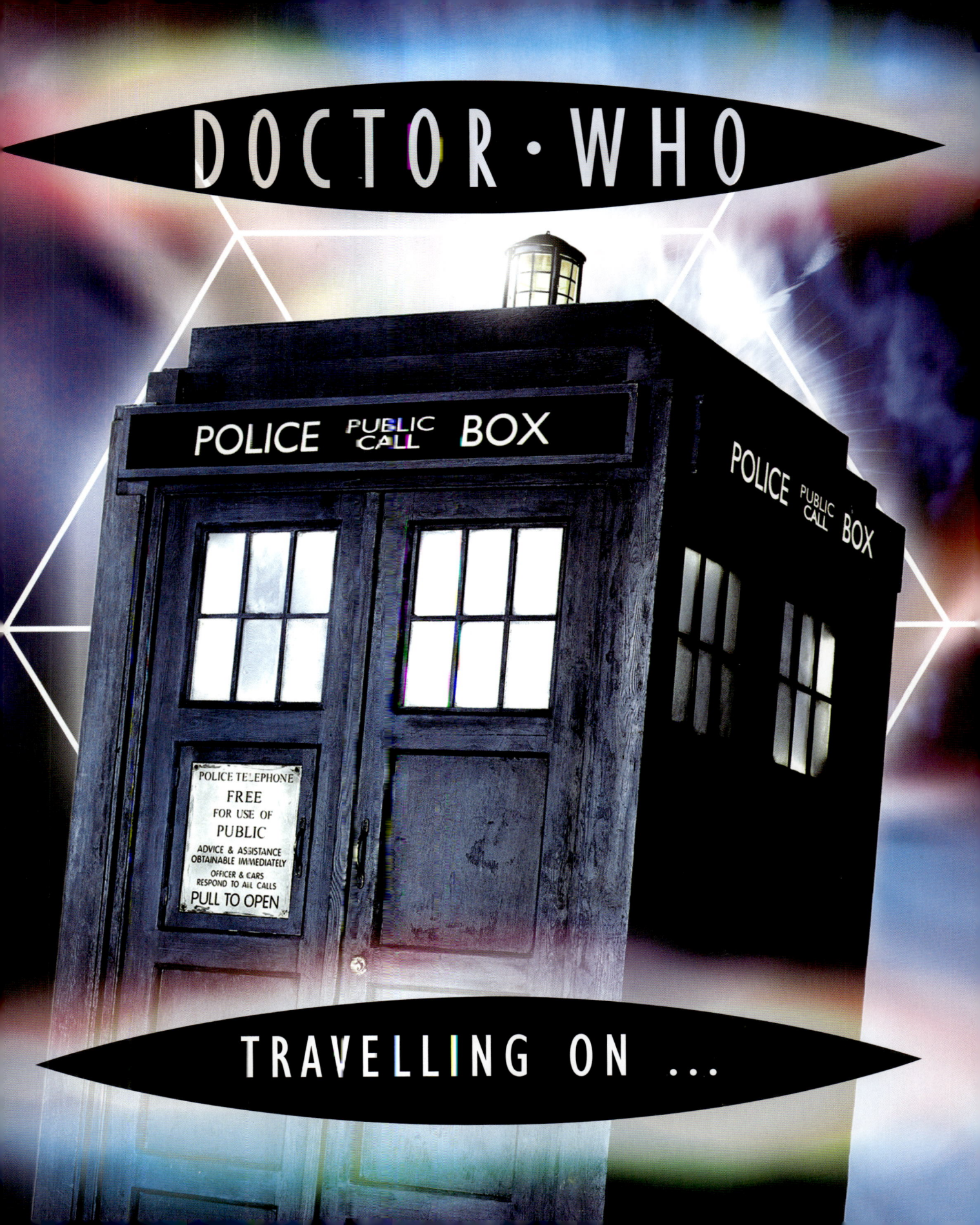

TRAVELLING ON ...

488 THE CHILDREN OF TIME

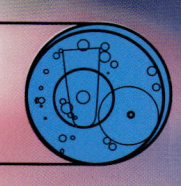

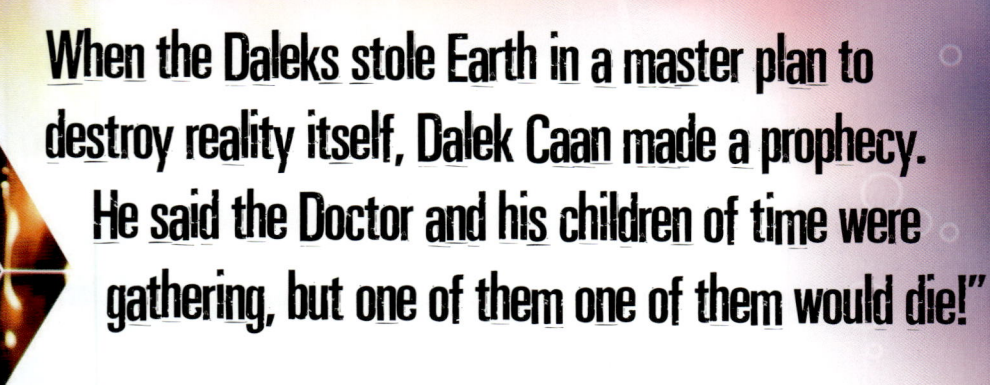

When the Daleks stole Earth in a master plan to destroy reality itself, Dalek Caan made a prophecy. He said the Doctor and his children of time were gathering, but one of them one of them would die!"

The Doctor located Earth with the help of Former Prime Minister Harriet Jones, Captain Jack, Martha and Sarah Jane. They got the whole world to call the Doctor at the same moment so that he could trace Earth through space and time.

But when the Doctor arrived on Earth and was about to be reunited with Rose, a Dalek exterminated him. Jack, Donna and Rose carried him into the TARDIS to regenerate. Meanwhile, Mickey, Rose's mum Jackie and Sarah Jane surrendered to the Daleks so that they could get on board the Crucible.

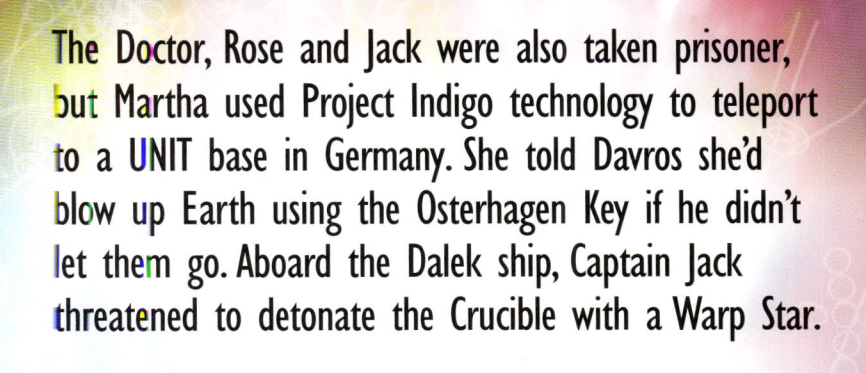

The Doctor, Rose and Jack were also taken prisoner, but Martha used Project Indigo technology to teleport to a UNIT base in Germany. She told Davros she'd blow up Earth using the Osterhagen Key if he didn't let them go. Aboard the Dalek ship, Captain Jack threatened to detonate the Crucible with a Warp Star.

But ultimately it was Donna who saved the day. When she touched the Doctor's spare hand, she became part Time Lord and was able to stop the Daleks with the press of a button. But Dalek Caan had foretold that one of the Children of Time would die. And after they towed Earth home in the TARDIS, Donna's brain began to malfunction. The Doctor was forced to wipe it of all their adventures together in order to save her life.

MARTHA JONES – DOCTOR JONES

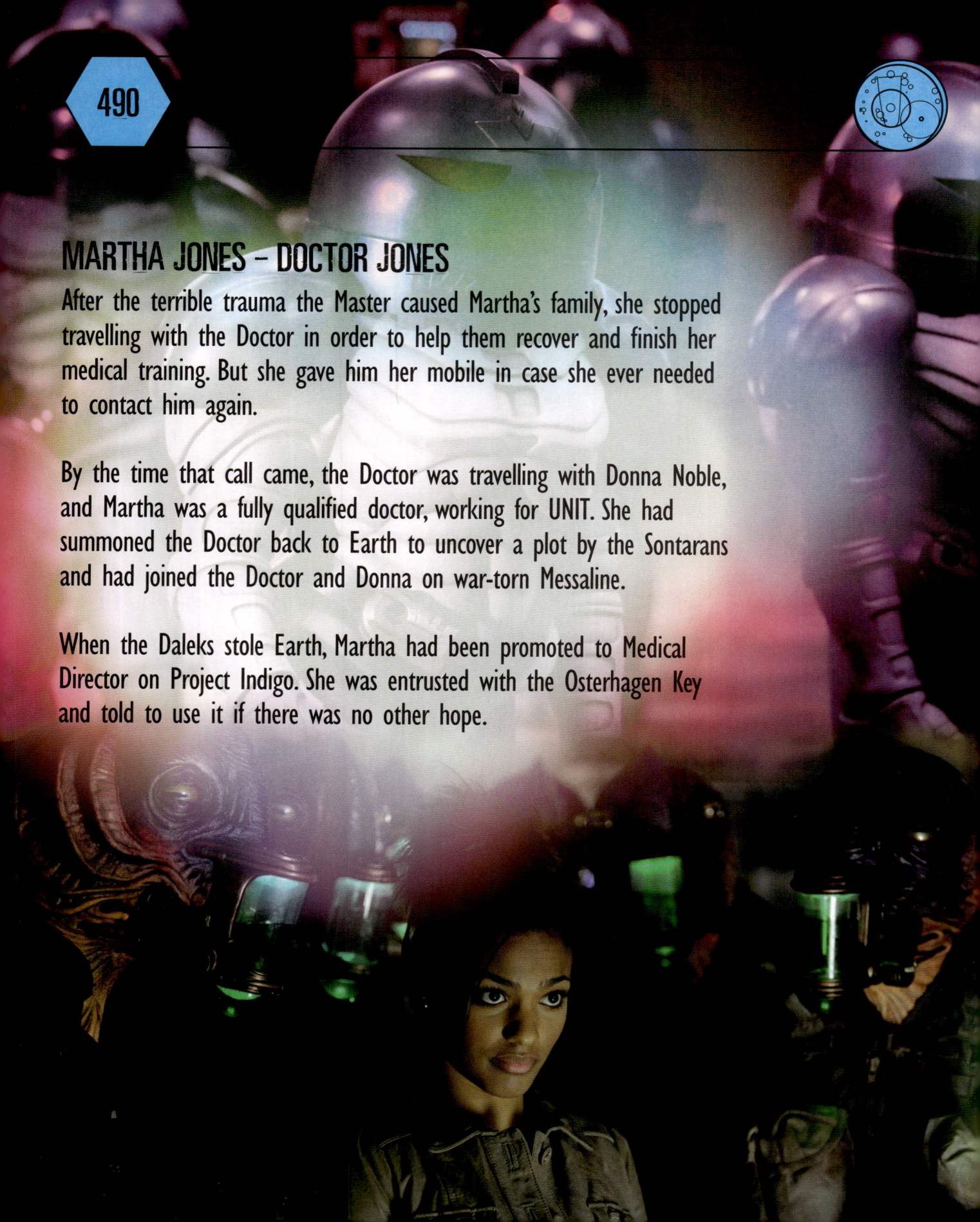

After the terrible trauma the Master caused Martha's family, she stopped travelling with the Doctor in order to help them recover and finish her medical training. But she gave him her mobile in case she ever needed to contact him again.

By the time that call came, the Doctor was travelling with Donna Noble, and Martha was a fully qualified doctor, working for UNIT. She had summoned the Doctor back to Earth to uncover a plot by the Sontarans and had joined the Doctor and Donna on war-torn Messaline.

When the Daleks stole Earth, Martha had been promoted to Medical Director on Project Indigo. She was entrusted with the Osterhagen Key and told to use it if there was no other hope.

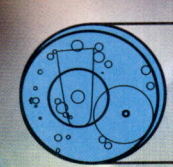

ROSE TYLER – PARALLEL WORLDS

The Doctor and Rose defeated millions of Cybermen and Daleks invading Earth in the Battle at Canary Wharf, but at a terrible cost. Rose got trapped in a parallel Earth without the Doctor.

In Rose's parallel Earth, she worked with UNIT to build a travel machine called a Dimension Cannon. She knew that the darkness was coming and that only the Doctor and Donna could stop it. As all the dimensions started to collapse, Rose travelled between the worlds looking for them.

When Rose was finally about to be reunited with the Doctor, a Dalek exterminated him! Instead of regenerating, the clever Doctor healed himself and put his excess energy into his spare hand. Later, Donna touched this spare hand, creating a new part-human Doctor. He looked identical to the original Doctor, and shared all the same memories but only had one heart. After they defeated the Daleks, the Doctor took the TARDIS back to the parallel Earth. Although it broke his heart to do it, he left Rose there to live out her life with the other Doctor and that reality sealed itself off once more.

492 THE DALEKS

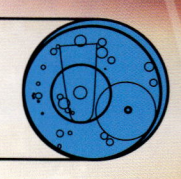

THE FINAL EXPERIMENT

The Dalek leader, Dalek Sec, decided the Children of Skaro must walk again in order for Dalek-kind to survive. He designed the Final Experiment, in which a new army of human Daleks would be born. Dalek Sec sucked a human called Mr Diagoras into his body and became Dalek Sec Hybrid — part human, part Dalek, all scary!

But the other Daleks did not want their race tainted by humans and exterminated him. Dalek Thay and Dalek Jast were destroyed by their own creations and Dalek Caan would have suffered the same fate but he performed an emergency temporal shift back to the Time War.

A NEW DALEK EMPIRE

Although the whole Time War was timelocked, Caan managed to rescue the creator of the Daleks from the jaws of the Nightmare Child and return him to the present. But it drove him insane! Davros built a new empire of Daleks, growing each one from cells from his own body and plotted to destroy the entire universe with a terrible weapon called the Reality Bomb.

493

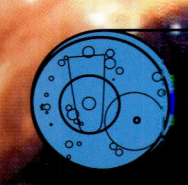

He would have succeeded in his dastardly plan had not Dalek Caan betrayed him. When Caan saw all that the Daleks had ruined through space and time, he decreed no more. He manipulated the Time Lines so that Donna would become the genius DoctorDonna and be able to vanquish the Daleks once and for all. When the Crucible blew up, the Dalek Empire was completely destroyed.

THE SUPREME DALEK

This ruthless, red monster was the leader of the new Dalek Empire. He commanded the Dalek battle fleet from the heart of the Crucible, ordering both the attack on Earth and the destruction of the TARDIS with Donna still inside. The Supreme One referred to Dalek Caan as 'The Abomination'. He believed the Daleks were unstoppable, but the DoctorDonna foiled their plans and Captain Jack shot him with a Defabricator Gun.

494 THE CYBERMEN

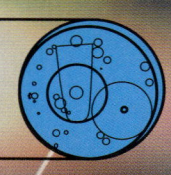

THE CYBERMEN

Unfortunately even though the Cybermen were beaten in the Battle at Canary Wharf and sent into the Void, a few of them escaped. The Reality Bomb had caused the walls between worlds to crumble and the last of the Cybermen fell back through time to Victorian England. There, they created a terrifying new breed of Cyber creature called Cybershades by converting the brains of cats and dogs. These hellish wall-scuttlers helped them gather a workforce of stolen children to build a giant CyberKing.

THE CYBERKING

A 60m tall Dreadnought class Cyber ship designed with one function in mind, conquering worlds. In its chest was a Cyber factory, capable of converting millions of humans into new Cybermen. Enthroned in its mouth was Miss Hartigan, a power-hungry workhouse matron who had been forced to become the CyberKing against her will.

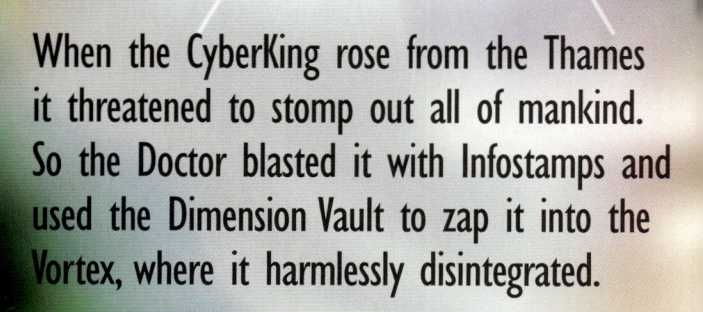

When the CyberKing rose from the Thames it threatened to stomp out all of mankind. So the Doctor blasted it with Infostamps and used the Dimension Vault to zap it into the Vortex, where it harmlessly disintegrated.

THE DOCTOR

495

THE TENTH DOCTOR

When the Doctor returned Donna to her home, her mind wiped of any memory of her adventures with the Doctor, he was alone again. Donna's granddad Wilfred promised to look out for the Doctor every night while he looks at the sky. The Children of Time had gathered to help save Earth and the Doctor, but ultimately, they all had to part ways. As the last of the Time Lords travels through time and space, he stands up for what is right.